D1029728

Property Threats and the Politics of Anti-Statism

Tax revenues have risen robustly across Latin America in recent decades, casting doubt on the region's reputation for having states too poor to finance economic and social development. However, dramatic differences persist in the magnitude of national tax burdens and public sector size, even among seemingly similar countries. This book examines the historical roots of this variation. Through in-depth case studies of Argentina, Brazil, Chile, and Mexico, as well as evidence from Ecuador and Guatemala, Ondetti reveals the lasting impact of historical episodes of redistributive reform that threatened property rights. Ironically, where such episodes were most extensive, they hindered future taxation by prompting economic elites and social conservatives to mobilize politically against state intervention, forming peak business associations, rightist parties, and other formal and informal organizations that have proven to be remarkably enduring.

Gabriel Ondetti is Professor of Political Science at Missouri State University. He is the author of *Land, Protest and Politics: The Landless Movement and the Struggle for Agrarian Reform in Brazil* (2008).

Property Threats and the Politics of Anti-Statism

The Historical Roots of Contemporary Tax Systems in Latin America

GABRIEL ONDETTI
Missouri State University

CAMBRIDGE
UNIVERSITY PRESS

CAMBRIDGE
UNIVERSITY PRESS

University Printing House, Cambridge CB2 8BS, United Kingdom

One Liberty Plaza, 20th Floor, New York, NY 10006, USA

477 Williamstown Road, Port Melbourne, VIC 3207, Australia

314–321, 3rd Floor, Plot 3, Splendor Forum, Jasola District Centre, New Delhi – 110025, India

79 Anson Road, #06–04/06, Singapore 079906

Cambridge University Press is part of the University of Cambridge.

It furthers the University's mission by disseminating knowledge in the pursuit of education, learning, and research at the highest international levels of excellence.

www.cambridge.org
Information on this title: www.cambridge.org/9781108830850
DOI: 10.1017/9781108914147

© Gabriel Ondetti 2021

First published 2021

A catalogue record for this publication is available from the British Library.

ISBN 978-1-108-83085-0 Hardback

To Indira and Ben, with love

Contents

List of Figures   *page* viii
List of Tables   ix
Preface and Acknowledgments   x

1   Introduction   1
2   Historical Property Threats and Contemporary Tax Burdens   26
3   Chile: Allende, Counterrevolution, and Sustained Neoliberalism   66
4   Mexico: *Cardenismo*, Reaction, and Low-Tax Stability   106
5   Brazil: Moderate Statism and Public Sector Expansion   149
6   Argentina: Populism, Divided Elites, and Heavy Taxation   191
7   Conclusions   234

Appendix: Interviews   264
References   268
Index   303

Figures

1.1 Summary of the argument   *page* 18
2.1 Historical tax burden trajectories, 1900–2017 (decadal
    averages)   59
3.1 Evolution of Chile's tax burden, 1900–2017   69
3.2 Share of votes won by right in Chilean Chamber of Deputies
    elections, 1937–2013 (percent)   100
4.1 Evolution of Mexico's tax burden, 1900–2017   109
5.1 Evolution of Brazil's tax burden, 1900–2017   152
6.1 Evolution of Argentina's tax burden, 1900–2017   194
6.2 Annual inflation rate and the tax burden in Argentina,
    1945–1988   201

Tables

1.1 Average tax burden and tax structure, 2013–2017   *page* 5
1.2 Selected tax rates, *c.* 2015   5
1.3 Theories of the tax burden summarized   13
2.1 Trade openness, agricultural dependence, and inflation,
      2013–2017   28
2.2 Fiscal revenue and spending, 2013–2017   30
2.3 Regime characteristics as of 2017   32
2.4 Subnational government revenue by source, 2014–2015   35
2.5 Summary of contemporary statist/anti-statist power balance   44
3.1 Distribution of seats in the Chilean Congress by term
      and chamber, 1990–2018 (percent)   88
4.1 Distribution of seats in the Mexican Congress by election
      and chamber, 1997–2018 (percentages)   139
5.1 Electoral performance of Brazil's PT, 1985–2016   183
6.1 Distribution of seats in the Argentine Congress by term
      and chamber, 2003–2015 (percentages)   221

Preface and Acknowledgments

When I began researching tax policy roughly a decade ago, my intention was to leave behind land reform, a topic that had dominated my earlier scholarly work but whose relevance in Latin America seemed to be waning. However, land reform and the broader issue of property redistribution refused to be left behind. Within a few years, I had come to realize that attempts to restructure property relations had played a fundamental role in creating the surprising differences in taxation I was trying to explain. By threatening property rights, left-leaning governments in some Latin American countries had inadvertently given rise to anti-statist political blocs that posed a lasting obstacle to taxation. My foray into the realm of fiscal politics had, equally inadvertently, brought me back full circle to the question of property redistribution. This book is the end product of that circuitous intellectual journey.

I have accumulated many debts along the way. Two people have been especially important to the successful completion of this project: my former dissertation advisor Evelyne Huber and my wife and colleague Indira Palacios-Valladares. Evelyne provided detailed comments on the entire manuscript and has been a vital source of advice and encouragement. Indira went over multiple versions of each chapter and put up with my often-cranky responses to her criticisms. She has also supported this project in many other ways – so many that it is not possible to mention them all here. I am also grateful to our son, Ben, for tolerating my research-related absences, both physical and mental.

A number of other professional colleagues also deserve thanks. Matt Carnes, Tasha Fairfield, Gustavo Flores-Macías, Jim Mahon, Fabrício Augusto de Oliveira, Luiz Carlos Bresser-Pereira, Jenny Pribble, Aaron Schneider, and Mónica Unda have provided valuable comments on my previous work on this topic. Gustavo also invited me to a 2014 workshop on the politics of Latin American taxation at Cornell University, which provided very useful feedback and resulted in an excellent edited volume. A number of researchers located in Latin America gave me crucial assistance in obtaining and interpreting fiscal data, most notably Luis Aboites, José Roberto Afonso, Oscar Cetrángolo, Juan

Carlos Gómez Sabaini, Michael Hanni, and the aforementioned Fabrício Augusto de Oliveira. I am also grateful to Benjamin Davy, Ulrike Davy, and Lutz Leisering for inviting me to participate in the "Understanding Southern Welfare" research group at the Center for Interdisciplinary Research (ZiF) at the University of Bielefeld in Germany, which contributed to my thinking about the politics of redistribution.

Sara Doskow, my editor at Cambridge University Press, has been very supportive of this project and exceptionally efficient at moving it toward publication. In addition, I must thank the two anonymous reviewers she engaged, who provided rigorous critiques of the manuscript, helping me improve it substantially. My graduate assistants, especially Mason Gaspard, Corbett McKinney, Trinh Nguyen, Stephen Rowe, and Sirvan Salehzadeh, have also been a great help.

The extensive fieldwork I conducted in Argentina, Brazil, Chile and Mexico was made possible by grants from the American Philosophical Society, the American Political Science Association, and Missouri State University. It was also facilitated by visiting affiliations with the Centro de Investigación y Docencia Económicas (CIDE) in Mexico, the Instituto de Ciencia Política of the Pontificia Universidad Católica de Chile and the Escuela de Gobierno of the Universidad Torcuato Di Tella in Argentina, as well as the flexibility of my department head, George Connor, and dean, Victor Matthews. Finally, I owe a debt of gratitude to the eighty-six people (listed at the end of the book) who took time from their often-hectic schedules to sit for interviews. This book might not have been published without their contributions and, if it had, it would surely have been a much poorer work.

1

Introduction

Recent decades have seen large increases in taxation in Latin America. The average tax burden in the region has risen by almost a third since 2000 and now stands at more than 20 percent of gross domestic product (GDP). The conventional wisdom that Latin American tax systems generate too little revenue to promote economic and social development seems harder to sustain today than in the past.[1] What continues to be striking about the region's tax burdens, however, is the great disparity between them. While countries like the Dominican Republic, Guatemala, Mexico, and Panama have tax revenues of 13–16 percent of GDP, which is indeed a low level of taxation by international standards, in Argentina, Bolivia, Brazil, and Uruguay the burden is roughly double that amount.

The purpose of this book is to shed light on the origins of these differences. That goal is not grounded in the assumption that more taxation is necessarily better. Public revenues are not always spent in judicious or public-spirited ways, and Latin America faces longstanding problems with clientelism and corruption. In addition, taxation has done relatively little to promote social equity in this highly unequal region, both because it tends to rely heavily on regressive levies and because much of the resulting revenue flows to relatively well-off groups. Nevertheless, a productive tax system provides at least the potential for effective state intervention, something lacking in low-tax countries like Guatemala and Haiti. It also guards against problems of unaccountable governance that scholars have sometimes attributed to reliance on "unearned" income like natural resource rents and foreign aid (Moore 2008). Finally, even fiscal systems that are inefficient from an equity perspective may effect some redistribution if they collect enough revenue. It is

[1] The observation that Latin American tax burdens are unusually low, or lower than would be ideal, can be found in many studies, including Bird and De Wulf (1973), Inter-American Development Bank (1998), Bird (2003), and Gómez Sabaini (2006).

no accident that the Latin American countries with the largest tax burdens are also the ones in which the fiscal system is most equalizing (Hanni et al. 2015; Lustig 2016, 2017).

Admittedly, this is not the first scholarly work to tackle the puzzle of tax burden variance in Latin America. A handful of other studies have done so (Cetrángolo and Gómez Sabaini 2007a; Martín-Mayoral and Uribe 2010; Dioda 2012). In addition, several works have integrated the Latin American countries into broader analyses of this question (Lotz and Morss 1970; Gupta 2007; Pessino and Fenochietto 2010). Nevertheless, almost all these studies rely exclusively on large-N statistical methods. This is the first book-length study dedicated to explaining the determinants of taxation level in Latin America using qualitative comparison.[2] To be sure, there is a growing body of qualitative research on the politics of taxation in Latin America, which has generated valuable insights, but this literature focuses mainly on particular types of taxes, especially more progressive "direct" taxes, rather than the overall tax burden (Lieberman 2003; Fairfield 2010, 2015; Flores-Macías 2014). This difference is significant because countries with larger and more redistributive public sectors tend to rely mainly on indirect and social security taxes, rather than direct ones (Kato 2003; Beramendi and Rueda 2007).

More specifically, the question of tax burden variance is investigated here through an in-depth comparison of four countries: Argentina, Brazil, Chile, and Mexico. Despite sharing several theoretically relevant characteristics, including a substantial level of economic development by regional standards, a political regime widely regarded as democratic, a presidential system of government, and a similar history of external military conflict, these countries have sharply divergent levels of contemporary taxation. Brazil and Argentina have the largest tax revenues in Latin America relative to GDP. Mexico, despite a recent uptick, has a tax burden well below the regional average. Chile is an intermediate case. Why, the book asks, do these otherwise fairly similar countries have starkly different tax burdens?

Most existing theories of taxation shed little light on this puzzle. While some of the independent variables they propose are controlled by the case selection, even those that are not are generally unconvincing. For example, established variables such as trade openness, dependence on agriculture, and federalism are flatly contradicted by the cases. Nevertheless, some others do illuminate aspects of this question. Perhaps the most obvious is nontax revenue from natural resource extraction, often seen as depressing taxation by providing an

---

[2] Some other book-length studies use qualitative comparison to address related questions. Schneider (2012) examines (among other variables) the increment in the tax burden in recent decades in Central America. Kurtz (2013) explores the roots of longstanding differences in general state capacity among the South American countries. Although Kurtz views the contemporary tax burden as largely reflecting underlying state capacity, this book will challenge that notion.

alternative means for financing public spending. Such revenues clearly help explain the especially light taxation in Mexico.[3] However, for reasons elaborated later, resource revenues constitute only a very partial solution. Some other theories, including path dependence theory, power resources theory, and recent work on business elites and taxation, are also useful, but their contribution can best be appreciated not in isolation but as part of a broader account that traces a causal connection between the occurrence of property reform and the state's subsequent ability to tax.

To be more specific, the argument developed in the book emphasizes the political impact of historical episodes of large-scale redistribution, especially ones that substantially menaced private property. Such episodes shaped taxation indirectly by influencing in an enduring manner the balance of power between actors favorable and opposed to state intervention in the economy. Ironically, where threats to property were most serious, they had the unintended effect of hindering future taxation by promoting the emergence of interest groups, parties, and other actors deeply committed to combatting state intervention in the economy. In contrast, where such threats were more limited, an anti-statist political bloc of comparable strength failed to arise, and taxation eventually reached a higher level.

Although it weaves together a number of existing strands of scholarship, this argument's emphasis on the lasting impacts of conservative backlash against property reform is new to both the literature on taxation and the broader body of scholarship on Latin American political economy and state formation. While it cannot, by any means, explain all the variance in the level of taxation across the region, it does shed considerable light on the roots of tax burden differences elsewhere in Latin America. It also raises crucial questions, which this book tentatively seeks to answer, about the viability of different approaches to achieving greater social equality in this deeply inequitable region.

The rest of this introductory chapter is divided into five sections: the first provides a concise overview of Latin American tax systems, the second reviews the existing literature on the determinants of the tax burden, the third sketches the argument of the book, the fourth explains the research design, and the fifth provides a map of subsequent chapters.

1.1 TAXATION IN LATIN AMERICA

Tax systems vary on a number of major dimensions, including the volume of revenue they collect, the degree to which collection is centralized in the national government, and the types of taxes that produce the bulk of the revenue. This book focuses exclusively on explaining differences on the first

---

[3] Natural resource extraction plays an even larger role in Chile's economy but, for reasons discussed in Chapter 2, nontax revenues from this sector make a much smaller contribution to Chile's fiscal system than Mexico's.

of these. Nevertheless, it is useful to begin by providing a broader perspective on Latin American tax systems, both because some theories view the tax burden as partially determined by the degree or character of fiscal centralization, and because, as this book argues, the relative weight of different types of taxation reflects political dynamics shaping the size of the tax burden. In addition, it will enhance the reader's general comprehension of the text to have a basic understanding of how taxation works in the region. The discussion highlights both region-wide patterns and cross-national differences. It also attempts to situate the four case study countries within the broader regional context.

1.1.1   The Tax Burden

Latin American countries have on average brought in slightly over 20 percent of GDP in tax revenue in recent years (see Table 1.1).[4] This is more than a third less than the corresponding figure (34 percent) for the generally far richer countries that comprise the Organisation for Economic Cooperation and Development (OECD).[5] However, it is substantially higher than in the past. The average tax burden in the region increased from 13.6 percent of GDP in 1990 to 15.8 percent in 2000 to 20.8 percent in 2017 (OECD 2019, p. 135) even as the OECD average remained relatively stagnant.[6] The average Latin American tax burden is also higher than the average of developing countries outside the region.[7] As noted earlier, there is much diversity within Latin America, with tax burdens ranging from about 13 percent of GDP to more than 32 percent. The set of countries examined in this book expresses this diversity. Brazil and Argentina are the two most heavily taxed countries in the region. Despite a significant increase beginning in 2015, Mexico is among the more lightly taxed. Chile is an intermediate case with revenues almost identical to the regional average.

Variance in the tax burden reflects key differences in tax policy. Brazil and Argentina have a larger number of significant taxes. For example, Brazil has essentially two different corporate income taxes and two value-added taxes (one each at the national and state levels), while Argentina has an important tax on bank transactions and high taxes on commodity exports. No comparable measures exist in Chile or Mexico. Argentina and Brazil also apply higher rates

---

[4] Cuba is excluded from regional calculations because its still largely socialist economy makes comparison with other countries complicated.

[5] Chile and Mexico are both part of the OECD, an organization devoted to studying development issues, but they are, along with Turkey, the poorest of its 34 members.

[6] The average OECD tax burden was 31.9 percent of GDP in 1990, 33.8 percent in 2000, and 34.2 percent in 2017 (OECD Global Revenue Statistics Database, www.oecd.org/tax/tax-policy /global-revenue-statistics-database.htm).

[7] The average tax burden in 2017 for non-high-income countries outside Latin America was 19.6 percent (OECD Global Revenue Statistics Database).

TABLE 1.1 *Average tax burden and tax structure, 2013–2017*

Country	Tax revenue/ GDP (%)	Type of tax (% of total tax revenue)				Level of government (% of total tax revenue)	
		Direct	Indirect	Social security	Other	Central	Subnational
Argentina	31.0	28.4	47.3	22.3	2.0	83.2	16.8
Brazil	32.1	30.2	41.3	26.1	2.4	68.3	31.7
Chile	20.1	38.6	53.8	7.1	0.5	92.4	7.6
Mexico	15.1	47.7	36.7	14.3	1.3	94.1	5.9
Regional average[a]	20.1	31.5	47.5	19.2	1.8	90.8	9.2

Sources: CEPALSTAT (estadisticas.cepal.org/cepalstat/portada.html?idioma=english); OECD (2015, 2016, 2017, 2018)
[a] Data for the Dominican Republic, Haiti, and Venezuela exclude subnational governments.

TABLE 1.2 *Selected tax rates, c. 2015*

Country	Personal income tax (minimum/ maximum)	Corporate income tax (standard)	VAT (general)	Social security (% average wage)	Import tariff (average)
Argentina	9/35	35	21	44.5	13.0
Brazil	7.5/27.5	34	28[a]	43.2	13.5
Chile	4/40	22.5	19	23.7	6.0
Mexico	1.9/35	30	16	25.5	8.6
Regional average	9.8/26.6	26.1	15.8	27.5	8.5

Sources: Inter-American Center of Tax Administrations (CIAT) Database (https://www.ciat.org /ciatdata/?lang=en); KPMG (2016); Alaimo et al. (2017); Ernst and Young (2017); OECD (2018).
[a] Combines the state and federal VAT-type taxes. Although most states use a 17 percent rate, the largest ones use 18 or 19 percent. The figure here is based on 18 percent. The federal tax has no general rate, so the value used is a rough average (10 percent) calculated by the accounting firm KPMG (KPMG 2016, p. 4).

for some key taxes (see Table 1.2). Finally, the mandatory pension systems in Argentina and Brazil are wholly public, so all contributions flow into state coffers. In contrast, all but a small percentage of Chile's pension contributions go to private investment funds. Mexico's system is a hybrid, with about 70 percent of revenues entering the public sector.

1.1.2   Centralization

As a rule, tax collection in Latin America, as Table 1.1 shows, is overwhelmingly concentrated in the national government. Even in some countries that are nominally federal in constitutional structure, such as Mexico and Venezuela, tax collection is highly centralized (Díaz-Cayeros 2006, pp. 2–9). In several Latin American countries, subnational governments have come in recent decades to wield substantial control over key policy areas, such as education and health care, and to account for a large share of public spending (Eaton 2002; Falleti 2010). However, even in these countries, states and municipalities obtain their revenues mainly from fiscal transfers from the central government, rather than their own tax collection efforts (Corbacho et al. 2013, pp. 81–83).

The major exception to the rule of tax system centralization is one of the case study countries, Brazil. Both states and municipalities have substantial tax authority and together they bring in about 30 percent of total tax revenue. After Brazil, the countries with the most decentralized tax systems are Argentina and Colombia, where subnational governments account for upward of 15 percent of total tax revenues (OECD 2018). In the Argentine case, it is mainly the provincial governments that matter, since municipalities generally have little tax authority. Mexico and Chile, in contrast, join other Latin American countries in concentrating tax collection overwhelmingly at the national level.

1.1.3   Type of Taxes/Progressivity

Latin American tax systems have been criticized for collecting too little revenue from income and property taxes, which are generally more progressive than other types (Tanzi 2000; Flores-Macías 2019). Known as "direct" taxes because their onus is borne by the payer rather than being passed on to consumers, these taxes contribute less than a third of total tax revenues (see Table 1.1). This figure is lower than the corresponding one for the OECD, as well as Africa and Asia (OECD Global Revenue Statistics Database).[8] In addition, income tax revenues in Latin America come primarily from the corporate income tax, which is often viewed as less progressive than the personal income tax (Mahon 2019). Instead of relying on income taxation, Latin American countries derive the bulk of their revenues from taxes that tend to be neutral or regressive. Most important are "indirect" taxes, a category that includes both taxes on consumption, such as value-added taxes (VATs) and "excise" taxes on specific products, and taxes on foreign trade. In addition,

---

[8] In 2016, for example, direct taxes contributed 30.8 percent of tax revenues in Latin America, 39.3 percent in the OECD, 36.0 percent in Africa, and 46.6 percent in East Asia (OECD Global Revenue Database).

a substantial amount of revenue comes from the payroll taxes that fund social security systems.

Although the share of revenue derived from direct levies is generally low, it varies substantially across the region, with values ranging from 15 to almost 50 percent. As Table 1.1 shows, the countries examined in depth in this book reflect at least some of this diversity. Mexico and Chile are among the countries in which direct taxes contribute the largest share. Argentina and Brazil do not rank at the bottom, but they are well below the other two.[9] These differences mainly reflect the relative weight of income taxes, since property taxes play a minor role in Latin America.[10] The personal and corporate income taxes contribute roughly similar amounts of revenue in Argentina, Mexico, and Brazil, but corporate taxation is more dominant in Chile, due to its unusual "integrated" income tax regime (discussed in Chapter 3).[11]

It should be noted that, although direct taxes tend to be more progressive, the fact that a country relies heavily on them does not necessarily mean that its fiscal system has a strong redistributive impact, since other variables also affect progressivity.[12] First, both direct and indirect taxes can vary in their distributional consequences, depending on specific design attributes.[13] Second, the impact of revenue also depends on how it is spent. Both the distribution of spending among policy areas and how specific programs are structured are important.[14] Finally, the volume of revenue matters. A fiscal system that taxes and spends progressively may still have little redistributive impact if it brings in only a small amount of revenue. Conversely, one whose design is only mildly redistributive may have a significant impact if it handles a large quantity of resources.

That the magnitude of the tax burden is relevant for equity is reflected by the fact that the Latin American fiscal systems with the largest tax revenues

[9] Nevertheless, given their heavier tax burdens, Brazil and Argentina have somewhat larger direct tax revenues relative to GDP. Between 2013 and 2017, Brazil's averaged 9.7 percent of GDP, Argentina's 8.8 percent, Chile's 7.8 percent, and Mexico's 7.2 percent (CEPALSTAT).

[10] Property taxation is more significant in Argentina, but this is mainly due to a tax on bank transactions, rather than more conventional taxes, like those on real estate or inheritance.

[11] Between 2013 and 2017, personal income tax revenues averaged 50.8 percent of total income tax revenues in Mexico, 46.4 percent in Brazil, 46.3 percent in Argentina, and 23.7 percent in Chile (CEPALSTAT).

[12] "Redistributive" and "progressive" are used interchangeably here to describe policies that tend to promote greater socioeconomic equality.

[13] For example, as mentioned, the personal income tax is generally viewed as more progressive than the corporate version. With regard to indirect taxes, the regressivity of consumption taxes like the VAT may be attenuated by exempting staple goods like food and medicines.

[14] Spending on primary education and preventive health care is especially redistributive because poorer people use those services more than the richer ones. Policy design also matters. For example, policies that transfer cash to individuals can have very different distributive effects, depending on whether they require prior payment of payroll taxes and whether they employ a means test.

(Argentina, Brazil, and Uruguay) also achieve the greatest reduction in income inequality (Lustig et al. 2014; ECLAC 2015, pp. 94–95; Hanni et al. 2015; Lustig 2016, 2017). None of them has a significantly redistributive tax system, but all collect substantial revenue and a good part of it is spent on policies with a redistributive impact.[15] On the other extreme, the countries whose fiscal systems effect the least redistribution tend to be the same ones (e.g., the Dominican Republic, Guatemala, and Paraguay) that collect the least revenue. Mexico and Chile are in the middle of the regional pack, although Chile consistently ranks higher. Despite this variation, even the most progressive Latin American fiscal systems achieve less redistribution than the OECD average, owing both to a lower level of taxation and less progressive tax and spending structures (Hanni et al. 2015, pp. 12–14).

1.2 EXISTING THEORIES

Existing scholarship offers a variety of theoretical tools for solving the puzzle addressed by this book. Although research specifically on the roots of Latin American tax burdens is limited, the broader literature is large and diverse, reflecting the centrality of this question to social science research.[16] Chapter 2 evaluates this literature in light of the cases, but for the purpose of introducing the arguments and research design of the book (in subsequent sections) it is useful to provide a brief overview here. While the focus is on general theories, the discussion also refers to some of the more prominent arguments proposed for specific countries under study here. Others are dealt with in later chapters.

Extant theories can be thought of as falling into three broad categories – economic, institutional, and actor-centric – depending on the causal variable they primarily emphasize. Each of these categories is discussed in turn.

First, though, it is important to touch on an issue that cuts across them. Variance in the tax burden most obviously reflects differences in the legal tax code. However, it can also reflect the degree of compliance with that code (Levi 1988). Noncompliance, or, in other words, tax evasion, is a common phenomenon in developing countries. Numerous studies have underscored its importance in Latin America (Alm and Martinez-Vazquez 2007; Bergman 2009; Gómez Sabaini and Morán 2016). Nevertheless, an emphasis on evasion begs the question of why this problem is more serious in some societies than others. Thus, to the extent that they touch on the subject at all, theories of taxation and overall public sector size portray evasion as a result of

---

[15] Argentina and Brazil, for instance, boast the region's heaviest spending on targeted anti-poverty programs, especially noncontributory pensions (Arza 2017, p. 15) and conditional cash transfers (Cecchini and Atuesta 2017, p. 31).

[16] The tax burden scholarship is integrated into a broader debate on the "size of government." Spanning the fields of economics and political science, this literature treats taxation and spending as aspects of one variable: the fiscal magnitude of the state. Thus, a few studies cited here operationalize the dependent variable as total public spending, rather than taxation.

deeper causes, including the structure of the economy, the perceived legitimacy of political institutions, and the general efficacy of the state in penetrating society and enforcing the law. Following this logic, the discussion here treats evasion not as a separate explanation of tax burden variance, but rather as a variable that plays a mediating role in some theories.

1.2.1 Economic Theories

A variety of economic conditions have been seen as influencing the level of taxation. Probably the most widely acknowledged is economic development. While there are differing accounts of the causal links involved, development is broadly viewed as promoting greater taxation by boosting societal demand for public goods, such as economic regulation, education, and social protection, which require revenues for their provision (Wagner 1883; Lotz and Morss 1970; Pessino and Fenochietto 2010). Consequently, richer societies should be expected, other things being equal, to have heavier tax burdens. Scholars have also argued that openness to international trade tends to increase public sector size, mainly by generating demands for social insurance against external shocks (Rodrik 1998). Although some studies cast doubt on this relationship (Benarroch and Pandey 2012), most find support for it, at least under certain conditions (Ram 2009; Farhad and Jetter 2019; Ferreira de Mendonça and Oliveira 2019). Moreover, those conditions, including democracy, volatile export prices, and developing country status, generally hold for the countries under study here.

While development and trade integration are usually viewed as promoting heavier taxation, some other conditions are believed to inhibit it. Strong dependence on agricultural production reduces the tax burden because it is harder for the state to enforce compliance in agriculture than in other sectors (Piancastelli 2001; Gupta 2007). Price inflation is sometimes associated with lighter taxation because of the so-called Olivera–Tanzi effect, in which the time lag between a taxable event and the state's receipt of the corresponding revenues undermines the latter's real value (Tanzi 1977; Cetrángolo and Gómez Sabaini 2007a).[17] Scholars view state-controlled natural resource wealth as inhibiting taxation by providing an alternative revenue source that is politically less costly and requires less bureaucratic capacity (Patrucchi and Grottola 2011; Crivelli and Gupta 2014). Finally, at least one study of Mexico argues that the country's proximity to the United States prevents heavier taxation in two ways (Elizondo Mayer-Serra 2014). First, the threat of contraband from the United States puts pressure on Mexican authorities to keep consumption taxes low in border

---

[17] There are also ways in which inflation can contribute to higher taxation, such as by triggering tax reform (Mahon 2004) or causing income tax "bracket creep" (as discussed in Chapter 6). However, at least in the developing country context, the predominant hypothesis in the literature is that it hinders tax collection.

regions. Second, income taxation is inhibited by the risk of capital flight into the United States.

1.2.2   Institutional Theories

Scholars have also advanced explanations of the tax burden based on the characteristics of a country's political institutions. Most of these emphasize relatively formal differences in decision-making processes, but others focus on the capacity to exert effective governance, which is seen as flowing mainly from deeply rooted informal traditions.

A perspective that falls more clearly into the first category involves the macro-institution of regime type. A common argument is that democracy favors the expansion of spending and taxation, both by granting poorer citizens opportunities to press demands for redistribution and by legitimizing the state's own demands for revenue, thus enhancing compliance (Boix 2001; Besley and Persson 2013; Bird et al. 2014). A more nuanced version argues that under democracy public sector size is a function of income inequality (Meltzer and Richard 1981). When the median voter's income is below average, he or she tends to vote for measures that redistribute income downward through taxation and spending.

These theories focus on democracy writ large. Nevertheless, even among democratic regimes, there are major differences in institutional design. Students of fiscal policy have offered several arguments about how these differences affect public sector magnitude, most of them taken from the experiences of developed countries. One is the proposition that parliamentary democracies tend toward larger public sectors than presidential ones because the separation of powers inherent to the latter makes it harder for politicians to extract rents from the state (Steinmo 1993; Persson and Tabellini 2003). Another is that proportional representation (PR) systems for electing legislators favor higher taxation and spending (Steinmo and Tolbert 1998; Persson and Tabellini 2003). The logic is essentially that PR favors a party system based on multiple competitive parties, while first past the post (FPTP) tends toward a two-party system. Multiparty systems, in turn, facilitate the creation of center-left governing coalitions that strive to redistribute income (Iversen and Soskice 2006).

Other theories emphasize the effects of federalism versus more centralized systems. The classical argument is that, by allowing individuals and businesses to shop around for the lowest tax rate, federalism puts pressure on subnational governments to keep their taxes low and thus leads to a lighter tax burden overall (Brennan and Buchannan 1980). However, other scholars have argued that federalism may lead to greater taxation if spending is decentralized more than taxation (Stein 1999; Rodden 2003). Where such a "vertical fiscal imbalance" exists, subnational governments may be tempted to spend irresponsibly, knowing that the economic and political costs of paying for their outlays will be incurred by national authorities.

Finally, with regard to formal institutional design, analysts of Brazil and Chile have advanced theories based on idiosyncratic aspects of their respective constitutions. In the former case, they assert that the constitution ratified in 1988, shortly after Brazil's democratic transition, led to heavier taxation, mainly by creating a series of new social spending commitments (Melo et al. 2010; Afonso 2013). These commitments are particularly extensive and costly in the case of pensions. With regard to Chile, the argument focuses on institutional structures left over from the 1973 to 1990 military regime that were designed to bolster rightist influence. Until their elimination in 2005, these "authoritarian enclaves" helped to slow fiscal growth by keeping center-left governments from fully capitalizing on majorities won at the polls (López 2013). Especially important were the nine senators appointed (rather than elected) to office by other state institutions.

Capacity-based explanations suggest that the tax burden is determined not so much by formal institutional structures as by deep-seated norms that shape the state's ability to govern. While some states boast institutions that both obey the law themselves and enforce it consistently on society, others are captive to rent-seeking interests that divert them from their public purpose and engender social apathy or resistance. An inability to tax effectively is viewed as one of the consequences of state weakness. Scholars differ in their accounts of the roots of state capacity. Perhaps the best-known perspective portrays it as a by-product of involvement in external war (Hintze 1975; Tilly 1990). When they do not destroy the state, wars augment its capacity by fostering a general willingness to sacrifice for the good of the nation and forcing leaders, under threat of military defeat or even death, to develop robust mechanisms for extracting revenue from individuals and organizations within their territories. A more recent theory, derived from Latin American experiences, focuses instead on a number of domestic variables, especially the character of labor relations and the degree of cooperation between regional elites in the decades following national independence, and the way in which non-elite groups were subsequently incorporated into the polity (Kurtz 2013).

1.2.3 Actor-Centric Theories

Actor-centric perspectives view the extent of taxation as a function of the influence of certain political actors. Some scholars argue that taxes are higher where left parties control government because such parties desire generous social policies, which in turn require revenue (Cameron 1978; Stein and Caro 2013). At least one study has indicated that strong labor unions, which are sometimes allied with left parties, are also associated with heavier taxation (Steinmo and Tolbert 1998). Although they focus on taxation, these arguments concur with the central theme of the well-known "power resources" school of social policy research, which views the size and characteristics of welfare states as a reflection of labor and left-party strength (Stephens 1979; Korpi 1983; Huber and Stephens 2001, 2012).

In recent years, a number of studies based wholly or partly on Latin American cases have stressed the influence of economic elites on tax policy, a theme not previously prominent in the literature (Lieberman 2003; Fairfield 2010, 2011, 2015; Schneider 2012; Flores-Macías 2014). With one exception (Schneider 2012), these works focus exclusively on direct taxes, rather than the overall tax burden. It is not self-evident that the determinants of these two variables should be the same, since higher-tax countries tend to rely less on direct taxes than do lower-tax ones (Steinmo 1993; Kato 2003). Nevertheless, it is worth touching on these works, both because they focus on Latin America and because some of the arguments they advance end up shedding considerable light on the issue explored in this book.

All these works stress the degree to which a country's economic elites are politically united. However, they contrast sharply in terms of the significance attributed to this variable. On the one hand, Lieberman, Schneider, and Flores-Macías all suggest that elite cohesion facilitates revenue-raising reform by helping the collective interest of the private sector in a more effective state prevail over the individual interest of particular firms in avoiding heavier taxation. On the other hand, Fairfield argues that because business leaders tend strongly to oppose taxation, the more unified and politically connected they are, the harder it is to raise taxes.[18] This argument is, in a sense, the flip side of the power resources perspective: while power resource-type arguments suggest that a well-organized working class encourages heavier taxation, Fairfield's argument suggests that a highly organized capitalist class discourages it. Table 1.3 provides a summary of existing theories of the tax burden.

1.3 ARGUMENT OF THE BOOK

This book generally does not find much evidence for the economic and institutional explanations discussed earlier. Instead, it elaborates a central argument that mainly echoes key themes from the actor-centric literature. It also draws on theoretical work on path dependence, which, despite some inconsistencies in conceptualization (discussed in Chapter 2), provides useful tools for clarifying the roots of divergence among these cases. The discussion in this section touches very briefly on the theories that do not appear to provide much leverage on this set of cases, but dwells mainly on laying out the core argument. It also addresses an important potential objection to that argument, related to the issue of tax progressivity.

---

[18] Fairfield (2010, 2015) also views the "structural" power that business wields through the threat of disinvestment or capital flight as a check on revenue-raising tax reform. However, since this power varies greatly depending on the timing and specific characteristics of the proposed reform, her argument about cross-national differences in reform success focuses on the political influence of business, or what she refers to as "instrumental" power.

TABLE 1.3 *Theories of the tax burden summarized*

Type	Variable	Representative works
Economic	Economic development	Wagner (1883), Lotz and Morss (1970), Pessino and Fenochietto (2010)
	Trade openness	Rodrik (1998), Ram (2009)
	Weight of agriculture	Piancastelli (2001), Gupta (2007)
	Price inflation	Tanzi (1977), Cetrángolo and Gómez Sabaini (2007a)
	Natural resources	Patrucchi and Grottola (2011), Crivelli and Gupta (2014)
	Proximity to United States (Mexico)	Elizondo Mayer-Serra (2014)
Institutional	Democracy	Boix (2001), Besley and Persson (2013), Bird et al. (2014)
	Democracy-inequality interaction	Meltzer and Richard (1981)
	Presidentialism v. parliamentarism	Persson and Tabellini (2003)
	Electoral system	Steinmo and Tolbert (1998), Persson and Tabellini (2003)
	Federalism	Brennan and Buchannan (1980)
	Vertical fiscal imbalance	Stein (1999), Rodden (2003)
	1988 constitution (Brazil)	Melo et al. (2010), Afonso (2013)
	Authoritarian enclaves (Chile)	López (2013)
	State capacity	Tilly (1990); Kurtz (2013)
Actor-centric	Labor/left-party strength	Cameron (1978), Steinmo and Tolbert (1998)
	Economic elite cohesion	Schneider (2012); Flores-Macías (2014); Fairfield (2015)

1.3.1 Limitations and Strengths of Existing Theories

For the most part, existing theories of the tax burden do not shed much light on the empirical puzzle addressed here. To some extent, of course, this is because the research design largely controls for the causal variables they propose. Variables like economic development, presidentialism (versus parliamentarism), electoral system design, contemporary political regime, and involvement in external war do not get a truly fair test. However, even some that are not well controlled for, including trade openness, inequality, proximity to the US border, federalism, and postindependence labor relations, do not provide a compelling explanation. In some instances, the tax burden outcomes unambiguously clash with theoretical expectations. In others, the outcomes are superficially more consistent with expectations, but closer scrutiny reveals that the causal mechanisms they posit are contradicted by the empirical evidence.

Nevertheless, some other variables highlighted by the literature do illuminate certain aspects of the empirical puzzle addressed here. These include, most clearly, nontax natural resource revenues, labor/left-party influence, economic elite organization, and the idiosyncratic constitutional design features emphasized by scholars of Chile and Brazil.

The tax-depressing impact of nontax resource revenues stands as a separate explanation to the more clearly political one emphasized in this book. There can be little doubt that nontax revenues from resource extraction help explain the especially light tax burden in Mexico, where the state oil company plays a crucial role in funding the public sector. Nevertheless, as Chapter 2 demonstrates, even if we take nontax sources into consideration, Mexico's fiscal revenues are only about equal to those of Chile and far smaller than those of Argentina and Brazil. Hence, the substitutive effect of nontax revenue constitutes no more than a first approximation at solving the puzzle posed by this book.

The role of the other variables mentioned earlier can best be understood not individually but as components of a broader explanation of tax burden variance that melds actor-centric variables with insights from the path dependence literature. That argument, which stresses the enduring impact of instances of sharp distributive conflict on the relative influence of statist and anti-statist actors, is outlined briefly in the next subsection.

1.3.2 Property Rights Threats and the Tax Burden

The book argues that tax burden variance among the case study countries is largely a function of the occurrence or nonoccurrence of earlier episodes of major redistributive reform, especially ones that deeply threatened, but did not eliminate, private property. Where they occurred, such episodes affected later taxation levels by spurring economic elites to mobilize against state intervention and join forces with social conservatives, who were also alarmed by the changes. These historical episodes of reform and reaction left lasting legacies of anti-statist political thought and organization that have constituted a hindrance to public sector growth, not only by opposing it directly but also by taking measures to weaken its proponents, especially organized labor. In contrast, where such an episode did not occur, economic elites remained more accepting of state intervention and failed to organize effectively to resist it. The result, eventually, was the robust growth of tax revenues.

Anti-statism, it should be underscored, is not simply a dislike of paying taxes, but rather a general wariness of the effects of state economic intervention. Anti-statists tend to oppose all sorts of taxes, not just the more redistributive ones, because taxation provides public authorities with the fiscal resources necessary to shape the economy and society and to build a constituency for subsequent and perhaps more aggressive interventions. Given their distrust of the public sector, anti-statists prefer to "starve the beast" (to use a phrase coined by US conservatives) by denying it revenue. They also resist a greater state role in non-fiscal areas, such as trade protection, domestic regulation, and production of goods and services. Thus, where anti-statism is strong, the tendency for the public sector to grow as society becomes richer may be attenuated.[19]

The terms statist and anti-statist as used here are mostly, but not entirely, equivalent to left and right. Some political groups not usually described as leftist because they reject Marxism and embrace relatively conservative social values are nevertheless statist because they prefer interventionist and redistributive policies. Argentine *peronismo* (as the followers of former populist leader Juan Perón are collectively referred to) is the key example among the cases. The flip side of the coin consists of actors with relatively liberal social values but a strong preference for market-based policies. Such groups may be commonly described as centrist, but their views about the state's role in accumulation and distribution place them in the anti-statist category. Examples include parties like Argentina's Republican Proposal (Propuesta Republicana, PRO) and Chile's National Renewal (Renovación Nacional, RN).

This argument is actor-centric in focusing on the relative power of certain political actors as the key determinant of the tax burden. It acknowledges both the tax-increasing effects of worker organization (as in power resource-type arguments) and the tax-inhibiting impact of economic elite organization (as in Fairfield's recent work), portraying them as components of a more general balance of power between statist and anti-statist forces. However, it puts primary emphasis on the latter, since elites that are broadly mobilized to resist the state can make it difficult for workers even to organize themselves. Although the distinctive constitutional features fiscal scholars have emphasized in the Brazilian and Chilean cases are indeed significant, the argument portrays them largely as reflections of underlying power structures that support and oppose, respectively, statist policies.

The concept of path dependence is useful for understanding the connections between instances of extensive redistribution and subsequent anti-statism. While there are significant differences in how path dependence is understood, scholars generally seem to agree that this concept refers to instances in which historical events give rise to formal and informal institutions that, due to certain

---

[19] Anti-statists do not necessarily reject the use of state power to repress political dissent. However, their support for such measures is generally motivated by the goal of defending capitalism from statist threats.

self-reinforcing qualities, are stubbornly resistant to change (Mahoney 2000; Pierson 2000; Capoccia and Kelemen 2007; Slater and Simmons 2010). Versions that emphasize the power of ideas (North 1990; Mahoney 2000; Pierson 2004) in stabilizing a specific path find particularly strong echo here, since perceptions about the state play a key role in the causal process. Where it occurred, major property rights redistribution had path-dependent effects in terms of strengthening anti-statist actors in an enduring, self-perpetuating fashion. Broad, multi-sector business organizations and strong right parties emerged and became permanent fixtures of the political landscape. Moreover, sustained anti-statist influence on public policies weakened labor, reinforcing a balance of power that leans toward anti-statism.

1.3.3   How the Cases Fit into the Argument

Of the four country cases examined in depth in the book, two, Chile and Mexico, belong to the first category described earlier, in which instances of sharp redistribution provoked the formation of a strong anti-statist coalition that subsequently helped keep the tax burden light. In the other two, Brazil and Argentina, no such episode occurred and, at least partly as a result, taxation has risen to high levels. To be sure, the country pairs are not homogeneous. Chile's political trajectory differs from Mexico's in crucial ways and the same can be said of Brazil and Argentina. Nevertheless, each pair evidences a similar causal process with regard to taxation that is at the same time distinct from the other pair.

Chile can be thought of as the "easy" case with regard to the first analytic category, since the events involved are especially dramatic. Between 1970 and 1973, Socialist president Salvador Allende implemented a series of major reforms, including land reform and expropriation of urban businesses, that deeply menaced private property and helped provoke the rise of a conservative military regime that would devastate labor and the left and eventually bring a sharp tax reduction. Although the military left power in 1990, the mobilization against Allende left a legacy of rightwing civilian political organization that survived the transition. Since then, a highly organized business sector and strong partisan right with solid ties to conservative sectors of the Catholic Church have worked effectively to moderate tax increases and discourage the reemergence of the alliance of unions and programmatic left parties that had protagonized state expansion during the years of redistributive reform. Both the origins of the Chilean constitution, forged in 1980, and the persistence of its key conservatizing features until 2005 expressed the strength of anti-statist forces post-Allende.

Mexico is a subtler case, since the conservative backlash against redistribution did not topple the old political regime, which would survive until the 1990s. The underlying causal process is nonetheless similar in crucial respects. Changes implemented under Lázaro Cárdenas (1934–1940), including

Latin America's first major land reform and the state's seizure of the crucial oil industry, forged a cohesive anti-statist bloc among key economic elites, with strong links to Catholic social conservatives. This bloc wielded great influence over the state after 1940, pushing authorities both to moderate taxation and to divide and weaken the popular forces Cárdenas had unleashed. It was largely because of its power that the tax burden stagnated, turning Mexico into a case of exceptionally light taxation. In the 1980s and 1990s, in a context of economic crisis and pressures for democracy, anti-statist elites would transform the National Action Party (Partido Acción Nacional, PAN) from a token opposition into one of Latin America's most successful rightist parties. As in Chile, democratization since the 1990s has not kept anti-statist forces, including the PAN (which held the presidency from 2000 to 2012) and an exceptionally well-organized business elite, from continuing to exercise great influence and impeding more substantial expansion of the public sector.

Among the countries in which no major property threat arose, Brazil is the case that contrasts most clearly with the Chilean and Mexican experiences. Despite some episodes of mild social reformism, Brazilian elites have never faced a government both willing and able to implement major redistributive change. As a result, they have remained relatively complacent and politically unorganized in the face of rising taxation. Compared to Chile and Mexico, Brazil boasts neither strong business organization nor programmatic rightist parties. Instead of acting collectively to block public sector expansion, Brazilian elites have generally tried to profit from it through rent seeking. Even the 1964–1985 military regime, widely regarded as pro-business, had a strongly statist orientation. Albeit unintentionally, elite acceptance of state-led development has created a permissive context for labor unions and associated parties to grow and become a force for greater public spending (and consequent taxation), particularly since the democratic transition of the 1980s. Brazil's constitution, drafted during that period, has facilitated public sector growth, but both its original provisions and the ways it has been amended reflect a preexisting power balance favoring statism.

The Argentine case differs from the Brazilian one in some ways, including the greater instability of the tax burden and the greater strength of organized labor and an associated populist electoral coalition. However, it shares with Brazil the crucial fact that no government has advanced a reform project that seriously menaced private property. Even Perón, who implemented major labor and social policy reforms during his first two presidencies (1946–1955), left property rights largely inviolate and portrayed himself as a bulwark against socialism and a champion of domestic industry. Rather than uniting capitalists in a solid anti-statist bloc, Perón aggravated existing divisions. Although subsequent military regimes sometimes repressed labor and sought to reverse public sector expansion, conflicts between statist and anti-statist factions of the business community hindered the consolidation of a stable liberal development model and engendered acute instability. Since the 1980s, moreover, democratic consolidation has gradually allowed the statist-leaning power balance to influence public policies in a more

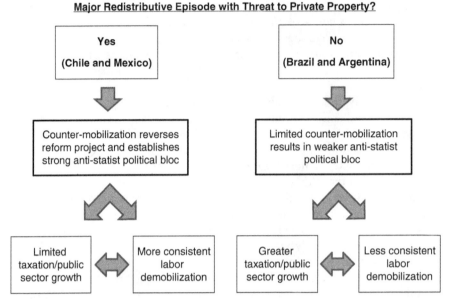

FIGURE I.I Summary of the argument

sustained fashion, resulting, as in Brazil, in the formation of a substantial welfare
state supported by heavy taxation. Figure I.I graphically depicts the overall
argument, with the arrows indicating causal relationships.

I.3.4 Progressivity and Tax Burden Magnitude

This book is not primarily an attempt to explain differences in the relative
weight of different types of taxes, but it is important to touch briefly on this
variable, since there is an important potential objection to the book's argument
that is related to it. The fact that statism is associated with strong labor
movements and leftist or populist parties and anti-statism with well-organized
economic elites might lead one to expect a polity that tilts in a statist direction to
also rely more heavily on progressive taxes, in order to maximize redistribution.
However, as pointed out earlier, that is not the case among the countries
analyzed here. In fact, in the countries with heavier tax burdens, Argentina
and Brazil, direct taxes bring in a significantly smaller share of total revenue
than in the others.

An initial retort to this objection is that the relationship it implies between the
tax structure and public sector size is not generally observed in other countries,
either. Previous research, especially on OECD countries, has shown that
societies with heavier tax burdens tend to rely on direct taxes for a smaller

share of their revenues (Huber and Stephens 2001; Kato 2003; Beramendi and Rueda 2007; Joumard et al. 2012). These countries also tend to have more extensive welfare states, which consume large quantities of revenue. Of course, the reliance on regressive taxation blunts the redistributive impact of spending (Timmons 2005). However, it does not negate it entirely. The cases under study here fit this broader trend. Compared to Chile and Mexico, Argentina and Brazil not only have substantially heavier tax burdens but also have more regressive tax structures and much greater spending on social programs. Although they redistribute far less income than the large European welfare states, they appear to do so more than the other countries examined in this book.

Why do countries with heavy tax burdens and extensive welfare states not generally rely mainly on progressive taxation? For the most part, the literature suggests that this pattern reflects a kind of structural requisite of capitalism (Przeworski and Wallerstein 1988; Lindert 2004; Beramendi and Rueda 2007). It is difficult to both extract large amounts of revenue and do so in a way that disproportionately burdens economic elites because the latter may respond by curtailing investment, moving capital abroad, or using their resources to exert political pressure on the government. Put more generally, any fiscal arrangement that sharply and systematically takes from one social group to give to another is hard to sustain (Timmons 2005). There must be an implicit "fiscal contract" in which roughly the same group that pays the bulk of the taxes also receives most of the benefits, be they social programs (in the case of non-elites) or secure property rights (in the case of elites).

These observations tell us why heavy taxation and strong progressivity tend not to go together, but they do not tell us why some countries choose the path of a large public sector funded by a more regressive tax structure, while others settle on a smaller state sustained by more progressive taxation. The arguments advanced in this book suggest a possible answer: the long-term impact of sharp redistributive conflict. Attempts to redistribute on a large scale, especially when they involve major threats to property, may foment such mistrust of the state among economic elites that they become wary of endowing it with substantial resources, even through non-direct forms of taxation. In contrast, where such conflict has not occurred, elites are more tolerant of public sector growth, as long as it is paid for primarily by indirect and social security taxes. The result is a state that can potentially be far larger but, mainly because of its funding source, may not be markedly more redistributive.

1.4 RESEARCH DESIGN

Methodologically, the most distinctive aspect of the present study is its use of a purely qualitative, case study-based approach, since existing scholarship on the tax burden leans rather heavily on statistical methods. Although this point was raised near the outset of this chapter, it is worth spelling out the justification for this choice of approach and further clarifying some other aspects of the research design, in particular, how the dependent variable is operationalized, the logic of the case selection, and the data sources.

1.4.1   Benefits of Qualitative Comparison

Without a doubt, quantitative analysis can be a very powerful research strategy, especially when it comes to testing hypotheses that are readily quantifiable and for which appropriate data are available. By drawing on a large universe of cases, statistics can offer the advantage of strong external validity or, in other words, generalizable findings. It also yields precise estimates of the amount of variance explained by each causal factor.

Nevertheless, there are good reasons to complement statistical work with a smaller-N approach. The debate launched in response to King, Keohane, and Verba (1994), an influential methodological treatise often criticized for implying that statistical methods are inherently superior, has made it clearer than ever that case-oriented research has its own distinctive logic and strengths. Both qualitative and quantitative researchers have argued that this approach generates causal inferences in a way that is essentially different from statistics. In particular, it relies heavily on within-case observation of causal processes that unfold over time (George and Bennett 2005; Brady and Collier 2010). Through this method, the researcher eliminates hypotheses that imply mechanisms different from the ones observed, gradually settling on an explanation consistent with the evidence.

The small-N approach also has its own distinctive advantages over statistics. Because the researcher can learn more about each case, the small-N approach provides greater internal validity. It puts the researcher in a better position to tease out complex or subtle causal relationships that would be hard to perceive from the bird's-eye view of quantitative analysis, as well as to test theories that are difficult to operationalize statistically. It also makes the researcher less vulnerable to the weaknesses of large cross-national data sets, because he or she can triangulate between different sources of information.

Of course, a mixed-methods strategy can potentially combine some of the advantages of both statistical and qualitative work (Seawright 2016). However, given the dozens of statistical studies that have already been conducted on the roots of tax burden variance (including a handful specifically on Latin America), the time seems ripe for a study wholly dedicated to using qualitative analysis to explore this issue. In addition, it is not clear that the argument advanced by this book could be tested statistically, since longitudinal data are lacking to operationalize such variables as the ideological inclinations of business organizations and the extent of their ties to parties, think tanks, and other actors.

1.4.2 Further Specifying the Dependent Variable

This book's dependent variable is the contemporary tax burden, understood as total tax revenues as a share of GDP averaged over the five-year period from 2013 to 2017. The values on this variable for the case study countries are displayed in Table 1.1. A range of years is used because the tax burden can fluctuate somewhat from year to year based on economic conditions, even without changes in tax policy. However, the relationship between the cases would be essentially the same for any individual year within this range, or even a number of years earlier.[20]

Tax revenue refers to payments made compulsorily by private individuals and organizations to the state in fulfillment of laws intended mainly to endow the state with revenue. This definition includes taxes imposed by both the national and subnational (i.e., state/provincial and municipal) governments. It also encompasses the entire spectrum of types of taxes, including direct, indirect, and social security taxes. What it does not include are payments made to public sector entities for the purchase of goods and services, including natural resources such as oil and gas, as well as payments that are mandated by law but ultimately go to non-state entities, such as private pension funds.[21] The former are excluded because they do not involve legal coercion, the latter because they do not fund the public sector.

While this is a conventional definition of taxation, similar to the ones used by international agencies like the United Nations Economic Commission for Latin America and the Caribbean (ECLAC), the International Monetary Fund (IMF), and the OECD, it is worth elaborating on certain aspects of it, since some scholarly studies adopt narrower definitions.

Cross-national analyses of taxation level have at times focused exclusively on central government revenues. This approach is probably based mainly on subnational data scarcity, since revenue raised by subnational governments indisputably plays a crucial role in funding major public policies in some countries. For example, in Argentina and (especially) Brazil, subnational taxes provide a significant share of the funding for policies that are wholly or almost wholly funded by the national government in more centralized countries, including health care, policing, and higher education. It does not make sense

---

[20] The ordinal ranking of the cases with respect to their tax burdens goes back to about the early 1990s. However, as Chapter 6 makes clear, since the early 2000s Argentina's tax burden has gone from being closer to Chile's to being similar to Brazil's much heavier one.

[21] Unfortunately, official data sources classify some of the fiscal revenue from state-owned natural resource companies as tax revenue, contradicting the definition used here. Furthermore, they do not permit precise separation of these revenues from those paid by private resource extraction firms. However, rough estimates based on the relative weight of public firms in the extractive sector suggest that "taxes" on state-owned firms contributed significantly less than 1 percent of GDP on average in all four countries between 2013 and 2017. In addition, in every case except Chile, these revenues came mainly from indirect taxes, the onus of which is ultimately borne mostly by private consumers.

in these cases to only consider revenues collected by the national government. Moreover, if light taxation in Chile and Mexico is due in part to the force of anti-statist ideology among key actors, as this book argues, the effects are unlikely to be restricted to the national level.

It is probably even more common to exclude social security. The rationale is usually not explicit and may, again, involve data limitations. However, if there is a theoretical justification, it is probably that social security payroll contributions more closely resemble payments for a service than a tax. This view is unconvincing, both because such payments are legally required and because the financing of social security programs is often deeply intertwined with the broader tax system. On the one hand, general tax revenues are sometimes used to compensate for the insufficiency of social security taxes and, on the other, the latter have been known to be diverted to other purposes. The Argentine and Brazilian cases, as well as that of Chile before its 1980 social security reform, will provide examples of these phenomena.

1.4.3   Case Selection

In qualitative research design, the selection of cases to be studied is a crucial decision, since it impacts what variables can reasonably be tested, the reliability of the findings, and other issues. This book adopts what Przeworski and Teune (1970) refer to as a "most-similar systems" design, which involves selecting cases that resemble each other with respect to a number of theoretically relevant independent (i.e., causal) variables but have different values on the dependent variable. By controlling for independent variables that are well established in the literature, this approach allows the researcher to focus on others, including ones that may have not been identified or highlighted by previous scholarship.

Despite having disparate tax burdens, Argentina, Brazil, Chile, and Mexico share a number of characteristics that previous work suggests are relevant to this variable. For the most part, the cases are not actually identical with regard to these characteristics, something that is difficult to achieve in the social sciences. However, they are similar enough to cast serious doubt on the idea that the variable in question can explain marked differences in the tax take.

First, the cases share a relatively high level of development by Latin American standards. Every country but Chile has been classified by the World Bank as "upper middle income" in recent years. Chile was in that category until 2011 but was subsequently reclassified as "high income." Second, over the last two decades, all four countries have generally been considered democracies by scholars and regime indices like those of Freedom House and the Polity V database. Third, all four countries (like the rest of Latin America) have presidential constitutions. Fourth, with one partial exception, they use PR for electing legislators. Mexico is the exception, but rather than using FPTP, it uses a hybrid system (Kerevel 2010). Moreover, in recent decades, Mexico has had a multiparty system with a relatively clear left, right, and center, much as one would expect under PR. Fifth, the countries share a rather similar history of interstate war. All four became embroiled in significant cross-border conflicts during the mid-to-late nineteenth century but have enjoyed largely peaceful relations with neighboring countries since then (Centeno 2002). Brazil and Mexico actively supported the Allies in World War II, but their involvement was too limited to significantly affect their fiscal systems. Similarly, Argentina's involvement in the 1982 Malvinas/Falkland Islands War with Great Britain was too brief (nine weeks) to transform its tax collection apparatus.

Finally, it is worth noting that all four countries are also part of one region, Latin America, comprising societies that share a similar cultural and historical background. All were colonized by a Catholic, Iberian power (Spain or Portugal) during the sixteenth century and gained their independence during the early nineteenth century. While there are no explicit theories linking Iberian colonialism to the extent of contemporary taxation, it is plausible that this background has an influence that has not yet been clearly perceived by scholars. If so, that influence is controlled for by the case selection.

Several of the other variables reviewed in the previous section do vary considerably between the cases, including fiscal centralization, natural resource revenues, trade openness, inflation, and income inequality. One might argue, then, that the research design suffers from a "degrees of freedom" problem (i.e., having more potential causal variables than cases). However, most of the variables that vary do so in ways that contradict theory. In addition, the in-depth "process tracing" method used to investigate the cases facilitates the weeding out of explanations inconsistent with the processes observed in the case study, even when the values on the dependent variable are seemingly consistent with the theory's predictions.

1.4.4 Data Sources

In investigating these cases, the study taps three main types of sources. First, it makes intensive use of the scholarly literature on all four countries, including works from political science, history, economics, and other disciplines. The secondary literature is crucial for understanding the causes and consequences of historical events, which end up playing a central role in the book's argument.

Second, it employs data sets and reports published by governments and multilateral organizations like ECLAC, the IMF, the World Bank, and the Inter-American Development Bank (IDB). It should be noted that some categories of tax data are difficult or impossible to obtain for earlier decades, with subnational and social security taxes posing the biggest problems. There are also problems of conflicting sources, lack of transparency or consistency in aggregating different types of revenue, and unreliable GDP estimates. The approach adopted to dealing with these difficulties is to use data that seem roughly consistent with other available sources, to exercise transparency in reporting the limitations of the data, and, where possible, to use data sets collected by international organizations, since they (more than national government agencies) use standardized methodologies to calculate the tax burden and disaggregate revenue sources.

Finally, the study makes use of information drawn from in-depth, open-ended interviews conducted by the author with current and former legislators, executive branch officials, interest group officials, and tax consultants. A total of 86 interviews were conducted, including 23 in Argentina, 25 in Brazil, 15 in Chile, and 23 in Mexico. With two exceptions, the interviews were conducted in person. The Brazilian interviews were carried out in 2015, while the rest occurred in 2014. Some interviewees requested anonymity because of the sensitivity of the issues discussed. They are listed in the text by the names of their organizations. The interview data are used, along with media coverage, primarily to understand recent events.

1.5 PLAN OF THE BOOK

The arguments outlined in this introduction are elaborated over the course of six additional chapters. Chapter 2 evaluates existing theories of the tax burden through a comparative analysis of the four country cases. Based on that analysis, as well as insights derived from path dependence theory, it further develops the explanation of tax burden variance sketched in this chapter.

Chapters 3, 4, 5, and 6 delve more deeply into the cases of Chile, Mexico, Brazil, and Argentina, respectively. They flesh out with greater empirical detail and nuance the book's argument about the path-dependent effects of sharp redistributive change. While the analysis could potentially have been organized differently, dealing with each country as a whole helps underscore the power of historical legacies. The sequence in which the cases are presented emphasizes three key points: (1) the similarities between Chile and Mexico, despite the fact that these countries are often viewed as having dissimilar political trajectories; (2) the striking contrast between both of these cases and Brazil; and (3) the fact that Argentina, despite experiencing major redistributive change under Perón, nonetheless conforms more closely to the Brazilian model than the Chilean and Mexican one, due mainly to the lack of property rights threat.

Chapter 7 concludes the book by extending its argument in three ways. First, it examines the argument's broader applicability within Latin America through a comparison of two countries, Guatemala and Ecuador, at lower levels of development than the core cases. Second, it evaluates how well the argument travels beyond Latin America. Finally, since the argument could be seen as implying a somber view of the prospects of achieving substantially greater socioeconomic equity in Latin America, it closes by reflecting more explicitly on this vital question. This chapter suggests that the book's central argument is compelling in the cases of Ecuador and Guatemala, but does not perform as well beyond Latin America because it is embedded in certain distinctive socioeconomic and political characteristics of this region. It also advances the view that in the Latin American context gradual reformism mainly through the fiscal system represents the "least bad" path to greater equality.

2

Historical Property Threats and Contemporary Tax Burdens

The introductory chapter outlined in a preliminary fashion an explanation of differences in the contemporary tax burdens of Argentina, Brazil, Chile, and Mexico. This chapter elaborates that argument further by empirically evaluating existing theories of the tax burden and using that analysis as the basis for constructing an explanation of variance among this set of countries.

It argues that the large majority of explanations offered by the literature are unconvincing in the context of this comparison. For the most part, the actual outcomes are simply not consistent with their predictions. Even when there are specific country cases that do seem to fit, deeper scrutiny fails to turn up clear evidence of a causal connection. Nevertheless, there are a number of theories that do shed light on the cases. While none is satisfying on its own, collectively they provide a rough preliminary account, comprised of three major components, one economic in nature and the other two more clearly political.

The economic component involves state-controlled natural resource extraction, which depresses taxation by providing an alternative source of revenue. Of the two political components, the first consists of specific aspects of the constitutional structures of Brazil and Chile, which have had the effect of increasing and reducing taxation, respectively. The second consists of an expanded version of the power resource perspective, which brings the traditional emphasis on left-labor power and Fairfield's focus on right-business power under one conceptual roof. This theory suggests that national tax burdens reflect the balance of power between statist and anti-statist actors. It is the most crucial aspect, since it can both compensate for the limited explanatory power of the natural resource argument and place the case-specific institutional explanations within a broader political context that makes the origins and persistence of these institutions more understandable.

The major weakness of this account is that it cannot effectively explain the roots of variation in the power structures underlying contemporary tax burdens. The chapter, therefore, develops such an explanation. It argues that differences in the balance of power between statist and anti-statist actors reflect the impact of historical episodes of profound redistributive change, or their relative absence. Paradoxically, where such episodes were most extensive, and especially where they involved widespread threats to private property, they had the effect of strengthening anti-statist actors in an enduring way. In contrast, where redistribution was limited to fiscal and regulatory policies, a strong anti-statist bloc failed to emerge. Chile and Mexico comprise the first category, while Argentina and Brazil make up the second. In developing this argument, this chapter draws on ideas from the literature on path dependence, which highlights how partly contingent events can give rise to political arrangements with self-reinforcing qualities that encourage their long-term persistence.

It is organized according to the two key tasks it addresses. The initial section tests existing theories of the tax burden and derives from that analysis an account stressing the importance of the statist versus anti-statist power balance. The second taps path dependence theory to develop an explanation of the roots of that balance.

2.1 ASSESSING EXISTING EXPLANATIONS

The theories of the tax burden outlined in Chapter 1 are evaluated here, beginning with the two categories (economic and institutional) that, on the whole, provide less explanatory power, then moving on to the one (actor-centric) that offers more. Theories that are largely controlled for by the case selection are excluded, with the exception of the idea that democracy favors heavier taxation. The reason for this exception is that, although all four countries have widely been considered democracies in recent decades, there are differences in the quality and age of the current regimes, as well as in the cumulative historical experience of each country with democratic politics, that are potentially significant. While the section finds that extant theories from all three major categories contribute to our understanding of tax burden variance, it argues that an actor-centric account emphasizing the relative influence of statist and anti-statist forces provides the most explanatory leverage.

It should be noted here that, whatever the causes of tax burden variance, they appear to operate mainly through differences in the legal tax system rather than evasion. The most current comparable data show little correlation between evasion rates and revenue production among this set of countries. For example, high-tax Argentina and Brazil have evasion rates for the VAT and both the personal and corporate income taxes that are similar to or even higher than those of low-tax Mexico (ECLAC 2017a, p. 44). Economic informality, which can be seen as a rough proxy for evasion by smaller businesses, is also not clearly correlated with the tax burden. For instance, Brazil has a higher overall informality rate than either Chile or Mexico, but also has a vastly heavier tax burden (Gómez Sabaini and Moran 2012, p. 21; Corbacho et al. 2013, p. 68).

Hence, although noncompliance with the tax code is a significant problem in all four countries, it does not determine the diversity in their tax burdens.

2.1.1   Economic Theories

Most of the economic explanations outlined in Chapter 1 can be dealt with briefly because actual tax burdens among the cases unambiguously contradict their predictions. Trade openness is widely viewed as promoting heavier taxation (Rodrik 1998; Ram 2009) but, as Table 2.1 indicates, low-tax Mexico and Chile have considerably more open economies than Brazil and Argentina. These differences are longstanding. While all four countries have liberalized trade over the past few decades, Chile's opening was especially early and decisive.[1] Mexico began liberalizing later, but even during the pre-1980s era of import-substitution industrialization (ISI), its economy was more open than those of other large Latin American countries (Graham 1982, p. 25; Ros 1993). The negative correlation between openness and the tax burden is no mere coincidence. To a large extent, as this book should make clear, both trade policy and tax policy have reflected broader ideas about the role of the state in development.

Dependence on agriculture, which is generally believed to impede taxation, also fails to shed light on the differences among these countries. As Table 2.1 demonstrates, the correlation between farm sector size and the tax burden is nearly the opposite of what theory would lead us to expect: Argentina derives the largest share of GDP from agriculture, followed by Brazil, Chile, and

TABLE 2.1 *Trade openness, agricultural dependence, and inflation, 2013–2017*

Country	Exports and imports/ GDP (%)	Agricultural product/ GDP (%)	Annual inflation (%)
Argentina	26.3	6.0	27.4[a]
Brazil	25.2	4.5	6.7
Chile	60.1	3.8	3.3
Mexico	70.8	3.2	3.9

Source: World Bank Database (https://data.worldbank.org/); Cavallo and Bertolotto (2016)
[a] Official Argentine price data for this period do not follow international norms, so this figure is derived from estimates by Cavallo and Bertollotto (2016).

[1] Chile's liberalization occurred mainly in the second half of the 1970s, while Mexico's happened between the mid-1980s and early 1990s. Argentina began its trade opening in the late 1970s, but this change was not as radical or sustained as in Chile. Most of the liberalization occurred in the early 1990s. Brazil, finally, opened its trade mainly during the early 1990s (Agosín and Ffrench-Davis 1995).

Mexico. As with trade, these differences are not new, since Argentina and Brazil, with more favorable environmental conditions, have long had more dynamic farm sectors.

Price inflation, for its part, has indeed undermined taxation in some of these countries in the past. As Chapter 6 argues, the Olivera–Tanzi effect is an especially important concept for understanding the evolution of taxation in Argentina. Nevertheless, inflation cannot account for contemporary variance in the tax burden, both because none of these countries has experienced truly extreme inflation since the early 1990s and because, as can be seen in Table 2.1, contemporary differences on this variable contradict theoretical expectations. Brazil and (especially) Argentina have had higher inflation in recent years than the other two countries, yet also have much heavier tax burdens.

The argument linking Mexico's light taxation to its proximity to the United States is also, on the whole, unconvincing. It is true that, until 2013 (when it passed a tax reform law discussed in Chapter 4), Mexico had a lower VAT rate in border regions, based on the nominal goal of avoiding an influx of goods from neighboring countries, where taxes on consumption are lower than Mexico's general VAT rate. Nevertheless, the impact of this measure was small. A top Mexican finance ministry official interviewed for this study said the elimination of the special border rate was expected to yield only 0.1 percent of GDP in revenue (SHCP1 2014, interview).[2]

There is also little empirical evidence to support the hypothesis that proximity to the United States suppresses direct taxation through the threat of capital flight. Mexico has indeed suffered major episodes of capital flight in recent decades, but other Latin American countries far more distant from the United States, including Argentina, have seen much larger outflows relative to GDP (Owens 2017, p. 10). Studies that explain differences in the volume of capital flight across the region attribute it not to location, but to either policy choices, such as an overvalued exchange rate and weak capital controls (Pastor 1990; Mahon 1996), or political factors, including instability and pressures for redistribution (Fatehi 1994; Owens 2017).

A more convincing explanation of Mexico's light taxation comes from the notion that nontax revenue from state-controlled natural resource extraction depresses tax revenues (Patrucchi and Grottola 2011; Crivelli and Gupta 2014). As Table 2.2 demonstrates, Mexico is both the country with the lightest tax burden among this group and the one with easily the largest flow of nontax revenue from resource production.[3] Such revenues come almost entirely from the state-owned oil

---

[2] The actual increase in VAT revenues since the reform has been about 0.2 percent of GDP, compared to the average during the five years preceding the reform (CEPALSTAT), but it cannot be assumed that all this increment is due to the higher border rate.

[3] These figures do not include nontax revenues from sources other than natural resources, but such revenues are insignificant among these countries. In some Latin American countries, they are more important. For example, Panama receives substantial revenue flows from the Panama Canal and Paraguay from the Itaipu Dam.

TABLE 2.2 *Fiscal revenue and spending, 2013–2017*

Country	Nontax natural resource revenues/ GDP (%)[a]	Tax revenues/ GDP (%)	Total fiscal revenue/ GDP (%)	Total public spending/ GDP (%)
Argentina	0.4	31.0	31.4	39.9
Brazil	0.6	32.1	32.7	38.2
Chile	0.5	20.1	20.6	24.5
Mexico	6.0	15.1	21.1	27.3

Source: CEPALSTAT; IMF World Economic Outlook Database (www.imf.org/external/pubs/ft/
weo/2018/02/weodata/index.aspx)
[a] Data are from 2013 to 2016.

company, Mexican Petroleum (Petróleos Mexicanos, PEMEX), and are equivalent
to almost 40 percent of tax revenues. There is a broad consensus among scholars of
Mexico that oil revenues have the effect of discouraging heavier taxation
(Martínez-Vazquez 2001; Tello and Hernández 2010; Elizondo Mayer-Serra
2014) and, indeed, it is hard to imagine a country at Mexico's level of
development maintaining such a light tax burden in the absence of these
revenues. It is also notable that the significant spike in Mexico's tax burden (of
more than 2 percent of GDP) in 2015 coincided with a sharp drop in oil revenues,
suggesting that the high oil prices of the previous decade had helped keep the tax
burden light.

   Nevertheless, the natural resource variable can offer no more than a very
partial explanation of the variance in tax burdens among the cases. The main
reason can easily be gleaned from Table 2.2. Natural resource revenues can
potentially account for the difference in tax burdens between Mexico and Chile,
in the sense that once nontax resource revenues are included, the total fiscal
revenues of the two countries are quite similar.[4] However, they cannot account
for the vast gap in fiscal resources separating both countries from Brazil and
Argentina. Not surprisingly, the latter two countries also have much higher
public spending. In other words, Argentina and Brazil are not just countries
with heavier taxation than Mexico and Chile, they are countries with far larger
public sectors, a circumstance that contradicts the substitution mechanism at
the heart of the natural resource explanation.

   There are also reasons to believe that Mexico's heavy fiscal reliance on
PEMEX is partly a result, rather than just a cause, of the state's inability to tax.
First, Mexico's emergence as an unusually lightly taxed country significantly

---

[4] Natural resource extraction, especially copper mining, plays a major role in Chile's economy.
   Nevertheless, about two-thirds of production is in private hands (Cademartori et al. 2014,
   p. 300), so fiscal revenue from that sector enters the state principally through taxation.

predates its modern rise as a major oil producer. By the late 1940s, as Chapter 4 demonstrates, Mexico's tax burden was already falling visibly behind those of the other three countries. By 1960, it was even lighter than that of many poorer Latin American countries. Although oil had been a major source of revenue in the late 1910s and 1920s, its importance faded thereafter. PEMEX, which monopolized oil production after Cárdenas' 1938 nationalization, made a modest contribution to revenues for its first few decades (Farfán Mares 2011). It was not until the discovery of new oilfields in the mid-1970s that the company became a crucial source of public funding. PEMEX's share of federal revenues shot up from just 3.9 percent in 1972 to 38.1 percent ten years later (Chávez 2005, p. 274).

A second indication that Mexico's reliance on oil revenues reflects the difficulty the state has faced in extracting tax revenues from society is the fact that its fiscal exploitation of its natural resource wealth is unusually intense. Compared to other state oil companies (including Brazil's Petróleo Brasileiro or PETROBRAS), PEMEX transfers a disproportionate share of its earnings to the treasury (Wainberg and Foss 2007; Musacchio and Lazzarini 2014, p. 383; Ramírez-Cendero and Paz 2017, p. 480). For example, a study comparing the state oil companies of Brazil, China, Mexico, and Norway found that, although they had comparable earnings, PEMEX's fiscal contribution was far larger than the others (Wainberg and Foss 2007, p. 21). Because the vast majority of its profits are syphoned off to support spending by other state institutions, PEMEX has been sorely lacking in capital to develop new sources of oil (Penchyna Grub 2014, interview; Tacuba and Chávez 2018). This knowing overexploitation of the state oil company bespeaks a state politically unable to tax its citizens and firms.

2.1.2 Institutional Theories

As mentioned in Chapter 1, the macro-institution of democracy is sometimes viewed as promoting heavier taxation (Boix 2001; Besley and Persson 2013). While there is some evidence in the present comparison that seems consistent with that belief, there is too much that goes in the opposite direction to embrace it as an important cause of variation across the cases.

The case selection does not include countries that currently have authoritarian regimes. However, there are arguably significant differences in both the age of these democracies and their quality or depth. Perhaps more importantly, there is a large amount of variation in the length of time that each country has lived under a democratic regime during its history. Table 2.3 summarizes these differences, drawing on widely used regime indices.

Argentina's current democracy is the oldest of this group, dating back to 1983, when the military junta that had held power since 1976 relinquished it to civilians and elections were held. Brazil's democracy is the second oldest, but its transition was more gradual. The leadership of the armed forces, which had seized power in 1964, conducted elections for state governors in 1982 and permitted a civilian

TABLE 2.3 *Regime characteristics as of 2017*

Country	Age of current democracy (years)[a]	Quality/depth of current democracy			Total time under democracy (years)	
		Polity V (10 = most democratic)	Freedom House (1 = most democratic)	Economist Intelligence Unit (10 = most democratic)[b]	Low bar (democracy> authoritarian)	High bar (democracy score ≥5)
Argentina	35	7.8	2.1	6.8	102	52
Brazil	33	7.9	2.4	7.1	51	50
Chile	28	9.1	1.5	7.8	118	80
Mexico	21	7.7	2.7	6.7	24	21

Sources: Center for Systemic Peace (www.systemicpeace.org), Economist Intelligence Unit (www.eiu.com), author's calculations, Freedom House (www .freedomhouse.org)

[a] Based on transition dates of 1983 for Argentina; 1985 for Brazil; 1990 for Chile; and 1997 for Mexico.

[b] Limited to 2006–2017.

electoral college to choose the president in 1985.[5] It was only in 1989, however, that the country held a popular election for president. Chile ended seventeen years of military rule in 1990, when it elected a civilian president and legislature. The Mexican case is less clear-cut because its old regime was a semi-authoritarian hegemonic party system, rather than a military dictatorship. However, its transition to full democracy is usually seen as having occurred during the 1990s, culminating with the long-ruling Institutional Revolutionary Party's (Partido Revolucionario Institucional, PRI) loss of its congressional majority in 1997 and its defeat in the 2000 presidential election.

There is also variation in the quality or depth of these regimes. All major indices clearly rate Chile's regime highest but, with the exception of Freedom House (which rates Mexico's lower), do not draw sharp distinctions among the others. Cumulative years under democracy is potentially a more important variable, since the ranking of these countries with respect to the tax burden largely precedes the current democratic period.[6] Whether one uses a low bar, in which democratic characteristics simply outweigh authoritarian ones, or a higher one, in which the regime must be at least in the middle of the democracy scale, makes little difference. By both standards, Chile boasts easily the longest democratic tradition, followed in order by Argentina, Brazil, and Mexico.

The Mexican case is consistent with the idea that democracy encourages heavier taxation. Not only is its current regime younger than the others, but it is of somewhat lower quality and the country's overall experience with democracy is briefer. Of course, Mexico is also the most lightly taxed country. Otherwise, however, there is little support for this notion. Chile, the country with easily the best record in terms of the quality of the current regime and the length of its democratic tradition, has a tax burden much lighter than that of Argentina or Brazil. Brazil, the country with the heaviest tax burden, has the second shortest overall experience with democracy, and its current regime is rated lower than Chile's. Furthermore, as will be discussed in future chapters, Argentina and Brazil have experienced robust tax burden growth under both authoritarian and democratic regimes.

An interpretation based on Meltzer and Richard's theoretical model, in which democracy interacts with income inequality, is, on balance, no more compelling. It is true that the Brazilian case is on the surface quite consistent with this theory. The country with the heaviest tax burden of the group, Brazil has also had the highest level of income inequality, both since its democratic transition and since 2013.[7] However, Argentina, which has clearly the lowest

---

[5] Brazil's Congress was closed for only three years, but during most of the regime it operated under strict limits and with a party system imposed by the military.

[6] There has been only one sustained change in the ranking since the mid-1980s, when Argentina surpassed Chile to become the second most heavily taxed country (see Figure 2.1).

[7] Since 2013, Brazil's Gini coefficient for income has averaged 52.5, Mexico's 50.3, Chile's 45.8, and Argentina's 41.6. The averages since their respective democratic transitions are: Brazil, 56.4; Chile, 51.0; Mexico, 50.5; and Argentina, 46.5 (CEPALSTAT; World Bank Database).

inequality by both of these measures, should have the lightest taxation, yet its tax burden is similar to Brazil's and much heavier than Mexico's or Chile's.

Moreover, even the apparently good fit in the Brazilian case proves to be, on closer inspection, illusory. For one thing, the Meltzer–Richard model cannot explain why Brazil was already the most heavily taxed country in this group by the early 1980s, given the country's limited experience with democracy and the fact that a substantial portion of the lower class – in theory, the group most desirous of redistribution – was excluded from the suffrage by a literacy requirement. In fact, Brazil would only remove this requirement in 1985, later than any other country in Latin America (Lapp 2004, p. 25).

In addition, public opinion research does not uncover the expected link between income level and attitudes toward redistribution. For example, studies conducted by the polling firm Latinobarómetro in the late 1990s and 2000s show that better-off Brazilians consistently view the income distribution as more unjust than do people of lower socioeconomic level.[8] The firm's research also turned up no clear relationship between income and self-placement on a left-right ideological scale.[9] Similarly, there was no consistent relationship between the socioeconomic level of the interviewee and likelihood that he or she would rank poverty, inequality, or social injustice as Brazil's "most important" national problem.

That the democracy-based theories do not seem to explain the variance between the cases does not mean that regime type is irrelevant to the tax burden. As subsequent chapters show, where lower-class organization is strong and economic elites are politically fragmented, a democratic transition can, indeed, encourage the emergence of a larger and more redistributive public sector. However, where those conditions do not obtain, democratization is likely to have little effect on these variables.

The foregoing discussion has examined the relevance of differences in regime type, as well as the possible interaction between regime type and social inequality. However, there are also some arguments suggesting that differences in institutional structure within the category of democracies may affect the tax burden. Some of these are controlled by the case selection, but those that focus on fiscal centralization are not. Nevertheless, the observed variance quite clearly contradicts theoretical expectations.

The traditional view of federalism, based largely on the experience of developed societies like the United States and Switzerland, is that it tends to reduce overall taxation (Brennan and Buchanan 1980; Steinmo 1993; Mueller

---

[8] The data can be accessed at: www.latinobarometro.org/latOnline.jsp. The data discussed here refer to those studies in which socioeconomic level was assessed by the interviewer, based on the dwelling, the furnishings inside the dwelling, and the interviewee's physical appearance. Beginning in 2011, studies appear to include only a self-evaluation by the interviewee. The former approach seems more likely to yield reliable results.

[9] Over the period for which data are available (1995–2010), the average scores of people in the top two (of five) economic categories were virtually identical to those in the bottom two.

TABLE 2.4 *Subnational government revenue by source, 2014–2015*

Country	Own-source revenues (% GDP)	Total revenues (% GDP)	Own-source revenues/total revenues (%)
Argentina	6.3	15.2	41.4
Brazil	10.9	14.2	77.1
Chile	2.2	3.7	59.5
Mexico	1.4	9.8	14.4

Source: ECLAC (2017a), p. 100; OECD (2017), p. 112

2003). Clearly, the cases assembled here defy this prediction, since the two most decentralized countries, Brazil and Argentina, have the heaviest tax burdens. State-level officials in Brazil do sometimes complain, in line with Brennan and Buchanan's classic argument, that competition between the states to attract investment undermines revenue, since it often involves tax concessions (Tostes 2015, interview). However, this dynamic has not kept state governments from collectively raising over 8 percent of GDP in taxes, more than in any other Latin American country.

The more recent view, that federalism encourages heavier taxation if subnational entities rely disproportionately on central government transfers to support their spending, is also not convincing. As Table 2.4 demonstrates, it is actually in Mexico that we find easily the largest gap between subnational governments' own-source revenues and the total revenues they have at their disposal. In contrast, heavily taxed Brazil has the smallest such imbalance. Brazilian subnational governments do enjoy large fiscal transfers, but they also collect very high revenues of their own, mainly through a VAT-like tax imposed by the states.

Capacity-based institutional perspectives are also unsatisfying. As noted in Chapter 1, the external war variable is effectively controlled by the case selection. The more domestically rooted determinants of state capacity emphasized by Kurtz (2013) do vary among the cases, but in a way that is inconsistent with his argument. A major problem involves variation in postindependence labor relations. While Kurtz argues that a coercive labor regime impeded the emergence of a strong state, this set of cases does not support that view. In particular, Brazil, which had clearly the most coercive labor system (i.e., outright slavery) of the countries under study here during the nineteenth century, would also become the most heavily taxed.

However, there is a more basic problem with this account, one that also extends to other capacity-based arguments. While Kurtz suggests that variation in the contemporary tax burden in Latin America reflects underlying differences in state capacity, the evidence does not back that claim up. For example, Chile, which he views as having a highly capable state, actually has a much lighter tax burden today than Argentina, which he sees as suffering from a relatively weak state. Similarly, most scholars of the region would undoubtedly view Chile as ranking higher than Brazil on such capacity-related characteristics as the rule of law and the existence of a rational, "Weberian" bureaucracy. Yet, Brazil also has a far heavier tax burden. These observations suggest a need to analytically separate the fiscal magnitude of the public sector from the transparency and efficacy of state action.

Of the institutional explanations of tax burden variance, the most convincing are the ones offered in the specific cases of Brazil and Chile, which focus on distinctive aspects of their respective constitutions. It is hard to argue with the contention that Brazil's 1988 constitution, which is exceptionally detailed and policy oriented, tends to favor a large public sector. Its generous pension provisions for both private and public sector workers contributed to a sharp rise in pension spending, which by the early 2000s had reached 10 percent of GDP, an unusually high level relative to the country's wealth and age structure (Costanzi 2015, p. 12). In addition, the constitution gave federal authorities the ability to create new "contributions," a type of tax earmarked for a specific spending area. Under pressure to keep up with rising spending commitments, presidents created new contributions or raised the rates of existing ones, making this the fastest growing source of revenue. There is broad agreement among politicians, policymakers, and scholars that the constitution is an important cause of Brazil's heavy tax burden (Afonso and Serra 2007; Melo 2010 et al.; 2015 interviews: Appy, Hauly, Maciel).

Likewise, there are good reasons to believe that Chile's "authoritarian enclaves" made it harder for center-left Concertación governments to raise revenue, since these provisions bolstered the influence of rightist forces in Congress. The appointed, or "designated," senators were particularly important, since without them the coalition would have wielded a consistent majority in both legislative chambers prior to 2005. In her in-depth research on efforts to boost income and wealth taxation, Fairfield (2015, pp. 77–78) argues that the Concertación's inability to achieve a Senate majority during this period discouraged it from even presenting legislation that would substantially raise revenues.

Nevertheless, the explanatory power of both these institutional arguments is limited by the fact that they cannot account for crucial characteristics of the respective case. In the Brazilian case, a focus on the constitution's fiscal provisions cannot explain why the country's tax burden was already the heaviest in Latin America even before 1988. It also cannot explain why these provisions were included in the constitution, given that their effects were (as Chapter 5 demonstrates) largely foreseen. Finally, it cannot explain why political elites have not done more to change them, given that Brazil's constitution has been amended almost continually since the early 1990s (Arantes and Couto 2009).[10]

---

[10] As Chapter 5 explains, Brazil's Congress has passed amendments to fiscal provisions of the constitution, including three pension reforms and a federal spending cap. However, with the

Similarly, the argument regarding Chile's "authoritarian enclaves" cannot explain why Chile entered its current democratic period with tax revenues of about 15 percent of GDP, a low level for a relatively prosperous country. In addition, it cannot explain why taxation did not increase substantially after most of the enclaves, including the designated senators, were eliminated through constitutional reforms in 2005 (López 2013). Finally, even the modest pace of revenue increases between 1990 and 2005 cannot be wholly ascribed to the authoritarian enclaves since the original cohort of designated senators was replaced in 1998 with a group less committed to preserving the military regime's legacies (Fairfield 2015, p. 77). In fact, a number of politicians interviewed for this study on both left and right argued that the major obstacle to increased taxation was the Concertación's own reluctance to propose substantial reform, whether out of fear of a negative response from business or a belief among top policymakers that revenues were already adequate to the country's needs (2014 interviews: Dittborn, Ominami, UDI).

2.1.3 Actor-Centric Theories

As the preceding discussion has suggested, state-controlled natural resource wealth and two case-specific institutional variables provide some leverage on the problem explored here, but they leave several important questions unanswered. Some of the variables drawn from the actor-centric category provide powerful tools for addressing these questions. In particular, those that in one way or another emphasize the relative power of statist and anti-statist actors ring true with respect to the cases under study in this book.

2.1.3.1 *A Balance of Power Perspective*
A group of actor-centric arguments that clearly does not resonate with these cases consists of those that posit that a cohesive economic elite with close ties to governing parties facilitates revenue-raising reform (Schneider 2012; Flores-Macías 2014). In fact, there is a strong negative correlation between elite cohesion and the electoral success of rightist parties, on the one hand, and tax burden magnitude, on the other. As discussed later, low-tax Mexico and Chile stand out in Latin America for having politically cohesive private sectors united by strong peak organizations. In both cases, business has close ties to programmatic rightist parties that are among the most successful in the region. In contrast, Brazil and Argentina, the two countries with heavier taxation, are both characterized by organizationally fragmented business communities and party systems in which programmatic rightwing actors have traditionally been weak. Admittedly, there are situations in which a right-leaning government with unified business support can find it easier to

exception of the spending cap, these measures have been incremental in nature. Moreover, the spending cap is quite recent (2017) and is unlikely to permit a reduction in taxation.

implement tax reform than a leftist one that has an antagonist relationship with business. However, since such governments do not embrace a long-term project of expanding the state's role in society, those reforms are likely to be isolated responses to crisis situations.

More convincing with regard to the current comparison are two other actor-centric perspectives discussed in Chapter 1. One focuses on labor and left-leaning parties, which, in the power resources tradition, are viewed as increasing the tax burden mainly by pushing for social and labor market policies that require funding. The other perspective, associated mainly with Fairfield's work, stresses the negative impact of strong business organization on taxation. Admittedly, Fairfield focuses specifically on direct taxes, not on the tax burden. However, her analysis of her cases (including Argentina and Chile) makes clear that the same forces that oppose direct taxes also tend to oppose *any* tax increase and, indeed, virtually any expansion of the public sector (Fairfield 2015, pp. 74–75, 80, 82, and 102). Consequently, although Fairfield does not herself do so, her argument can readily be extended to encompass the overall tax burden. Moreover, because they are (as noted in Chapter 1) essentially two sides of the same theoretical coin, these perspectives can be combined into a single theory that portrays the tax burden as a function of the balance of power between the actors they each stress.

While Fairfield and some works in the power resources tradition portray these actors largely in social class terms, it would seem more accurate to frame them ideologically, as statist or anti-statist actors. Doing so acknowledges two important, interrelated facts. First, social class falls well short of fully determining ideology. Workers do not necessarily embrace statist views and business owners and other elites do not always staunchly oppose state intervention. As this book stresses, the extent of adherence to these views can be deeply influenced by contingent historical processes. Second, those collective statist and anti-statist actors that do exist are not necessarily homogeneous in social class terms. For example, while their core constituencies may be comprised mainly of elites, anti-statist parties must inevitably curry the support of non-elites to win elections. At the same time, some of the most committed statists often belong to groups, such as civil servants, autoworkers, and college students, whose personal or family incomes place them in the upper half (at least) of the income distribution in the Latin American context.

Thus, the synthesis of the power resources and Fairfield perspectives proposed here specifies that the size of the tax burden reflects the balance of power between statist and anti-statist forces, rather than between labor and capital or poor and rich people. The loose or contingent relationship it posits between class position and ideology also tends to distance it from Marxist approaches, although in its emphasis on ideological conflict and the role of civil society (e.g., business associations, labor unions, and religious groups) in that conflict it does bear a certain resemblance to Gramscian theory (Gramsci 2000).

This ideological balance of power theory is compelling among the cases assembled here and helps fill gaps left by the scholarship evaluated earlier. From this point of view, taxation is heavier in Argentina and Brazil than in Mexico and Chile largely because, for a number of decades, the balance of power has tilted less toward the anti-statist side. Not only are programmatically right actors weaker, but also labor unions are stronger and more militant. To some extent, the partisan left is also stronger. Chile is something of an exception to the latter rule, since at least nominally left parties have enjoyed considerable electoral success there since 1990. However, the reticence of center-left governments to raise taxes can be understood in large part as a function of the electoral, lobbying, and media power of the right.

2.1.3.2 *Cross-Case Variance in the Power Balance*
The clearest differences among these cases involve the strength of actors embodying anti-statist views and policy goals. As mentioned, Mexico and Chile have more organizationally unified business sectors than Brazil and Argentina (Schneider 2002, 2004; Fairfield 2015). Both of the former two countries have unusually strong peak associations that represent businesses across different regions and sectors. Mexico has three such associations: the Employers' Confederation of the Mexican Republic (Confederación Patronal de la República Mexicana, COPARMEX), the Coordinating Council of Business (Consejo Coordinador Empresarial, CCE), and the Mexican Business Council (Consejo Mexicano de Negocios, CMN). Each has a distinctive role in representing the business community, but they have shared some of the same leaders and have often collaborated closely, especially in times of crisis. In recent decades, Chile's Confederation of Production and Commerce (Confederación de la Producción y del Comercio, CPC) has likewise played a strong leadership role representing the private sector as a whole (Silva 1996; Fairfield 2015). The Society for Industrial Promotion (Sociedad de Fomento Fabril, SOFOFA) is also important and has a somewhat broader scope than its name implies.

In contrast, the business communities of Brazil and Argentina are notoriously fragmented (Schmitter 1971; Schneider 2004; Fairfield 2015). There are essentially no significant organizations beyond the sectoral level, and even sectoral entities are often divided or unrepresentative. In Brazil the business association most frequently described as the country's most powerful, the Industrial Federation of the State of São Paulo (Federação das Indústrias do Estado de São Paulo, FIESP), represents only one sector in a single state (albeit a very important one). Argentina has some strong sectoral organizations, most notably the Argentine Rural Society (Sociedad Rural Argentina, SRA), but there are no enduring multi-sector groups of any real significance. Moreover, the broadest industrial association, the Argentine Industrial Union (Unión Industrial Argentina, UIA), has long been riven by factionalism (Dossi 2010). These differences are not merely institutional. Rather, they represent longstanding contrasts in the private sector's attitudes toward the state. In Chile and Mexico, class-wide collaboration among capitalists is driven by a deeply ingrained wariness of state intervention. The existence of strong peak associations both reflects and serves to propagate a defensive attitude toward the public sector. Chilean business's unified rejection of state intervention has been well documented by scholars (Silva 1995; Silva 1996; Fairfield 2015). Mexico's private sector is more ideologically diverse, at least in part because the country is larger. However, there is a current of virulent anti-statism that has long been highly influential (Shafer 1973; Martinez Nava 1984; Luna 1992). Its major carriers have been the Monterrey Group, an informal network of major businesses based in the northern state of Nuevo León; COPARMEX; and the Confederation of National Chambers of Commerce, Services and Tourism (Confederación de Cámaras Nacionales de Comercio, Servicios y Turismo, CONCANACO). These entities have played key roles in the creation and leadership of the largest of the peak organizations, the CCE.

Ideological commitment to small-state policies is weaker among the two cases in which business is more fragmented. For decades scholars have noted Brazilian business elites' relatively accepting attitude toward state economic intervention (Schmitter 1971; Diniz and Boschi 1978; Evans 1979). Perhaps because of the lack of elite sponsorship, free-market ideas have had comparatively little influence in Brazil (Sikkink 1991, p. 67). Argentine business is more ideologically heterogenous and some entities, most notably the SRA, have traditionally preferred liberal policies. However, more interventionist groups have wielded strong influence, especially in manufacturing but also in other sectors like commerce and even agriculture (Olivera 2004; Brennan and Rougier 2009).

Programmatic rightist parties have also had more electoral success in recent decades in Chile and Mexico. Along with El Salvador, these countries represent the clearest examples of successful rightwing party-building among Latin America's contemporary democracies (Luna and Rovira Kaltwasser 2014). Chile has two competitive parties that consistently embrace market principles: the socially conservative Independent Democratic Union (Unión Demócrata Independiente, UDI) and the more liberal National Renewal (Renovación Nacional, RN). Together, they comprise a coalition that has consistently garnered around 40 percent of the vote and held the presidency from 2010 to 2014 (and again since 2018). Mexico's National Action Party (Partido Acción Nacional, PAN) also combines social conservatism with support for market-based policies. Although for many years it functioned as a largely symbolic opposition to the PRI, it has been a competitive party since the 1980s. It controlled the presidency from 2000 to 2012 and since the mid-1990s it has usually held 25–30 percent of the seats in Congress.

Recent upsurges in anti-statist sentiment notwithstanding, neither Brazil nor Argentina has a tradition of fielding electorally competitive anti-statist parties. Non-left parties have generally prevailed in Brazilian elections (especially for legislative seats), but these have for the most part not been ones that consistently endorse anti-statist positions (Montero 2014). Rather, they are either clientelistic parties lacking a clear ideology or ones that embrace centrist positions, like the Party of Brazilian Social Democracy (Partido da Social Democracia Brasileira, PSDB), which held the presidency from 1995 to 2002. Argentina has also never developed a competitive, enduring conservative party (Gibson 1996).

Because of their common viewpoints, business and rightist parties have worked closely together in Mexico and Chile. Business provides funding, favorable media coverage, and other forms of support and, in return, is frequently consulted on policy issues. There is an especially close relationship between COPARMEX, perhaps the most overtly ideological of any major business association among these four countries, and the PAN (Wuhs 2010). In fact, many PAN politicians have also occupied leadership positions in COPARMEX. In Chile such ties have been less conspicuous, at least in recent decades, but the scholarship leaves little doubt that there has been close collaboration between business and conservative parties, particularly the hard-right UDI (Pollack 1999; Luna 2014).

Argentine and Brazilian business associations also engage in electoral politics, but, given the lack of a clear pro-business party, their partisan loyalties are weaker and more diverse. In Brazil, as a well-known work on Latin American parties put it, "[l]inkages between business organizations and parties are virtually nonexistent. The former may tap individual politicians, but they eschew being tied to any particular party" (Mainwaring and Scully 1995, p. 13). This statement, which remains accurate today, also roughly describes the situation in Argentina (McGuire 1995; Fairfield 2015). While the jury is still out on Republican Proposal (Propuesta Republicana, PRO), a pro-market party that arose in the mid-2000s and held the presidency from 2015 to 2019, there is little reason to believe it will develop the tight business-party linkages seen in Chile and Mexico, since those, as argued later, arose in distinctive historical circumstances.

As this discussion suggests, Chile and Mexico both boast longstanding, programmatically anti-statist political blocs that do not exist to nearly the same extent in Argentina and Brazil. These blocs are mainly composed of parties and business associations, but, as subsequent chapters demonstrate, they also include other institutions, especially think tanks and universities. On the statist side, the differences between these two groups are less clear-cut, but are nonetheless significant, particularly with regard to labor unions. At least in recent decades, the Argentine and Brazilian labor movements have been considerably stronger and more militant than their Chilean and Mexican counterparts (Cook 2007; Niedzwiecki 2014; Bensusan 2016).

Argentina has long been considered to have the strongest labor movement in the region, with high unionization rates and, notwithstanding recurring factionalism, considerable organizational centralization in the form of the General Confederation of Labor (Confederación General del Trabajo, CGT) (Collier and Collier 1991; Cook 2007). Although not traditionally among the strongest in the region, Brazil's labor movement grew in organization toward the end of the 1964–1985 military regime. Since about the 1980s, Brazil has had among the highest rates of unionization in Latin America (Blanchflower 2006, p. 31; Roberts 2012, p. 6). There is no national confederation as dominant as Argentina's CGT, but the Unified Workers' Central (Central Única dos Trabalhadores, CUT) clearly has the largest number of members and is less factionalized than the CGT.

While the Chilean and Mexican labor movements have roughly similar levels of organizational centralization as Argentina and Brazil, they currently suffer from lower membership. Once among the most unionized societies in the region, Chile and Mexico have seen their unionization rates drop greatly in recent decades (Bensusán and Middlebrook 2013, p. 53; Durán and Kremerman 2015, p. 5). Data on unionization in Latin America are notoriously fragmented and unreliable, but available comparative figures consistently show that membership rates are lower in these two countries than in Brazil and far lower than in Argentina.[11]

Like business associations, labor unions vary in their views and policy positions. Although Brazilian and Argentine unions have different ideological perspectives, in both cases unions generally favor an active state. Over the past several decades, Brazil has had the most left-leaning movement among these countries, since its largest organization (the CUT) has a clear leftist orientation. In a sense, Argentine labor is different, since it has long been dominated by *peronismo*, which rejects socialism and tends to focus on wages and benefits rather than broader issues. At the same time, however, *peronismo* favors a state that protects domestic firms and implements worker-friendly policies (Recalde, interview, 2014). Moreover, Argentine unions have a tradition of militantly opposing spending cuts and market-oriented reforms. Hence, although Argentine unionism is less anti-capitalist than its Brazilian counterpart, it is not clearly less statist and organizationally it is stronger.

Mexican and Chilean labor once had strong combative, leftist currents, but in both countries they eventually lost ground to more pragmatic forces focused on incremental gains and maintaining good relations with authorities.

---

[11] For example, Bensusán (2016, p. 157) reports union membership rates for wage workers of 37.6 percent in Argentina, 20.6 percent in Brazil, 17.0 percent in Mexico, and 11.5 percent in Chile. The rates for total employees are 17.8 percent in Brazil, 13.6 percent in Chile, and 11.2 percent in Mexico (there is no figure on this variable for Argentina). A report prepared by a coalition of Latin American labor unions gives rates (relative to wage employment) of 48 percent in Argentina, 20 percent in Brazil, 18 percent in Chile, and 14 percent in Mexico (Confederación Sindical de Trabajadores de las Américas 2016, p. 200).

In Mexico, this transition began in the 1940s and 1950s as leftist leaders were replaced by so-called *charros* beholden to the state and management (Collier and Collier 1991, pp. 408–416). It deepened in the 1980s and 1990s in the context of economic crisis and liberalizing reform. Combative unions continue to exist even today but, on the whole, Mexican unionism is depoliticized. The largest organizations, especially the Confederation of Mexican Workers (Confederación de Trabajadores de México, CTM), are widely viewed as disinterested in mobilizing workers (Bensusán and Middlebrook 2013; Bensusán 2016). Chile's combative unionism disappeared under military rule and never recovered, despite re-democratization (Julián Vejar 2014). Instead, a more cautious leadership current emerged that focused on improving collective bargaining outcomes and avoiding an even larger membership decline. It came to dominate the largest confederation, the Unitary Workers' Central (Central Unitaria de Trabajadores, CUT).

The superior force of statist actors in Argentina and Brazil is less clear in the realm of party politics, since in Chile a center-left coalition anchored by the Christian Democratic and Socialist parties has controlled the presidency for all but about six years since the return to democracy. The first four center-left governments were based on the Concertación coalition, while the fifth (2014–2018) was rooted in the New Majority (Nueva Mayoría), which differed from its predecessor mainly in that it included the Communist Party (Partido Comunista de Chile, PC). The Concertación enjoyed majorities in both legislative chambers only in 2006 and 2007, while the Nueva Mayoría did so throughout its time in government.

Nevertheless, statist parties have clearly had more success in Argentina and Brazil than Mexico during the current era of competitive elections. Brazil's major leftist party, the Workers' Party (Partido dos Trabalhadores, PT), has been a strong competitor in presidential elections since 1989 and held that office continuously from 2003 to 2016. Given the extreme fragmentation of Brazil's party system, it never held more than about 25 percent of the seats in either house of Congress. However, during its presidencies, it was able to cobble together working majorities by allying with other leftist and centrist forces. In Argentina, parties associated with *peronismo* have tended to dominate elections, winning all but three presidential contests since 1983. Admittedly, the *peronista* governments of the 1990s embraced market-oriented reform. However, this decision constituted a sharp departure from *peronismo*'s statist and nationalist tradition, one induced by the devastating effects of hyperinflation. The collapse of this experiment in the early 2000s opened the way for a resurgence of that tradition. From 2003 to 2015, the presidency was controlled by a left-leaning faction of *peronismo* committed to statist and redistributive policies. These governments were usually able to muster working majorities in the Congress, mainly by uniting different factions of *peronismo* (Zelaznik 2014).

TABLE 2.5 *Summary of contemporary statist/anti-statist power balance*

Country	Strong business organization	Strong right parties	Strong labor movement	Strong left/ populist parties	Balance of power
Argentina	No	No	Yes	Yes	Statist
Brazil	No	No	Yes	Yes	Statist
Chile	Yes	Yes	No	Yes	Anti-statist
Mexico	Yes	Yes	No	No	Anti-statist

Mexico's main leftist party in recent decades, the Party of the Democratic Revolution (Partido de la Revolución Democrática, PRD), emerged to challenge the PRI during the late 1980s, when the latter openly embraced liberalizing economic reforms (Bruhn 1996). However, it has never been able to win the presidency and, despite competing in a far less fragmented party system than Brazil's PT, it has been unable to win more than about a quarter of the seats in Congress. Among the obstacles it has faced is the lack of a strong labor base, given Mexico's low unionization rate, as well as lingering corporatist ties between unions and the PRI (Bensusán and Middlebrook 2012, pp. 73–77). The weakness of leftist or populist parties in Mexico was dramatically reverted in 2018, when the National Regeneration Movement (Movimiento Regeneración Nacional, MORENA) won the presidency and captured a legislative majority. This change, however, does not negate the fact that Mexican politics has long been dominated by centrist and rightist forces.

These differences in the power balance between statist and non-statist actors, which are summarized in Table 2.5, can largely explain why Chile and Mexico have lighter tax burdens than Argentina and Brazil. In addition, they situate the constitutional provisions emphasized by scholars in the Brazilian and Chilean cases within a broader causal process that accounts for their origins and persistence over time. The links between the balance of power and tax outcomes will be explored in depth in the country chapters, but in the interest of clarifying the overall argument, some comments about each case are made here.

2.1.3.3   Links between the Power Balance and Policy Outcomes

Chile's persistently light taxation reflects the strong influence of anti-statist forces in the private sector, civil society, and party system, which has counterbalanced the electoral success of non-right parties. The country's tax burden plummeted during the military era and failed to rebound to its former level thereafter. The Concertación managed to hold on to the presidency for the first twenty years of democracy, but it was intimidated by the business community's unified opposition to any significant departure from former dictator Augusto Pinochet's liberal development model. This position was strongly supported by the rightist party coalition, influential think tanks, and the media.

In the face of this situation, the Concertación governments adopted a "consensus" strategy in which any significant policy change was discussed with leaders of business and the partisan right and amended to address their objections before being publicly unveiled or sent to Congress (Garretón 2012; Sehnbruch and Siavelis 2014). To further reassure business, Concertación presidents placed in key economic policy posts people with strong credentials in neoclassical economics. Consequently, while there were debates about fiscal policy within the Concertación, proposals to substantially raise the tax burden generally never saw the light of day (Fairfield 2010, 2015; 2014 interviews: Ominami, Budget Department). Labor's weakness both facilitated this strategy and made pursuit of alternatives risky.

While they lasted, the designated senators raised the barriers to increased taxation by denying the Concertación a legislative majority. However, their existence was itself a reflection of the influence of rightwing views in Chilean society. The authoritarian enclaves persisted intact for the first fifteen years of democracy, despite their obvious intent to mitigate the impact of popular elections, because the Concertación was reluctant to challenge the anti-statist bloc. In the early going, its hesitancy had to do partly with fears of military unrest, but by the late 1990s it mainly reflected a desire to avoid undermining business confidence and provoking conflict with the right. The fact that the Concertación continued to hew to its tradition of consensus-based politics and market-oriented economics even after achieving a congressional majority in 2006 attests to this idea.

The influence of rightwing actors over the Chilean state was attenuated by the unprecedentedly massive student-led protests of 2011, which prompted the Concertación leadership to expand their coalition to the left and adopt some of the movement's proposals (Palacios-Valladares and Ondetti 2019). Consequently, the Nueva Mayoría government passed the most significant set of statist reforms since 1990, including tax reform. However, the tax law faced determined opposition from business and conservative politicians and its revenue impact has been minimal. Moreover, the rightwing coalition returned to the presidency in 2018 and promised to stabilize the tax burden at its current level.[12]

Mexico's light taxation is the product of a political system that has tilted to the right for an even longer period. Although the PAN was not well represented in government until the late 1980s, intense business mobilization scuttled or diluted numerous revenue-raising tax reforms proposed by PRI officials going back to the 1940s (Aboites 2003; Ondetti 2017). The most significant proposals were advanced by presidents Adolfo López Mateos (1958–1964) and Luis

---

[12] *La Tercera*, March 15, 2018. Nevertheless, as discussed in Chapter 3, recent protests have forced President Sebastián Piñera to consider measures to increase revenue.

Echeverría (1970–1976), who sought to shift Mexico onto a more redistributive, welfare-oriented development path, in part by endowing the state with greater revenue. Despite the PRI's dominance of state institutions, these attempts were thwarted by determined private sector resistance, aided by other rightist forces (Martínez Nava 1984; Elizondo Mayer-Serra 1994).

While there were theoretical reasons to believe that the transition to more genuine electoral competition in the 1990s would lead to increased taxation, the change has been slow in coming. The power of anti-statist forces is, again, crucial. Since 2000, the presidency has mainly been controlled by the conservative PAN. Although the two PAN governments did attempt to boost revenues, their anti-statist ideology and close ties to the most right-leaning sectors of business meant that they lacked a broader project for transforming the state in a more activist direction. Their modest proposals faced internal resistance and failed to convince society that the revenues would contribute to the general welfare. Only minor changes were approved and even these failed to increase the tax burden.

Recent years have brought a shift away from rightist governance. The centrist PRI held the presidency from 2012 to 2018, and in 2018, as mentioned earlier, MORENA won that office. Accordingly, the tax burden has increased. A wide-ranging reform passed in 2013 and a decline in oil revenues (which appears to have brought stronger enforcement of the tax code) helped tax revenues reach a level probably unprecedented in Mexico. However, resistance to taxation remains strong, as evidenced by the fact that even Andrés Manuel López Obrador, Mexico's nominally leftist president, pledged repeatedly to business leaders during the election campaign not to raise taxes.[13]

In Brazil, in contrast, the longstanding weakness of rightwing actors and the growing importance of the left since the early 1980s have contributed to a long-term rise in taxation. While many Latin American countries pursued state-driven industrialization programs between the 1930s and 1980s, in Brazil the construction of a large state with vast fiscal resources was facilitated by the absence of strong opposition to state intervention within the private sector or among other actors (Schmitter 1971; Sikkink 1991). In contrast to Chile's conservative military regime, which reduced taxation, Brazil's actually raised it substantially, perpetuating a trend going back decades (Oliveira 1991). As a result, Brazil entered its current democratic period already having the heaviest tax burden in the region.

Since the 1980s the dynamic of public sector growth has changed somewhat (Ondetti 2015). Rapid industrialization and urbanization under military rule helped give rise to a stronger labor movement and a party, the PT, with close ties to it. Democratization gave these actors opportunities to shape policy through elections and protest. While the weakness of anti-state forces continued to favor

---

[13] *La Jornada*, December 8, 2017; *El Sol de Tlaxcala*, June 6, 2018.

public sector expansion, now demands for social protection became an additional force driving it forward (Afonso and Serra 2007; Ondetti 2015). The character and persistence of the fiscal provisions of the 1988 constitution can be better understood in light of these observations. This document's generous social provisions, as well as the tax instruments it provided to fund them, reflected the influence of an increasingly organized civil society seeking to reverse the military regime's favoritism toward capital. Business and conservative politicians mobilized to block provisions that most clearly threatened property rights and workforce control, but there was little conflict over social provisions, especially those that would soon push pension spending to exceptionally high levels (Martínez-Lara 1996; Afonso and Serra 2007). That same statist-leaning balance of power has insured that, in subsequent decades, change to crucial fiscal provisions of the constitution has generally only occurred at the margins.

In the Argentine case, a statist-leaning balance of power has also fueled taxation, but the dynamics of that process are somewhat different. Since the mid-twentieth century, the partly labor-based *peronista* movement has been a strong force in favor of an interventionist state. Every time it has controlled government, spending and taxation have risen, albeit less robustly during the 1990s. An ideologically divided, organizationally fragmented elite has lacked the ability to counteract *peronismo*'s electoral and mobilizational power through democratic, constitutional means (Gibson 1996; Mora y Araujo 2011).

For decades anti-statist forces coped with this dilemma by making recourse to military intervention, giving rise to a series of authoritarian regimes. However, lacking either broad elite consensus or popular legitimacy, these civil-military coalitions were unable to restore in an enduring way the liberal development path Argentina had left behind decades earlier. The result was extreme political and macroeconomic instability reflected in a tax burden that fluctuated greatly between the 1950s and 1980s.

Since the 1980s, changes in domestic and international norms have rendered the military strategy obsolete (Mainwaring and Pérez Liñan 2013), allowing *peronistas* to serve five full terms in the presidency. Initially, that shift did not result in a major increase in taxation, mainly because hyperinflation led President Carlos Menem (1989–1998) to adopt an exceptionally rigid stabilization regime that made state-expanding proposals unviable. However, the collapse of that strategy in the early 2000s allowed *peronismo* to return to its statist traditions. Under the presidencies of Néstor Kirchner (2003–2007) and his wife Cristina Fernández de Kirchner (2007–2015), Argentina's tax burden rose by about 50 percent, helping fuel a major increase in social and other types of spending. The right-leaning government of Mauricio Macri (2015–2019) attempted to pare back taxation, but lacked the political support to do so, and was replaced by a new *peronista* government.

Thus, the actor-centric perspective outlined earlier provides a powerful explanation of the differences in the tax burden between Chile and Mexico, on the one hand, and Argentina and Brazil, on the other. It complements the natural resource-based and case-specific institutional accounts discussed earlier, compensating for the limited explanatory leverage of the former and placing the latter within a broader context that makes the origins and persistence of the constitutional provisions in question more understandable.

At the same time, however, it suffers from a major limitation. While it highlights the ideological power balances underlying tax burden variance among the cases, it does not explain the origins of those balances. In other words, it does not tell us *why* the Chilean and Mexican political systems lean more toward anti-statism than those of Brazil and Argentina. This is a crucial question for this book since whatever forces determine the balance of power between statist and anti-statist forces also determine, albeit indirectly, the variance in tax burdens. The next section addresses this question directly.

2.2   EXPLAINING THE BALANCE OF POWER

Anti-statist forces are stronger in Chile and Mexico, the book argues, because left-leaning governments in those countries undertook major redistributive reforms, especially widespread expropriation of private property, in a context of pronounced ideological polarization and widespread popular mobilization. The perceived threat to basic aspects of capitalism inadvertently provoked a broad-based backlash that became institutionalized in the strong anti-statist actors described earlier. These actors have fought taxation not only directly but also indirectly, by pushing authorities to repress and demobilize workers and thus weakening labor as a political force. Although the roots of the power balance in Argentina and Brazil differ in important respects, these two cases share the fact that the lack of an acute threat to property inhibited the emergence of an anti-statist bloc comparable to those of Mexico and Chile.

While it suffers from certain conceptual disagreements or inconsistencies, the body of scholarship on path dependence provides some powerful ideas that can help to flesh out and reinforce the logic of this empirical argument. For that reason, this section begins with a discussion of path dependence and then employs that concept and some closely related ideas from the literature to further elaborate the causal connection between past property threats and the strength of contemporary anti-statism.

2.2.1   The Concept of Path Dependence

Since the late 1980s, when it was popularized by the seminal contributions of economic historians (David 1985; Arthur 1989), "path dependence" has become a commonly used term to characterize situations of continuity in economic, social, or political phenomena over extended periods. It is a core concept in the field of comparative historical analysis (Mahoney and Thelen 2015) and it has been the subject of a lively theoretical debate (Mahoney 2000;

Pierson 2000, 2004; Capoccia and Kelemen 2007; Slater and Simmons 2010; Soifer 2012). While there is a certain consensus about what path dependence means, there are lingering disagreements on significant issues. This section briefly summarizes both the agreements and points of discord and clarifies the understanding employed in this book.

The most basic agreement is that path dependence refers to situations in which the outcome of some historical process takes on a self-perpetuating dynamic and thus places enduring constraints on future outcomes.[14] As a result, subsequent changes in variables that theory or common sense indicates should influence the outcome do not produce the expected effects. The initial outcome becomes "frozen" or "locked in." Path dependence challenges approaches assuming a fluid response of one variable to another, emphasizing instead the potential "stickiness" of sociopolitical arrangements once established. The outcomes path dependence analyses are interested in are described as "institutions," but they are not necessarily formal institutions. Instead, they can range widely, from explicit laws and legally established organizations to unwritten conventions and traditions.

There is also substantial agreement regarding both the origins of particular institutional "paths" and the mechanisms leading to their persistence over time. With regard to the former, scholars recognize that even outcomes that endure for long periods and have a major impact on society can potentially be at least partially the result of random or unpredictable events, such as natural disasters or the decisions of individual leaders acting under conditions of limited information. At the time that they occur, the events in question may not even appear to be particularly momentous. They may only be identified as "critical junctures," or events that establish enduring new outcomes, long after the fact.

With regard to institutional reproduction, there is broad acceptance that a variety of mechanisms may potentially be at work. Early research in this area by economic historians stressed the notion of "increasing returns" (David 1985; Arthur 1989). It argued that path dependence occurs when the emergence of a new way of doing things leads actors to make adaptations specific to that innovation. Over time, change becomes increasingly difficult because it might render those adaptations irrelevant. Thus, even if it is clear that the approach adopted is less inefficient than an alternative, actors may resist change for fear of undercutting their individual well-being. In other words, the original path generates "positive feedback" that militates in favor of its own persistence.

Political scientists and sociologists who have subsequently written on path dependence have accepted that this type of process is one of the mechanisms through which outcomes may persist in the political realm (Mahoney 2000; Pierson 2000). Political institutions, like technologies, reward certain types of capabilities, and actors who have attained positions of advantage within

---

[14] This idea echoes Stinchcombe's (1968) earlier distinction between "constant" and "historical" causation.

a particular context may be unwilling to put their own gains at risk by accepting change. At the same time, a consensus has emerged among students of politics that the notion of increasing returns, at least in a narrow utilitarian sense, does not exhaust the mechanisms through which a path can be reproduced.

For example, institutional outcomes may also endure because they are supported by ideas. The course of historical events gives rise to "subjective models of reality" (North 1990, p. 112), "mental maps" (Pierson 2000, p. 260), or "orientations or beliefs about what is appropriate or morally correct" (Mahoney 2000, p. 523) that can stubbornly resist change. Since reality is complex enough to admit various interpretations, there is little reason to believe that social learning will necessarily lead to a convergence of ideas or regression to some ideological mean. Information that might contradict a particular interpretation of socioeconomic or political processes can be systematically ignored, downplayed, or framed in a way that skews its significance (Pierson 2000, pp. 260–261). Specific ways of understanding the world may also be reinforced by their embeddedness in organizations, which can provide a variety of normative and material incentives (e.g., belongingness, money, social prestige) for individuals to hew to orthodoxy (Stinchcombe 1965; Stevens 2002).

Particular institutional paths may also persist because they embody self-reinforcing power dynamics (Mahoney 2000; Pierson 2015). If an initial outcome confers influence on a specific political actor, that actor may subsequently be able to shape policies, institutions, and even norms and beliefs in a way that prolongs or reinforces its own power. As Pierson (2015, p. 133) aptly puts it, "power can beget power."

Despite the relative consensus on the aforementioned points, there are also disagreements. One involves the role of contingency or randomness in the critical junctures that initiate a path-dependent process. Some scholars have insisted that, for a process to be considered path dependent, the emergence of the path in question must necessarily be contingent, in the sense that it could not have been predicted based on initial conditions (Mahoney 2000; Mahoney and Schensul 2006; Capoccia and Kelemen 2007). The reason would seem to be that if the episode that established the new path was a theoretically foreseeable result of antecedent conditions, then the explanatory buck cannot stop at those events but must be passed back further into history. Other analysts acknowledge that contingency can play a role but fall short of making it a defining aspect of path dependence (Collier and Collier 1991; Slater and Simmons 2010; Soifer 2012). For them, it is mainly the fact that a historical episode marks a point of institutional divergence that makes it critical (Soifer 2012, p. 1593).

A related disagreement revolves around the issue of whether critical junctures necessarily involve a slackening of "normal" structural constraints on political actors. Authors like Capoccia (Capoccia and Kelemen 2007; Capoccia 2015) and Soifer (2012) take this position, arguing that it is only during such extraordinary instances of systemic crisis or disequilibrium that political leaders can exercise enough agency to establish an enduring new path. However, others are silent or noncommittal on this idea (Mahoney 2000; Pierson 2000, 2004; Mahoney and Thelen 2015) or explicitly rebut it, suggesting that it exaggerates the amount of agency needed to produce a critical juncture (Slater and Simmons 2010, p. 890).

A third point of discord involves what Mahoney and his collaborators have called "reactive sequences": situations in which an initial outcome sets in motion a "chain of tightly linked reactions and counter-reactions" (Mahoney 2000; Mahoney and Schensul 2006). These authors argue that such processes should be viewed as path dependent because the initial outcome largely determines subsequent outcomes, even though the latter may differ drastically from the former. Other scholars recognize that such sequences occur, but some prefer to reserve the term path dependence exclusively for situations in which an initial outcome persists through some self-perpetuating or self-reinforcing dynamic (Pierson 2004, p. 21; Sarigil 2015, p. 223). They do so both for reasons of conceptual parsimony and because reactive sequences are especially vulnerable to "infinite regress," or the limitless push backward in time in search of the "definitive" cause of some outcome.

Having summarized key divisions in the literature, it is now important to clarify how the book positions itself relative to them. On the question of contingency, the perspective adopted is that it is unnecessary to choose between the views presented earlier because the difference between them is, at bottom, one of emphasis rather than substance. Fundamentally, both sides view the outcomes of critical junctures as resulting from a combination of, on the one hand, preexisting constraints or opportunities and, on the other, events occurring during the juncture that are not predetermined and end up prodding institutional development in a particular direction. Slater and Simmons (2010) stress the former, or what they refer to as "critical antecedents," and scholars like Mahoney (2000) and Capoccia and Kelemen (Capoccia and Kelemen 2007; Capoccia 2015) the latter. However, neither side goes so far as to deny the significance of the other type of determinant. Likewise, this book views path-dependent processes as being initiated by contingent events that produce changes within boundaries set by preexisting conditions. Neither the events nor the preexisting conditions are fully determinative of the outcome. Moreover, the precise balance between the two is an empirical question rather than one to be decided a priori.

While this definition reserves a place for contingency in the initiation of path-dependent processes, the position adopted here rejects the idea that critical junctures must necessarily result from instances when the usual constraints on action are briefly relaxed. A problem with this distinction is that it would seem to unambiguously fit only situations in which some external shock disturbs the domestic status quo. Otherwise, how can we distinguish normal from abnormal times? Relatedly, this perspective seems to exclude the possibility, which is both logically compelling and borne out by events discussed in this book, that decisions made by political leaders or even voters during the course of "normal" politics can themselves give rise to a critical juncture that changes the course of a country's political development. Thus, the perspective adopted here is that the relaxation of normal constraints is a possible, but not a necessary cause of a critical juncture.

Finally, and mainly for the sake of conceptual clarity, this book endorses the view that the label path dependence should be applied only to cases in which an outcome endures through some sort of self-reinforcing process. Nevertheless, the concept of reactive sequences is a useful one for characterizing backlash processes that may unfold during or in the aftermath of a critical juncture and ultimately set in place the self-reinforcing path that will endure into the future. Collier and Collier (1991, p. 37) seem to be making this point when they observe that

> ...to the extent that the critical juncture is a polarizing event that produces intense political reactions and counter-reactions, the crystallization of the legacy does not necessarily occur immediately but rather may consist of a sequence of intervening steps that respond to these reactions and counter-reactions.

This insight, as this chapter and subsequent ones demonstrate, sheds considerable light on some of the cases discussed in this book.

Thus, the term path dependence as employed here refers to situations in which some blend of preexisting conditions and contingent events produces a transformation in societal institutions, broadly defined, which subsequently persists for an extended period due to a self-reinforcing process that may rely on a variety of mechanisms. The new arrangement does not necessarily consolidate itself immediately, but rather may result from some action-reaction sequence. It is worth noting here that, unlike some works in the path dependence genre (Collier and Collier 1991; Mahoney 2001; Kurtz 2013), this one does not focus on explaining different national responses to the same critical juncture. Rather, it identifies a specific type of event (i.e., reformist episodes that threatened but did not abolish property rights) that occurred during different historical periods, or not at all, in different countries, but which had the same path-creating impact where and when it did occur. This is perhaps an unorthodox use of the concept, but there seems to be no logical reason not to employ it in this way. The understanding of path dependence sketched here is used in the next two subsections to assist in the elaboration of an argument linking historical instances of property rights threat, or their relative absence, to the contemporary balance of ideological power among the case study countries.

2.2.2 Strong Property Rights Threat and Anti-Statist Predominance: Chile and Mexico

The relative superiority of anti-statist forces in Chile and Mexico today can be traced to the path-dependence-inducing effects of earlier episodes of redistributive reform that posed acute threats to private property. These episodes, which constituted critical junctures in the development of anti-statism, were deeply influenced by antecedent conditions, but their occurrence was not inevitable. In both cases, they could have been smaller in scale or more gradual, so that they never appeared to constitute a systemic challenge. Yet, once they occurred, they initiated reactive sequences that, rather ironically, ended up strengthening anti-statist actors. That transformation subsequently persisted because of a combination of self-reinforcing mechanisms, most notably ones involving ideas and power. The causal process was more obvious in the Chilean case because the reformist government was more radical and the backlash against it involved violent regime change, something that did not happen in Mexico. However, essentially the same process unfolded in Mexico in a subtler fashion.

The key episodes of redistributive reform occurred during different periods in the two countries but shared key characteristics, including extensive state expropriation of private property, intense popular mobilization, and a prominent role for Marxist groups either in the government or its support coalition in civil society. These characteristics mattered because they generated a sense of intense threat, suggesting that fundamental aspects of the capitalism system, most notably the existence of private property, were at risk. It is hard to determine their relative importance, since their effects fed off each other. However, the occurrence of actual property seizure on a large scale was probably the most crucial, since it demonstrated a willingness and ability on the part of authorities to transcend mere leftist rhetoric.

In Chile, the Allende government (1970–1973) deepened an existing expropriation-based land reform and forcibly seized property from hundreds of nonfarm businesses, including the US firms that controlled the crucial copper industry. The alarm generated by these measures was compounded by the fact that the governing coalition consisted mainly of parties committed to socialism and that the period was marked by widespread protests intended to accelerate reform. More than three decades earlier, Cárdenas (1934–1940) had undertaken a similar set of reforms, including Latin America's first large-scale land reform and its first major expropriation of foreign corporations. As in Chile, Mexico's reform process was accompanied by popular mobilization in the form of peasant land invasions, union organizing campaigns, and strikes. While Cárdenas did not clearly embrace socialism, some of his key allies did, including the Communist Party and the leaders of the largest labor confederation.

The origins of these episodes cannot be explained without reference to certain "critical antecedents." One involves the role of extractive industries. Resource extraction has played a more important role in Chile and Mexico than in the other two countries. Mining has been central to Chile's economy since the 1880s, when the country took control of rich nitrate fields in the War of the Pacific (1879–1884). Although demand for nitrates faded after World War I, their crucial role was replaced by copper. Mexico experienced its first oil boom beginning in the late 1910s as the revolution wound to a close. At its peak in the early 1920s, Mexico was the world's second largest producer (Rubio 2003, p. 2). Output declined beginning in the mid-1920s, but oil was still an important sector of the economy in the 1930s. In contrast, Brazil and Argentina have never been among the regional leaders in hydrocarbon or mineral production, at least relative to GDP or total exports. The prominence of extraction in Chile and Mexico, and the fact that the key extractive industries were dominated by foreign corporations, meant there was greater potential for resource nationalism to be stoked politically to promote change.

Another critical antecedent involves the socioeconomic characteristics of the agricultural sector. All four countries have traditionally had highly unequal landholding structures (Eckstein et al. 1978, p. 2), but they have differed on other variables. Both Chile and Mexico have relatively limited amounts of arable land and extensive regions in which the farm sector has been dominated by labor-intensive forms of production, meaning that there was substantial pressure on land resources. Mexico, moreover, has an especially large indigenous population, particularly in the center and south of the country. As a result, there are regions in which indigenous peasant communities have had longstanding claims to specific tracts of land. Over time, and particularly during the late nineteenth and early twentieth centuries, when export agriculture expanded rapidly, much formerly indigenous land came under the control of well-off, nonindigenous landowners, giving rise to resentments and conflict (Womack 1968). In both countries, but especially in Mexico, these conditions created the underlying potential for a major land reform.

Argentina presents the clearest contrast. The lack of a large indigenous population and the absence of a labor-intensive farm economy have meant that Argentina's rural population has always been comparatively small and there has been less pressure on land resources than in the other countries. Brazil, on the other hand, does have regions in which the rural population is relatively dense, due to a history of labor-intensive plantation agriculture (in the coastal northeast) or the migration of European peasants seeking land (in the south). However, demand for land redistribution has arguably been attenuated by the existence of a vast rural hinterland, consisting mainly of the Amazon River basin. Even before authorities began to proactively attract settlers to the Amazon through official colonization programs, the region received a flow of migrants seeking land and opportunities to engage in extractive activities like rubber tapping. Thus, the Amazon has served as a "safety valve" for land-related pressures in other parts of Brazil (Perdigão and Bassegio 1992, p. 169).

In both Mexico and Chile, natural resource nationalism and demands for land redistribution had contributed to political mobilization and some policy reform even before the redistributive episodes highlighted earlier. Land reform and state control over natural resources had emerged as key issues during Mexico's 1910–1920 revolution and were enshrined in the pioneering 1917 constitution. Tentative efforts at addressing both, but particularly land reform, had emerged in the 1920s, contributing to the gradual weakening of the agrarian elite (Katz 1996, pp. 32–33). In Chile, land reform and copper nationalization had also been debated for decades, but mobilization around these issues intensified during the 1960s. Responding to these pressures and seeking to harness them for political gain, President Eduardo Frei Montalva (1965–1970) had broken up some extensive rural properties and negotiated the state's purchase of large shares of the major foreign copper enterprises (Fleet 1985).

Although these antecedent conditions made it more likely that a major threat to private property would arise in Chile and Mexico than in Argentina and Brazil, they did not guarantee that such an event would occur. In both cases, an examination of the events immediately preceding these episodes suggests that history could plausibly have played out quite differently had individual political leaders or relatively small groups of voters made different decisions. Contingency, in other words, played an important role. The circumstances surrounding the reforms are discussed at greater length in subsequent chapters, but some brief comments are appropriate here to underscore this point.

In the Mexican case, choices made by President Cárdenas were pivotal. Under the leadership of strongman Plutarco Elías Calles, the country had taken a conservative, pro-business turn in the late 1920s and early 1930s. The "maximum leader" had distanced himself from erstwhile labor allies and criticized land reform. A Calles protégé, Cárdenas was widely expected to follow largely in his mentor's footsteps (Hamilton 1982, p. 104). That he instead turned on Calles, forced him into exile, and proceeded to implement easily the most extensive reforms since the revolution was thus quite surprising.

Allende's decision to pursue radical reforms was less surprising, given the longstanding commitment of his leftist coalition to pursuing a peaceful road to socialism. However, his rise to the presidency was by no means a foregone conclusion. In fact, Allende won the 1970 election by only 1.3 percent of the vote, edging out a far more conservative candidate. He might still have been denied the presidency by Congress (which was constitutionally obliged to choose between the top two vote-getters) had it not been for a badly botched attempt by the US Central Intelligence Agency (CIA) and domestic rightists to promote a military coup (Kornbluh 2003, p. 29).

Of course, we cannot know what would have happened had Cárdenas taken a more moderate path or Allende fallen short of winning the presidency. Major property reforms might have occurred anyway under a future government. However, it is also possible that one or both countries would have implemented more limited property reforms or spaced them out over several governments, with none advancing reforms deep enough to be perceived as a fundamental threat by economic elites. For example, given the broad popular consensus behind it in both countries, it is plausible that the nationalization of natural resources industries could have been accomplished by a centrist government otherwise respectful of private property.[15] Such a turn of events would have deprived leftists of a major political banner and meant that land reform, had it occurred, might have been perceived as a more isolated initiative, rather than part of a broad assault on property.

Once they were set in motion, however, these reform waves triggered reactive sequences whose ultimate result was to strengthen anti-statism, as well as at least partially reverse the reforms. In both countries, elites engaged in unprecedented mobilization intended to thwart proposed changes. Business leaders who had once sought to extract rents from the state now rejected interventionism and embraced doctrines vilifying it as the source of nearly all social maladies. Frightened by the specter of godless Marxism, religious conservatives also sprang into action to defend Christianity and "Western values." Because they faced a common threat, these groups joined forces to fight back against it. In the heat of the conflict, new organizations were forged and old ones became imbued with new meanings linked to the struggle against a hostile state. Due to their superior political resources and newfound unity of purpose, the anti-statist blocs generated by these counterreactions eventually prevailed, putting a halt to reform and, especially in Chile, largely reversing it.

The counterreaction to Allende's reforms was particularly powerful because of the clarity of the threat, given the overtly socialist character of the government. Business leaders engaged in new forms of collective action that sought to unify small and large businesses and overcome other traditional divisions (Campero 1984; Silva 1996). The CPC, previously overshadowed by sectoral organizations, gradually took on the role of mouthpiece of the private sector as a whole. New bonds were also forged between business and two political actors whose ideological positions had previously put them outside the mainstream: a conservative Catholic student movement called *gremialismo* and a network of neoclassical economists that became known as the "Chicago Boys," because of degrees earned at the University of Chicago, a bastion of free-market thought (Valdés 1995; Pollack 1999). The anti-statist bloc created by this countermobilization provided much of the civilian support necessary for the 1973 coup d'état and, subsequently, the military regime's radical neoliberal restructuring.

Although Mexico was not as polarized during the Cárdenas years as Chile under Allende, the reaction against *cardenismo* was nonetheless intense (Hamilton 1982; Contreras 1989). The most prominent opposition group was probably the industrialists of Monterrey, then the country's manufacturing hub (Saragoza 1988). The Monterrey elite resurrected COPARMEX, an

---

[15] Cárdenas' oil expropriation, though unsettling for economic elites, was quite popular (Gilly 2013, pp. 196–197). Similarly, despite the overall polarization of the party system, Allende's copper nationalization law was approved unanimously by Congress, reflecting a solid societal consensus on the issue (Moran 1974).

organization created in 1929 to oppose labor code reform, in order to mobilize business against the government. They were aided by Catholic activists frightened by the reforms, as well as by the anti-clerical thrust of Cárdenas' educational policies. Street protests, fascist thuggery, electioneering, and an armed uprising signaled widening discontent with the president's policies, widely viewed as "communist" (Contreras 1989). The PAN was created at the apex of this reaction, uniting business elites and social conservatives. Although the reaction did not, as in Chile, result in the government's overthrow, it did force Cárdenas to back off his reformism and accept a moderate as his successor. The conservatizing shift would be deepened during the 1940s, as the ruling party strove to restore business confidence.

While the reactions triggered by these reforms were perhaps predictable, what is more surprising is that the anti-statist blocs endured and grew in influence after the reformist challenge had been beaten back. Instead of fading away, anti-statism became embedded in a network of formal and informal organizations dedicated to resisting state intervention. This network acquired greater density and breadth over time, and its influence was reinforced by the growing weakness of organized labor, a key force behind the earlier reformist drives. In other words, the episodes of reform and backlash discussed earlier proved to be historical turning or branching points at which strong anti-statist blocs began to emerge and grow, tipping the balance of power rightward in a lasting fashion.

In Chile, the emergence of the CPC as an effective peak business organization, a phenomenon that had accompanied the growing redistributive threat, was consolidated after the coup (Silva 1996). Chile became one of the relatively few Latin American countries with a business association capable of speaking authoritatively on behalf of capitalists as a class (Schneider 2004). Moreover, as the military regime began to face popular challenges in the 1980s, anti-statists founded the UDI and RN, parties designed to defend rightist positions in a more competitive environment. Largely the same groups behind the CPC and rightist parties also created powerful think tanks during this era that continue to exist today. The relative influence of this bloc has been heightened by the debility of Chile's labor movement, which never fully recovered from repression suffered under military rule (Sehnbruch 2012; Julián Vejar 2014). Partly as a result, the left-labor alliance that had underpinned the Allende reform project has not been reconstituted.

The strength of anti-statism in post-reform Mexico is less easily perceived, due to the lack of effective party competition until the 1990s. However, business anti-statism flourished during the era of PRI hegemony (Martínez Nava 1984; López Portillo 1995; Gauss 2010). The Monterrey Group and COPARMEX, which had led the resistance to *cardenismo*, anchored a network of anti-state activism that fiercely opposed interventionist initiatives (limiting Mexico to a relatively liberal version of the post–World War II import-substitution policy regime) and played leading roles in the creation of the CMN in 1964 and the CCE in 1976. Beginning in the 1980s, in the context of economic crisis and rising pressures for democratization, the same forces would revitalize the PAN, transforming it from an ineffectual opposition into a competitive national party. At the same time as this anti-statist bloc consolidated itself, Mexico's labor movement, among the strongest in Latin America under Cárdenas, declined as a political force. It lost its autonomy to resist conservative policies and eventually its organizational density, as well. By the 2000s, it was one of the weakest movements among the more developed Latin American countries (Bensusán 2016).

Theoretical discussions of the mechanisms of reproduction behind path dependence shed considerable light on these outcomes. Signs of an increasing returns dynamic can be detected to some extent. The relatively liberal economic policy regimes consolidated in Mexico and (especially) Chile after their anti-reform backlashes favored some economic interests over others. Compared to those of Argentina and Brazil during the same periods, these regimes fostered firms less dependent on state assistance and more integrated into foreign markets. Other things being equal, such firms are less inclined to support policies that discourage trade and foreign investment, rely on high taxes to provide subsidized credit and energy, or foment domestic consumption. Hence, initial policy decisions tended to shape interest group pressures in the direction of preserving a market-oriented economy.

Nevertheless, other mechanisms are more compelling. The role of ideas seems especially important. Consistent with arguments advanced by scholars like Mahoney (2000) and Pierson (2000, 2004), the anti-statist ideas that arose or were popularized during processes of mobilization against reformist threats persisted because they became the prism through which influential actors interpreted the world. For organizations like UDI and COPARMEX (as explained in Chapters 3 and 4, respectively), opposition to state economic interference is not merely a desirable goal but their very reason for being. It is a fundamental aspect of the identity that was imprinted on them through their participation, or that of their founding leaders, in the counter-reform struggle. At the same time that they embody anti-statist ideas, these entities also use their resources to propagate those ideas in the wider society by influencing intellectual debates and media coverage and occupying public offices. While presumably not wholly impervious to shifts in the sociopolitical environment that might favor interventionism, the anti-statism of these groups is stubbornly resistant to them, due to the relative ease with which events can be interpreted to fit their own ideological schemas.

The idea that "power begets power" also sheds light on the lasting character of post-reform anti-statism. In particular, anti-statist blocs have used their influence to press for policies that weaken organized labor or discourage its resurgence as an actor with sufficient power to support a statist revival. In Chile, business and the right have steadfastly resisted reform of the anti-union labor code established under military rule (Ensignia 2017) and lent their support to an extremely liberal trade policy that, in effect, discourages workers from making

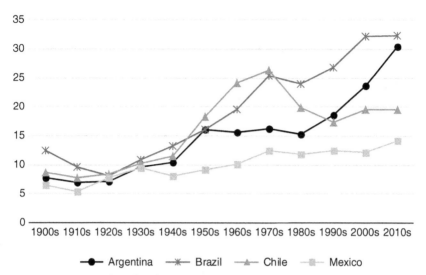

FIGURE 2.1 Historical tax burden trajectories, 1900–2017 (decadal averages)
Sources: Administración General de Ingresos Públicos (AFIP); CEPALSTAT/ECLAC;
IBGE Estatísticas do Século XX (http://moxlad.cienciassociales.edu.uy/en); World Bank
(1961, 1966, 1970, 1984); Camelo and Itzcovich (1978); Braun-Llona et al. (1998);
Diaz-Cayeros (2006); Cetrángolo and Gómez Sabaini (2007b)

demands on employers. A roughly similar dynamic can be found in Mexico. Responding in part to private sector pressures, after 1940 PRI presidents turned against the activist union leaders who had supported Cárdenas, replacing them with compliant and business-friendly *charros* (Collier and Collier 1991, pp. 579–587). A divided, coopted labor movement helped slow the growth of the welfare state and would eventually facilitate neoliberal reform, which further undermined workers' capacity for collective action (Zepeda Martínez 2009).

The lasting political impact of episodes of acute property rights threat in Chile and Mexico is reflected in the trajectories of their tax burdens, displayed in Figure 2.1.[16] Mexico's burden had tended to rise during the 1920s and 1930s, following the end of the revolution, and was not strikingly different from those of the other countries. However, beginning in the early 1940s, it stagnated relative to the others, reflecting the rising influence of anti-statism. By the 1960s, Mexico's tax burden was on average only about 60 percent of Argentina's, 50 percent of Brazil's, and 40 percent of Chile's. Oil revenues do

---

[16] While the figure paints a broadly accurate portrait of historical trends, the pre-1990 data suffer from limitations worth noting. In the Argentine case, pre-1930 data are only available for selected years and the 1930–1950 figures exclude subnational revenues. Chilean data prior to 1990 do not include subnational governments and social security revenue is only included from 1950 on. In the Mexican case, data are wholly or partially lacking for some of the revolution years and social security revenues do not appear in fiscal data until 1965.

not explain the gap, since they played a modest role in Mexico's fiscal system during these years. The tax burden would fluctuate somewhat in subsequent decades, but Mexico has remained a low-tax country. A roughly similar phenomenon can be observed in Chile, where revenues had grown robustly throughout most of the post-World War II era. The tax burden plateaued in the years following the 1973 coup, then dropped in the 1980s as a result of revenue-reducing pension and income tax reforms. It has grown only moderately since the 1990 democratic transition, never recovering its pre-coup level.

2.2.3 Weak Property Rights Threat and Statist Predominance: Brazil and Argentina

While strong property rights threats in Chile and Mexico set in motion path-dependent processes that strengthened anti-statist actors, in the other two countries the relative absence of such threats has favored statism. Brazil provides the clearest contrast, in that elites have never faced a major redistributive reform episode of any kind and have thus remained comparatively lackadaisical and unorganized in the face of public sector expansion. Argentina, in contrast, did experience substantial reform under Juan Perón (1946–1955). However, because it did not menace property, that wave failed to provoke the formation of a cohesive anti-statist bloc. In addition, it gave rise to a powerful populist coalition with statist proclivities. While the initial impact of Perón's reforms was to trigger a reactive sequence that destabilized Argentine politics, in the longer term it gave rise to path-dependent effects favoring statism.

As noted, the antecedent conditions that inclined Chile and Mexico toward property reform did not exist to the same extent in Brazil and Argentina. Consequently, they have been less politically salient. Natural resource nationalism, in particular, has been a minor phenomenon in both countries due to modest or inaccessible endowments of extractable resources. Insofar as resource nationalism has existed at all, it has mainly involved petroleum. Authorities did appeal to nationalist sentiments in founding state oil companies in Argentina in the 1920s (Bernal 2005) and Brazil in the 1950s (Rodrigues Neto 2005). However, since the oil sector was either small (in Argentina) or essentially nonexistent (in Brazil), these initiatives involved limited conflict with foreign corporations.

With regard to land reform, a distinction must be made between Argentina and Brazil. Land reform has simply not been a major issue in the former. In contrast, land reform activism has been an important phenomenon in Brazil during certain periods. However, perhaps because of the frontier "safety valve" and its conscious use by authorities to blunt demands for land redistribution, it emerged relatively late in historical and developmental terms. There was an outbreak of protest for land in the early 1960s that provoked concern among landowners and political conservatives, but it was less intense than the one that arose in Chile a few years later (Houtzager and Kurtz 2000, p. 399). A well-organized grassroots land reform movement would only take shape in the 1990s, when roughly 75 percent of the population already resided in urban areas – a condition that limited its potential extent and consequences.

While it is theoretically possible for major challenges to property relations to arise even when structural conditions are not especially favorable, in these two cases they have not. Brazil has seen occasional spates of social reformism, most recently under PT rule. However, all have been relatively mild, and none involved major property threats. The most significant occurred under Getúlio Vargas (1930–1945 and 1951–1954), who laid the foundations of the country's social security system and instituted a labor code with substantial benefits for workers. However, Vargas never implemented land reform and undertook no high-profile expropriations in other sectors. In contrast to Allende and Cárdenas, he had an antagonistic relationship with the Marxist left. In addition, Vargas did not seek to mobilize workers against employers or political opponents, but rather to guarantee labor peace through corporatist controls (Malloy 1979).

Perón implemented more extensive social and labor reforms than Vargas and more aggressively courted workers, in the process creating an enduring cult of personality. At the same time, however, he avoided land reform and undertook virtually no major expropriations other than the railroads, which were already partly nationalized (Mallon and Sourrrouille 1975). Moreover, as a career military officer with fascist sympathies, Perón presented himself to elites as a barrier to working-class radicalization. It was at least partly for this reason that he initially benefitted from considerable support from the Catholic Church and the armed forces (Waisman 1987), and that his nationalist economic policies were well received by a substantial sector of Argentine business (Brennan and Rougier 2009).

Because he brought more jarring change, Perón triggered a more pronounced reactive sequence than Vargas, or any other Brazilian president. Although Vargas certainly had enemies, his relations with the private sector and conservative Catholics, actors at the forefront of the mobilizations against Allende and Cárdenas, were relatively non-conflictual. Anti-Perón groups, in contrast, would engineer a military coup against the president, send him into exile, and, for nearly two decades, insist on either military rule or a limited democracy in which *peronista* parties were banned. Their intransigence engendered a seesaw struggle between the two sides that made Argentina nearly ungovernable. It was only in the 1980s that they would learn to coexist democratically and even today the *peronista* versus *antiperonista* cleavage is a highly salient one in Argentine politics.

What is important to emphasize, however, is that Perón generated such a protracted reactive sequence partly because his reforms were not profound enough to forge a cohesive anti-statist bloc of the kind that sprung up in response to Allende and Cárdenas. By sparing private property at the same time that he promoted industrialization through tariffs and subsidies, Perón aggravated divisions within the private sector, setting domestically oriented businesses against those better prepared to thrive in an open economy (Schneider 2004; Brennan and Rougier 2009). Although he would ultimately become embroiled in a damaging dispute with the clergy, his government's relative conservatism meant that it did not engender a reactionary grassroots Catholic movement on the scale of those seen in Chile and Mexico. Thus, *peronismo* was destabilizing as much for what it did not do as for what it did.

Because they have not experienced reform waves that deeply threatened private property, neither Argentina nor Brazil has witnessed the emergence of a cohesive anti-statist bloc capable of consistently impeding public sector expansion. As suggested earlier, there is no real analogue in either country to Mexico's COPARMEX, CCE, and PAN or Chile's CPC, UDI, and RN, organizations with broad social bases and an abiding commitment to defending free enterprise. Their absence is especially marked in Brazil, where there are hardly any longstanding political actors that espouse an anti-statist worldview and where elites have historically devoted far more effort to extracting benefits from the state than halting its expansion (Schmitter 1971; Sikkink 1991). Argentina does have some strong liberal interest groups at the sectoral level, but divisions within the business community have impeded the long-term consolidation of more encompassing ones (Schneider 2004). Admittedly, recent years have seen upsurges of anti-statism in both countries. However, it is by no means clear that these trends will ultimately result in a sustained increase in the influence of anti-statist actors, as discussed in Chapters 5 and 6.

In both countries, the lack of a cohesive anti-statist bloc has favored the emergence and persistence of labor unionism as a significant force. Certainly, unions have sometimes faced strong repression, especially under military rule. However, the generally more statist brand of policymaking in Brazil and Argentina has created opportunities and incentives for union organizing by fomenting more protected manufacturing sectors and larger state bureaucracies and by providing extensive social insurance for formal sector workers. In addition, the limited power of anti-statism has resulted in labor codes that are friendlier to unions, especially compared to the Chilean case (Cook 2007; Bensusán 2016).

While neither Brazil nor Argentina has experienced a critical juncture that put it on a sustained path of strong anti-statism, it is worth noting that the concept of path dependence does shed light on the origins of the contemporary balance of power in these countries.

Argentina is a more complex but possibly more compelling case in this sense. Although the immediate effect of Perón's reformism was to plunge Argentina into a period of destabilizing conflict, in the longer run it laid the foundation for statist predominance. It did so in two ways. First, it aggravated divisions within the private sector by encouraging the rise of a well-organized faction ideologically committed to a statist, nationalist economic model (Brennan and Rougier 2009). Second, it helped forge a strong and cohesive labor movement that could serve as the anchor of a broader electoral coalition. Because union ideology was not anti-capitalist and because labor and the statist business faction both desired policies fomenting industrial job creation and domestic consumption, these two groups repeatedly joined forces to combat liberalization of the Argentine economy (O'Donnell 1977).

That these transformations did not initially result in sustained public sector growth was due to the ability of anti-statist civilian actors to enlist the support of the armed forces. While it was unable to craft a stable liberal alternative, military intervention prevented *peronismo* from exercising extended control of the state from Perón's fall until the return to democracy in the 1980s. In addition, the instability and institutional decay generated by the attempt to exclude the country's largest faction plunged Argentina into such a profound economic crisis that the first *peronista* president of the democratic era, Menem, found himself obligated to adopt neoliberal reforms, rather than the statist policies traditionally embraced by his movement.

Eventually, however, the forces that had counteracted statism faded and the power of the statist bloc asserted itself more effectively. The authoritarian exclusion of *peronismo* proved unsustainable beyond the early 1980s and the movement's crisis-driven embrace of liberalism was discarded in the early 2000s in favor a much more statist orientation. During the 2000s and much of the 2010s, a *peronista*-based coalition controlled the central government and most of the provinces, with labor support. While protesting some of the more aggressively statist initiatives, a divided business community proved unable to halt the massive expansion of the public sector, including a major and thus far sustained tax increase.

The staying power of the statist coalition and its superiority over anti-statist forces reflect largely the same mechanisms behind the persistence of anti-statist influence in Mexico and Chile. Ideas have played a key role. *Peronismo*, with its connotations of social justice, nationalism, and state paternalism, has retained its mass appeal, despite dramatic changes in the political and social context (Mora y Araujo 2011; Calvo and Murrillo 2012). Although *peronismo* has never become strongly institutionalized as a party, many top political leaders embrace it, as do the large, resource-rich unions. Economic elites, in contrast, continue to be weakened by divisions traceable at least in part to the Perón governments of the 1940s and 1950s (Schneider 2004). Power has also begotten power to some extent. For example, the strength of statist forces has prevented substantial reform of the country's pro-union labor code, helping preserve labor as a major actor (Cook 2007; Etchemendy 2011).

In Brazil, no historical episode can be identified that so clearly led to change in the ideological balance of power as the Allende, Cárdenas, and Perón governments. Nevertheless, it can be argued that Getúlio Vargas' gradual public sector expansion in the midst of the Great Depression played a crucial part in establishing statism as a predominant force in that country. By coming to the assistance of urban workers and industrialists without menacing the vital interests of other groups, most notably the powerful agricultural elite (Schmitter 1971; Fausto 2006), Vargas founded a business-friendly brand of statism that has proven remarkably enduring. Vargas' approach was self-reinforcing in part because it fomented a comparatively trusting attitude toward the public sector among economic elites, which led them to organize to extract advantages from it rather than to halt its expansion. In addition, Vargas' statism strengthened groups (both elite and non-elite) with a material interest in the persistence of state intervention. Over the years, these groups have consistently sought to defend or increase their state-provided benefits, in classic increasing returns fashion.

The causal dynamics described earlier are reflected (with a caveat noted later) in the tax burden trajectories displayed in Figure 2.1. Although both Brazil and Argentina have seen periods in which taxation did not grow, or even fell, neither country has ever adopted a sustained path of light taxation of the kind seen in Mexico and Chile following their major episodes of property rights threat. Brazil's tax burden has grown in fits and starts since the end of World War I, with no sustained declines. By the mid-1980s it was already the most heavily taxed country in the region (in part because of the tax cuts in Chile, the previous leader), but a new surge of revenue growth beginning in the mid-1990s consolidated this status. Argentina's tax trajectory has been more unstable, due largely to the conflicts unleashed by *peronismo*, but has never taken the form of a long-term pattern of light taxation. After several decades of volatility beginning in the mid-twentieth century, the tax burden stabilized in the 1990s and grew rapidly during the 2000s and early 2010s, almost catching up with Brazil's. It should be noted that the decadal averages used in this graph do not capture the instability of Argentina's tax burden for nearly four decades after Perón's 1955 ouster. However, that pattern can be fully appreciated in Figure 6.1 in Chapter 6, which uses annual data.

2.3 CONCLUSION

This chapter has elaborated an explanation of differences in the tax burden among Argentina, Brazil, Chile, and Mexico that underscores the enduring impact of major redistributive reform waves involving widespread expropriation of private property, intense popular mobilization, and significant influence of Marxist groups on governing authorities. In the two countries in which they occurred (Mexico and Chile), these waves erected imposing obstacles to future taxation by steeling economic elites to resist state intervention and prompting them to forge stronger ties to social conservatives, who also felt threatened by the state's offensive. The anti-statist blocs that emerged from these episodes subsequently fought taxation not only directly by combatting efforts to raise taxes but also indirectly by pushing authorities to adopt or retain policies weakening labor.

In Brazil and Argentina, in contrast, the absence of reform waves of this magnitude meant that elites and social conservatives never coalesced into a cohesive anti-statist bloc capable of acting as an enduring barrier to public sector growth. The relative lack of such a bloc has created a more permissive context for statist actors to organize and exert influence over policy, eventually giving rise to a heavy tax burden.

While most extant theories of taxation and public sector size are unconvincing among this set of cases, the account sketched here either complements or encompasses within it a number of other explanations scholars have offered. It accepts that state-controlled natural resource wealth explains some of the variance among the cases, although the explanatory leverage this variable provides is limited. The complementary political account it emphasizes builds on earlier work on the institutional roots of fiscal policy in Brazil and Chile, as well as broader arguments focusing on the power of business, labor, and associated political parties. In developing the historical aspect of the argument, the chapter has also drawn on the scholarship on path dependence, which provides useful tools for understanding the potentially enduring impact of relatively contingent events.

3

Chile

Allende, Counterrevolution, and Sustained Neoliberalism

Considering that Chile is among the wealthiest countries in Latin America, its tax revenues are low. In recent years, its tax burden has been far below those of Argentina and Brazil and is even surpassed by those of some much poorer countries, like Bolivia, Ecuador, and Honduras (CEPALSTAT). A law passed in 2014 promised to boost revenues significantly, but as of 2017 it had not done so.[1] This chapter seeks to explain Chile's light tax burden, fleshing out the skeletal account provided in the preceding chapters.

Resource extraction plays an important role in Chile's economy, but it cannot explain the country's light tax burden since, as discussed in Chapter 2, nontax revenues from such activities amount to a modest 0.5 percent of GDP.[2] Rather, the explanation developed here emphasizes politics. The central argument is that light taxation reflects the indirect impact of a major redistributive reform wave that unwittingly tilted the balance of power in Chilean society in favor of anti-statist forces in an enduring manner. It did so in the short term by providing the impetus for a radical state retrenchment program under military rule, and in the longer term by fomenting the rise of actors and institutions capable of sustaining anti-statism as an influential force under more democratic conditions.

Although significant redistributive reforms began in the mid-1960s under President Eduardo Frei Montalva of the Christian Democratic Party (Partido

---

[1] The 2017 tax burden (20.1 percent of GDP) was slightly higher than in 2014 (19.6 percent) but slightly lower than the average (20.3 percent) during the three years (2012–2014) prior to implementation of the reform (CEPALSTAT).

[2] Even total fiscal revenue (including taxes) from mining averaged less than 2 percent of GDP between 2013 and 2016 (OECD 2015, 2017, 2018). During the peak of the 2000s commodity boom mining's contribution was greater, but that surge is largely reflected in tax revenues, since the state-owned National Copper Corporation of Chile (Corporación Nacional del Cobre de Chile, CODELCO) accounts for only a third of copper production.

Demócrata Cristiano, PDC), it was their intensification under Allende in the early 1970s that was most crucial in mobilizing and unifying economic elites and social conservatives. The leftist government's attempts to restructure property ownership amid acute polarization and popular mobilization profoundly alarmed these groups, as well as many people of more modest means, generating a climate propitious for the diffusion of radical anti-statist ideas and policy proposals. The military regime that arose in the wake of Allende's ouster seized on these ideas and proposals to undertake a neoliberal counterrevolution that dramatically reshaped the state. An aspect of this change was a sharp reduction in Chile's previously heavy tax burden.

Democratization might have been expected, following theoretical ideas described in Chapter 1, to bring a robust renewal of public sector growth. However, the actual change has been rather modest. Between 1989 and 2017, tax revenues increased by only about 4 percent of GDP, considerably less than in Argentina or Brazil since their democratic transitions. The major reason for the relative stability of the tax burden is that anti-statist forces have retained great influence in Chilean society. While center-left coalitions have controlled the presidency for most of the democratic period, vehemently anti-statist views have been well represented in Congress and the private sector. In addition, organized labor, once a key statist actor, has never recovered from the harsh blows it was dealt under military rule.

The persistent strength of anti-statism in democratic Chile is a path-dependent consequence of the earlier backlash against Allende's government. That experience inspired a deep desire, especially among economic elites, to insure themselves against a relapse into statism and, largely as a result, facilitated the military regime's construction of Latin America's most coherent free-market development model. Together, deep-seated fears of a statist resurgence and positive evaluations of the economic model have sustained Chile's rightist bloc for many years, thwarting efforts to raise taxes. The strength of anti-statism has also hindered policy changes that might revive labor unionism, further reinforcing the neoliberal status quo. Institutional structures left over by the Pinochet regime have contributed to tax burden stability, but, as this chapter argues, they are best understood as the reflection of a broader strengthening of anti-statist forces stimulated by redistributive threats.

The rest of the chapter is divided into two major sections: the first analyzes the causes of the sharp decline in the tax burden under authoritarian rule and the second explains the relative stability of that burden under the subsequent democratic regime.

3.1 THE DECLINE OF TAXATION UNDER MILITARY RULE

By the early 1970s, Chile was the most heavily taxed country in Latin America, fruit of a long process of sustained public sector expansion. Over the next two decades, however, taxation would first stagnate and then be dramatically rolled back, eventually falling to less than 60 percent of its previous peak. While remarkable, this change was only one component of a wider neoliberal reform wave undertaken by the 1973–1990 military regime, which also involved profound trade and financial liberalization, privatization of state-owned enterprises (SOEs), and labor market deregulation, among other reforms (Ramos 1986; Ffrench-Davis 2010). Hence, the approach adopted in this section is to explain this larger transformation while focusing particular attention on the roots of the policy changes that reduced taxation.

The argument emphasizes the role of threats to property rights in providing the political impetus for change. A rapid, fundamental transformation of the economic model was perhaps not an inevitable result of the 1973 coup. Nevertheless, there can be little doubt that the profound statist reforms that preceded that event played a crucial role in inspiring and sustaining the military regime's policies. They did so mainly by increasing the willingness of economic elites to accept a radical change of course, despite its inevitable costs for some of them. Redistributive reforms implemented by the center-left Frei government (1965–1970) contributed to this transformation, prompting an incipient mobilization of business owners and other conservative actors in defense of property and free enterprise. More crucial, however, were the deeper transformations implemented by Allende, which struck at fundamental pillars of capitalism and gave credibility to an emerging ideology that viewed the state as the basic source of Chile's economic and political woes.

3.1.1   The Rise of Heavy Taxation

To understand the decline in Chilean taxation under military rule, it is important to first examine the dynamics of the process of public sector expansion that preceded it. The focus of the analysis is mainly on the period between the end of World War II and 1970, which saw a sustained increase in the tax burden. Growing taxation during these years was driven by rising social demands from an increasingly organized society and a development strategy that prioritized the state's role in spurring investment. However, it was also facilitated by the lack of strong resistance to state intervention, even among economic elites, who would later become the central pillar of the anti-statist coalition. While in some cases uneasy about public sector growth, elites were lulled into relative passivity by the fact that it did not jeopardize their vital interests, especially their right to property.

Due at least in part to its early consolidation of postindependence political stability, by the beginning of the twentieth century, Chile had one of the more productive tax systems in Latin America (Kurtz 2013, p. 82). During the first decade and a half of the century, it collected an average of 9–10 percent of GDP in revenue, second only to Brazil among the countries examined here. However, as Figure 3.1 shows, the tax burden would increase only modestly over the next thirty years, in part because a series of external shocks (i.e., World War I, the

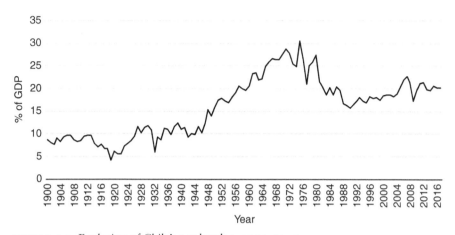

FIGURE 3.1 Evolution of Chile's tax burden, 1900–2017
Sources: CEPALSTAT/ECLAC; World Bank (1961, 1966, 1970, 1984); Braun-Llona et al. (1998)

Great Depression, and Word War II) disrupted trade flows and the revenues stemming from them. Chile was highly vulnerable to these events because at least two-thirds of its fiscal revenue in the early decades of the century came from trade levies, especially taxes on nitrate exports (Bowman and Wallerstein 1982, p. 448; Luders and Wagner 2003, p. 794).

Nevertheless, repeated crises did have the salutary effect of stimulating a gradual shift toward less volatile domestic taxation. The country's first permanent, general income tax was created in 1924 and a broad-based consumption tax was introduced in 1936. While import tariffs continued to be a significant revenue source, export taxes were virtually extinguished. Copper, which by the 1930s had replaced nitrates as Chile's main export, continued to be an important revenue generator, but instead of entering state coffers through export taxes copper revenues now entered mainly through levies on the income of private, mainly US-owned mining companies. Beginning in the 1920s, the creation of contributory pension and healthcare systems meant that an increasing amount of revenue came from social security taxes. By the late 1940s, only about 20 percent of tax revenues came from trade (Escalona 2014, p. 11).

While important changes occurred during the 1920s and 1930s with regard to the types of taxes used to gather revenue, Chile's tax system preserved the highly centralized character imprinted on it during the early decades of the nineteenth century (Espinoza and Marcel 1994, p. 23). Municipalities achieved some tax authority during the late 1800s due to a brief civil war that resulted in certain institutional reforms (Eaton 2004, p. 43), but Chile, unlike the other countries discussed in this study, never developed regional governments with any degree of fiscal autonomy. As data presented in Chapter 1 suggest, centralization has remained a constant characteristic of Chile's tax system.

Beginning after World War II, Chile embarked on a more sustained trajectory of tax burden growth. Revenues increased from 10 to 12 percent of GDP in the mid-1940s to more than 27 percent in 1970. The latter figure was the highest in the region (Ondetti 2015, p. 754). Growth was driven mainly by indirect and social security levies. Notwithstanding some increases in income taxation under Frei (who sought to reverse the relative decline of this tax after World War II), direct taxes accounted for less than a fifth of total tax revenues in the late 1960s and early 1970s (World Bank 1984; Braun-Llona et al. 1998). Revenues from such taxes were substantial by Latin American standards relative to GDP, but their contribution was outweighed by that of other levies, especially social security taxes, which by 1970 brought in close to 10 percent of GDP, or almost 40 percent of total tax revenues.

Increasing taxation was just one aspect of a general expansion of the public sector (Ffrench-Davis 1973; Stallings 1978). The Chilean state sought to promote industrial growth through high tariffs, subsidized inputs, and direct ownership of a variety of industries. The latter two aspects were mainly the responsibility of the Corporation for Production Promotion (Corporación de Fomento de la Producción, CORFO), perhaps the most powerful public development agency in Latin America. Under Frei the state also acquired partial ownership of the crucial copper mining industry. Another central aspect of state expansion was the growth of social security. By the 1960s, Chile's social security spending was rivalled in Latin America only by Uruguay's (Mesa Lago 1978, table 7–15). In fact, total social spending in 1970 was similar to the OECD average, at about 20 percent of GNP (Arellano 1985, p. 397). Thus, even before Allende, the Chilean state "played a greater role in the nation's economy than it did in the economy of any other Latin American country with the exception of Cuba" (Valenzuela 1978, p. 13).

Public sector growth was driven by a combination of factors. Demands for spending on social policies such as pensions, health care, and education played a key role. Stiff competition for votes in a relatively democratic system motivated political elites to offer social benefits in return for support (Valenzuela 1978). However, this process might not have resulted in an extensive welfare state had it not been for the influence of organized groups who demanded inclusion in the social security system or upgrading of their benefits (Mesa-Lago 1978, pp. 25–30). Labor unions were crucial in this sense. Chile had one of the strongest labor movements in Latin America during these decades and many unions had ties to left parties, especially the Communist Party (Partido Comunista de Chile, PC) and Allende's Socialist Party (Partido Socialista, PS). Although the left was excluded from most postwar governing coalitions, its support among organized workers and the threat that it might come to power pressured other parties to create or expand social programs. By the 1960s, this had become an "almost compulsory" objective of all Chilean parties (Stallings 1978, p. 123).

In addition, the postwar consolidation of an import-substitution industrialization (ISI) development strategy favored the emergence of a substantial state apparatus. While advocates of this approach (including economists associated with ECLAC) did not necessarily endorse heavy taxation, the activist role they envisioned for the state in promoting and channeling investment required fiscal resources and tended to invite pressures from businesses seeking to profit from protectionism, subsidized credit, public infrastructure, and so on. Along with pressures for welfare state expansion, ISI helped create a dense "state-centered matrix" in which authorities were constantly striving to arbitrate between the demands of different groups for public benefits (Cavarozzi 1992).

However, just as important as these positive pressures for state economic intervention was the lack of political resistance to it (Stallings 1978; Kurtz 2013). Until at least the late 1950s, Chile's state-led development model faced relatively little opposition from the country's economic elite. While not exempt from disagreements and tensions, the relationship between the state and the owners of capital was generally a cooperative one. Even the agricultural sector, which arguably had the least to gain from a model emphasizing industrialization and mineral extraction, was generally not a frontal opponent of the model. As one scholar has noted, "elite reactions to this turn to the mixed economy and substantial protectionism ranged from muted opposition to open support" (Kurtz 2013, p. 146).

Underlying this situation was the fact that the state did not significantly threaten the elite's core interests, especially with regard to property. Despite originating in a series of center-left governing coalitions during the late 1930s and 1940s, interventionism was generally pro-business. The state came to control a substantial share of industry but did so mainly through joint ventures between CORFO and the private sector in which the former contributed most of the capital and assumed much of the risk (Stallings 1978, pp. 47–49). In most cases firms created through such partnerships were eventually privatized entirely, often on terms highly favorable to the buyers. Land reform had been discussed in Chile since at least the 1920s, resulting in vague progressive language being inserted into the constitution (Mirow 2011). However, until the mid-1960s nothing of significance was done in this area.

To be sure, there were currents within the private sector and the two traditional parties that anchored the political right, the Conservative and Liberal parties, concerned about public sector expansion. They felt excessive interventionism was the underlying cause of the chronic inflation and lackluster growth that had afflicted the economy since the mid-1950s (Ffrench-Davis 2002, pp. 4–5). In 1958, an alliance of these two parties managed to elect businessman Jorge Alessandri as the president of Chile. Alessandri was committed to reducing the state's role in the economy by, among other things, reducing the tax burden (Stallings 1978, pp. 64–65). He initially had the support of much of the private sector, but in practice business was unwilling to bear the costs associated with his program of currency stabilization and trade opening, which would inevitably hurt some firms, at least in the short run. By the end of Alessandri's term in 1964, economic policy remained largely unchanged and the tax burden was somewhat higher than at the outset of the government (see Figure 3.1).

Symptomatic of the lack of acute business concern with Chile's economic strategy was the political fragmentation of the private sector. Chile did have a peak business association, the Confederation of Production and Commerce (Confederación de la Producción y del Comercio, CPC), which had been created in 1933 in the wake of the "Socialist Republic," a military regime with strong leftist leanings that existed from June to September 1932 (Schneider 2004, p. 154). However, over the next three decades, the CPC was generally overshadowed by some of the sectoral entities that composed it, especially the Society for Industrial Promotion (Sociedad de Fomento Fabril, SOFOFA) and the National Society of Agriculture (Sociedad Nacional de Agricultura, SNA). The private sector preferred to work through sector-specific groups, probably because they represented firms with more homogeneous interests. Thus, at least through the mid-1960s, the CPC "never became a very effective tool for the representation of entrepreneurial interests" (Cavarozzi 1975, p. 110). Moreover, even the sectoral organizations represented mainly large businesses (Schneider 2004, p. 157). Smaller firms either belonged to entities unaffiliated with them or were not members of any association.

To some extent, private sector fragmentation was also reflected in partisan ties. Business generally was closer to the Conservative and Liberal Parties than to those of the left or to the Radical Party (Partido Radical), the traditional representative of the educated, secular middle class. However, there was a sectoral division within the private sector, with agriculture being closer to the Conservative Party and industry and finance (i.e., urban sectors) to the Liberals (Stallings 1978, p. 41). The creation of the centrist PDC in the late 1950s and its subsequent rapid growth added to the diversity. At least until the second half of the 1960s, when the PDC's leftward turn under Frei began to scare them off, large industrialists were attracted to the Christian Democrats' modernizing agenda and played a crucial role in directing the party (Stallings 1978, pp. 61–62).

Thus, as this section has argued, the growth of Chile's tax burden during the decades preceding Allende's rise to power was the product of both forces favoring increased public spending, including strong unions, competitive labor-based parties, and a state-led development strategy, and the relative weakness of anti-statism, given the lack of acute threats to core elite interests. This statist-leaning power balance would begin to decay in the late 1960s, but would only definitively collapse in the 1970s, as discussed in the next section.

3.1.2   Property Rights Threat and Rising Anti-Statism

Statist predominance in postwar Chile was ultimately destroyed by the perception that the state was advancing toward a socialist system that would curtail property rights, as well as religious and other freedoms. Such fears, rooted in the identity and actions of public authorities and their supporters in civil society, fueled a countermobilization of economic elites and social conservatives and legitimized rightwing views that had previously been considered extreme. Support for, or acquiescence to, state expansion gave way to a determination to fight it. This change began during the PDC government, but would probably have been a transitory phenomenon had that government not been followed by one with far more radical goals and policies: that of Allende's Popular Unity (Unidad Popular, UP) coalition.

Compared to the Radical Party, which had previously been Chile's major centrist force, the PDC had a clearer progressive agenda (Valenzuela 1978; Fleet 1985). Although the party was not free of factionalism, on the whole it supported a strong state role not only in pursuing growth but also in promoting equity. Frei had a broad reform agenda involving increased progressive taxation, incremental nationalization of copper (meant to extract more fiscal resources from this sector), increased social spending, expanded educational access, and land reform. However, it was this last item that was most controversial and would ultimately provoke greatest resistance. Although his land reform fell well short of the one undertaken during the next government, Frei did expropriate about 1,000 properties with a collective area of more than three million hectares (Valdés and Foster 2014, p. 4). To prepare the way for this reform, he pushed through Congress a constitutional amendment that loosened property rights protections, making it easier and less expensive to expropriate land.

Frei's government also brought an intensification of labor and peasant mobilization (Stallings 1978, ch. 5; Valenzuela 1978). The Christian Democrats sought to establish a stronger grassroots base by fomenting the growth of allied labor unions, chipping away at the traditional dominance of the PC and PS in this area. They also tried to mobilize peasants and the urban shantytown dwellers, groups largely neglected by the left. Threatened by these initiatives, left parties redoubled their own organizational efforts and sought to differentiate themselves from the PDC by radicalizing their positions. Union membership grew (mainly because of the growth of rural unionism) and strike activity intensified (Angell 1972; Larraín and Meller 1991, p. 177). In spite of the PDC's grassroots organizing efforts, the PS and PC continued to control the Unified Workers' Central (Central Única de Trabajadores, CUT), the country's only broadly cross-sectoral labor confederation. Moreover, in a climate of growing polarization, groups began to emerge that rejected the traditional leftist parties' embrace of democratic competition (Valenzuela 1978, p. 38).

Private sector elites were alarmed by the shift toward the left within the state and larger society and sought to organize themselves to defend their interests. Of particular concern was the threat to property implied by land reform and the constitutional amendment passed to facilitate it (Kaufman 1972). Although industrialists had, in some cases, expressed sympathy for land redistribution, their commitment withered as this policy unfolded in practice. Sensing a general threat to private property, in the wake of the amendment's passage in early 1967, SOFOFA joined forces with the SNA and other sectoral groups to launch a propaganda campaign in defense of free enterprise. One of the key themes was that the private sector was not limited to large firms, but also included hundreds of thousands of store owners, street vendors, taxi drivers, and other small businesses (Stallings 1978, pp. 111–113). The CPC played an important role in this campaign, presaging its later prominence.

Business mobilization was accompanied by other shifts that underscored a growing concern with the extent and character of state intervention. One was the 1966 merger of the Conservative and Liberal parties into the new National Party (Partido Nacional, PN). Both parties had supported Frei's candidacy in order to avoid a leftist victory. However, their own poor performance in the 1965 legislative elections and the reality of the PDC's reformism led them to unite, along with some smaller rightist groups, in a single party (Valenzuela 1995, pp. 42–44). The PN developed a hostile relationship with the PDC, making the renewal of the center-right coalition in the 1970s elections increasingly unlikely.

Another aspect of the growing rightist mobilization was the emergence of grassroots conservative movements. Probably the most important was a student movement rooted in the Catholic University of Chile, one of the country's two most prestigious (Pollack 1999). The Movimiento Gremial, or syndical movement, emerged in reaction to left-leaning student protests that sought to increase university autonomy and student governance, with some support from the Frei government (Fuentes 2011). Led by the charismatic intellectual Jaime Guzmán, *gremialismo* (as it was often referred to) rejected the university reform movement as a stalking horse for the PDC's leftist agenda. It was able to win control of the Catholic University's student government association in 1969. As we shall see, members of this movement would come to play important roles in both the Pinochet regime and the subsequent democratic right.

Had Frei's government been replaced by a more conservative one, it seems likely that the incipient mobilization of the right would have dissipated, leaving few lasting traces. Frei had moderated his policies in the last three years of his presidency and relations with the private sector had improved moderately (Stallings 1978, pp. 113–115). In contrast to what had happened in the 1930s, and would happen again under Allende, no new entities were created during this period to represent capitalists as a class. The Frei years had given rise to a new conservative party, but the PN had not yet developed a strong identity, which helps explain its rapid postcoup dissolution. Frei could have potentially had an impact roughly analogous to that of João Goulart's in Brazil, his approximate contemporary. Goulart, as Chapter 5 shows, provoked some rightist countermobilization but left no lasting sequelae in terms of elite economic ideology or organization.

Such an outcome was by no means out of the question. The 1970 presidential election ended up being a three-way race among Allende of the leftist UP, a coalition composed mainly of the PS, PC, and Radical parties; Radomiro Tomic of the PDC; and former President Alessandri, who ran as an independent backed by the PN. The failure of the PDC and PN to reach an agreement on a center-right coalition similar to that of the 1965 election (as well as some previous contests) made Allende's victory more probable. However, on the eve of the election, most polls suggested that Alessandri would win (Valenzuela 1978, p. 41). Allende pulled off a victory, but with a margin of little more than 1 percent of the vote.

Furthermore, since no candidate had secured a majority, it was up to Congress to decide the winner, choosing from the top two vote-getters. When such situations had arisen in the past, Congress had chosen the candidate who had won more votes, but this was no ordinary situation, since the winner was a Marxist advocating a transition toward socialism. Given their position in the center of the political spectrum, the Christian Democrats would decide the outcome. However, they were deeply divided (Valenzuela 1978, p. 49). Allende ultimately secured their support by agreeing to a constitutional amendment amounting to a pledge to follow the constitution. Even this agreement might have been derailed by military opposition had it not been for a failed attempt by an extreme rightist group with CIA ties to kidnap General René Schneider, commander of the Chilean army. Details of the plot, which led to Schneider's death, would only be uncovered years later, but it was clear that the general, who opposed intervention, had been targeted to clear the way for a coup that would keep Allende from the presidency. The surge of pro-democracy sentiment that resulted rendered such a move unviable (Valenzuela 1978; Kornbluh 2003, p. 29).

Once in office, Allende initiated a series of radical policy changes that would ultimately forge a stronger anti-statist bloc by further unifying elites and legitimizing an emerging ideological synthesis of extreme economic liberalism and Catholic social conservatism. Instead of attenuating the polarization of Chilean society, the 1970 election ended up exacerbating it greatly, facilitating a profound transformation of the political system and, ultimately, of the development model pursued since the late 1930s.

Despite having won only a narrow plurality of the presidential vote and lacking majorities in either legislative chamber, the UP government set about fulfilling its promise of pursuing a peaceful, gradual path to socialism.[3] There were numerous policies during this period that raised the hackles of the private sector and conservative actors, including large minimum wage increases, price controls, increases in spending, and, ultimately, rationing of essential goods to cope with acute shortages.[4] However, undoubtedly the most important aspect

---

[3] Following the 1969 legislative elections, the left controlled 40.0 percent of the seats in the Senate and 40.7 percent in the Chamber of Deputies.

[4] As Figure 3.1 suggests, the UP government did not bring a substantial tax increase. In fact, the tax burden declined in 1973, probably due to exceptionally high inflation.

from both the economic and political perspectives was a major shift in property rights affecting several sectors of the economy (Meller 1998, ch. 2).

Authorities sought to assert control over the "commanding heights" of the economy (mainly manufacturing and banking) by creating both fully state-owned firms and public/private partnerships in which the state would hold a majority stake. The government ended up exceeding even its own ambitious plans due to a wave of worker takeovers of industrial firms, which pushed authorities to use various means to bring those firms under state control. By December 1972, 250 companies had been seized, raising the state's share of total industrial capital from 28 to 45 percent (Stallings 1978, pp. 156–157).[5] In the farm sector, Allende greatly deepened Frei's land reform, expropriating more than 4,200 properties with a collective area of over 5.4 million hectares (Valdés and Foster 2014, p. 4). By mid-1972 the "latifundium" had been essentially eradicated from Chile (Winn and Kay 1974, p. 142).

The government's property initiatives both provoked and were driven forward by a rising tide of grassroots mobilization in the city and countryside. As mentioned, workers responded to the UP government by trying to accelerate the socialist transition through factory occupations. Over time, this tactic developed into a broader strategy of forming regional "industrial cordons," in which workers from multiple occupied factories collaborated and were sometimes joined by local community organizations and even peasant groups, if the factories were located near a rural area (Castillo 2010). Land reform efforts also spurred peasant land seizures, which pushed the government to intensify its efforts in this area (Winn and Kay 1974). While UP authorities, who had formed a solid alliance with the CUT (Gaudichaud 2004, pp. 29–32), sympathized with these actions, they contributed to a climate of chaos and polarization that frustrated the goal of an orderly transition.

If Frei's reformism had provoked an embryonic mobilization of anti-state forces, Allende's far more radical moves inspired a full-blown rightwing opposition movement determined to rid itself of the UP government by constitutional or unconstitutional means.

As state property seizures mounted, elites came to perceive that they were facing a threat to their survival as a social class and made unprecedented efforts to organize resistance (Campero 1984, p. 62). SOFOFA, traditionally the most powerful business association and one that had typically operated mainly behind the scenes, named a new, more aggressive president and resolved to go on the offensive (Stallings 1978, pp. 138–139). However, realizing that an open confrontation between big capital and the pro-worker government would not be beneficial, business leaders sought to bring entities representing smaller firms into the fold. Together, associations of large and small businesses created an

---

[5] The seizures included the US-owned copper mining companies Anaconda and Kennecott, but these were among the least controversial nationalizations since they were supported by a broad consensus and were approved unanimously by the Chilean Congress.

umbrella organization called the National Private Sector Front (Frente Nacional del Área Privada, FRENAP). In forming FRENAP, the major associations "appealed to the interests that large and small businessmen most had in common: private property" (Silva 1996, p. 48). This alliance would coordinate a number of protest activities, most notably two national producer strikes, in which truckers played a particularly crucial role because of their ability to block highways. "The Allende experience," as Silva notes, "had sharpened the class consciousness of capitalists and fortified their capacity for collective action" (Silva 1996, p. 90).

Increasingly, business collaborated with other forces to combat the government and work toward Allende's removal (Campero 1984, p. 69). There is evidence of ties between big business and the Nationalist Front for Fatherland and Liberty (Frente Nacionalista Patria y Libertad), an extreme right group formed in 1971, which was accused of acts of violence and sabotage against the government (Stallings 1978, p. 149). Following the legislative elections of 1973, which dashed hopes of removing Allende through constitutional methods (due to the UP's solid performance), efforts intensified to form a civil-military coup coalition including leaders of the private sector, political parties, and armed forces. The coup plotters were in contact with the US government, which had been working systematically since the 1970 election to thwart the UP's ambitions through both overt and covert means. These efforts included secretly funding *El Mercurio*, Chile's largest-circulation newspaper and a fierce opponent of the socialist government (Kornbluh 2003, pp. 91–94).

Within this context of marked polarization, groups propounding ideological perspectives previously at the margins of Chilean society gained wider acceptance (Valdés 1995; Moulian 1997, pp. 196–201). On the right, the most important were the largely student-based Movimiento Gremial and a network of mainly US-trained professional economists deeply committed to free-market policies. In the highly charged atmosphere that characterized the UP government, the two of them not only increased their influence over business, the media, the armed forces, and other actors but also began to merge their seemingly disparate ideologies into a single socially conservative, economically liberal worldview (Pollack 1999).

Previously confined to the Catholic University, *gremialismo* not only consolidated its grip over that institution but also expanded outward to others (Huneeus 2001, pp. 13–14). Jaime Guzmán, its major ideologue and spokesman, became a well-known political figure due to his impassioned and lucid criticism of the UP government and his regular appearances in the media (Monckeberg 2017). His celebration of civil society groups and the Catholic principle of "subsidiarity," which holds that the state should not make decisions that can be made by such groups, influenced business leaders, who employed it rhetorically in their own organizing efforts. *Gremialismo* was important to the opposition because it framed mobilization against Allende as the defense not only of capital and the rich, but also of values deeply embedded in Chilean society, including family, religion, and personal freedom.

A network of liberal economists that would later come to be known collectively as the "Chicago Boys" also had close ties to the Catholic University (Valdés 1995). It arose out of a program in the late 1950s and 1960s that allowed Chilean students to pursue graduate studies at the University of Chicago's Department of Economics, a renowned bastion of neoclassical, free-market thought. On their return to Chile, the Chicago Boys took positions in the private sector and universities. Several developed ties to the Grupo Edwards, the large conglomerate that owned *El Mercurio*, working as executives, writing columns for the newspaper, or conducting research for a pro-market think tank bankrolled by the conglomerate (Pollack 1999, pp. 41–47).

The approximation of the Chicago Boys and *gremialistas* began during the late Frei years, when members of the two groups launched a magazine that synthesized their views in a broad critique of the growing politicization and state dominance of Chilean society (Gárate 2012). However, their interactions intensified under Allende as the phenomena they decried grew in importance and other actors sought them out as allies in their struggles against the government (Pollack 1999). At first blush, the *gremialista*'s Hispanic corporatist ideas would seem an odd fit with the Anglo-Saxon liberalism of the Chicago Boys. Nevertheless, Guzmán's emphasis on subsidiarity and the role of civic groups had some affinities with the economists' anti-statism. More importantly, the Chicago Boys offered the *gremialistas* something they lacked: a clear policy package backed by a sophisticated rationale, a valuable tool in their battle against leftism and statism. In essence, the *gremialistas* were "neoliberalized" in the course of the political struggle (Vergara 1985).

Although business had resisted incorporation of the Chicago Boys' ideas into Alessandri's 1970 campaign platform (Pollack 1999, pp. 44–45), three years later circumstances had changed. As business elites, the partisan right and members of the armed forces began to prepare for a coup in late 1972; they secretly turned to members of the Chicago Boys for an economic plan to guide the new regime (Silva 1996, pp. 68–78). Guzmán, who was close to some of the economists, also participated in their meetings (De Castro 1992, p. 10). The resulting document, codenamed "the brick" (*el ladrillo*), constituted a roadmap not only for reversing Allende's policies but also for transitioning to a far more liberal development model than the one pursued over previous decades. It would become a key influence on the military regime's policies. If implemented, the strategy laid out in "the brick" would impose major costs, even bankruptcy, on many firms. However, as a study of the Chicago Boys points out, the larger context helped make these ideas more widely acceptable:

Gradually, the fundamental deterioration in society's economic, social and political situation made extreme solutions appear "more realistic." The same radical force that sapped the prestige of moderate politicians and intermediate political solutions also assisted the rise of radical economists, who advocated the reduction of the role of government as part of the confrontation between the state and the market. (Valdés 1995, p. 245)

3.1.3 Military Rule and Tax Reductions

The authoritarian regime established as a result of the September 11, 1973 coup d'état would bring about a drastic reduction in state intervention in the Chilean economy, including a sharp decline in taxation. While this transformation was influenced by conjunctural factors, including General Augusto Pinochet's success in concentrating power in his own hands, the fact that it occurred in the wake of a major statist reform wave that profoundly threatened property rights and gave credibility to a virulently anti-statist ideology goes a long way toward explaining its deep and sustained character. In a pendular fashion, the radicalism of the shift toward state control of the economy under Allende created the momentum necessary for an equally radical move in the opposite direction.

Chile's new military authorities did not immediately implement sweeping market reforms. For over a year following the coup, economic policymaking focused mainly on short-term goals, like reducing inflation and returning expropriated property to its former owners (Moulian and Vergara 1980, pp. 71–86). However, beginning in April 1975, the regime embarked on a more decisive liberalizing course that would lead it to reform numerous aspects of the economy, including trade, financial flows, ownership of productive assets, the labor market, social security, and education. Although many other Latin American countries would eventually also adopt market reform projects, none would prove as sweeping, coherent, and sustained as the one implemented by Chile's military regime.

This transformation eventually came to include a sharp drop in taxation. However, facing a large fiscal deficit left by the preceding government (which had contributed to inflation of about 500 percent in 1973), authorities initially focused on making taxation more efficient (Cheyre 1986, p. 12). The most important change during the 1970s was the introduction in 1974 of a VAT, which replaced the existing consumption tax. The advantages of the VAT, which had already been adopted by many European countries and some Latin American ones, were that it was less distortive of the economy and included certain built-in incentives for business compliance (Larraín and Vergara 2001, p. 81).[6] Despite significant declines in social security revenues due to reduced employer contributions, the VAT helped keep taxation at a level roughly

---

[6] Because they tax each transaction in the process of producing and distributing a good, sales taxes cause taxation to cumulate, creating nonmarket incentives for firms to vertically integrate in order to reduce the number of transactions. A VAT avoids this problem by only taxing the value added by each firm. In addition, since businesses must present receipts of their input purchases to the

comparable to that of the Allende and Frei governments. In addition, during the 1970s, the state enjoyed unprecedentedly high nontax revenues, due to the copper nationalization and strong global prices for this commodity.[7]

Nevertheless, the 1980s brought two policy shifts that extended the state-reducing reform wave decisively into taxation, even as nontax revenues were also declining. The first was a pioneering transformation of the pension system, implemented in 1981 after several years of incremental change. Chile's massive public, pay-as-you-go system was transformed into one in which worker contributions flowed into individual retirement accounts managed by private firms and employer contributions were eliminated (Borzutzky and Hyde 2016). The state's role was reduced mainly to regulating the private system, in addition to providing minimal pensions to informal sector workers and topping off the pensions of formal sector workers whose individual savings fell below a legally defined minimum. Although existing workers were given the option of continuing in the public system, financial incentives and propaganda were designed to make transitioning to the new one more attractive. Contributions to the public system declined from 5.6 percent of GDP in 1980 to only 1.8 percent in 1989 (World Bank 1984; CEPALSTAT).

The second major reform involved the corporate income tax. In 1984, the tax was restructured so that firms would pay a much lower effective rate on earnings that were retained rather than distributed to shareholders, the purpose being to spur investment (Hsieh and Parker 2006). In addition, shareholders would be able to deduct the corporate income tax they paid from their personal income tax liability, thus avoiding "double taxation" (Larraín and Vergara 2001, p. 87). Mainly as a consequence of this reform, the income tax rate on retained corporate earnings dropped from nearly 50 percent at the beginning of the decade to only 10 percent in the second half. Four years later, it was temporarily reduced to zero, presumably for electoral reasons (Vergara 2010, p. 724). The result was not only an investment boom, but also a public sector with reduced fiscal resources. Because of the pension and income tax reforms, as well as a 1988 reduction of the VAT rate from 18 to 16 percent, Chile's tax burden declined steadily over the course of the 1980s. In 1990, the year of the democratic transition, it was less than 16 percent of GDP (see Figure 3.1), or roughly 40 percent below its pre-coup peak.

How can we explain this profound transformation of the Chilean economy, including an impressive decline in taxation? As mentioned earlier, the military regime's embrace of profound, rapid state retrenchment was arguably not inevitable. The members of the military junta by most accounts possessed

state in order to receive tax credits for them (and thus only be taxed on the value added), there is a built-in incentive for compliance.

[7] According to Braun-Llona et al. (1998), between 1900 and 1972, nontax revenues had averaged about 1 percent of GDP, but during the following decade they rose to about 7 percent.

neither expertise nor strong convictions regarding economic policy. Given their diverse material interests, business leaders were also not homogenously committed to radical reform (Silva 1995, p. 4). Accordingly, the first year or so of the regime was characterized by jockeying between different groups within and outside the state to influence policy, and the outcome involved moderate reforms that mainly sought to address particularly urgent problems, such as inflation.

The turn to more radical change beginning in mid-1975 can be explained in part by two interrelated processes operating within the state. First, despite having joined the coup coalition only days before Allende's overthrow, General Pinochet ascended to a position of clear leadership within the military junta. By December 1974, he had convinced the group to name him the president of Chile (Cavallo et al. 1997). Second, once consolidated in power, Pinochet sought to address the persistent economic problems by elevating the Chicago Boys, several of whom were already working in the government, to higher positions, including Minister of the Economy and President of the Central Bank. With Pinochet's blessing, they launched an initial series of major reforms, including sweeping trade liberalization, privatization, and spending cuts.

Nevertheless, the extreme and sustained character of Chile's neoliberal transition cannot be adequately understood without appreciating the various ways in which the UP government's reforms and the intense conservative countermobilization against them impacted this process.

First, the trauma of this period and the fear of a return to socialist governance led propertied groups to deposit great trust in the military regime (Silva 1991, 1995). For many Chileans, the armed forces had saved the country from totalitarianism and they were both thankful and desirous of continued protection. This effect helps explain the impressive autonomy bureaucrats enjoyed in implementing reforms that were costly, if not deadly, to many firms. Second, the UP government had made elites acutely aware of the dangers of an interventionist state. While there was disagreement about how rapid and drastic liberalization should be, there was broad support for the kinds of reforms outlined in "the brick." Defenders of a mere return to the pre-Allende status quo were "completely isolated. They had no allies in government and precious few outside of it" (Silva 1996, p. 89). As the costs of liberalization mounted, support for reform became more concentrated in internationally competitive firms, but the private sector's basic sympathy for Pinochet's market-oriented project remained solid throughout the military era (Silva 1995; Campero 2003).

Finally, the struggles of the pre-coup years had given rise to a coherent rightwing ideology embedded in organized groups and social networks and possessing a clear vision of what post-Allende Chile should look like. The core of this "new right," as it has been described, was composed of the *gremialista* movement and the Chicago Boys (Pollack 1999). Members of both groups assumed important roles in the military regime.[8] Chicago Boys largely dominated the top economic posts from 1975 on (Silva 1991, p. 391). Many *gremialistas* served as mayors and in other political posts. Guzmán never took an official position but was a trusted advisor to Pinochet and played a key role in drafting the 1980 constitution, still in force today. While we cannot know for sure why Pinochet allied himself with these groups, it seems likely that the clarity of their views was appealing, since it could endow the regime with a sense of direction and purpose and, consequently, reinforce his own power.

Thus, while the turn to radical liberalization was by no means fully determined by the statist offensive that preceded the military coup, it was certainly deeply influenced by it. In fact, it is hard to imagine Chile's military regime having made such sweeping changes had it come to power in a less polarized setting. As one of the most prominent Chicago Boys, Sergio de Castro, has argued, "Allende gave the best economic lessons on what not to do. After that, the path was clear. Without Allende, Pinochet would not have existed and without Pinochet the free market would not have existed."[9] Of course, this dynamic bears a close resemblance to the concept of the reactive sequence (Mahoney 2000), in which an initial action in one direction largely determines a subsequent action in the opposite direction.

The reforms that contributed most to the reduction of the tax burden both occurred during the 1980s but corresponded to different phases of the regime and involved somewhat different political dynamics. While pension reform was initiated during a period of strength, in which the regime basked in the glory of a long-awaited economic recovery, the income tax reform was largely a defensive reaction to the acute recession that broke out in the early 1980s and led to vocal complaints, even among some regime loyalists.

That the pension system would be targeted for reform is not surprising. Relative to GDP, Chile's social security expenditures, of which pensions were easily the largest component, were at a level characteristic of far more developed societies (Wallich 1981, p. 6). By the 1970s, moreover, because of rapid benefit growth and the failure to raise revenues proportionately, the state was heavily subsidizing the system with general revenue. Chile's pension system was also highly fragmented and bureaucratically complex. While employer contributions were high and pension coverage broad by regional standards, pensions were not even readily defensible on equity grounds, due to great variation in benefit levels among different categories of workers (Borzutzky and Hyde 2016, p. 59).

Pension reform began incrementally in the mid-1970s with moves to limit benefit growth and ease the burden on employers in order to foment job

---

[8] An attempt to quantify the presence of different groups in the military regime's cabinets found that, other than the Army (22.0 percent), the Chicago Boys (17.0 percent) and *gremialistas* (12.5 percent) held the largest share of posts (Huneeus 2001, p. 9).

[9] *The Clinic*, April 7, 2015.

creation (Kritzer 1996, p. 46). Social security tax revenues declined relative to the Frei and Allende years, but the basic structure of the system remained intact. Reform took a more radical turn in 1980 when the government, buoyed politically by three years of solid economic growth, approved a law transforming Chile's fully public, pay-as-you-go pension system into one based on individual investment accounts managed by private firms. The amount of a worker's pension would now depend almost entirely on their own savings, since employer contributions were eliminated. The reform, it was argued, would boost job creation by unburdening employers, "depoliticize" pension provision by removing it from the state's grasp, and deepen capital markets with an inflow of forced savings (Kurtz 1999, pp. 416–418).

In contrast to pension privatization, a relatively autonomous initiative of the state technocrats during good times, the income tax reform was implemented to recapture business confidence in the wake of the calamitous economic crisis that broke out in 1982. In that year, Chile was struck by the same debt crisis that was sweeping through much of the rest of Latin America. A combination of rising interest rates, weakened demand for their commodity exports, and the unwillingness of foreign banks to extend new loans forced these countries to adopt harsh austerity measures or face the grim prospect of debt default. Although it ultimately recovered more quickly than some other countries, in the early going Chile was among the worst hit, as the economy shrunk by more than 10 percent in 1982.

Pinochet came under pressure to adopt measures to protect businesses against further losses and stimulate a recovery. Led by the CPC, business associations sought a number of policy shifts, including debt relief, higher tariffs, a less austere fiscal policy, and lower corporate income taxation (Silva 1996, p. 176). While these proposals did not challenge the basic liberal framework of the regime's economic strategy, officials were initially resistant to them, since they would attenuate the hardnosed austerity championed by the Chicago Boys. Nevertheless, the outbreak of mass protest against the regime in 1983 raised the stakes by creating the possibility that elements of the private sector might ultimately side with rising calls for democratization (Silva 1996, pp. 182–192). Consequently, beginning in 1984, authorities implemented many of the changes demanded by capitalists.

Among these was the income tax reform described earlier, whose main provision was to greatly reduce the taxation of corporate profits that are reinvested rather than distributed to shareholders. While the reform was made under pressure, it clearly obeyed the anti-interventionist, pro-market logic of the military regime's overall economic strategy. The additional reduction in corporate taxation, as well as the VAT, during the late 1980s represented further efforts to secure business support for continued military rule.

As this section has argued, the pronounced reduction in Chile's tax burden during the Pinochet-led military regime must be understood as symptomatic of a powerful backlash against the statist, anti-capitalist onslaught of the Allende years, which deeply threatened well-off Chileans and made more acceptable anti-statist views that had previously occupied a relatively marginal place in Chilean society. Those views were eventually embraced by a regime leadership that lacked its own economic ideology and was searching for a way to address deep economic problems and legitimize its rule.

3.2   THE SLOW GROWTH OF TAXATION UNDER DEMOCRACY

The general literature on taxation tends to associate both democracy and left party strength with higher taxes, and the Latin American experience of recent decades seems to bear those relationships out. Tax burdens have increased substantially since the "third wave" of democratization and have tended to do so particularly rapidly under leftist rule (Stein and Caro 2013). Chile, however, is an anomaly relative to both variables. The country returned to democracy in 1990 and since then an evolving coalition of center and left parties has been the predominant political force, at least in presidential contests. This coalition, known as the "Concertación" until 2013 and "Nueva Mayoría" from 2013 to 2018, won five of the seven presidential elections, including the first four. Yet, despite the approval of a number of reforms, tax revenues have increased at a slow pace compared to both the region as a whole and Argentina and Brazil in particular.

The persistence of light taxation in democratic Chile, it is argued here, primarily reflects a balance of power within the national legislature and the larger society that has favored anti-statism and thus imposed constraints on government action. The relative superiority of anti-state forces is, in turn, a reflection of the enduring impact of the conservative backlash against the radical reformism of the pre-coup era. That backlash not only sustained the military regime's profound neoliberal counterrevolution but also laid the foundation for a long-term increase in the influence of anti-statist views in Chilean society, thus preventing a strong movement back in the direction of greater state intervention.

3.2.1   Continued Neoliberalism and Light Taxation

Although Chile's tax system has undergone a variety of reforms since re-democratization, those initiatives have not brought about a major increase in the tax burden, which remains light relative to both the country's wealth and its past levels of taxation. The failure to substantially boost tax collection is consistent with a broader pattern of preserving the core aspects of the neoliberal model established under authoritarian rule.

Chile has seen two relatively broad-based tax reforms and a variety of narrower changes since returning to democracy. The first important reform occurred in 1990 under President Patricio Aylwin of the centrist PDC, the first of four consecutive Concertación presidents. Seeking to address what were widely seen as acute problems of poverty and social equity stemming from the dictatorship's austere policies, Aylwin championed a reform intended to increase both revenues and progressivity (Boylan 1996; Marcel 1997). The package that was ultimately approved had two key features: an increase in the rate of corporate income taxation from 10 to 15 percent and an increase in the VAT rate from 16 to 18 percent. Largely as a result of the reform, the tax burden had risen by about 2 percent of GDP (to 18.0 percent) by 1993. However, macroeconomic fluctuations and subsequent tariff reductions meant that revenues fell below that level on a number of occasions during the 1990s (see Figure 3.1).

The decade that followed brought little change to the tax code, but after 2000 governments did make a series of reforms. President Ricardo Lagos (2000–2006) implemented anti-evasion measures affecting both direct and indirect taxation, an increase in the VAT rate from 18 to 19 percent, and a small new tax on private mining companies (Sánchez 2011, pp. 70–85; Fairfield 2015, chs. 3 and 4). Somewhat surprisingly, the next significant tax reform was undertaken not by the Concertación but by President Sebastián Piñera (2010–2014) of the rightist coalition. In 2010, in response to a major earthquake, Piñera pushed through Congress an increase in the corporate income tax from 17 (the lowest in Latin America) to 20 percent. The tax was supposed to raise funds for reconstruction and was explicitly temporary. However, in 2012 the government (pressured by massive student protests, discussed later) made the new rate permanent. Although the increase was partially offset by cuts in the personal income tax and some other taxes, it still raised direct tax revenues by about 0.3 percent of GDP (Fairfield 2015, p. 270).

Seemingly more significant, however, was a tax law passed in 2014 by the Nueva Mayoría government (2014–2018) led by Michelle Bachelet of the PS. Bachelet had done little to change the tax system during her first term as president (from 2006 to 2010), but at the outset of her second she announced a reform whose objective was to increase revenues by 3 percent of GDP by 2018, mainly through heavier income taxation (Fairfield 2014, 2015). It would do this by attenuating the 1984 corporate tax reform that shielded reinvested profits from taxation and prevented "double taxation" of corporate income by allowing corporate tax payments to be deducted from shareholders' individual tax bills. The existing system had been criticized for providing both incentives and opportunities to disguise personal income as corporate income (IMF 2014, pp. 37–38), leading to legal tax avoidance as well as illegal evasion.

After a difficult negotiation, a reform was approved creating a complex hybrid income tax system in which corporations can choose between a regime similar to the existing one but with a higher rate, and one that levies a lower rate but limits the ability of shareholders to discount corporate tax payments from their personal tax bills (World Bank 2016, ch. 3). Despite accepting major changes to its original proposal, the government stood by its initial revenue projection. Nevertheless, as of 2017 Chile's tax burden remained largely unchanged relative to the pre-reform years. Even income taxation, the central focus of the reform, had not increased. The new rightist government that took power in 2018 (headed, again, by Piñera) initially said it would pursue a revenue-neutral reform focused on simplifying the tax code. However, large protests and a controversy aroused by the state's harsh repression of them subsequently pushed Piñera to advance a project that includes a modest (0.6 percent of GDP) revenue increase.[10]

All told, in more than a quarter century, the tax burden has risen by about 4 percent of GDP, a substantially smaller increase than in democratic Argentina or Brazil. As can be seen in Figure 3.1, it remains well below its level under Allende or Frei, despite the fact that Chile's real per capita GDP is now more than three times its 1973 level (World Bank Database), a difference that would lead us to expect considerably heavier taxation. In 2006–2007, Chile experienced a spike in its tax revenues to as high as 22.7 percent of GDP, but this phenomenon was due to an extraordinary rise in global copper prices and was not sustained.

Moderate tax burden growth has been part and parcel of a broader pattern of relative policymaking stability. Pinochet's rigorously market-oriented, small-state model has been largely preserved. Such emblematic reforms as pension privatization have so far survived with only modest alterations. In some areas, such as foreign trade, liberalism has even been reinforced. Reform has occurred mainly at the margins (Fazio and Parada 2010; Landerretche 2013) and has primarily involved targeted spending on poor and vulnerable groups (Marfán 2014, interview). Admittedly, the 2014–2018 Nueva Mayoría government made more significant changes than its predecessors (Palacios-Valladares and Ondetti 2019). However, these were mainly limited to education, reflecting the crucial role that the massive student-led protests of 2011 played in the coalition's creation.

3.2.2 Anti-Statist Power in Democratic Chile

Analyses of the reasons behind neoliberal continuity in democratic Chile have sometimes suggested that the leaders of the Concertación, swayed by the grave economic problems of the Allende period and the sustained growth achieved beginning in the mid-1980s, simply bought into the neoliberal model and thus did not seek to alter it. While this view was mainly advanced by leftist critics of the coalition (Fazio 1996; Riesco 2007; Ominami interview, 2014), some conservative politicians and policy experts interviewed for this study expressed a similar perspective, arguing that top Concertación policymakers had held economic views largely convergent with their own (2014 interviews: Dittborn, Lagos, Larroulet).

---

[10] *Gestión*, February 25, 2020.

This argument cannot be dismissed out of hand. Undoubtedly, some ideological change did occur within the left-leaning parties. Nevertheless, policy continuity cannot be reduced to a symptom of the ideological conversion of former leftists. Although there were certainly a good many Concertación leaders who were comfortable with Pinochet's development model, particularly within the centrist PDC, many were clearly uncomfortable. The debates between these two factions, popularly known as the "self-satisfied ones" (autocomplacientes) and the "self-flagellating ones" (autoflagelantes), respectively, at times grew heated and public (Garretón 2012, pp. 88–93). To a large extent, the formation of Nueva Mayoria in 2013 represented the triumph of the more critical currents within the coalition (Palacios-Valladares and Ondetti 2019).

More important than a lack of statist convictions among center-left leaders is a society-wide balance of power that favors anti-statism and thus makes it difficult for progressive governments to advance their preferred policies. The relative power of anti-statism is manifested mainly in three features of Chilean politics since the return to democracy: the strong representation of programmatic right parties in the national Congress (due to both electoral performance and institutional design), the unified opposition of the private sector to any substantive deviation from Pinochet's market-based approach, and the weakness of organized labor, potentially a key source of support for a more interventionist policy tack.

While the center-left coalitions have generally controlled the presidency, their position in the national legislature has been weaker, as Table 3.1 suggests. Between 1990 and 2018, they held majorities in both chambers of Congress for only two periods, 2006–2007 and 2014–2018. The Concertación captured majorities in both houses in the 2005 elections, but the defection of two senators (both of whom became independents) at the end of 2007 deprived them of their already slim majority in that chamber.

To some extent, the Concertación's lack of legislative control has been a product, not of its electoral performance, but of the structure of Chile's representative institutions. The most important feature in this regard was the "designated" senators that existed between 1990 and 2005. Under this arrangement, nine of the forty-seven members of the Senate were appointed by other state institutions rather than popularly elected. Two were chosen by the president, three by the Supreme Court, and four by the National Security Council. Each National Security Council nominee had to be a former commander of one of the security forces. Like their elected counterparts, the designated senators served eight-year terms. This institution lasted until 2005, when it was removed from the constitution along with a number of other "authoritarian enclaves" left over from the military regime (Fuentes 2015).

Although the designated senators were formally nonpartisan, they generally favored the right. This was especially true of the first cohort, which was chosen in 1989 by authorities of the outgoing regime. The designated senators appointed in 1998 were on the whole less rightist, since they were chosen

TABLE 3.1 *Distribution of seats in the Chilean Congress by term and chamber, 1990–2018 (percentages)*

Coalition/category	1990–1994 COD[a]	1990–1994 Sen	1994–1998 COD	1994–1998 Sen	1998–2002 COD	1998–2002 Sen	2002–2006 COD	2002–2006 Sen	2006–2010 COD	2006–2010 Sen[b]	2010–2014 COD	2010–2014 Sen	2014–2018 COD	2014–2018 Sen
Center-left	57.5	46.8	58.3	44.7	57.5	40.8	51.7	41.7	54.2	52.6	47.5	50.0	55.8	55.3
Right	40.0	34.0	41.7	36.2	39.2	34.7	47.5	37.5	45.0	44.7	48.3	42.1	40.8	42.1
Other	2.5	0	0	0	3.3	2.0	0.8	0	0.8	2.6	4.2	2.6	3.3	2.6
Designated		19.1		19.1		18.4		18.8						
Ex-president[c]						4.1		2.1						
Total	100	100	100	100	100	100	100	100	100	100	100	100	100	100

Source: Servicio Electoral de Chile (www.servel.cl/)

[a] "COD" stands for Chamber of Deputies and "Sen" for Senate.

[b] The center-left coalition lost its majority in December 2007 when two senators became independents.

[c] As Footnote 11 indicates, until 2005 ex-presidents were given a seat in the Senate. For 1998–2002, the table counts both Pinochet and Eduardo Frei Ruiz-Tagle (1994–2000), although the latter assumed his position in the middle of that period. For 2002–2006 only Frei is counted since Pinochet resigned his seat in early 2002.

either by President Frei or by institutions with a substantial number of Frei or Aylwin appointees. However, the right was still well represented in both the Supreme Court and the National Security Council, so the senators those institutions appointed continued to be a conservatizing force. If we assume that the designated senators and the elected senators of the rightist coalition formed a single bloc until 1998, then that bloc enjoyed solid majorities. The senators appointed for the 1998–2006 term were less loyal to the right, so during that period the two coalitions were essentially tied (Fuentes 2015, p. 112). Hence, although the balance of power in the Senate was becoming more favorable to the Concertación, the designated senators still deprived the coalition of the solid majority they otherwise would have enjoyed in both chambers.[11]

The unusual "binomial" electoral system in place until 2014 has also been seen as benefitting the right (Garretón 2012, p. 98). However, its effects were much less important than those of the designated senators. Under this system, each electoral district had two seats. For one party or coalition to capture both, it had to win at least two-thirds of the vote, an imposing challenge. Otherwise, the top two parties or coalitions would split the seats. There is considerable evidence that this system, created under military rule, was designed in part to boost conservative party representation (Polga-Hecimovich and Siavelis 2015). As it turns out, though, it actually benefitted both party coalitions roughly equally (Carey 2006). Hence, although electoral engineering increased the right's legislative force, its impact largely ended in 2005.

A more constant obstacle has been the success of rightwing parties in elections. Virtually all the elected seats not held by the center-left have been held by two programmatic rightwing parties, the Independent Democratic Union (Unión Demócrata Independiente, UDI) and National Renewal (Renovación Nacional, RN). While UDI is further to the right on both economic and (especially) social issues, both parties are deeply skeptical of state intervention in the economy and have rarely supported measures to raise taxes. Together, they form one of the most successful rightist partisan blocs in modern Latin America (Luna and Kaltwasser 2014). Although RN was the stronger of the two during the early years of democracy, since 1997 UDI has tended to win a larger share of the legislative vote.[12]

---

[11] Until the 2005 constitutional reform, ex-presidents were granted lifetime seats in the Senate. Overall, this provision ended up favoring the Concertación slightly. Pinochet assumed his seat in 1998, after retiring from his position as commander of the armed forces but, as discussed later, he was soon engulfed in a controversy that prevented him from participating in the Senate and ultimately led to his resignation in 2002. Frei assumed his seat in 2000 and served until it was eliminated.

[12] Their performance in Senate elections since 1997 has been, on average, nearly identical. However, UDI has performed better in the Chamber of Deputies, winning an average of 20.9 percent of the vote, versus 16.0 percent for the RN. If we exclude the 2017 election, which is irrelevant to the average 2013–2017 tax burden, UDI's advantage is even greater and extends to both chambers.

Adding to the difficulties faced by center-left governments has been the unified opposition of the private sector to any substantial modification of the free-market, small-state economic model established under Pinochet (Arriagada 2004; Fairfield 2010, 2015; Gárate 2012; Undurraga 2015). To be sure, businesses in virtually all societies tend to be skeptical of the benefits of state intervention and resistant to handing over their profits to the state. Nevertheless, as subsequent chapters make clear, there are significant cross-national differences in the degree of opposition, as well as the ability of the private sector to act collectively to pressure authorities against taxation. At least among the Latin American countries, Chile's private sector stands out in terms of both its organizational cohesion and its ideological commitment to economic liberalism.

As Schneider (2004) argues in his wide-ranging comparison of Latin American business organizations, Chile's private sector ranks among those with the most encompassing associative structures. Unlike many other countries in the region (even relatively small and economically homogeneous ones like Uruguay and Ecuador), Chile has a nationwide, multi-sector business association that enjoys widespread support from business. That organization is the CPC, which, as mentioned earlier, dates to the 1930s. While the CPC has not always played a prominent political role, during the current democratic period it has been a very important voice in expressing the collective opinion of private enterprise (Fairfield 2015, p. 74). Sectoral organizations also play important roles and there is a certain rivalry between SOFOFA and the CPC (2014 interviews: Lizana, SOFOFA). However, there is enough consensus between the six sectoral groups comprising the CPC that the latter has been able to credibly represent the business community as a whole. That ability gives the CPC great political clout, despite not possessing a large budget or permanent staff.

The adhesive that binds the private sector together, endowing it with a common purpose and collective identity, is a commitment to preserving Chile's free-market system. While association officials argue that business leaders are unideological, they admit that there is great unity within the private sector regarding the importance of resisting efforts to create a larger, more interventionist state (2014 interviews: Lizana, SOFOFA). Scholars have sometimes contrasted the Chilean case to that of neighboring Argentina (discussed in Chapter 6), where business is both less homogenously committed to economic liberalism and lacking in cross-sectoral organizations of any real significance (Fairfield 2010, 2015; Undurraga 2015). Of course, the consensus is not total. Manufacturing, in particular, has at times desired a less aggressive brand of liberalism, especially with regard to trade (Silva 1996). However, on most major issues, including resistance to taxation, the degree of consensus within Chile's business community is impressive (Brzovic 2014, interview).

The private sector's unity has helped make it an imposing political force. Interviewees associated with the Concertación noted that coalition policymaking was affected by a pervasive fear of eliciting negative reactions from business. This sentiment was most intense during the early years of democracy, when memories of business mobilization against the UP government were still relatively fresh (Ominami 2014, interview). However, even during the first Bachelet government (2006–2010), the coalition was restrained by an "inertial fear" of business that caused it to tread lightly policy-wise in order to "make a good impression" (Budget Department 2014, interview). It was this imperative that led the president to appoint Harvard professor Andrés Velasco, a mainstream neoclassical economist with strong ties to international financial institutions, as Minister of Finance. As a PDC legislator observed, "She put him in to signal to the market that there would not be big changes" (Ortiz 2014, interview).

Although there is no formal relationship between business associations and parties, they have clearly worked closely together since the democratic transition. Business has at times, especially during the 1990s, supported right candidates rhetorically and it has continued to do so financially, which has allowed these parties to enjoy richer campaign war chests than those of the center-left.[13] For example, in the 2009–2010 elections, the conservative parties received a volume of "reserved donations," a type of contribution likely to come from business, 125.5 percent higher than that of the Concertación (Agostini 2012, p. 18).[14] UDI, which is widely viewed as being especially close to business, has enjoyed a particularly large advantage in fundraising. Its reserved donations were twice as large as RN's and four times that of the best-performing Concertación party, the centrist PDC (Agostini 2012, p. 18).

Another aspect of business-party collaboration involves think tanks. Chile has some of the largest and most sophisticated rightist think tanks in Latin America (Flisfisch et al. 2013; McGann 2017). Particularly prominent are Freedom and Development (Libertad y Desarrollo), which is informally but closely linked to UDI; the Jaime Guzmán Foundation (Fundación Jaime Guzmán), which is formally tied to UDI; and the Center for Public Studies (Centro de Estudios Públicos), which is ideologically close to RN. Right-leaning think tanks are financially supported by business and individual donations, as well as research services they provide to the private sector (Flisfisch et al. 2013; Fairfield 2015, p. 75). As with think tanks elsewhere,

---

[13] Beginning in the early 2000s, the major business associations began to lower their political profiles, especially in electoral politics, reflecting the perception that vocal defense of conservative positions was no longer necessary and could be damaging to both business and rightist parties (Lizana 2014, interview; Fairfield 2015)

[14] Chilean law allows three types of campaign donations: (1) small ones whose origin the candidate is aware of but does not have to publicly disclose; (2) medium-sized ones made to the electoral agency and subsequently distributed to the candidate without revealing their source (to avoid undue influence); and (3) large ones whose origins are publicly disclosed. The "reserved" contributions are the second category and they constitute the most important source of campaign funding overall (Agostini 2012).

Chile's wield influence by crafting evidence-based positions on policy issues. Their work informs party platforms and legislative agendas, contributes to business association strategizing, and is diffused to the media and academia through conferences, reports, and blog posts.

A final factor contributing to anti-statist predominance in Chile has been the lack of pressure for statist policies emanating from civil society. Particularly important in this regard is the debility of organized labor. While Chile once had one of Latin America's most powerful and militant labor movements, today labor is structurally weak (Niedzwiecki 2014, p. 35; Durán and Kremerman 2015; Bensusán 2016). Compared to Argentina and Brazil, union density is lower, collective bargaining is rarer, and strikes and other forms of collective action are more infrequent. The difference with regard to collective bargaining is particularly striking. Fewer than 10 percent of Chilean workers' wages are determined by collective bargaining, compared to more than 50 percent in both Argentina and Brazil (Durán and Kremerman 2015, p. 14).

Largely as a result of these weaknesses, Chile has a "stagnant, feckless labor movement, incapable of compelling government to promote its core interests" (Posner 2017, p. 247). Leaders of the CUT, still the most important labor organization,[15] have sometimes threatened the government with national mobilizations but, knowing they could not deliver, have almost always refrained from doing so (Frank 2015). Center-left governments have feigned a willingness to make policy in conjunction with both labor and business but, in reality, only the latter's opinion has had real weight on most major issues (Insunza 2014, interview).

Admittedly, the rise of a massive student-led protest wave in 2011 helped counterbalance the weakness of other statist forces in civil society. Hundreds of thousands of students and sympathizers took to the streets during the second half of that year to demand a more assertive state role in education supported by increased revenue. Its positive reception by the general public was widely interpreted as a powerful blow to neoliberalism (Mayol and Azócar 2011; Cárdenas and Navarro 2013). The student movement's impact reverberated within the party system and state. In response, Concertación leaders moved forward with a long-debated expansion of the coalition to the left, integrating the PC and two smaller left parties (Palacios-Valladares and Ondetti 2019). For the 2013 elections, this Nueva Mayoría coalition adopted a more ambitious platform than the Concertación, including key student demands. Its solid triumph in that contest, which gave it control of the presidency and both chambers of Congress, put it in a favorable position to advance its reforms.

Nevertheless, the power shift provoked by the student movement proved fleeting. While the movement continued after 2011, protest activity dropped off to only a fraction of its former level (Palacios-Valladares and Ondetti 2019,

---

[15] The original CUT was dismantled by the military regime, but the confederation was refounded (with a slightly different name but the same acronym) in 1988.

p. 643). As pressure on governing elites to fulfill the movement's demands waned, opposition from actors like the partisan right, business associations, the news media, and sectors of the Catholic Church involved in education took on greater weight. In addition, cracks appeared within the ruling coalition itself between the PDC and its leftist partners, which limited the depth of the reforms approved. By the end of President Bachelet's term, Nueva Mayoría was both unpopular and internally divided, facilitating the right's return to the presidency.

3.2.3 Anti-Statist Influence and Tax Policy

The relative predominance of anti-statist actors in democratic Chile has worked to attenuate the extent of tax increases. In line with their broader ideological perspective, right parties, major business associations, and conservative think tanks have all consistently opposed efforts to augment the tax burden. This statement applies not only to progressive taxes but also to other types (Fairfield 2014, p. 3; Fairfield 2015, p. 102), reflecting the broad, ideologically based opposition of these groups to state intervention in the economy. UDI leaders interviewed for this study were particularly adamant that public revenues should increase through economic growth not tax hikes (2014 interviews: Dittborn, Larroulet). In fact, a longtime UDI legislator stated proudly that his party had voted against virtually every tax-raising measure during his time in Congress (Dittborn, interview 2014). Business association officials and corporate tax consultants were less adamant in this regard, but they also expressed the broad view that all taxes have a negative impact on the economy and that taxation should therefore be as light as possible (2014 interviews: Brzovic, Lizana, SOFOFA).

The most obvious channel through which anti-statist actors affected tax policy is control of public office. While center-left coalitions have usually held the presidency, the fact that almost all legislative seats outside the ruling coalition have been controlled by programmatically anti-statist parties is important. Had the opposition been substantially composed of centrist or nonprogrammatic parties, then it might not have been difficult to craft makeshift coalitions to pass spending and tax increases. In some cases, such as the 1990 tax reform, which occurred in a context of exceptionally light taxation and obvious deficits in social spending caused by the military regime's austerity, the Concertación was able to gain the support of the RN, effectively isolating UDI (Boylan 1996). However, on most issues involving taxation or other key features of the development model, the two conservative parties have hung together, presenting a united front (Sanchez 2011, p. 68; Fairfield 2015, p. 76).

Anti-statist influence has operated less directly, but no less importantly through pressures exerted by business, media, and think tanks. As with the partisan right, the key to the influence of non-electoral actors has been their cohesive and often vehement support of market-friendly, low-tax policies. The chorus of voices arguing that any substantial increase in taxation would kill the goose that laid the golden egg of Chile's rapid post-1985 economic growth has drowned out contradictory messages, making such proposals appear rash or irresponsible. No government wants to be blamed for undercutting growth and job creation. That this unified message is accompanied in some (though not all) cases by seemingly credible threats of lower investment should a revenue-raising reform occur has only compounded the difficulties faced by center-left governments (Fairfield 2015).

Of course, the lack of strong countervailing voices in Chile has contributed mightily to the neoliberal "consensus." Good arguments exist to oppose this discourse, including the lack of clear correspondence between taxation level and economic growth and the existence of real-world examples of small, open economies that thrive despite heavy taxation. However, Chilean democracy has lacked prestigious, resource-rich actors to make these arguments. A strong labor movement with associated think tanks and close ties to a left-leaning or populist party would be the most obvious candidate to do so, but Chilean unionism, as noted, has remained weak throughout the democratic period. Moreover, leftist parties, in part because of labor's debility, have been intimidated by the anti-statist bloc and hesitant to frontally attack it.

The superiority of anti-statist forces has not usually been reflected in high-profile defeats of proposals to raise taxes. Instead, at least until the Nueva Mayoría government, the predominant pattern under center-left governments has involved introducing relatively narrow reforms that were sometimes further diluted in the legislature, but ultimately approved. To a large extent, the absence of major legislative defeats reflects the Concertación's adoption of practices designed to attenuate conflict (Garretón 2012; Fairfield 2015). First, presidents filled key economic posts with individuals whose neoclassical educational background and past work experience (e.g., positions with the IMF and top US universities) would reassure the private sector and its allies of continued adherence to market principles. Former Minister of Finance Velasco, mentioned earlier, is a good example. Second, in an approach often referred to as "democracy by agreement," officials would engage in extensive consultation with business and the right even before introducing a bill into Congress (Siavelis 2016, pp. 72–73; Marfán 2014, interview). As a result of these mechanisms, proposals that might have generated conflict were for the most part simply suppressed (Fairfield 2015, p. 101). The government, as a PDC technocrat put it, "exercised prior self-censorship" (Budget Department 2014, interview). "The attitude was 'I'm probably going to lose, so I'm not going to risk it.'"

Even the 1990 reform, which has been lauded for increasing revenues and promoting greater equity (Marcel 1997; Weyland 1997), followed this pattern closely. The reform progressed rapidly through Congress because by the time it was introduced an extensive process of negotiation between the Concertación and RN (which consulted frequently with business leaders) had already occurred. In fact, the discussion was initiated even before the Concertación assumed office (Garretón 2012, p. 104). In the process, an increase in the VAT, which the center-left alliance had originally opposed, was incorporated into the bill, the corporate income tax increase was scaled back, and the projected revenue increase fell from 3 to 2 percent of GDP (Boylan 1996, p. 24). The result was a reform that, though important, was rather modest given the center-left character of the governing coalition and the sharp decline in revenue in the years preceding its approval.

The Nueva Mayoría's 2014 reform effort initially broke with the traditional pattern. Instead of naming a prominent neoclassical economist to lead the Ministry of Finance, as in her first term, Bachelet appointed Alberto Arenas, a low-profile technocrat known for his loyalty to the president and her progressive agenda (2014 interviews: Central Bank, Marfán). Arenas pushed boldly ahead with his bill, rather than engage in lengthy private discussions with groups that might oppose it. Business leaders and conservative politicians were deeply unhappy with this turn of events, which they characterized as a major shift in the center-left's approach to governance (2014 interviews: Dittborn, Larroulet, SOFOFA). Even some former Concertación finance ministers were leery of the change (2014 interviews: Marfán, Aninat).

Nevertheless, opposition eventually pushed the process toward a compromise reminiscent of previous reforms. Conservative parties and business associations were deeply critical of Bachelet's proposal because it deviated from the sacrosanct principle of avoiding "double taxation" of income and promised to significantly increase revenue. In congressional debates, as well as electronic pamphlets and online videos meant to shape public opinion, they cautioned that it would undermine investment and job creation.[16] Polls showed a decline in public support for the reform from 52 percent when it was introduced in early April to only 33 percent in late June.[17] Fearful of advancing a divisive and unpopular reform, the government found itself forced to negotiate a complicated compromise that allowed it to claim victory but promised to be hard to implement. The extent of its concessions was reflected in the fact that the law was approved virtually by consensus, even receiving support from UDI.[18]

Moreover, lingering business discontent with Arenas' leadership of economic policy led to his removal only a few months after the bill's approval and his replacement with an individual whose resume, including a PhD from the Massachusetts Institute of Technology and work experience at the IMF, was similar to the Concertación finance ministers of the past.[19] The new minister, Rodrigo Valdés, promptly introduced a proposal to simplify the reform, which was passed in 2016. Although the original projected revenue increase of

---

[16] *Diario Universidad de Chile*, June 16, 2014; *Tele 13*, September 11, 2014.
[17] *Tele 13*, September 11, 2014.　　[18] *Radio Cooperativa*, September 10, 2014.
[19] Arenas himself later commented that "with my exit the government opted to signal that the promised reforms would be attenuated" (*Tele 13*, September 25, 2016).

3 percent of GDP was never officially abandoned, by the end of Bachelet's term it was clear that the reform was not having the purported effect on revenues, which should have increased by almost 2.5 percent of GDP by 2017 (Ministério de Hacienda 2014) but were essentially stagnant.

Thus, although the process through which the Nueva Mayoría reform was approved was initially different, reflecting Bachelet's commitment to advancing the reform agenda embraced by the 2011 student protestors, the end result in terms of the state's extractive capacity appears rather similar to the past. Chile's anti-statist political bloc worked steadily and effectively to limit the "damage" from the reform push. Although the Piñera government is currently facing pressures to increase spending, its ideology and support base, along with the modesty of the recently approved tax reform, would seem to foretell tax burden stability.

3.2.4 The Path-Dependent Roots of Anti-Statist Influence

The persistent power of anti-statist forces, despite the transition to democracy, is a path-dependent product of the conservative backlash against the statist reformism of the late 1960s and, especially, the early 1970s. As argued earlier, rejection of the reforms provided the foundations for the sweeping transformation of Chile's economic model that would occur under military rule. However, it also created the basis for a more enduring anti-statist shift in the balance of power in Chilean society, one that would survive regime change. While the persistence of anti-statist power reflects a variety of different mechanisms of reproduction, the most crucial involves the interaction between ideas and political organization, which is thus the focus of the analysis developed in this section.

The UP presidency triggered an important ideological change in two closely interrelated but analytically distinct ways. First, the assaults on property rights, employer control of the labor force, and other aspects of capitalism during these years had made well-off Chileans considerably warier of the state than in the past (Moulian 1997). They came to view the expansion of its resources and authority as a kind of slippery slope leading to the "politicization" of economic policy, rising redistribution, and, ultimately, radical reforms to property and privilege. They were joined in this perspective by social conservatives, for whom the attack on capitalism was not just a threat to the economy but also to what they saw as Chile's fundamentally Christian and Western values (Pollack 1999; Cristi 2000).[20]

Second, because it conferred upon the authoritarian state a mandate to transform the economy, the reaction against Allende allowed it to implant a uniquely coherent set of market-oriented reforms that provided a sound

---

[20] This view was clearly stated in the regime's 1974 "Declaration of Principles of the Government of Chile," which was drafted at least in part by Jaime Guzmán (Cristi 2000).

basis for economic growth. While the debt crisis cast doubt on the future of the reforms, the regime's broad civilian support, gained from having "saved" Chile from socialism, helped it to weather the crisis and to stay, with some adjustments, the liberalizing course. The result was a development model that by the end of the 1980s had generated high and sustained growth. Business elites had especially strong incentives to protect the model because of its pro-growth and pro-capital bias. Nevertheless, despite the sharp increase in income inequality under military rule, many ordinary Chileans clearly felt they were benefitting as well, as suggested by the fact that, in a 1988 plebiscite on whether Pinochet should continue as the president, 44 percent of voters cast their ballots in favor of the dictator.

Thus, the strength of anti-statism has been sustained by both negative views of the UP period and positive evaluations of *pinochetista* policies. In the end, though, even the positive aspect must be traced to the backlash against Allende's reforms, since the latter provided the political energy behind Pinochet's neoliberal counterrevolution. To paraphrase the statement by Sergio de Castro quoted earlier: Pinochet created the economic model, but Allende, however unwittingly, created the political conditions under which he could do so.

Two of the three aspects of the anti-statist power imbalance highlighted in the previous section of this chapter, the legislative strength of programmatic rightwing parties and the business community's unified commitment to free-market economics, can be traced directly to these effects of the anti-Allende backlash. The third, persistent labor weakness, is probably best seen as a derivative of the other two and reflective of the theoretical notion that power, once attained, can be used in ways that make it self-reinforcing.

As discussed earlier, the legislative strength of the right is the product of a combination of the designated senators and the parties' success in appealing to voters. Both aspects have their roots in the conservative reaction against the UP government. The creation of the designated senators and other "authoritarian enclaves" reflected the Pinochet regime's desire to keep the armed forces from being punished for crimes committed during and after the coup and to hinder any movement away from the market-oriented and private property-based policies that were its core legacy (Garretón 1995). However, the fact that these limits survived the democratic transition and persisted for fifteen years thereafter also reflects the strong civilian support the military enjoyed as a result of having reversed the socialist transition and implemented what turned out to be a successful economic model.

The enclaves were embedded in a new constitution drafted in the late 1970s by a team of jurists led by Jaime Guzmán. This document laid out a gradual path to regime transition in which, depending on the results of the 1988 plebiscite, Pinochet would either remain as the president for another decade with an elected legislature or a fully elected government would take power in 1990. However, even if opposition forces won both the plebiscite and subsequent elections, their ability to promote change would be hamstrung by clauses limiting majority rule and endowing the armed forces with autonomy from the civilian leadership. The constitution was ratified in 1980 through a referendum, but the difficulty of campaigning against it meant that its democratic legitimacy was highly questionable (Heiss and Navia 2007).

Given both the restrictive character of the constitution and its authoritarian origins, democratic opposition groups might well have refused to follow its transition guidelines. Moreover, even if they agreed to participate in the plebiscite, they might have insisted in the wake of their victory that the limitations on majority rule be eliminated. Instead, they essentially acquiesced to a 1989 constitutional reform that attenuated but did not eliminate some of them and strengthened others (Heiss and Navia 2007). The nine designated senators were retained, but their influence was diluted by increasing the number of elected senators. Meanwhile, the military's autonomy was increased through a number of provisions, and the rules for amending the document were made more stringent.

While critics chastised the leaders of the opposition coalition for abdicating their responsibility to seek unfettered democracy (Moulian 1997, pp. 52–53), their decisions made sense in a context characterized by a unified military leadership with a solid civilian support base, especially among the economically powerful. As one scholar of business politics has argued, the tight bond between the private sector and the regime left opposition parties with little leverage. "It gave the regime the fortitude to resist opposition demands for a rapid transition to full democracy. Pinochet and his supporters could bide their time and insist on a political transition within the institutional confines of the 1980 constitution ... " (Silva 1996, p. 226). In addition, although the victory of the "no" option in the plebiscite gave democratic forces momentum, the fact that not far from half the voters cast their ballots for Pinochet in a relatively free and fair election demonstrated that the regime also enjoyed the backing of many non-elites.

Retrospective civilian support for the regime also played a role in the persistence of the authoritarian enclaves for the first fifteen years of democracy. To be sure, the direct cause was institutional in nature. Constitutional amendment required a 3/5 majority in both chambers of Congress, more seats than the Concertación ever controlled. However, the enclaves also endured because the positive image the military regime enjoyed made it politically viable for rightist parties to defend its democratically questionable institutional legacies.

Indirect but powerful evidence for this assertion is the fact that the enclaves' removal would come only after external events seriously tarnished the regime's image (Fuentes 2015, pp. 110–111). The most important was Pinochet's detention in London from late 1998 until early 2000 on order of a Spanish judge investigating atrocities committed during the dictatorship. Although Pinochet was eventually released for health reasons, this episode created momentum leading to his subsequent prosecution in Chile, something that had previously been nearly unthinkable. Also significant was a 2004 US Senate investigation of Washington, DC-based Riggs Bank, which revealed that Pinochet and his family had maintained clandestine accounts with too much money to have resulted from legitimate activities. Because a reputation for probity had helped to counterbalance the military regime's violence and authoritarianism, the revelation was politically potent. These blows to the regime's image made it desirable for rightist parties to distance themselves from its political legacies, and the 2005 constitutional reform removing the designated senators and other enclaves provided a convenient method for doing so.

Thus, as argued in earlier chapters, the designated senators should be seen not merely as an institutional barrier to change but also as a symptom of a broader political reaction to the UP government that shifted the power balance in Chilean society. Similarly, the strength of programmatic rightwing parties in democratic Chile is a legacy of the anti-Allende backlash in the sense that the latter influenced both the ideology of these parties at the leadership level and their enduring success in attracting votes.

Both contemporary right parties trace their roots to 1983, when Chile was in the midst of its debt crisis and economic discontent threatened to bring a faster political transition than envisioned in the constitution. In this context, civilian regime supporters began to prepare for a more competitive environment (Moulian and Dujisin 1988; Pollack 1999). UDI was created in September and two months later a group was formed called the "Movement for National Unity" (Movimiento de Unidad Nacional, MUN). In preparation for the upcoming plebiscite, in 1987 UDI and MUN merged into one organization, National Renewal. However, UDI broke off the following year, leaving what had essentially been the MUN with the RN moniker.

Despite what were in some ways common origins, RN and UDI differed in their ideologies. RN had ties to the former PN, which had been dissolved following the 1973 coup.[21] Its relatively pragmatic economic liberalism and at least theoretical support for democracy likened it to the old Chilean right, although it was arguably less tolerant of state intervention (Pollack 1999). However, UDI was clearly a newer phenomenon, which embodied the marriage of the *gremialismo's* Catholic social conservatism and the Chicago Boys' fundamentalist economic liberalism. It was led by Guzmán, a key regime ideologue, and many of its cadres were former *gremialista* activists whose worldview had been forged "in the fires of the struggle against Popular Unity" (Valdivia 2008, p. 145). UDI was wholly uncritical of the military regime and vehemently committed to preserving its legacies. Its commitment to economic liberalism was, and still is today, more sweeping than that of any of the major party organizations that existed prior to Allende's overthrow.

---

[21] For example, Andrés Allamand, a cofounder of the MUN and still a major RN leader, was chief of the PN youth organization at the time of the coup.

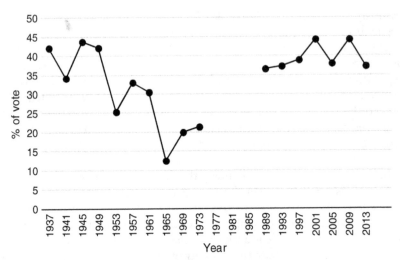

FIGURE 3.2 Share of votes won by right in Chilean Chamber of Deputies elections, 1937–2013 (percent)
Sources: Servicio Electoral de Chile; Valenzuela (1978), p. 35

In addition to being more ideological than their pre-coup counterparts, the contemporary conservative parties have also been more successful electorally, at least compared to the post-1950 period. With regard to presidential elections, right party performance is roughly similar across the two periods.[22] However, contemporary conservative parties have performed better in legislative elections, as Figure 3.2 suggests. The pre-1973 parties were strong until the end of the 1940s, but they declined thereafter, reaching a nadir in 1965, when they won only 12.5 percent of the vote. The right rebounded after the creation of the PN, but even that party's best performance was much weaker than the right's in any election since 1989.

The success of the contemporary right cannot be attributed purely to its ideological or programmatic appeal. As Luna (2014) has shown, UDI has effectively deployed a "segmented" strategy in which it courts the well off with programmatic messages and the poor with personalism and petty clientelism. The latter tactics have helped it build an urban political machine second to none among Chilean parties. Nevertheless, ideology and the programmatic messaging are crucial aspects of the right's success. Opinion polls suggest that even people of modest income understand what UDI represents ideologically. Both the general public and party sympathizers correctly identify UDI as the most right-leaning of the major parties (Siavelis 2009, p. 18; Morales 2014, p. 75). Moreover, the

---

[22] Until the 2017 election, which it won, the right had captured the presidency only once since 1990. However, during the four-decade stretch of democracy between 1932 and 1973, the right also won only twice and one of those victories was in 1932.

success of the clientelistic strategy depends on both the financial resources the party receives from its wealthy supporters and a network of local political bosses based to a substantial extent on the former *gremialista* movement. Both groups are loyal to the party because of what it stands for. Finally, it is generally accepted that RN, whose supporters are wealthier and more educated than UDI's on average, attracts votes more through programmatic appeals than clientelism.

That a rightist, pro-market ideology holds considerable attraction for many Chileans is due in no small part to the trauma of the UP years and the significance it still holds in the collective memory. Of course, for many people the Allende government represents a brave quest for social justice and equality. For others, though, it was an era of great peril, a time when the country barely escaped falling victim to Cuban- or Soviet-style communism. For the latter group, the Pinochet regime, for all its repressiveness, was a necessary corrective. Loxton (2014) categorizes both UDI and RN as successful cases of "authoritarian successor parties," or ones that compete in elections based at least in part on their links to a prior and relatively popular dictatorship. UDI is a particularly clear-cut case because of its more fervent defense of Pinochet's legacy and *gremialismo*'s role in the regime. Loxton (2014, p. 130) argues that UDI has been successful because it has been able to appropriate the military regime's appeal: "If an authoritarian successor party like UDI can transfer this popular brand to itself, it is born with a ready-made partisan base in the electorate."

Chilean business was also deeply impacted by the UP episode, and its cohesion today reflects that experience (Schneider 2004, p. 153). As touched on earlier, the political fragmentation of the post-World War II private sector was symptomatic of its acceptance of an assertive state role in development. As long as its fundamental interest in safeguarding property rights was not threatened, there was little incentive to put aside sectoral differences and construct a class-wide alliance against state intervention. Political action thus focused on extracting sectoral, subsectoral, and even firm-specific advantages. That began to change under Frei, but it was during the UP era that business came to perceive an existential threat and mobilize as a class (Campero 1984; Silva 1995). The UP government, with its property seizures, worker mobilization, and general macroeconomic disorder, left capitalists shaken. That episode would contribute, along with the eventual success of Pinochet's reforms and the decline of formerly protected industries, to the emergence of a stronger class consciousness tied to a deep-seated rejection of state interference in the economy and a glorification of free enterprise (Undurraga 2015). The Allende government, a SOFOFA official observed of business leaders, "is still in their minds – the expropriations, the growth of the state. The feeling is that no one wants to live through that experience again" (SOFOFA 2014, interview).

The rise of the CPC as a strong peak association able to speak credibly on behalf of the private sector is an aspect of this transformation. The CPC began assuming a more prominent role during the late 1960s and early 1970s because it offered a tool for cross-sector coordination to oppose state actions of concern to business in general (Silva 1996; Schneider 2004). That transformation was interrupted temporarily by the military seizure of power. For years, business collective action was discouraged not only by authoritarian controls but also, and more fundamentally, by the credibility enjoyed by the regime. Firms whose interests were affected negatively by its policies found themselves isolated, their protests feeble and largely ignored (Silva 1995). With the outbreak of the debt crisis, however, capitalists once again found it necessary to band together to defend class-wide interests and the CPC assumed a central role in representing them (Silva 1996). What motivated them this time was not threats to property but rather a too-rigid embrace of macroeconomic austerity and free trade during a time of acute vulnerability for many firms. The CPC became the key interlocutor between a private sector panicked by mounting losses and an economic team struggling to recapture business confidence.

Despite this context of mobilization against Chicago Boy policies, the revitalization of the CPC in the 1980s still reflected the impact of the anti-Allende struggle. Its purpose was not to overturn the free-market model but to save it from itself through pragmatic adjustments. Once growth had been reinitiated, business was quite willing to support new structural reforms and a tough fiscal policy that reduced revenues to levels not seen in decades. The CPC, SOFOFA, and other groups firmly supported Pinochet in the plebiscite and their resolute rejection of economic policy changes essentially forced the Concertación to publicly pledge not to substantively alter it (Silva 1996, pp. 224–226). Thus, the elected political leadership that took power in 1990 faced a private sector that was both highly unified and willing to defend with tooth and nail the policies established during the preceding two decades.

Labor's enduring weakness in democratic Chile is, to a large extent, a reflection of the relative predominance of anti-statist forces. Although labor unionism suffered grievous blows under military rule, there were reasons to believe that a more open political environment would allow workers to revive their organizations and the political role they had enjoyed during the pre-coup years. Instead, labor has been caught in a vicious circle: its weakness relative to anti-statist actors has prevented it from substantially altering the liberal economic and labor model inherited from the Pinochet years. The persistence of that model, in turn, has reinforced its structural weakness (Sehnbruch 2012, p. 5).

Labor unions had been important actors in pre-coup Chile, both in terms of representing workers vis-a-vis management and supporting left-of-center parties. Left-leaning governments, in turn, had aided unions through legislation and support in industrial conflicts (Frank 2015). Under the dictatorship, however, many unions were brutally repressed, and their leaders fired, imprisoned, or killed. In 1979, the regime announced a profoundly anti-union labor code reform. Among other things, it outlawed negotiations beyond the firm level, limited the length of strikes, narrowed the scope of negotiations to wages, outlawed public sector unions, facilitated termination, and banned the CUT (Frank 2015). These changes made it harder for unions to use strikes as bargaining leverage and impeded collective action between unions. The labor code added to existing problems related to the regime's economic reforms, especially deindustrialization. Between 1973 and the mid-1980s, union density declined by almost two-thirds (Durán and Kremerman 2015, p. 5).

The democratic transition and the Concertación's victory in the 1989 elections encouraged hopes of union revival, since it was supposed that a democracy would be more responsive to worker demands (Zapata 1992, p. 711). Unionization did grow at the outset of the Aylwin government, but the trend did not last (Durán and Kremerman 2015, p. 5). The reasons behind labor's weakness are complex. As with their Concertación counterparts, CUT leaders may have moderated their views in response to the traumatic events of the 1970s and not pursued worker mobilization with as much vigor as in the past (Julián Vejar 2014). However, contextual constraints have also been at work. In particular, the same right-leaning power balance that impeded higher taxation also hindered the expansion of unionism by preventing labor market and economic reforms capable of strengthening union bargaining power and capacity for collective action (Posner 2017).

With regard to the labor code, center-left governments have admittedly made some changes. Probably the most important occurred under President Aylwin, who removed the time limit on strikes, increased severance pay, and relegalized the CUT, among other reforms (Frank 2015, pp. 186–188). The Lagos and second Bachelet governments made further incremental changes, including placing stronger limits on employers' ability to fire striking workers (Ensignia 2017). However, core aspects of Pinochet's labor code remain, especially the unusual prohibition on collective bargaining beyond the firm level, which some experts believe is a key obstacle to a stronger movement (Ensignia 2017).[23] In addition, the labor code continues to facilitate outsourcing and precarious forms of employment, such as part-time and temporary work, which are ineligible for collective bargaining (Posner 2017).

While labor scholars sometimes blame the center-left governments for being complacent about labor, there is also considerable recognition that opposition from anti-statist actors has played a major role in limiting union-strengthening change (Ensignia 2017; Posner 2017). As with taxation, labor reform has been impeded by unified business resistance, the strong presence of right parties and conservative appointees in the legislature, and, ironically, the weakness of the

---

[23] At least among OECD countries, Chile is unique in confining collective bargaining to the firm level. Durán and Kremerman (2015) also include Japan in this category, but Japan has a system of informal coordination that makes collective bargaining in effect highly centralized (Kenworthy 2001).

labor movement itself. One labor scholar describes the evolution of labor reform under the Concertación as

...a tale of high expectations of social justice on the part of workers and an almost paranoid fear of regulation on the part of employers, which has led successive Concertación governments to engage in endless negotiations and continuous compromise, but one that has ultimately resulted in the dissatisfaction of all the social actors involved in the process. (Sehnbruch 2006, p. 48)

While this analysis is more than a decade old, Ensignia (2017) describes the Nueva Mayoría's modest labor reform in much the same terms. He argues that the coalition's reform was foiled in part by a business elite and partisan right "determined to defend at all costs" the economic model, leading to a law that altered the regulatory framework only marginally and which satisfied neither labor nor business.

However, the limited extent of labor code reform is only part of the reason for union weakness. The broader continuity in economic policy is also crucial. In Latin America strong unionism has been associated with statist policies that protect and subsidize domestic firms. Unlike in Europe, where unions have thrived in small, open economies, in Latin America there are few cases of strong unionism under free trade conditions. Organized labor emerged as a significant force with the diffusion of ISI-type development strategies beginning in the 1930s (Collier and Collier 1991). The trade liberalization of the past few decades has taken a heavy toll on them by undermining employment in firms where they were strong and pressuring employers to minimize labor costs in order to survive in a more competitive environment (Bogliaccini 2013). Trade liberalization has negatively impacted unions in all four countries under study in this book, but the damage has been greatest in Chile and Mexico, where the liberalization was deeper and more sustained.

The small size of the Chilean state also limits union power. Public sector unions play crucial roles in the overall labor movement in Argentina and Brazil, since they tend to be both well organized and militant (Jard da Silva 2015; Cardoso and Gindin 2017). While public servants are also well organized in Chile, they are far less numerous. Public sector employees make up a smaller percentage of the workforce in Chile than in any of the other case study countries.[24] Thus, anti-statist forces' success in preserving the small-state model inherited from military rule has had the additional benefit (from their perspective) of helping to limit the influence of labor unions and thus reinforcing their own power.

---

[24] According to the International Labor Organization database (https://ilostat.ilo.org/), in 2016 14.8 percent of Chile's employed population worked for the public sector. The most recent figures for the other countries were 27.7 percent in Argentina (2014), 19.3 percent in Brazil (2009), and 16.4 percent in Mexico (2016).

3.3 CONCLUSION

This chapter has argued that Chile's light taxation is largely the product of a sustained conservative backlash against the redistributive reform wave that preceded the 1973 coup d'état. Fear of socialism and rejection of state intervention in the economy fueled the profound neoliberal restructuring of the economy under military rule, including a sharp decline in the tax burden. While democratization might have been expected to bring a reversal of Pinochet's low-tax policies, that has not occurred. The reason is that the intense anti-statism that emerged from the UP experience and the success of the military regime's economic reforms has continued to exert great influence over Chilean society. It has operated through party, interest group, and think tank organizations, benefitting, for a time, from representative institutions designed to bolster its power. Anti-statist forces have successfully used their resources to prevent substantial tax increases. Their influence has also kept organized labor weak, a condition that has reinforced the stability of the liberal, small-state model.

This case provides strong evidence in favor of the ideological balance of power perspective sketched in previous chapters. The stability of light taxation under democracy in Chile cannot be understood by dwelling on the influence of one particular actor or one side of the ideological spectrum. Instead, it is a function of a combination of interconnected conditions that shape the ideological power balance, including a private sector with a unified commitment to economic liberalism, political parties that are both programmatically rightist and competitive in national elections, and a labor movement undermined by low union and collective bargaining density and the proliferation of precarious employment.

This chapter has also illustrated the utility of the concept of path dependence for understanding the roots and persistence of the anti-statist balance of power. The rise of a major threat to private property was neither a random occurrence nor one wholly predetermined by structural factors. It resulted, rather, from a blend of critical antecedents and contingent events, namely Allende's narrow electoral victory and the clumsy attempt to preempt his inauguration through a military coup. Once it occurred, however, the UP government's radical redistributive reforms laid the groundwork for a sustained rise in anti-statist influence by stimulating economic elites and social conservatives to organize more effectively and embrace views about the state previously considered extreme. Their countermobilization against threats to property and other aspects of capitalism came to be embedded in a network of prestigious, resource-rich organizations that have worked together to defend a vision of Chilean society based on competition, market efficiency, and a residual state.

4

Mexico

Cardenismo, *Reaction, and Low-Tax Stability*

Even more than Chile, Mexico is a case of light taxation. Although its tax burden has increased recently, it remains well below the regional average. The large flow of nontax revenue from PEMEX helps explain this situation, permitting a higher level of public spending than would be possible if the state relied exclusively on taxes. However, as discussed in Chapter 2, Mexico's light taxation is not simply a product of reliance on oil. If it were, Mexico's total fiscal revenues would be roughly comparable to those of the other countries. They are indeed comparable to Chile's, but some 35 percent lower than Brazil's and Argentina's. The unusual intensity with which Mexico fiscally exploits PEMEX also suggests that reliance on nontax revenues reflects at least in part a political inability to obtain adequate amounts of revenue through taxation. This chapter thus develops a political explanation of Mexico's light tax burden to complement the natural resource-based one.

Mexico's political trajectory is in some ways starkly different from Chile's. Its violent 1910–1920 revolution and the subsequent rise of a semi-authoritarian, hegemonic party regime that would persist for most of the twentieth century set it clearly apart from the Southern Cone country. Unlike Chile, Mexico would experience neither a long stretch of competitive, multiparty politics nor an outright military dictatorship. Only in the 1990s would their regime trajectories converge, as both transited to greater democracy.

Nevertheless, this chapter argues that the causal dynamics behind Mexico's light tax burden are quite similar to the ones operating in Chile in two crucial respects. First, light taxation reflects a sustained power imbalance favoring anti-statist actors. Second, this imbalance is largely an unintentional, path-dependent consequence of efforts by a left-leaning government to redistribute property in favor of workers. The reformist episode, which resulted partly from contingent decisions by political elites, set in motion a reactive sequence whose result was subsequently reproduced through self-reinforcing mechanisms involving ideas and power.

More specifically, the argument emphasizes the enduring impact on the tax system of postrevolution reforms, mainly under President Lázaro Cárdenas (1934–1940). Because they seemed to endanger essential features of capitalism, especially private property, the Cárdenas reforms provoked a potent countermobilization that deeply affected the attitudes of economic elites toward the state and strengthened their ties to social conservatives. Although some of the organizations that anchor Mexico's anti-statist bloc today would only emerge decades later, the Cárdenas period was a turning point, in that it fomented a disposition among key elites to view the state with suspicion and to react forcefully to even modest attempts to expand its resources. The tight anti-statist network that emerged from this struggle would subsequently play a central role in limiting taxation, weakening labor, and crafting an ever-stronger coalition of interest group, party, and intellectual organizations to support its objectives. Thus, Mexico entered its current democratic period with both an extremely light tax burden and an ideological power balance resistant to increasing it significantly.

This chapter is divided into three major sections, each of which attempts to explain the trajectory of the tax burden during a specific period: the first focuses on the striking stagnation of tax revenues during the 1940s and 1950s; the second examines the failure of a number of attempts to raise taxes during the 1960s and 1970s; and the third tries to explain why democratization since the 1990s has not, contrary to theoretical expectations, produced a substantial increase in taxation.

4.1 WHY MEXICAN TAXATION FELL BEHIND

Among the most puzzling aspects of Mexico's tax trajectory is the stagnation of revenues beginning in the 1940s. From being a country that seemed to be on a relatively "normal" fiscal development path, over the next two decades Mexico was transformed into one with an exceptionally light tax burden. The timing corresponds to what is commonly viewed as a key moment in the country's political development, when the ruling party abandoned *cardenista* radicalism and adopted pro-business policies. This correspondence is no accident: light taxation was a core aspect of the change. Thus, in order to account for the stagnation of the tax burden, we must explain the broader change in policy orientation, its persistence over time, and the role that taxation played in it. That is the purpose of this section.

Studies that highlight Mexico's post-1940 conservatism sometimes stress the emergence of an implicit pact between the state and business (Reynolds 1970; Hansen 1971; Kaufman Purcell 1981). Under this so-called alliance for profits, the leadership of the Institutional Revolutionary Party (Partido Revolucionario Institucional, PRI) provided highly favorable conditions for doing business and in return the private sector steered clear of politics, acquiescing to or even endorsing the PRI's power monopoly. While correctly emphasizing both the great lengths to which authorities went to encourage investment and the relative lack of overt business-state strife compared to other periods, this perspective is unsatisfactory in two ways. First, it cannot explain why the supposedly close relationship between the public and private sectors required restrictions on state intervention that went beyond those of other middle-income Latin American countries. Second, it exaggerates the degree of consensus and cooperation between the state and business (Gauss 2010, pp. 2 and 229).

The view developed here is that the relatively timid expansion of the public sector reflected authorities' attempt to cope with an anti-statist backlash caused by previous state initiatives, particularly under Cárdenas. As in Chile under Allende, threats to property stimulated a countermobilization by economic elites and social conservatives. Although the ruling party would eventually back down from its reformism, completing the reactive sequence, the injuries and insults these groups suffered during the reform wave were not easily forgotten. They shaped business identity, ideology, and policy preferences in enduring ways, forcing the state to adopt particularly austere versions of the developmentalist and welfarist policies diffusing across Latin America in the postwar era, and to crack down on groups, most notably labor unions, that resisted this orientation.

4.1.1 Tax Burden Growth and Stagnation

Despite suffering through a far more tumultuous early history than Chile, Mexico by 1940 seemed to be developing along a roughly similar fiscal path. It had initiated a transition toward greater domestic taxation and its tax burden had grown rather steadily during the 1920s and 1930s. However, in the early 1940s, the tax burden declined somewhat and it subsequently stagnated. Since taxation in Latin America was generally rising during this period, by the early 1960s, Mexico was one of the lightest-taxed countries in the region. Tax policy, moreover, was not an isolated phenomenon. Although Mexico adopted the same ISI model as Chile and the other countries examined here, its version was an unusually liberal one.

Mexico consolidated a national tax system later than Chile, due to the great instability and recurrent armed conflict that afflicted the country during the half century following its 1821 independence from Spain (Tenenbaum 1986). Nevertheless, under the leadership of Porfírio Díaz (1876–1910), Mexico constructed a solid national fiscal system (Carmagnani 1994). As Figure 4.1 suggests, the combined revenues of national and subnational governments during the early twentieth century amounted to a little over 6 percent of GDP. While this was less than in Chile, a larger share of revenues came from more dependable domestic taxes. Between 1900 and 1911, trade taxes accounted for 50.9 percent of federal tax revenue (INEGI 2015). Since subnational governments contributed approximately a third of the total (Diaz-Cayeros 2006, p. 36) and do not appear to have imposed significant foreign trade

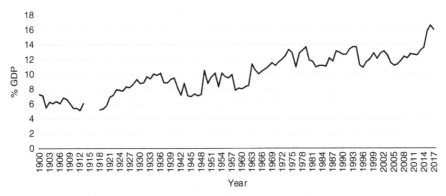

FIGURE 4.1 Evolution of Mexico's tax burden, 1900–2017[1]
Sources: CEPALSTAT/ECLAC; Diaz-Cayeros (2006)

taxes, the overall contribution of such taxes was probably lower. In contrast, trade tax revenues comprised roughly two-thirds of the total in Chile, as well as Argentina and Brazil, during these years (Marquez 2005, p. 158).

Over the next decade, tax revenues would suffer from both the civil war that broke out in 1910 and the trade breakdown caused by World War I. However, revenues rebounded in the 1920s and continued to grow during the 1930s. Domestic taxation received a boost from the creation of Mexico's first income tax in 1925 – a year after Chile created its own such tax.[2] Cárdenas focused more on asset redistribution than taxation, but did pass an excess profits tax in 1939 that boosted direct taxation (Unda 2010, ch. 5).[3] By the second half of the 1930s, trade taxes accounted for only a third of federal revenues and about a quarter of total tax revenues (Diaz-Cayeros 2006, p. 36; INEGI 2015). Tax revenues averaged 7.8 percent of GDP in the 1920s and 9.4 percent in the 1930s, levels roughly in line with the other countries (see Figure 2.1).

During the late 1930s and early 1940s, the tax system also became somewhat more centralized, due to the growing importance of the income tax and the transfer of some indirect taxes to the federal level, a process that was negotiated with the state governments on a state-by-state basis (Aboites 2005, p. 199). However, states and municipalities continued to account for about a quarter of

---

[1] Data for 1900–1979 are estimated from Figure 1.1 in Diaz-Cayeros (2006). Alternative sources suffer from aggregation problems among different levels of government, as Aboites (2003, p. 32) notes. Data are missing for 1914–1917 due to the Mexican Revolution. Social security revenues were included in fiscal data beginning in 1965.

[2] Taxes on foreign oil companies made an important contribution in the early 1920s, when the sector was booming, but faded to only 2 percent of tax revenues by the end of the decade, partly because of declining production (Rubio 2003, p. 9).

[3] This tax, which supplemented the corporate income tax, affected firms with unusually high profits. Such taxes became common during the early twentieth century but were usually levied during war time.

total tax revenues (Díaz-Cayeros 2006, p. 36). More decisive centralization would not come until some decades later.

Mexico's seemingly steady fiscal growth ground to a halt after 1940. The tax burden dipped in the early 1940s, then grew only fitfully during the rest of the 1940s and 1950s. As a result, Mexico came to lag far behind the other countries examined here, especially Chile and Brazil. By 1960, the latter two countries had tax burdens of 17–18 percent of GDP, roughly double that of Mexico.[4] In fact, region-wide data collected by ECLAC suggest that in that year Mexico's nonsocial security tax burden was the single lightest in Latin America (ECLAC 1979, p. 99). Including social security would probably not make much difference, since available data indicate that Mexico's system was small, with contributions of little more than 1 percent of GDP in 1960 (World Bank 1964, Appendix D, Table 16). A World Bank report noted that Mexico's tax burden was "among the lowest in the world" and urged a "tax readjustment to bring about a substantial increase in revenues" (World Bank 1962, pp. 12–14).

Stagnation was evident at all levels of government. The balance between national and subnational revenues did not change significantly during this era (Díaz-Cayeros 2006, p. 36). However, there were some differences in revenue growth among types of taxes. Income tax revenues increased at a faster pace than other taxes. By 1960 direct taxes played a larger role in Mexico's tax system than in those of the other countries analyzed here (Fitzgerald 1978, p. 132). While these data do not include social security taxation, including it would probably only widen the gap, since the available evidence suggests that Mexican social security revenues were smaller, especially relative to Chile (Mesa-Lago 1978, p. 284). The larger share of direct taxation in Mexico was not due to a heavy direct tax burden, but to the failure of other taxes to expand at the same pace as elsewhere (Reynolds 1970, pp. 274–275).

To be sure, some measures were taken, especially during the 1940s, to boost revenues. A 1941 reform implemented by President Manuel Ávila Camacho (1940–1946) raised income tax rates and increased revenues from this tax (Unda 2010, ch. 5). In 1943, the government introduced Mexico's first national social security program, a move that had been initiated by Cárdenas but subsequently abandoned (Dion 2010, pp. 64–68). Under Miguel Alemán (1946–1952), the federal government raised export taxes and created both a national sales tax, called the Mercantile Revenue Tax, (Impuesto sobre Ingresos Mercantiles, ISIM) and a tax on windfall profits.

Nevertheless, these measures, especially the ones involving non-direct taxes, had little effect, due to a combination of low rates, limited tax bases, exemptions, and evasion. One of the key failures involved the ISIM, which was supposed to replace some existing federal and state levies with the purpose of both raising revenue and simplifying the overall system (Martínez de

---

[4] Argentina's 1960 tax burden was 14.1 percent of GDP, but five years earlier it had been 17.7 percent. The reasons behind this volatility are discussed in Chapter 6.

Navarrette 1973, pp. 48–49; Aboites 2003, pp. 210–212). State governments willing to relinquish some of their own taxes would gain a share of its revenues. However, the tax did little to achieve either goal since the rate applied was low and most major states turned down the offer.[5] Ávila Camacho's social security program excluded public sector workers, and coverage of the private sector was extended very slowly. Even by the 1960s, coverage was only a third of the Chilean level and half the Argentine (Mesa-Lago 1978, p. 267). Contribution rates for both workers and employers were also much lower, especially compared to Chile (Mesa-Lago 1978, p. 284).

Tax revenue stagnation in post-1940 Mexico was reflected in very low public spending (Hansen 1971, chs. 3 and 4). For example, total current public expenditure relative to GDP in 1960 was 60.2 percent of Argentina's, 51.3 percent of Brazil's, and only 43.3 percent of Chile's (ECLAC 1979, p. 104). Social spending was particularly low. Mexico lagged considerably behind the other countries examined here in both education and health spending (ECLAC 1979, pp. 42 and 54). In fact, Mexico's combined public health and pension spending relative to GDP was lower than health spending alone in both Brazil and Chile.

Mexico's fiscal dwarfism would seem to clash with the common depiction of the country as pursuing state-led development during the post–World War II era (Fitzgerald 1978; Babb 2001; Tello 2010). To some extent, this reflects inaction specifically in the social sphere. However, Mexico was in some ways less economically interventionist, as well. Compared to Brazil, Mexico had a smaller state-owned enterprise (SOE) sector and the state played a lesser role in capital formation (Graham 1982). Mexico's state development bank, Nacional Financiera, was an important lender but less so than its Brazilian counterpart (Etchemendy 2011, p. 295). The pre-Pinochet Chilean state was even more interventionist, especially with regard to ownership of industry (Etchemendy 2011, p. 293).[6] Finally, Mexico's trade protection, while high by rich country standards, was modest by those of Latin America and developing countries in general (Ten Kate and Wallace 1980; Ros 1993). In sum, although Mexico did possess many features of ISI, its version was a relatively market-oriented one.

4.1.2 Postrevolution Reforms and Countermobilization

To understand the unusually liberal character of Mexico's development path after 1940, it is first necessary to examine the redistributive initiatives of

---

[5] The rate was set at 3 percent in states that accepted the federal government's offer and 1.8 percent in those that did not.

[6] State economic intervention would increase greatly in Argentina under Juan Perón (1946-1955), far surpassing the Mexican case. However, its expansion thereafter would be less steady than in Brazil or pre-1973 Chile.

preceding decades and their political impacts. Efforts to implement the progressive, nationalist promises of the Mexican Revolution began in the 1920s but expanded greatly during the Cárdenas years (Córdova 1974; Collier and Collier 1991). The seriousness of the challenge to elite economic interests during this period and the sense that Mexico could be moving toward socialism polarized the country and provoked a widening countermobilization in which elites, social conservatives, and other groups were involved (Hamilton 1982; Martínez Nava 1984).

Although the moderate "Constitutionalist" faction triumphed in the revolution, the pioneering 1917 constitution integrated some key demands of the peasant and worker groups that fought in the conflict and thus provided the legal basis for a highly interventionist state (Ankersen and Ruppert 2006; Gargarella 2014). Article 27 vested ultimate control of land, water, and mineral (including oil) resources in the state and called for the redistribution of large rural properties to the landless and land-poor. Article 123 granted extensive labor and social rights involving work hours, wages, health conditions, profit sharing, and other issues. The constitution also embodied the longstanding struggle of liberals to diminish the powers of the Catholic Church, especially in education.

Presidents Alvaro Obregón (1920–1924) and Plutarco Elías Calles (1924–1928) advanced some social reforms in alliance with popular sector groups. The former allied himself with peasant groups and implemented significant land redistribution, while the latter tilted more toward labor and, for a time, favored workers in conflicts with business. Calles' relationship with the Mexican Regional Labor Confederation (Confederación Regional Obrera *Mexicana*, CROM) afforded organized workers a degree of influence unprecedented at the time in Latin America (Collier and Collier 1991, p. 217). In addition, during the abbreviated presidency of Pascual Ortiz Rubio (1930–1932), the Congress approved a long-awaited labor law further elaborating some of the rights mentioned in constitutional Article 123. Efforts were also made to establish greater state control over oil (Brown 1993).

For the most part, however, reforms were moderate and tended to diminish in substance over time. Between 1928 and early 1934 (a period in which Calles dominated politics despite not being president), there was a clear conservative trend. Calles broke off his alliance with the CROM and declared his opposition to further land reform. Although a labor law was passed, the government ended up making important concessions to the private sector. Calles also de-escalated his previous struggle against the church, which had led to armed conflict with Catholic laymen in the 1920s. In some ways, Mexico seemed headed back to the Díaz era, when authorities governed in alliance with foreign capital and a compact group of domestic financiers, landowners, and industrialists, essentially ignoring social issues.

Thus, by 1934 the country appeared to be consolidating a reasonably stable political regime but one in which the progressive promises of the 1917 constitution would go largely unfulfilled. Cárdenas was not an obvious candidate to bring about a major break with this trend. Although identified with the *agrarista* (i.e., pro-land reform) wing of the ruling party, then known as the "National Revolutionary Party" (Partido Nacional Revolucionario, PNR), based on his land redistribution efforts as governor of Michoacán, he was also a Calles protégé and was widely expected to be another of his lackies (Medin 1971, p. 15; Hamilton 1982, p. 104; Knight 2016, pp. 106–107). Yet Cárdenas soon defied expectations by implementing a series of major changes that together represented a sharp lurch to the left (Collier 1982; Hamilton 1982).

Perhaps most emblematic was his land reform, easily the most extensive implemented in Latin America until the 1950s (Eckstein et al. 1978). The government redistributed 17.9 million hectares of farmland, more than double the total of all previous postrevolution presidents combined. By 1940, 47.4 percent of Mexico's cultivated land was in *ejidos*, the small, collectively held farms resulting from the reform (Hamilton 1982, p. 177). Just as importantly, Cárdenas did not limit himself, as had previous presidents, to expropriating low-productivity properties. As Allende would decades later, he also seized millions of hectares belonging to highly capitalized and irrigated commercial farms.

The Cárdenas government also implemented major reforms outside agriculture. It favored workers by encouraging unionization, taking the side of labor in industrial conflicts, and approving legislative measures to boost wages. Its professed goal was to strengthen workers relative to capital in order to increase the latter's share of the benefits of productive activity (Hamilton 1982, p. 142). While Cárdenas did not menace nonfarm property to the extent that Chile's UP would, he did seize "numerous industrial plants" (Story 1986, p. 40) and nationalized the already partly state-owned railroads. More importantly, in 1938, he dramatically expropriated the large British and US firms that dominated the oil sector, a move that constituted the first major nationalization in the region (Hamilton 1982, p. 220).

As in Chile, reform both encouraged and was pushed forward by popular mobilization (Córdova 1974; Knight 1994). Rural land invasions multiplied in many parts of the country, pitting peasants and landowners in bloody battles that prompted the government to organize armed peasant militias (Tai 1974, pp. 271–272). Strikes also grew rapidly in number, especially during the early years of the presidency (Hamilton 1982, p. 125). They were encouraged by the government's pro-worker interventions and rhetoric. In a famous 1936 speech to employers in Monterrey, Cárdenas defended labor militancy as socially just and provocatively suggested that factory owners who were "tired" of it could "turn over their firms to the workers or the government . . . " (Spenser 2007, p. 198).

Seeking to channel support for its reforms to maximum effect, the government spearheaded changes in political representation. It encouraged the formation of a new labor confederation, the Confederation of Mexican Workers (Confederación de Trabajadores de México, CTM), which quickly became the country's largest. It also forged a new peasant organization, the National Peasant Confederation (Confederación Nacional Campesina, CNC). Both would dominate their sectors for decades to come. Subsequently, Cárdenas restructured the party, replacing its geographical organization with a more corporatist one based on four sectors: labor, peasant, military, and "popular" (Hamilton 1982, p. 242).[7] The CTM, CNC, and other groups affiliated with the party through these sectoral entities.[8]

Unlike Allende, Cárdenas was not an avowed Marxist and his ruling coalition was ideologically heterogenous. Nevertheless, the president openly supported class struggle and had strong ties to leftists, including CTM leader Vicente Lombardo Toledano and the Mexican Communist Party, which overcame its initial skepticism to collaborate closely with the government (Hamilton 1982). In the countryside, radical schoolteachers played key roles in supporting land reform and implementing the government's "socialist education" policy, an attempt to purge Mexico's schools of church influences and promote a more collectivist worldview (Raby 1981).

Some scholars have downplayed the extent of change during this period, viewing the Cárdenas *sexenio* (six-year term) as merely an incremental step in the construction of industrial capitalism in Mexico (Anguiano 1984; Haber 1989). It is true that Cárdenas sought to tame, rather than eradicate capitalism, and provided assistance to private industry. Nevertheless, these observations should not obscure the fact that, as other scholars have argued, the government's policies were in some ways quite radical (Hamilton 1982; Knight 1994; Gilly 2013). They represented the most significant challenge Latin America had yet seen to the export-oriented, oligarchic order consolidated during the early twentieth century and, as subsequent chapters make clear, went far beyond those of other governments typically labeled "populist."

Not surprisingly, these policies also provoked intense resistance from a variety of groups. With regard to business, the most important source of opposition was the industrialists of Monterrey, capital of the northern state of Nuevo León (Saragoza 1988; Contreras 1989; Gauss 2010). Monterrey had emerged during the Díaz years as the country's major industrial center. Outraged by the government's support for labor activism and deeply concerned about what they viewed as an incipient socialist transition, *regiomontano* business leaders and their political allies fought back. They issued sharp public rebukes of the government; organized marches,

---

[7] The popular sector consisted of various entities representing largely middle-class groups, including teachers and other public employees and students.

[8] A corporatist entity was also created to represent business, and membership in the corporatist system became mandatory, but this sector was not represented within the ruling party.

demonstrations, and production strikes; engaged in lockouts and thuggery against the pro-government unions; and funded other anti-Cárdenas groups. They also used the Mexican Employers' Confederation (Confederación Patronal de la República Mexicana, COPARMEX), an organization created in 1929 to counter initial efforts at progressive labor reform, to push for wider business mobilization against the government.

The Monterrey Group, as this cohesive network of business leaders would become known, was able to thwart the pro-Cárdenas CTM's bid to organize Nuevo León's industrial workforce, an important victory (Collier and Collier 1991, p. 249). Its efforts to construct a nationwide business movement were less successful, due to the reluctance of many firms to openly challenge the government. Nevertheless, working through COPARMEX, it was able to forge a much broader alliance than during the earlier struggle against labor code reform and to become perhaps the single most important opposition actor. "By taking such a visible position against Cárdenas, the *regiomontanos* became a pole of attraction to which anti-Cárdenas sentiment gravitated regardless of the motivation" (Saragoza 1988, p. 182).

In the rural sector, there was no actor as prominent as the Monterrey Group, but landowners fiercely combatted land reform at the local and state levels and, in some cases, notched significant victories (Knight 1994, p. 102). They were aided by a largely rural social movement called the National Sinarquista Union (Unión Nacional Sinarquista, UNS), which organized protests and used strong-arm tactics against land reform activists and government workers. With ties to the Catholic Church and roots in the 1920s *Cristero* rebellion, the UNS represented a key expression of the social conservative reaction against *cardenismo*.

Opposition grew after the March 1938 oil nationalization. Although popular among ordinary Mexicans, the expropriations caused unrest among elites because of the bold affront they represented to private property and the prospect of retribution by foreign governments (Gilly 2013). One manifestation of this concern was the creation in 1939 of the Partido Acción Nacional (PAN), a party committed to defending free enterprise and religious faith (Loaeza 1974; Mizrahi 2003). Convinced that if left unchecked *cardenismo* "would ineluctably end up in socialism and dictatorship" (Arriola 1976, p. 248) the PAN sought to prevent its perpetuation beyond the approaching 1940 election. Another manifestation was the presidential candidacy of Juan Andreu Almazán, a popular military officer with ties to Monterrey. Almazán ran in opposition to the ruling party's candidate and attracted a great deal of support (Contreras 1989). He was initially backed by the Monterrey Group and its allies, although they would eventually (for reasons discussed below) shift to a neutral position. While the PAN did not officially endorse a candidate, many of its members favored Almazán. He would likely have won had it not been for the use of fraud by the ruling party (Hamilton 1982).

4.1.3   The Right Turn and Private Sector Mistrust

Beginning at the end of the Cárdenas era and accelerating during the 1940s, the ruling party's policies would turn in an anti-statist direction. Reflective of this shift, as noted earlier, was the stagnation of tax revenues. While it is clear that this right turn began as an attempt to placate opponents of *cardenismo*, its sustained character is remarkable. It can be understood as a reflection of the deep animosity and mistrust the events of the Cárdenas *sexenio* had inspired in economic elites, which forced state authorities to act unusually cautiously in their efforts to expand public sector resources and capabilities.

Although the turn away from reformism became clear in the 1940s, some aspects of it were already evident during the late Cárdenas years (Córdova 1974; Collier and Collier 1991, p. 403). Authorities became less supportive of strikes, land redistribution slowed, and a proposal to establish a social security system was shelved. Despite widespread expectations that Cárdenas would anoint a leftist successor, ruling party moderates secured the nomination for one of their own, Defense Minister Manuel Ávila Camacho. The candidate soon launched a behind-the-scenes campaign to reassure business of his good intensions. His efforts, along with the changes in government policy and the increasingly populist character of the Almazán campaign, convinced the *regiomontanos* to adopt a neutral stance (Contreras 1989). Their silence helped the ruling party get away with its fraudulent victory over Almazán.

The anti-statist trend continued during the presidencies of Ávila Camacho (1940–1946), Alemán (1946–1952), and Adolfo Ruiz Cortines (1952–1958). Ávila Camacho passed social security legislation, but he also deepened Cárdenas' tentative shift away from land reform and encouragement of labor activism. Lombardo Toledano, the most influential advocate of leftist unionism, was forced out of his position atop the CTM and eventually resigned the ruling party. The party itself was restructured to weaken the sectors and strengthen the central leadership (Collier and Collier 1991, p. 418). Its turn away from popular mobilization was symbolized by a new name, Institutional Revolutionary Party (PRI), which replaced the Cárdenas-era Party of the Mexican Revolution.

Under Alemán and Ruiz Cortines the conservative turn reached its apogee. The former moved aggressively to domesticate labor by forcibly removing combative union leaders and replacing them with more compliant individuals, known as *charros* (Middlebrook 1995, ch. 4). He also spearheaded a revision of constitutional Article 27 that provided greater security to many of the remaining private landowners (Niblo 2000, pp. 184–185). Spending on economic infrastructure increased, but social outlays stagnated along with taxation (Wilkie 1967, pp. 72–73; Hansen 1971). Ruiz Cortines had a more cautious style but continued his predecessor's pro-business policies. He is best known for establishing the disciplined, low-inflation macroeconomic policy known as "stabilizing development," which would last for two decades and distinguish Mexico from other similarly developed Latin American countries (Bazdresch and Levy 1991, pp. 230–235).

Scholars generally agree that the right turn was a response to the discontent generated by *cardenista* radicalism (Córdova 1974; Hamilton 1982; Contreras 1989; Collier and Collier 1991), in a rather clear example of a reactive sequence. By adopting less aggressively statist policies and abandoning popular mobilization, ruling party leaders sought to avoid the consolidation of an opposition coalition capable of ejecting them from power or instigating a civil war. They also wished to reestablish business confidence in order to spur growth and job creation.

What is striking, however, is how deep and enduring this change proved to be. As noted earlier, the "alliance for profits" perspective, which suggests that the Mexican state developed a close, symbiotic relationship with the private sector during this period, cannot entirely explain this phenomenon. One problem is that it is unclear why the consolidation of this alliance would require such strong constraints on state intervention. After all, statist perspectives on economic development were in ascendance throughout Latin America after World War II and did not necessarily encounter much resistance from business, especially among industrialists. For example, in both Chile and Brazil state intervention developed far more extensively than in Mexico and with considerable support from business (Schmitter 1971; Sikkink 1991; Kurtz 2013). The case of Brazil's 1964–1985 military regime, discussed in Chapter 5, is particularly impressive in this regard.

Just as importantly, the "alliance for profits" perspective exaggerates the degree of consensus and harmony that existed between the Mexican state and private business, even during the 1940s and 1950s, before significant attempts were made to chart a different course. On the one hand, there is little evidence that political and bureaucratic elites were themselves committed to maintaining an unobtrusive public sector. While more orthodox perspectives were well represented within the central bank, the heads of the powerful Secretariat of Finance and Public Credit (Secretaría de Hacienda y Crédito Público, SHCP), including Eduardo Suárez (1940–1946), Ramón Beteta (1946–1952), and Antonio Carrillo Flores (1952–1958), were pragmatists whose views on development largely paralleled the statist (or "developmentalist") perspective purveyed by ECLAC (Suárez 2006). A classic account of postwar Mexican economic policymaking offers a general characterization of the country's technocrats as believers in the virtues of state-led industrialization and income redistribution (Vernon 1963, pp. 136–149).

On the other hand, studies of the private sector reveal a very different perspective, one characterized by marked animosity toward state intervention. For example, an examination of business ideology during Alemán's presidency, widely considered the peak of state favoritism toward business, finds that most of the national associations expressed deep reservations, even alarm, about state intervention, viewing it not only as inefficient but also as dangerous, since it could lead to socialism (López Portillo 1995). This was true not only of the

Monterrey Group and COPARMEX, which had led the business countermobilization of the 1930s, but also of the national confederations of industry and (especially) commerce.

Moreover, business criticism of state intervention was not limited to subtle jabs or private warnings. For example, in 1948, the official magazine of the Confederation of National Chambers of Commerce (Confederación de Cámaras Nacionales de Comercio, CONCANACO) complained that, "The interventionism of those who govern in activities that should be left democratically to the citizens, to business and private capital, is an anticipation of Marxist socialism" (López Portillo 1995, p. 300). Similarly, in a 1950 speech, the president of the Confederation of Chambers of Industry of the United Mexican States (Confederación de Cámaras Industriales de los Estados Unidos Mexicanos, CONCAMIN) warned that the state's growing economic role could result in "abject servitude of individuals to an all-powerful state" and accused politicians of launching interventions "to realize demagogically what the private sector could accomplish in its normal functioning" (López Portillo 1995, pp. 194–195).[9]

A study of industrialists in four Mexican states reaches similar conclusions, emphasizing the wariness of business leaders and their political allies toward the federal government's interventionist initiatives during this era (Gauss 2010). Nowhere was this wariness more pronounced than in Monterrey. While not above lobbying for special treatment for their own companies, the *regiomontanos* opposed as a matter of principle initiatives that would expand the state's economic role. Even with regard to trade protection, the cornerstone of ISI, they expressed considerable skepticism, emphasizing the potential for inefficiency and politicization. Moreover, Monterrey elites continued, despite the strongly pro-business character of the Alemán government, to express strong doubts about the PRI's true intentions. According to the author,

... even as the PRI marginalized its leftist currents under President Alemán, members of the Monterrey Group continued to oppose corporatist labor relations and state economic intervention. In the late 1940s they recast this opposition to take advantage of the Cold War milieu by reinvigorating their historic antagonism to communism and tying it to the ruling party's class politics and statist aggressions against private property. (Gauss 2010, p. 239)

Admittedly, there was a sector of business, made up principally of small- and medium-sized manufacturing firms, that actively supported state intervention. These firms were mainly associated with the National Chamber of Manufacturing (Cámara Nacional de la Industria de Transformación, originally referred to as CNIT and later as CANACINTRA), created by Ávila

---

[9] Even the president of the normally more circumspect Association of Mexican Banks (Asociación de Bancos Mexicanos, ABM) warned at the group's 1951 annual convention that the state's efforts to control the economy, if not checked, could lead to totalitarianism (López Portillo 1995, p. 310).

Camacho in 1941 to provide a representative entity for industrialists that would not be dominated by Monterrey firms and other large businesses (Shadlen 2004). Unlike the other business associations, it openly supported the ruling party and had cordial relations with union leaders (Shafer 1973; López Portillo 1995; Shadlen 2004). Because of these positions, its leaders were sometimes derided by the other associations as "pseudo-communists" (Gauss 2010, p. 191).

CANACINTRA was no doubt symbolically useful to the PRI, but its actual influence was limited. When officials sought private sector support for policy initiatives, they had little choice but to curry the favor of larger companies (Shadlen 2004, ch. 2; Gauss 2010, pp. 173–175). Although some early scholarship had seen in CANACINTRA the future of Mexican industry, that view faded over time. According to a later assessment, "CNIT doctrine has utterly failed to win the hearts of Mexican business to it and it has had no effect on private enterprise attitudes toward government intervention, except possibly to make them more suspicious of government than they would have been if CNIT never had been founded" (Shafer 1973, p. 112).

Studies of the prerevolution era provide little evidence of widespread business anti-statism or efforts to organize politically (Saragoza 1988, ch. 2; Haber 1989; Riguizzi 2009). Rather, these phenomena were mainly a product of postrevolution reformism. While it would be an exaggeration to frame them purely as a response to *cardenismo*, since the more tepid reformism of the 1920s did elicit some organized resistance (Collier and Collier 1991; Gauss 2010), Cárdenas' bold reforms clearly had a major impact. Business leaders of the 1940s and 1950s portrayed the Cárdenas years as a time when the private sector had been fiercely attacked and narrowly escaped socialism (López Portillo 1995, pp. 11, 219, 235, 280; Dion 2010, p. 64). Among the factions most affected were the Monterrey industrialists, who consolidated during this period a distinctive political identity based on defense of free enterprise and a willingness to confront state authorities (Saragoza 1988, p. 1; Gauss 2010, ch. 6). As a result, the Monterrey Group (as well as COPARMEX) would become almost synonymous throughout Mexico with resistance to state interference in the economy.

Thus, the post-Cárdenas business-state relationship should probably be understood less as an alliance than a permanent (if generally manageable) state of tension between a party-state with a benevolent view of the public sector's ability to shape society and a private sector loath to concede it more authority or resources. This perspective is crucial for understanding the limited expansion of the public sector. While the PRI set out to regain the confidence of business elites after 1940, the latter, given their deep-seated mistrust of state intervention and the PRI, were not ready to grant it cheaply. They would extract a high price, not only with regard to opportunities to earn outsized profits but also in terms of depriving authorities of tools they could potentially use to direct the economy and provide benefits to supporters and society as a whole. In fact, the sacrifice they demanded even meant actively turning against erstwhile supporters in the labor movement and leftist sectors of the party itself, transforming the PRI-popular sector relationship into one based largely on clientelism, leadership co-optation, and occasional repression, rather than mobilization (Collier and Collier 1991, pp. 407–420).

4.1.4   Placating Business with Light Taxation

Few policy areas illustrate the relationship between business mistrust and limited intervention as effectively as taxation. Although conscious of the importance of gaining additional revenue, both for social and economic development purposes, Mexican officials of the 1940s and 1950s trod extremely lightly in this area for fear of further alienating a contentious private sector. Attempts were made to raise additional revenue, especially during the late 1940s, but they were of limited scope and were further diluted in response to private sector complaints, either through changes to proposed legislation or exemptions. The result was that tax revenues barely kept pace with GDP growth.

Top officials viewed the tax burden as insufficient to meet the state's needs to promote development and social equity. Presidents and finance ministers throughout the 1940s and 1950s repeatedly emphasized the importance of raising more revenue (Aboites 2005, p. 192). In the early 1950s, a joint Mexican government-World Bank commission, which had been created at Mexico's instigation to provide economic policy guidance, recommended a major tax reform to endow the public sector with greater resources for investment and social programs (López Portillo 1995, pp. 97–102). Similarly, a 1956 World Bank report remarked that the Ruiz Cortines government "has been well aware of the importance of raising the level of Government revenue," although officials were hesitant to do so for fear of disrupting economic growth (World Bank 1956, p. 7).

While authorities viewed greater tax collection as an important goal, business was skeptical. It not only opposed efforts to increase income taxation, particularly on capital and higher earners (Unda 2010, ch. 5), but also resisted paying higher indirect taxes, as evidenced by their rejection of Alemán's attempts to effectively enforce consumption taxation in the late 1940s (Aboites 2003, p. 211). Social security taxation was also resisted. An in-depth study of the politics of social security argues that, after grudgingly acquiescing to this program's creation under Ávila Camacho, the private sector steadfastly opposed its expansion (Dion 2010, p. 23). This perspective is consistent with business association pronouncements cited by López Portillo, which support social security in theory but argue against expanding it to new groups or increasing contributions until alleged flaws in the program were corrected (López Portillo 1995, pp. 211 and 232). An official report of the banking association ABM even cautioned that social security revenues might be used to "socialize the instruments of national production" (López Portillo 1995, p. 308).

Public officials were, of course, quite conscious of these sentiments. The slow growth of tax revenues during these decades reflected not only their desire to stimulate private investment, but also an awareness that doing so in their specific national context required a special sensitivity to private sector mistrust of the state.

One sign of this sensitivity was the concession of copious tax exemptions despite an already precarious revenue flow. This policy began under Cárdenas but was greatly expanded by both Ávila Camacho and Alemán (Gauss 2010, p. 75; Unda 2010, ch. 5). From 1939 to 1955 the value of exemptions was estimated at 15 percent of total revenue (Martínez de Navarrete 1967, p. 25). This policy came under sharp criticism from economists, who argued that it was unnecessary to stimulate investment, given the other advantages business enjoyed, and thus mainly served to boost profits (Kolbeck and Urquidi 1952; Aboites and Unda 2011, pp. 18–19). That the policy continued in the face of these criticisms suggests that it was motivated at least partly by a desire to placate a private sector deeply mistrustful of the state. This impression is reinforced by the fact that exemptions were increasingly handed out not to budding new industries but to large, well-established firms (López Portillo 1995, p. 87; Gauss 2010, pp. 85–86), precisely those that tended to be most skeptical of state intervention. In fact, Finance Secretary Beteta himself admitted in a speech that they were continued mainly to reassure business of the state's good intentions (Beteta 1951, p. 58).

Sensitivity to private sector mistrust was also reflected in a willingness to engage in extensive consultation with business before advancing tax reform proposals, in much the same way as the Concertación governments in Chile. This approach became quite evident under Alemán, who was both strongly committed to rebuilding business confidence (Aboites 2003, pp. 197; Unda 2010, ch. 5) and conscious of the state's need for additional revenue (Martínez de Navarrete 1973, p. 48). To gain business acquiescence to its proposed national sales tax, the government asked CONCANACO to organize an elaborate meeting, dubbed the First National Convention of Taxpayers, in which authorities would dialogue with business leaders (López Portillo 1995, pp. 289–290; Aboites 2003, p. 197). Two more conventions were held in subsequent years. Despite these efforts, business protested bitterly about the new ISIM, as well as an accompanying measure increasing penalties for evasion, when they were introduced. Their mobilization may have contributed to the adoption of a rate below the already modest one originally proposed (Aboites 2003, p. 212).

Close consultation with business continued to stifle efforts to increase taxation under Ruiz Cortines.[10] During this period, proposals were floated to reform the income tax in ways that would attenuate its "schedular" character,

---

[10] The discussion of this period is based mainly on Unda (2010), ch. 5.

which facilitated tax avoidance by applying different rates to different types of income. Influential bureaucrats believed that increasing taxation in this way could contribute not only to equity but also to growth, by allowing the state to channel corporate profits into infrastructural investment. Most other Latin American countries already had a mixed system of the kind proposed. However, discussions with private sector representatives led to a bill that omitted this aspect and tended to reduce the taxation of capital. In presenting the bill to Congress in 1953, Ruiz Cortines admitted that he had bowed to business preferences on this issue out of concern for promoting investment. Although some officials continued to champion a more global income tax, a 1955 reform also failed to include this measure.

4.2 THE FAILURE OF REFORM EFFORTS

The fiscally austere and strongly pro-business character of Mexico's postwar policies eventually gave rise to pressures for change, which presidents Adolfo López Mateos (1958–1964) and Luis Echeverría (1970–1976) sought to respond to by constructing a more activist state equipped with a greater capacity to extract revenue from society. Echeverría's successor, José López Portillo (1976–1982), had more limited goals, but his creation of the long-debated VAT in 1979 could potentially have endowed the state with a very potent revenue-raising tool. Nevertheless, all these efforts failed to decisively alter Mexico's low-tax path, and the growing gap between revenues and spending helped precipitate a severe debt crisis and eventually the frank abandonment of ISI.

There is considerable consensus among analysts of these events, including some who participated in them, that the failure to raise taxes more decisively was mainly due to intense private sector resistance (Martínez Nava 1984; Tirado 1985; Solís 1988; Elizondo Mayer-Serra 1994). Business reactions to reform efforts not only thwarted them but also prompted the rise of economy-wide associations that helped endow Mexican business with the exceptional degree of organization it boasts today (Schneider 2002, 2004). The analysis developed here concurs with this view but emphasizes, more than most works, the continuity between the mobilizations of the 1960s and 1970s and the attitudes and behavior of business in earlier decades. It argues that the same anti-statism that caused business leaders to view with mistrust even Alemán's highly favorable policies led them to react with panic and outrage to reforms proposed by López Mateos and Echeverría, despite their comparatively moderate character. López Portillo's VAT proposal did not elicit major protests, but business skepticism was instrumental in keeping it from having a greater revenue impact. In other words, the argument portrays the failures of reform as a path-dependent consequence of postrevolution threats to property, which gave rise to an enduring elite culture of anti-statism embedded in a powerful, expanding web of formal and informal organizations.

4.2.1 Discontent and Failed Attempts at Change

López Mateos and Echeverría came to office in the midst of political crises that threatened to undermine the revolutionary legitimacy crucial to the PRI's ability to monopolize state power with only limited use of violence or electoral fraud. They reacted to these pressures by undertaking reforms that sought to increase the state's ability to furnish social protection, attenuate inequality, and guide development. Revenue-raising tax reform was a priority for both. Coming to power after the intense state-private sector struggles of the Echeverría years, López Portillo had a more modest agenda. Yet, his tax reform proposals were centered on a new levy that had proven highly effective in generating revenue elsewhere, a fact that was probably not lost on either state officials or business leaders. Although these repeated efforts to increase revenues did yield some results, they were insufficient to significantly alter Mexico's status as a lightly taxed country.

Adolfo López Mateos, a former Secretary of Labor under Ruiz Cortines, was selected as the PRI's presidential candidate to reinforce the party's progressive image after years of conservative policies (Dion 2010, p. 91). Perhaps sensing an opportunity, independent labor unions launched a strike wave during the election year (1958) and the one that followed. The unions involved mainly represented public employees, who were upset about low wages, subpar benefits, and the state's authoritarianism. The strikes soon died down, but in the early 1960s a new wave of leftist organizing began, inspired in part by the 1959 Cuban Revolution. Even ex-President Cárdenas, who had remained largely silent in the face of the PRI's right turn, joined other politicians, intellectuals, and activists in denouncing the party's betrayal of its revolutionary heritage (Semo 1989). Throughout the late 1950s and early 1960s, peasant land invasions also multiplied and became increasingly organized outside of and in opposition to the corporatist CNC (Tai 1974, pp. 410–411).

Like previous presidents, López Mateos reacted to dissent with a blend of concession and repression while continuing the relatively austere "stabilizing development" policy. On the whole, however, his presidency was the most socially reformist since Cárdenas. He established a new social security program for public sector workers, implemented a profit-sharing system promised by the 1917 constitution, and revived land reform (Morett 2003, p. 104). The president also burnished his nationalist credentials by completing the nationalization of electric power generation (Story 1986, p. 40) and refusing to follow the US policy of isolating Cuba. In a further effort to accommodate disgruntled groups, his government reformed electoral law to allow parties winning only a small proportion of the national vote to assume seats in the Chamber of Deputies (Collier and Collier 1991, p. 593).

The López Mateos government also attempted a tax reform intended to raise additional revenue, principally through income taxation. In March 1960,

Finance Minister Antonio Ortiz Mena invited noted British economist Nicolas Kaldor to come to Mexico, conduct an in-depth study of the tax system, and develop recommendations for reform. Given Kaldor's left-leaning views, it was to be expected that he would recommend heavier taxation, and he did precisely that. Kaldor's report argued for a major tax hike, to be achieved mainly by replacing the schedular income tax with a universal one, creating a new wealth tax and giving the state more information about asset ownership (Aboites and Unda 2011, pp. 31–32). An interagency commission featuring some prominent officials was formed to study the recommendations and draft a bill.

However, the reform package finally sent to Congress in late 1961 bore little resemblance to Kaldor's proposal and had a relatively minor impact on revenues (World Bank 1964, appendix B, p. 4). The government announced a second income tax reform in late 1964, at the end of López Mateos' term, and a bill was pushed through Congress the following year (under President Gustavo Díaz Ordaz) that brought together all types of income under the same progressive rate structure (Aboites and Unda 2011). However, another law approved at the same time included a clause (supposedly temporary but renewed many times thereafter) that largely neutralized it by exempting capital income (Solís 1988). Thus, despite launching two different tax reforms, López Mateos brought only a moderate increase in Mexico's tax burden (Solís 1988; Aboites and Unda 2011, pp. 31–32).

Echeverría came to power in the wake of the most notorious act of official repression of the PRI regime, the 1968 massacre of student protestors in Mexico City. Criticisms of the state's abandonment of the values of the 1917 constitution were rife. Labor and peasant protest grew, as they had under López Mateos. The president's "shared development" program involved increased social security and educational spending, minimum wage hikes, and price controls on key commodities. Although he had not initially made land redistribution a priority, Echeverria ended up legalizing many peasant land invasions (Muñoz 2016, pp. 30–32). The public enterprise sector was expanded substantially, in part by taking over failing private companies to protect employment (Cypher 1990, ch. 4). The president's leftist orientation was also reflected in a foreign policy that featured support for the Non-Aligned Movement and good relations with Chile's UP government. He also was more tolerant of public protest and, like López Mateos, introduced mild measures to facilitate opposition party representation.

Facing powerful pressures for reform, the Echeverría government was less dedicated to fiscal prudence than its predecessors (Bazdresch and Levy 1981, pp. 240–241). However, from early on it made a number of attempts to increase tax revenues. The initial measures focused on raising indirect taxes, especially the ISIM and the excise tax on tabaco products (Martínez de Navarrete 1973, p. 55; Tello 2010, p. 40). In late 1972, it also advanced a proposal to reform income taxation in ways similar to the ones discussed in the early 1960s (Solís 1988, pp. 111–112). Like the López Mateos government, its objectives were both to increase revenues and to counteract the growing concentration of income.

Echeverría's tax reform efforts yielded mixed results. His efforts to increase indirect taxation, especially excise taxes and the federal sales tax, yielded some gains. For example, key states, enticed by more favorable terms, finally accepted the federal government's longstanding offer to suppress their sales taxes in return for a share of the federal ISIM (Aboites 2003). However, the president's income tax proposals were less successful. Progress was made in integrating some previously excluded income sources (e.g., rental housing) and modestly raising the top individual rate, but a more ambitious reform was abandoned (Elizondo Mayer-Serra 1994; Gil Díaz and Thirsk 1997).

José López Portillo backed away from his predecessor's support for progressive change, mainly because of the fierce opposition it had generated, as elaborated later. However, unlike his immediate successors, he did not seek to downsize the public sector. Spending continued to grow with the difference that now it was fueled by an oil boom based on both higher international prices and the discovery of huge new reserves in the Gulf of Mexico. Understanding the volatility of such revenues and the major deficiencies of the tax system, officials nonetheless sought to strengthen taxation, as well. Although they made some changes to income taxation, their focus was on creating a VAT, a tax that had already been adopted in much of Europe and Latin America (including Argentina, Brazil, and Chile) over the previous two decades and was increasingly viewed as a powerful revenue-raising tool (Kato 2003).

Although López Portillo ultimately succeeded in establishing a VAT, the basic rate of 10 percent was below what officials believed was needed merely to compensate for the taxes it would replace (Urzúa 1993, p. 19). Moreover, soon after its launch, the government succumbed to pressures to expand exemptions for foodstuffs (Gil Diaz and Thirsk 1997, p. 299). Hence, at least initially, it had little impact on the tax burden.

The reforms of the 1960s and 1970s did end up boosting Mexico's tax revenues from 8–9 percent of GDP to around 13 percent (see Figure 4.1), but the latter figure remained far below those of Brazil, Chile, and (in most years) Argentina. In addition, the rapid growth of public spending during the 1970s led to rising deficits and inflation, breaking with the relatively austere "stabilizing development" approach pursued since the mid-1950s (Bazdresch and Levy 1991). This problem was temporarily attenuated by the oil boom of the latter half of the 1970s, which transformed PEMEX into a central pillar of the fiscal system. However, the sharp decline in global petroleum prices in the early 1980s plunged Mexico into a severe fiscal and balance of payments crisis, pushing the previously moderate López Portillo to adopt extreme measures, including defaulting on the foreign debt and nationalizing the banks. This situation, as discussed later, would lay the groundwork for the neoliberal reforms that would dominate Mexican politics during the 1980s and early 1990s.

Although Echeverría and López Portillo failed to decisively transform Mexico's tax system in terms of revenue, they did substantially increase the federal government's role, consolidating the highly centralized system that exists today. The federal share of tax revenue increased from an average of about 75 percent during the 1960s to 90 percent in the 1980s (Díaz-Cayeros 2006, p. 36). This was mainly a result of changes to indirect taxation. Under Echeverría, as noted earlier, the remaining holdout states finally joined the ISIM regime (Aboites 2003). Centralization was further boosted by the VAT, which replaced that tax and eliminated some 300 state-level excise taxes (Gil-Díaz and Thirsk 1997, p. 298).

4.2.2   Business Mobilization and the Thwarting of Tax Reform

The failure of successive attempts to create the revenue base needed to sustainably increase state intervention is striking, given the PRI's near monopoly on institutional political power. It can be understood mainly as a consequence of the intense mobilization by the private sector (and some allied conservative actors) against these initiatives. Tensions between the state and business, especially under Echeverría, reached levels not seen since the Cárdenas era, prompting major innovations in business organization. While business mobilization against López Portillo was far less significant during the period in which he championed the VAT (it would intensify later), resistance to this initiative prompted concessions that blunted the tax's revenue impact.

During the early 1960s, conflict between the state and business escalated due to the latter's perception that they were witnessing a slide into a radical leftist regime. Their concerns were shaped by a combination of international and domestic factors. Cuba's transition to communism stimulated in Mexico, as elsewhere in Latin America, fears that similar events could occur at home. At the same time, domestic political mobilization, combined with the government's statist, pro-worker reforms, its friendly gestures toward Cuba, and its occasionally leftist discourse, suggested that the PRI itself might be moving to the left, reviving *cardenismo*. Business pronouncements and the more conservative media outlets became increasingly critical. In November 1960, CONCAMIN, CONCANACO, and COPARMEX jointly published a multipage paid advertisement in several major newspapers with the provocative title "By what path, Mr. President?" (Martínez Nava 1984, p. 143). In it, the associations assailed what they perceived as growing infringements on economic freedom and posed the rhetorical question, "Are we, through growing interventionism, moving toward state socialism?"

Several initiatives were undertaken to forge new associations to express business concern about the political climate and public policies (Tirado 1985; Martínez Nava 1984). While some openly criticized the government, the most enduring was one that operated almost exclusively behind closed doors. Founded in 1962 as the Council of Public Relations of the Pro-Mexico Private Sector, it was composed of about two dozen executives of Mexico's largest companies. Although framed innocuously as an effort to reassure foreign investors, its creation expressed alarm about the political situation and its members demanded from López Mateos a commitment to business-friendly policies (Valdés Ugalde 1997, p. 162). While not widely known at the time, this organization, whose name was changed to Mexican Council of Businessmen (Consejo Mexicano de Hombres de Negocio, CMHN) in 1967 and to Mexican Business Council (Consejo Mexicano de Negocios, CMN) in 2014, would become a major political actor.

The private sector was not alone in its struggle against the progressive tendencies of the government. It was increasingly joined in 1961 and 1962 by a wide variety of social conservative organizations, often with ties to the Catholic Church (Martínez Nava 1984; Tirado 1985). These groups included both existing organizations like the PAN and UNS and a series of new groups that arose as part of a growing wave of anti-communist fervor (Tirado 1985, p. 110). Mass protest movements flourished in a number of states, in many cases supported or even led by the business community (Tirado 1985, pp. 111–112).

In this climate, the government's attempts to craft a major income tax reform had little chance of prospering. The committee charged with drafting the bill was divided between a faction that wanted a reform incorporating core aspects of Kaldor's proposal, including the universal income tax, and another that preferred a more cautious, superficial one (Aboites and Unda 2011, pp. 35–36). Although proponents of large-scale change appear to have been a majority, Finance Minister Ortiz Mena sided with the other group. In a memoire published years later, he argued that, though he had personally favored a major reform, the private sector's deep mistrust of the government, due to the latter's progressive initiatives and rhetoric, had made advancing one "politically impossible" (Ortiz Mena 1998, p. 156). Doing so would have aggravated a "crisis of confidence" already affecting investment. Another high SHCP official of that period, Rafael Izquierdo, gives a similar account (Izquierdo 1995, pp. 70–75).

Private sector opposition also played a central role in thwarting the attempt to establish a progressive, universal income tax in 1964–1965. While a seemingly important reform bill was approved by Congress, its effect was blunted by a clause inserted into the annual budget law (Izquierdo 1995, p. 77). A former official of the Banco de México (the central bank) explains that this clause was not only written at the insistence of business but also drafted by representatives of the private sector itself (Solís 1988, pp. 43–44). Furthermore, Izquierdo (1995, p. 77) points out that a 1965 CONCAMIN report thanked SHCP for consulting extensively with the major business associations about the reform and adopting an "understanding attitude" toward their concerns. As these testimonials suggest, top public officials supported substantial reform and were frustrated by its defeat, which reinforces the notion that resistance from outside the state ultimately torpedoed it.

Private sector relations with the more conservative Díaz Ordaz government were smoother than under López Mateos, but business-state conflict escalated again under Echeverría, becoming an "almost permanent" feature of the *sexenio* (Martínez Nava 1984, p. 168). Skirmishes began early on and gradually evolved into an all-out battle between the private sector, led by what became known as its "radical" faction, consisting most prominently of the Monterrey Group and COPARMEX, and the government (Luna Ledesma 1992; Valdés Ugalde 1997, p. 184). Business fought the government with inflammatory public statements, rumor campaigns, and producer strikes in various parts of the country (Tirado 1985, pp. 113–114). In 1975 it also initiated a new organization, the Coordinating Business Council (Consejo Coordinador Empresarial, CCE) (Tirado 1985; Arriola 1988; Luna Ledesma 1992; Luna and Tirado 1992). The CCE was a confederation of all major business associations except CANACINTRA, whose alliance with the state precluded its membership.[11] Unlike the elitist and secretive CMHN, the CCE was constructed as a vehicle for mobilizing broad, public resistance to state initiatives. This difference probably reflected a greater perceived threat, given Echeverría's more sustained reformism and populist discourse.

Taxation was a major source of conflict between Echeverría and business and the latter largely succeeded in frustrating efforts to raise revenue (Tello 1979; Solís 1988; Elizondo Mayer-Serra 1994). The conflicts began only a few weeks after the president's inauguration, when key business associations sharply criticized the government for advancing a tax reform proposal, including a sales tax on luxury goods and a measure to remove the anonymity of stock ownership, without going through the usual prior consultation with business (Martínez Nava 1984, pp. 170–171). Their protests resulted in the watering down of the former provision (which had virtually no impact on revenues) and the abandonment of the second.

Business resistance also thwarted efforts to achieve a substantial income tax reform in 1972, according to an official involved in the process (Solís 1988). After the 1970 tax conflict, Echeverría had sought to cultivate good relations with key business representatives. However, when the government proposed a reform that would significantly increase taxation of capital and top incomes, even those leaders on friendly terms with him "hardened their positions to conserve the confidence of their members" (Solís 1988, p. 108). Officials

---

[11] The CCE was made up of ABM, the Mexican Association of Insurance Institutions (Asociación Mexicana de Institutos de Seguro, AMIS), CMHN, CONCAMIN, CONCANACO, and COPARMEX. They were joined in the 1980s by the newly formed National Council of Agriculture (Consejo Nacional de Agricultura, CNA). Previously, commercial agriculture had been represented mainly by COPARMEX (Trevizo 2011, p. 134).

attempted to convince them of the necessity of the project to preserve economic and social stability, but their arguments fell on deaf ears. In the end, the president, probably fearing a major conflagration with business (which ironically would come anyway soon after), quietly backed off his proposal.

From the beginning of his term López Portillo set out earnestly to mend relations with the private sector after the conflictive Echeverría presidency (Luna Ledesma 1992, p. 61). He largely succeeded and would not face aggressive business protests until 1982, when he reacted to massive capital flight by nationalizing the private banks. However, some of the president's initiatives did face considerable resistance, including the creation of the VAT. A VAT had initially been proposed in the late 1960s but "strenuous" business opposition led it to be shelved (Urzúa 1993, p. 6). It was floated by the SHCP again under Echeverría (Martínez Nava 1984, p. 191) but does not seem to have been endorsed by the president. When the López Portillo government broached the topic again in 1978, business objected, arguing that it would stoke inflation (Gil-Díaz and Thirsk 1997, pp. 297–298). Their opposition was implacable until SHCP offered to lower the basic rate from 12.7 percent, which it had projected was necessary just to maintain the existing revenue level, to 10 percent. "Although the basic rate was too low to have a revenue-neutral tax reform, the government chose it to make the introduction of the VAT more palatable to the private sector" (Urzúa 1993, p. 19).

4.2.3 Continuity with the Past

The conservative political mobilizations of the 1960s and 1970s were reactions to changes proposed by authorities during these periods. However, their intensity cannot be adequately understood without reference to previous decades, which established both the strongly anti-statist ideology of the business community and an extensive web of ties between key organizations and leaders. In essence, the reforms proposed by López Mateos and Echeverría provoked a potent response because they aggravated a sense of wariness that had persisted since the Cárdenas years, embedded in elite organizations and social networks.

To be sure, the reforms, especially Echeverría's, represented a policy shift relative to preceding governments. However, from most other perspectives, they were rather moderate. None of these governments proposed a redistribution of property rights on anything like the scale of the 1930s. Moreover, the increases in spending, taxation, and state control of production they sought were not unreasonable when compared to other countries in Latin America, including Chile (even pre-Allende) and Brazil, where the state apparatus was far more imposing (Graham 1982; Etchemendy 2012). While Argentina's instability prevented a comparably sustained public sector expansion, the tax burden in the early 1950s (as Chapter 6 documents) was already above the highest level experienced under Echeverría.

More than one author has remarked on the surprising intensity of private sector reactions to the reform initiatives of this period (Graham 1982, pp. 35–36; Martínez Nava 1984, p. 168; Basañez 1999, p. 57). Among the most telling of such analyses is one that compares the anti-Echeverría mobilizations to business protests against the expansion of state economic activity in Brazil during the same period. Although the Brazilian public sector was considerably larger than its Mexican counterpart on several dimensions, "in no way could either the criticisms or the concessions be compared to the private sector offensive that had been launched in Mexico. The Brazilian private sector critics were weaker, more defensive in their posture, and never went beyond the specifics of their complaints" (Graham 1982, p. 36).

How can we explain this reaction? Graham attributes it to preexisting traditions of state autonomy and interventionism in Brazil and private sector dominance and fiscal conservatism in Mexico. The author does not explore the roots of these differences, but his analysis is consistent with the idea advanced here that in Mexico business was already more hostile to state intervention and had organized itself more effectively to repel it. This chapter has already touched on post-Cárdenas business anti-statism, but the discussion here elaborates briefly on how the organizations and informal networks in which that perspective was embedded shaped resistance to statist initiatives under López Mateos and Echeverría.

Although the rise of CMHN and CCE would give Mexican business an exceptionally comprehensive organizational structure (Schneider 2002, 2004), even before these entities were created it enjoyed an impressive degree of coordination. For one thing, Mexico was one of the relatively few Latin American countries with an enduring national business association (COPARMEX) with a cross-sectoral membership. Brazil and Argentina lacked such an organization and until about the late 1960s Chile's CPC played a secondary role. COPARMEX was created to oppose labor reform, but it quickly developed under Cárdenas into a group devoted to "curbing state economic intervention more broadly" (Gauss 2010, p. 216). With about 10,000 member firms in the mid-1960s, it was far smaller than the state-sanctioned CONCAMIN and CONCANACO (Schneider 2002, p. 86). However, membership in COPARMEX, unlike these corporatist entities, was voluntary, so it implied a commitment to the organization's mission. In addition, although most of its members were small, COPARMEX attracted some of Mexico's largest firms, which of course increased its clout (Schneider 2002, p. 86).

By the 1960s, COPARMEX had local affiliates throughout much of the country and was no longer simply an instrument of the Monterrey Group. However, it continued to bear Monterrey's imprint, not only with regard to its top leadership, in which the *regiomontano* elite was still strongly represented, but also in terms of other characteristics, including its deep wariness of state intervention, its willingness to openly challenge authorities, its dedication to forging business unity, its ties to the PAN, and its rhetorical use of Catholic values to convey an image of employer paternalism toward workers. In some ways it resembled a social movement organization more than a business association. These qualities made it unusual among Latin American business associations (Schneider 2002, p. 85–86) and gave it an important leadership role (Valdés Ugalde 1997, p. 166; Shadlen 2004, p. 96).

Both COPARMEX and the Monterrey elite had close ties to CONCANACO and CONCAMIN, the national confederations of commerce and industry, respectively. For example, during the 1940s, two men served as president of both CONCANACO and COPARMEX and, during parts of the 1950s and 1960s, Monterrey business leaders served as presidents of both CONCANACO and CONCAMIN (Shafer 1973, p. 273, fn 13). In the name of promoting solidarity, Monterrey's monthly business magazine provided space for COPARMEX, CONCANACO, and CONCAMIN to express their views, and one of the intellectuals most closely associated with the Monterrey Group during the 1940s and 1950s, Jesús Guisa y Azevedo, was a regular contributor to CONCANACO's own publication (López Portillo 1995, pp. 217 and 264). These three associations frequently collaborated in efforts to influence policy during the 1940s and 1950s and shared a common antipathy toward CANACINTRA (Shafer 1973; Tirado 1985; Lopez Portillo 1995; Gauss 2010).

It was this preexisting network of business anti-state activism that sprang into action to oppose the reforms of the 1960s and 1970s. COPARMEX was particularly central to these efforts under both López Mateos (Valdés Ugalde 166–172) and Echeverría, when the rise to power of a hard-line faction pushed the organization even further to the right (Luna Ledesma 1992). Both COPARMEX and the Monterrey Group made voluntary contributions to the CCE, with the latter alone contributing roughly a third of the CCE's budget in its early years (Schneider 2002, p. 97). However, COPARMEX also worked closely with other associations, especially CONCAMIN and CONCANACO, as a study of López Mateos' profit sharing reform illustrates (Kaufman Purcell 1975). It was also closely tied to the CMHN, which supplemented COPARMEX's revenues (Schneider 2002, p. 88), and reportedly had a say in the selection of its president (Valdés Ugalde 1997, p. 173–175). Thus, the creation of the CCE in the mid-1970s was merely "the concretization, in the world of business institutions, of the unity and concertation of action and purpose that had already been achieved a long time before by employer organizations in Mexico" (Martínez Nava 1984, p. 224).

The stubborn persistence of anti-state activism is perhaps surprising, given the exceptionally favorable treatment business had received since 1940. It has been explained as a symptom of a constitution that grants the state considerable powers to intervene in the economy and property relations (Elizondo Mayer-Serra 1994, p. 169). However, there is reason to doubt that progressive constitutional provisions per se had a major impact. These provisions, especially Article 27, had been vigorously implemented only under Cárdenas.

Moreover, by the mid-twentieth century, several Latin American countries, including Argentina and Brazil, had altered their constitutions to more closely approximate the Mexican model and others would follow (Gargarella 2014, p. 12). Brazil's current constitution, ratified in 1988, offers an especially broad list of social guarantees and makes property ownership conditional on fulfillment of its "social function." Yet, as becomes clear in Chapter 5, Brazilian capitalists have been far more tolerant of state intervention than their Mexican counterparts.

More important than ongoing constitutional threats were ideas ingrained in formal and informal business organizations as a result of earlier conflicts with the state. The identities and ideologies of the most consistent opponents of state expansion had been forged in the struggles against postrevolution redistributive initiatives and especially *cardenismo* (Bravo Mena 1987; Saragoza 1988; Schneider 2002). Opposition to state intervention was part of their organizational DNA and something in which their leaders took pride. The captains of Monterrey industry viewed themselves as the defenders of freedom, morality, and hard work in the face of a corrupt, power-hungry state (Gauss 2010, pp. 206–207). Similarly, COPARMEX leaders wore their recalcitrance and ideological inflexibility as a badge of honor, portraying their organization as "the conscience of business" (Nuñez 2014, interview). While the activism of these groups was exceptional, their consistent ability to exercise a leadership role during periods of conflict with the state suggests that their viewpoint was widely shared. As a scholar of Mexican business associations pointed out in the early 1970s, "the legendary business conservatism of Nuevo León has always had plenty of counterparts elsewhere" (Shafer 1973, p. 105).

4.3   THE PERSISTENCE OF LIGHT TAXATION UNDER DEMOCRACY

Following these frustrated efforts to substantially increase tax revenues, Mexico settled back into a stable pattern of light taxation. This can be attributed in part to the crucial role that nontax oil revenues came to play in the fiscal system beginning under López Portillo. Nevertheless, as argued in Chapter 2, that variable is insufficient to explain the large gap in tax burdens between Mexico and the two high-tax countries examined in this book, Argentina and Brazil. That the tax burden did not increase during the peak years of liberalizing reform in the 1980s and 1990s is not surprising, since the purpose of the reforms was to limit the state's economic role. However, the fact that taxation has remained relatively light since the late 1990s is more noteworthy, given that the global neoliberal tide has slackened and, more importantly, the hegemonic party regime has given way to one based on fierce competition.

This section argues that relative tax burden stability reflects the power balance inherited from the old regime. While this balance clearly favored anti-statism even before the 1980s, the transformations of this decade and the 1990s aggravated the disadvantage faced by statist actors, largely because they were already too weak to defend their interests. As democratic competition heated up, the superiority of anti-statist forces became manifest in both the electoral and interest group arenas. Under the influence of relatively conservative governments and a well-organized and combative private sector, tax reform initiatives were generally timid and were diluted further during the legislative process, resulting in a tax burden that changed little until 2015, when nontax revenues declined sharply due to falling oil prices.

4.3.1 Crisis, Democratization, and Tax Burden Stability

As in much of Latin America, in Mexico the debt crisis of the early 1980s helped pave the way for both economic liberalization and political democratization. In the Mexican case, unlike some others (e.g., Argentina and Brazil), the economic transformation largely preceded the political one, although pressures to end PRI hegemony were already intensifying in the 1980s. While a transition to a less interventionist development strategy would not logically be expected to bring significantly heavier taxation, there are theoretical reasons (outlined in Chapter 1) to believe that democratization would. Yet, such a change has been slow to emerge. Mexico has remained a low-tax country.

Mexican policymaking during 1980s and 1990s was dominated by efforts to revive growth by adopting a more thoroughly market-based approach. While the country's policies were already less interventionist than those of some other Latin American countries, the governments of this era gave up even the pretense of pursuing state-led development. The three PRI presidents that followed López Portillo, Miguel de la Madrid (1982–1988), Carlos Salinas (1988–1994), and Ernesto Zedillo (1994–2000), all overtly embraced market economics and implemented extensive trade liberalization, privatization, deregulation, and spending cuts, in line with the "Washington consensus" (Ros 1993; Teichman 2001, ch. 6). The speed and extent of the transition, which left Mexico as one of Latin America's most liberal economies, was aided by both the semi-authoritarian character of the regime and the fact that Mexico's economy never reached the level of statism seen in Argentina, Brazil, and Chile.

In the area of taxation, the changes implemented by these presidents were aimed at closing the fiscal deficit, reducing distortions, and consolidating market reforms, rather than supporting increased state activity (Gil-Diaz and Thirsk 1997; Martínez-Vazquez 2001).[12] Facing an acute crisis, de la Madrid focused on increasing revenues by boosting the rates of excise taxes and the VAT, whose general rate rose to 15 percent. Salinas lowered some taxes, dropping the VAT back down to 10 percent and cutting income tax rates. However, he also introduced a corporate asset tax intended to reduce

---

[12] Such reforms, as Mahon (2004) notes, can enhance a state's ability to expand its activities in the future. However, the Mexican case illustrates that this is far from an inevitable outcome.

evasion by acting as a minimum income tax (Elizondo Mayer-Serra 1994).[13] Like de la Madrid, Zedillo faced serious problems caused by a financial crisis at the outset of his term. He responded with measures to strengthen Mexico's fiscal position, including returning the general VAT rate to 15 percent and raising income tax rates (Tello 2010, p. 41). The Zedillo government also undertook a social security reform with revenue implications. Influenced by the Chilean example, in 1995 it privatized the pension system for private sector workers, creating an individual account system (Madrid 2003). However, since existing workers were offered the option of staying in the old system (which many accepted), pension contributions did not fall nearly as precipitously as they had in Chile.

Despite implementing many piecemeal reforms, overall the neoliberal PRI governments changed the tax system relatively little. At 12.1 percent of GDP, the tax burden in 2000 was similar to that of two decades earlier and among the lowest in Latin America. Nontax natural resource revenues brought fiscal resources to 18.0 percent of GDP, but this figure was still lower than in Chile (19.1 percent) and Argentina (20.2 percent), to say nothing of Brazil (30.2 percent) (CEPALSTAT). As in earlier decades, direct taxes contributed a relatively large share of total tax revenues (46.2 percent) due to the small volume of other revenues. By 2000, taxation was more centralized than at the outset of the 1980s, but this was due mainly to López Portillo's VAT, rather than the policies of subsequent governments (SHCP2 2014, interview).

While PRI authorities were struggling to find a formula for returning to the strong economic growth of the pre-debt crisis period, they were also gradually relaxing authoritarian controls in response to pressures for democracy. Despite having resorted to fraud to hold onto the presidency in the 1988 election, during the course of the 1990s they implemented a series of reforms allowing greater competition. These changes led to the PRI's loss of its majority in the Chamber of Deputies (the lower house of Congress) in 1997 and the victory of the PAN's Vicente Fox in the 2000 presidential election. Although the PRI would return to the presidency in 2012, the one-party regime was finished.

Political regime change did not translate fluidly into change in the fiscal system, however. Through 2013 the tax burden remained essentially the same. Recent years have brought more robust growth, pushing tax revenues to 16.1 percent in 2017 (CEPALSTAT). However, this increase has occurred in the context of a slump in nontax revenues from oil, meaning that the public sector's fiscal resources have remained stable at 20–21 percent of GDP since the mid-2000s (CEPALSTAT). In fact, Mexico's total fiscal revenues in 2017 were virtually the same relative to GDP as at the outset of the 1980s, almost four decades earlier (World Bank 1984, p. 4).

---

[13] The tax consisted of a 2 percent levy on a firm's total assets. The amount paid was credited toward the corporate income tax, so firms reporting substantial earnings would pay no more than before.

Fox's government and that of his PAN successor Felipe Calderón (2006–2012) accomplished only minor tax reform. The former's *sexenio* was marked by the failure of repeated attempts to broaden the VAT to include previously exempt goods, especially food and medicine. Calderón proposed a reform in 2007 focused on direct taxation. It eliminated Salinas' corporate asset tax but introduced a corporate alternative minimum income tax and a tax on bank deposits (Díaz Pérez 2012). While these measures passed, the reform was unambitious and was further diluted during the legislative process. A subsequent reform undertaken to deal with the fiscal effects of the 2008–2009 economic crisis brought a small VAT increase and minor changes to income taxation, which merely stabilized revenues. Fiscal revenue grew by about 3 percent of GDP during the PAN years, but that increase was due mainly to strong oil prices.

The PRI returned to the presidency in 2012 with an ambitious reform agenda that included both pro-market and pro-equity measures. Of the latter, the most prominent was a tax reform that aimed to boost revenues through changes to both direct and indirect levies (Unda 2015; Ondetti 2017, p. 61). With regard to direct taxation, its main provisions were a hike in income tax rates for higher-income individuals, a new tax on corporate dividends, and the erosion or elimination of some business tax breaks. The proposed indirect tax reforms did not include the controversial broadening of the VAT, but they did include elimination of the lower border rate (extending the 16 percent rate nationwide), as well as new excise taxes on high-calorie foods. Despite meeting strong resistance, President Enrique Peña Nieto (2012–2018) gained approval for most of his original proposal. Taxes increased less than projected in 2014, but rose sharply in 2015, just as oil prices were plunging worldwide.

The 2018 election brought a seemingly important political change, as the PAN and PRI were defeated by the National Regeneration Movement (Movimiento Regeneración Nacional, MORENA), the electoral instrument of charismatic populist Andrés Manuel López Obrador, a former mayor of Mexico City. However, as of this writing López Obrador seems unlikely to significantly affect tax policy, since he has repeatedly promised, both during and after the election campaign, not to raise taxes.[14]

4.3.2 Neoliberal Transition and Reinforced Anti-Statism

Preceding sections of this chapter have underscored the role of a cohesive anti-statist bloc in establishing and maintaining light taxation in Mexico. Economic and political changes during the 1980s and 1990s would strengthen it further. While a new leftist party did arise in the late 1980s, the net effect of the changes of this period was to exacerbate the already marked power imbalance in favor

---

[14] *Milenio*, December 15, 2018.

of anti-statist actors. This transformation responded to new stimuli, but its direction was largely determined by preexisting power relations.

Mexico entered the 1980s with a well-organized private sector, fruit of the repeated confrontations with the state discussed earlier. Another such battle near the outset of the decade reinforced that structure by extending it more decisively into the electoral arena. The conflict in question involved López Portillo's 1982 decision to nationalize Mexico's banks. This move was a response to a massive capital outflow prompted by rising interest rates and falling export prices, which cast doubt on the sustainability of the fixed exchange rate. While the president had worked assiduously in previous years to mend relations between the state and the private sector, his bank takeover was viewed by the latter as a virtual declaration of war and additional evidence of the PRI's irremediable hostility toward private enterprise (Camp 1989, pp. 132–133). The bank takeover galvanized a major effort by businesspeople to transform the PAN into a legitimate electoral contender capable of countering the PRI's abuses (Loaeza 1987; Mizrahi 2003; Wuhs 2010, 2014).

For decades the PAN, a party founded for the purpose of combatting state control of the economy and defending Catholicism, had played a marginal role in Mexican politics (Loaeza 1987; Moctezuma 1997). While it developed a solid network of activists and supporters in several states and captured some mayoralties and legislative seats at the state and national level, it exercised little real influence (Loaeza 1974). Despite playing a crucial role in its founding, business had not for the most part invested heavily in the party after 1940, probably because an electoral road to political influence seemed both impractical, given the PRI's efficient control of the state, and unnecessary, given its ultimately market-friendly policies.

Business's interest in the PAN had already begun to increase under Echeverría, but it reached a new level after the bank nationalization (Tirado and Luna 1986; Loaeza 1987). From that point on, businesspeople flocked to the party, many of them intent on becoming candidates for public office. The rapidly growing business wing of the PAN, known as *neopanismo*, came disproportionately from northern Mexico and had strong ties to business associations, especially COPARMEX (Ard 2003, p. 99; Loaeza 2003, p. 225). An important figure in this movement was Manuel Clouthier, a commercial farmer and former COPARMEX president, who became the PAN's candidate in the 1988 presidential election. Although Clouthier lost, in the 1990s three other businessmen scored the PAN's first-ever victories in gubernatorial elections and *neopanismo* took control of the party's national committee (Wuhs 2010, p. 116). Moreover, one of those governors, former Coca-Cola executive Fox, would become the party's 2000 presidential candidate. Social conservatives remained a significant force within the party, but defense of business interests took on greater weight.

While the growing influence of *neopanismo* caused conflicts within the PAN (Mizrahi 2003), the private sector's rediscovery of the party during the 1980s no doubt strengthened it greatly as an electoral force by endowing it with material and human resources far beyond what it had previously enjoyed. Drawing on their money, connections, social prestige, and strong motivation to combat what they saw as an overbearing and despotic state, businesspeople transformed the PAN into a competitive national party, thereby extending their influence into the increasingly important electoral arena.

The PAN's rise did not mean that business wholly abandoned the PRI. Through its adoption of neoliberal reforms, the ruling party gradually increased its credibility with important sectors of big business (Heredia 1995; Thacker 2006). Business partnered with the *priísta* state to advance privatization, trade liberalization, and other reforms. The PRI also sought to counter the PAN's grassroots private sector backing by recruiting its own business candidates, and to some extent it succeeded (Heredia 1995, p. 207). Competition for its support between the two parties contributed to the private sector's growing political influence, since it now enjoyed both its own partisan vehicle and a greater voice within the PRI.

Both the starting point and the direction of change in the labor movement were essentially the opposite of business. Although some more structurally powerful unions had maintained a certain autonomy, decades of manipulation and selective repression had resulted in a movement that was fragmented and depoliticized (Bizberg 1990; De la Garza 2014). Many unions, especially those affiliated with the pro-government CTM, were led by people whose power stemmed from clientelistic ties to the state rather than grassroots support. Union leaders were bought off with the promise of legislative and bureaucratic positions and opportunities for personal enrichment. In return, they gave up the right to mobilize their members to collectively challenge the status quo. Labor was an important pillar of the PRI system, but it was incorporated in a subservient way. Isolated in the countryside and dependent on state subsidies, peasants were even weaker. While Echeverría had changed this relationship to popular sectors to some extent, tolerating greater pluralism and dissent, the system nevertheless remained largely intact after his *sexenio* (Collier and Collier 1991, p. 603).

The PRI's adoption of neoliberal reform beginning under de la Madrid both reflected the preexisting weakness of unions and aggravated it by undermining the structural bases of union organization. Or, to put it another way, labor's initial weakness begot even more weakness. The subjugation of the key unions to the ruling party helped PRI presidents purchase labor's acquiescence to state-reducing reforms at a relatively low price in terms of concessions (Burgess 1999). While the labor code was not significantly changed, other reforms, especially privatization and trade liberalization, undercut union density by precipitating the elimination, contraction, or rationalization of firms that had previously had large unionized workforces (Bensusán and Middlebrook 2012). Estimates of the change in unionization rates vary, but all show a sharp decline during the 1980s and 1990s.[15] Thus, Mexico went from having a solidly organized (by regional standards) but politically rather passive labor movement to having one that was both passive and weakly organized.

One bright spot for statists was the rise of a significant left party, the Party of the Democratic Revolution (Partido de la Revolución Democrática, PRD). The PRD was formed mainly by left-leaning PRI members disillusioned by the party's neoliberal turn and activists from a variety of social movements (Bruhn 1996). It arose in the wake of the 1988 presidential election, in which the independent candidacy of Cuauhtémoc Cárdenas, Lázaro's son and a dissident PRI leader, was foiled by massive fraud. Despite facing considerable repression, the PRD managed to achieve important victories in the 1990s, the highlight being the 1997 midterm elections, in which it won a quarter of the legislative vote, as well as the Mexico City mayoralty. However, as argued later, the party's lack of a solid labor base would contribute to its subsequent inability to go beyond its 1997 achievements.

4.3.3   Anti-Statist Predominance in the New Democracy

Largely as a result of the legacies described earlier, anti-statist forces have thus far exerted a predominant influence in Mexico's democracy. In the electoral arena, while much of Latin America shifted leftward during the 2000s, Mexico chose two consecutive presidents of the rightist PAN (Fox and Calderón), which thus controlled the executive for a dozen years. From 2012 to 2018, the presidency was held by Enrique Peña Nieto of the PRI, which by then had settled into a role as the major centrist party. While the PRD's López Obrador came close to winning the presidency in 2006, he ultimately lost to Calderón. It was only in December 2018 that he would become president, as candidate of the PRD splinter MORENA.

The PAN has been less successful than the PRI in legislative elections, but it has outperformed the PRD. Between 1997 and 2018, the PRI held on average about 40 percent of the seats in both chambers and the PAN about 30 percent (see Table 4.1). The PRD was the third major party, but its average share of legislative seats was much lower (17 percent). The fourth largest party, the Green Environmentalist Party of Mexico (Partido Verde Ecologista de Mexico, PVEM), is a rather conservative grouping motivated mainly by patronage. It allied itself with the PAN under Fox and with the PRI thereafter. The PT is a leftist party that has often allied itself with the PRD in presidential elections. Since neither the PAN nor the PRI ever had a legislative majority of their own, their governments depended on the support of other parties (Table 4.1).

The superiority of anti-statist forces is harder to assess precisely outside the electoral realm, but it is most likely even greater. Mexico's private sector is

---

[15] For example, one source reports that the share of unionized workers in the EAP dropped from 16.3 to 9.7 percent between 1978 and 2005 (Bensusán and Middlebrook 2012, p. 807).

TABLE 4.1 *Distribution of seats in the Mexican Congress by election and chamber, 1997–2018 (percentages)*

Party	1997		2000		2003	2006		2009	2012		2015	Average	
	COD	Sen	COD	Sen	COD	COD	Sen	COD	COD	Sen	COD	COD	Sen
PRI	47.8	60.2	42.2	46.9	45	20.8	25.8	47.4	42.4	42.2	40.6	40.9	43.8
PAN	24.2	25.8	41.2	35.9	30.4	41.2	40.6	28.6	22.8	29.7	21.8	30.0	33.0
PRD	25	12.5	10	12.5	19.2	25.2	22.7	14.2	20.8	17.2	12.2	18.1	16.2
PVEM	1.6	0.8	3.4	3.9	3.4	3.8	4.7	4.2	5.8	5.5	9.4	4.5	3.7
PT	1.4	0.8	1.6	0	1	3.2	1.6	2.6	3	3.9	0	1.9	1.6
Others	0	0	1.6	0.7	1	5.8	4.7	3	5.2	1.6	16	3.7	1.8

Source: Instituto Nacional Electoral (www.ine.mx/voto-y-elecciones/resultados-electorales/)
Note: "COD" refers to the Chamber of Deputies and "Sen" to the Senate.

among the most broadly organized in the region, with a single peak association (the CCE), to which all other major organizations are voluntarily affiliated (Schneider 2002, 2004). Although there are disagreements among associations, at least in recent decades these have not been strong or protracted enough to undermine the CCE's image as the public voice of Mexican business. As an official of this organization explained, "When the private sector wants to officialize something and exert pressure as a sector, it's the CCE that does it" (CCE and CMN 2014, interview). Other multisectoral entities, especially the CMN (formerly CMHN) and COPARMEX, both of which belong to the CCE, also continue to enjoy important roles, the first as a private interlocutor with top officials and the second as an aggressive watchdog against state intervention.[16] Thus, despite the greater regional and sectoral diversity of the Mexican economy, the private sector boasts an associative structure just as centralized as Chile's.

As in Chile, the adhesive that holds together Mexico's voluntary peak associations is a normative commitment to protecting free enterprise against state efforts to control or exploit it. Although there have been no business-state conflicts in recent decades as intense as the ones under Echeverría and López Portillo, the CCE, COPARMEX, and other organizations have expressed strong criticisms of some policies, including attempts to raise taxes. One reflection of the CCE's generally anti-statist orientation is the fact that three of its seven presidents since 2000 were formerly presidents of COPARMEX, still the most outspokenly anti-statist of the major associations. None of the other organizations has contributed more than one. In contrast, CANACINTRA, historically the most statist association, now has observer status in the CCE but still lacks voting rights (Luna and Tirado 1992).[17]

Both business associations and individual firms have increasingly invested their resources in lobbying and electioneering, reflecting Mexico's more democratic context (Gómez Valle 2008; Thacker 2012; Elizondo Mayer-Serra 2014). While it is hard to gauge the impact of these activities, there are indications that business support played a significant role in both of the PAN's presidential election victories. Mexican law provides for generous and relatively equitable public campaign funding and substantially limits private donations, but wealthy contributors have found ways to skirt these limitations. During the 2000 presidential race, an organization called "Friends of Fox" acted as a virtual parallel party to the PAN, effectively funneling millions of dollars into Vicente Fox's campaign (Tejeda 2005). In the closing weeks of the

[16] In recent decades, some individual businessmen have become significant political actors by accumulating unprecedented wealth, in part by taking advantage of privatization to acquire state assets. The paradigmatic example is Carlos Slim, widely considered to be among the world's richest people. While his economic power gives Slim an influential voice independent of the associations, the latter remain formidable forces (Wuhs 2010; Thacker 2012).
[17] It is formally represented by CONCAMIN, which does have voting rights, but in practice the latter mainly expresses the interests of larger manufacturers (Thacker 2006, pp. 147–148).

2006 election, the CCE sponsored a series of television advertisements that, without referring explicitly to López Obrador, reinforced the PAN's attempts to paint the PRD candidate as a dangerous radical (Gutiérrez 2007, pp. 46–54). In both cases, electoral authorities found that the law had been violated. The PAN was fined after the 2000 elections and the CCE ads were eventually taken off the air. In both instances, however, the tactics may well have affected the outcome.

Mexico's rightist think tanks are not as developed as Chile's, but some major business associations have strong research capabilities, including the CCE. In addition, the anti-statist cause benefits from the existence of highly prestigious private universities, especially the Autonomous Technical Institute of Mexico (Instituto Tecnológico Autónomo de México, ITAM) and the Institute of Technology and Higher Studies of Monterrey (Instituto Tecnológico y de Estudios Superiores de Monterrey, or Tec de Monterrey), whose teaching and research tends to support market-oriented policies. This is no lucky coincidence, since both were founded by business interests in the 1940s as an alternative to what they perceived to be the leftism of state universities (Babb 2001, pp. 70–71; Romero Sotelo 2011, pp. 35–37).

In contrast to business, Mexican labor has, if anything, grown even weaker. While it seemed reasonable to believe that the end of PRI hegemony would encourage a more autonomous and militant brand of unionism, that has not occurred (Bensusán and Middlebrook 2012). Strikes have been rare and the problem of "ghost unions" (ones formed without workers' knowledge simply to satisfy labor law) has reportedly grown. One scholar argues that the very meaning of unionism has been "inverted," with "union leaders defending the interests of the employers and the government before the workers, rather than the other way around" (Bensusán 2016, p. 144). Even the more independent unions, which had seemed to gain strength in the late 1990s, have lost momentum and political cohesion (De la Garza 2014, p. 230). While national organizations like the CTM and the Congress of Labor (Congreso del Trabajo, CT) continue to nominally represent substantial numbers of workers, they have little influence over national policies (De la Garza 2014; 2014 interviews: Alonso, Salinas).

Perhaps the biggest exception to the rule of union weakness is public-school teachers, represented nationally mainly by the National Union of Education Workers (Sindicato Nacional de Trabajadores de la Educación, SNTE). With more than a million members, the SNTE has unusual capacity to pressure the state. Nevertheless, it has not aggressively pursued benefits for the mass of teachers, let alone a broader agenda of progressive change. Instead, led by the notoriously corrupt Elba Esther Gordillo, it has mainly sought power and material benefit for its leaders, allying itself with the PRI or even the PAN. According to a longtime PRD legislator, "The big unions like the teachers and miners are totally controlled. They're corporatist unions that are tied to state power and use it to control their own people" (Alonso 2014, interview).

Just as business organizations seem to have contributed to the PAN's successes, so the weakness of labor is arguably a factor in the failure of the "pink tide" to wash over Mexico. To be sure, left-leaning parties can win elections even in the absence of solid labor support. However, unions can help by contributing leadership, legitimacy, campaign manpower, and other resources. With so few workers unionized, Mexican labor lacks the numbers needed to influence elections. In addition, the depoliticized character of most unions means that even organized workers tend to have little inclination toward left parties. Opinion polls show that the majority of people in union families either have no party preference or support non-left parties, most frequently the PRI. In fact, they even favored Calderón over López Obrador in the 2006 election (Bensusán and Middlebrook 2012, pp. 808–809).[18]

Within this context, MORENA's impressive victory in the 2018 elections, in which it won the presidency and majorities in both houses of Congress, represents a seemingly major change. However, the depth and character of this transformation remain uncertain. Most analyses seem to interpret MORENA's victory as a protest vote against the criminal violence that has afflicted Mexico in recent decades and the traditional parties' failure to effectively address it, rather than as a reflection of an ideological shift in the electorate.[19] In addition, despite his at times inflammatory populist rhetoric, López Obrador has demonstrated considerable pragmatism in dealing with business, including repeated promises not to raise the tax burden.[20]

4.3.4 Limiting Tax Reform

The superiority of anti-statist forces in democratic Mexico has worked against revenue-raising reform by shaping both the character of reform proposals put forward by authorities and their subsequent revision and implementation.

Before elaborating on that argument, it would be useful to touch on two competing explanations advanced recently by scholars. One is that taxation has been limited by the public's low opinion of the efficiency and honesty of the state, which makes them unwilling to pay higher taxes (Elizondo Mayer-Serra 2014; Flores-Macías 2018). In some ways, this argument rings true. Official corruption is undoubtedly a problem and its salience appears to have increased over time. In Transparency International's Corruption Perceptions Index (based on surveys of the public and business), Mexico generally ranks in the bottom third of Latin American countries.[21] Public opinion data also show that large majorities of Mexicans believe taxes are already high and have opposed

---

[18] The leader of the major independent labor federation, the National Union of Workers (Unión Nacional de Trabajadores, UNT), who once served as a PRD legislator, said the party did not even have close relations with independent unions (Hernández 2014, interview).

[19] *BBC News*, June 2, 2018.   [20] *Milenio*, June 5 and December 15, 2018.

[21] The data can be accessed at www.transparency.org/.

recent efforts to increase them (Elizondo Mayer-Serra 2014). Businesspeople interviewed for this book assailed the "low quality of public spending" and argued that taxation should not increase until spending improves (2014 interviews: CMN, Nuñez, Paredes).

Nevertheless, this is not a convincing explanation of Mexico's failure to increase taxes as much as Argentina and Brazil in recent decades. For one thing, there is no clear relationship between corruption perceptions and revenue increases among these countries. Argentina, where taxation has risen very sharply since the early 2000s, scores almost as poorly as Mexico on the Corruption Perceptions Index.[22] Meanwhile Chile, the only country with notably better scores, has maintained a light tax burden. In addition, the impact of corruption perceptions on tax revenues is usually held to operate largely through evasion, but, as noted in Chapter 2, Mexican compliance levels are no worse than Argentina's or Brazil's.

Another argument emphasizes the impact of judicial challenges to taxation using an instrument called *amparo fiscal* (or, roughly, "fiscal injunction") (Elizondo Mayer-Serra 2009, 2014). In Mexico taxpayers can file suit to impugn the legality of specific provisions of the tax code, based on a constitutional article stating that taxes should be "proportional and equitable." If a court grants an *amparo*, the petitioner is not only spared having to pay the tax in the future but also entitled to a refund of past payments.[23] The *amparo* stems from a judicial decision of the 1960s but came into common use in the 1990s (Elizondo Mayer-Serra 2009). Between 1996 and 2007 more than 180,000 *amparo* petitions were filed. The highest success rates were registered during the 2002–2004 period, when 50.8 percent were granted (Elizondo Mayer-Serra 2009, p. 367). There can be little doubt that the *amparo* has been a thorn in the side of fiscal authorities. However, its impact on revenues has not been very large. Even during the height of *amparo* victories in 2002–2004, the federal government was only forced to return 1.9 percent of the tax take, equivalent to less than 0.2 percent of GDP.[24] Moreover, between 2005 and 2007, the success rate dropped to only 17.4 percent (Elizondo Mayer-Serra 2009, p. 367). Data for more recent years are unavailable, but tax lawyers complain that winning an *amparo* has become rare (2014 interviews: Pérez, Real, Revilla).[25]

---

[22] The average scores between 2012 and 2016 were Chile, 70.4; Brazil 41.2; Argentina 34.2; and Mexico 32.8. A higher score indicates less perceived corruption.
[23] The judgment applies only to the party bringing the suit. However, after the courts have granted *amparos* on a particular aspect of the tax code five times, subsequent petitions are automatically granted. Those later *amparos* do not entitle the petitioner to a refund but grant protection from future payments (Elizondo Mayer-Serra 2009, p. 354).
[24] These figures were calculated based on data from Elizondo Mayer-Serra (2009), p. 367.
[25] While lawyers attribute this change to executive branch pressures on the judiciary, Elizondo traces it to a combination of greater state experience litigating these claims and greater judicial sensitivity to their fiscal impact (Elizondo Mayer-Serra 2014, p. 17).

Rather, the major cause of slow tax burden growth should be sought in the power imbalance between anti-statist forces and those favoring an activist state. One aspect of this imbalance is that the rightist PAN controlled the presidency from 2000 to 2012 and was then replaced by the centrist PRI, rather than a leftist force. All three presidents proposed revenue-raising reforms, but, especially under the PAN, these reforms were half-hearted and did not form part of an effort to build a larger, more activist state.

It is true, as scholars have pointed out, that the two PAN governments expanded social programs and sought to increase taxation (Romero Sotelo 2015; Fairfield and Garay 2017). In that sense, they resembled many left-leaning governments in Latin America during the same period. Yet, their efforts in both senses were comparatively limited, reflecting the party's underlying preference for small government and strong ties to a conservative business community. With regard to spending, Fox expanded an existing conditional cash transfer program and founded a health insurance program for the uninsured, while his successor created a pension program for the elderly poor. However, in all three areas, the allocation of fiscal resources and the extent of coverage were more limited than in countries like Argentina and Brazil, where they were undertaken mainly by left-leaning governments (Garay 2016; Borges 2018; Ponce de León 2018). For example, circa 2010 cash transfer programs reached about three-quarters of the informal sector poor in Argentina and Brazil, but less than 40 percent in Mexico (Garay 2016, p. 3). A similar gap existed for non-contributory pensions. Total spending on programs targeted at the poor was 2.4 percent of GDP in Brazil and 1.7 percent in Argentina, but only 0.7 percent in Mexico (World Bank 2015, Appendix D).

The PAN governments' efforts to raise taxes were equally modest, as well as less successful. At the beginning of his term, Fox proposed a reform whose core component was the extension of the VAT to previously exempt goods, including food and medicine (Pastor and Wise 2005). This measure would likely have generated less than 1.5 percent of GDP in revenue, so it would not have changed Mexico's status as a very lightly taxed country.[26] Furthermore, the patently regressive character of this narrowly based proposal left the government vulnerable to accusations of disregarding the interests of ordinary Mexicans. Fox promised that increased social spending would more than compensate for the reform's distributive effects, but this claim was not convincing, given the Mexican state's historic neglect of social problems and the PAN's conservative, pro-business ideology. Criticism soon began to mount. PRD legislators rejected the bill from the beginning. The PRI leadership initially pledged to support it but

---

[26] Ramírez Cedillo (2013) estimates an increase of 1.3 percent of GDP in revenue from extending the general VAT rate (p. 92) to excluded goods and cites a 2010 official estimate of 1.1 percent (p. 89).

later got cold feet, ensuring its demise (2014 interviews: Madero, Molinar Horcasitas). A later effort to revive this proposal suffered a similar fate.

Calderón was somewhat more successful in gaining legislative approval of his tax reforms, but his proposals were also modest. Having witnessed the debacle of VAT reform under Fox, Calderón focused his initial effort on direct taxes, including what was initially conceived of as a version of the "flat" tax championed by US conservatives (2014 interviews: Becerra and Sánchez).[27] However, his direct tax reform proposals had limited revenue-raising potential because they relied nearly exclusively on reducing avoidance and evasion, and eliminated the earlier corporate asset tax introduced by Salinas for the same purpose. In 2009, Calderón proposed additional tax increases, including a new 2 percent consumption tax, a small increase in the corporate income tax, and changes to the "fiscal consolidation" regime, which provides advantages to large holding companies. However, these were essentially emergency measures in the face of the 2008–2009 global financial crisis, which hit Mexico hard and undercut fiscal revenues (Madero 2014, interview). A diluted version was approved, which merely served to stabilize revenues.

Testifying to the importance of party ideology is the fact that the centrist PRI government proposed the most significant tax reform of the democratic period and passed it in alliance with a majority sector of the leftist PRD. Peña Nieto maneuvered early in his term to craft a loose coalition with both the PAN and PRD that would enable him to pass a series of major reforms despite the PRI's lack of a legislative majority. Within this scheme, the key incentive for the PAN was a liberalization of the oil sector to allow private investment, while the main reward for the PRD was a tax reform that would both exclude the regressive generalization of the VAT and include greater income taxation (2014 interviews: Madero, Delgado, Penchyna). The tax reform was by no means altogether progressive, since its major features included excise taxes on soft drinks and junk food, as well as a higher VAT rate in border areas, but it had enough progressive elements to satisfy a pragmatic sector of the PRD that agreed that the state needed greater fiscal resources (2014 interviews: Alonso, Salinas).

In contrast to earlier periods, since 2000 business protest has not been the most important factor impeding tax increases, mainly because the PAN held the presidency for much of this time. However, private sector resistance has served to limit the scope and impact of reform. Under Calderón business opposition diluted both the alternative minimum income tax and the changes in the consolidation regime proposed to deal with the 2008–2009 crisis (2014 interviews: Becerra, Foncerrada, Molinar). In fact, disagreement over the latter occasioned an acrimonious dispute between business leaders

---

[27] This tax would eventually morph into a minimum income tax whose effects were roughly similar to the existing corporate asset tax it replaced.

and the PAN president. The CCE launched a media campaign arguing that the government should rationalize spending, reduce corruption, and crack down on informality before asking "captive" formal sector taxpayers to contribute more (Consejo Coordinador Empresarial 2010, pp. 18–19). In response, a clearly frustrated Calderón publicly accused big business of "rarely paying taxes."[28] Nevertheless, his proposed consolidation reform was duly watered down.[29]

Although Peña Nieto ultimately succeeded in passing a tax reform, business opposition seems to have limited its impact to some extent. The government had initially proposed a package that would raise 1.4 percent of GDP the first year and 3.0 percent by 2018. However, changes made during the legislative process reduced those projections to 1.0 and 2.5 percent, respectively (SHCP1 2014, interview). A senior SHCP official suggested that pressures from business played a role in these alterations (SHCP1 2014, interview). Private sector protest against the reform was intense (2014 interviews: CCE and CMN, Paredes; Ondetti 2017, p. 26) and was echoed by the PAN, which voted as a bloc against it. Soon after the bill's introduction, both the CCE and COPARMEX released studies or statements lambasting it as unfair and anti-growth. During the two months the bill transited through Congress, the presidents of both groups were frequently quoted in the media making disapproving statements about it. Business anger was such that barely a month after its approval the president issued decrees temporarily softening aspects of it (Unda 2015). In 2014, moreover, the Secretary of Finance made a public pledge, clearly directed at business, not to raise taxes again during Peña Nieto's *sexenio* (Foncerrada 2014, interview).

That taxation has increased in Mexico since the 2013 reform is due not only to the reform but also, probably just as importantly, to the sharp drop in oil prices beginning in the second half of 2014, which deeply undercut revenues.[30] Scholars have noted in the past that Mexico's tax burden has tended to vary inversely with oil revenue, thus keeping fiscal resources relatively constant (Martinez-Vazquez 2001). This has been interpreted as a response to the private sector, which is willing to countenance increasing taxation when necessary for fiscal stability but resists a long-term increase in the tax burden (Moreno 2014, interview). Consistent with this perspective, in recent years fiscal experts have noted tougher enforcement of the tax code by the federal Tax Administration Service (Servicio de Administración Tributaria, SAT), which they interpret as an attempt to compensate for falling oil revenues and

---

[28] Proceso.com.mx, October 29, 2009.   [29] *La Jornada*, November 13, 2009.
[30] The price of crude oil dropped by more than 70 percent between May 2014 and February 2016 and has remained well below the levels of the 2000s commodity boom (https://tradingeconomics .com/commodity/crude-oil). Fiscal revenues from PEMEX fell from 8.4 percent of GDP in 2013 to only 4.1 percent in 2016 (CEPALSTAT).

avoid a destabilizing fiscal deficit.[31] Thus, the robust increase in taxation in recent years should not be interpreted as reflecting a major change in the political dynamics underpinning tax policy, but rather as a reaction to a steep fall in resource revenues after a long stretch of high oil prices, which had allowed a moderate increase in spending.

4.4 CONCLUSION

This chapter has argued that the causes of Mexico's light contemporary taxation are in crucial respects similar to the ones highlighted in the case of Chile. In both countries, this outcome was an unintentional, path-dependent result of an earlier redistributive reform wave that deeply threatened private property and thus gave rise to an enduring anti-statist coalition that has hindered public sector expansion. This coalition, rooted in a combination of interest groups, parties, and intellectual institutions, has thwarted revenue-raising tax reform both directly, by obstructing such proposals, and indirectly, by inhibiting policies that encourage worker organization and political mobilization.

In the Mexican case, the key episode in triggering the anti-statist backlash was the reform wave launched by Lázaro Cárdenas, who expropriated millions of hectares of farmland and the powerful oil industry in a context of widespread worker and peasant mobilization. Consistent with the discussion of path dependence in Chapter 2, this episode was the product of contingent decisions taken within a structural context broadly favorable to property rights change. Certain critical antecedents, including a large, foreign-controlled extractive sector and an agrarian structure vulnerable to conflict between peasants and large landowners, favored reform. However, the emergence of a broad threat to property was not foreordained. Cárdenas could easily have taken a more moderate approach. In fact, his bold reformism and his victory over *callismo* took many observers by surprise, including, reportedly, Calles himself (Medin 1971, p. 15). Of course, had his achievements been more modest, political space might have remained open for a later president to raise the banner of reform. However, it is by no means obvious that such a turn of events would have resulted in changes of the same magnitude. Other outcomes were certainly possible.

While their occurrence was not predetermined, once implemented the Cárdenas reforms provoked reactions that strengthened anti-statism in an enduring, self-reinforcing way. Their experiences during this period alienated many elites from the state, leading them to develop a mistrustful attitude toward it that became embedded in such actors as the Monterrey Group, COPARMEX and the PAN. The reflexive anti-statism of these groups caused later attempts at public sector expansion, even mild ones, to be interpreted as acute threats to

---

[31] *El Economista*, August 8, 2018.

private enterprise and thus to spur intense mobilizations that both thwarted them and resulted in further organization building in the form of the CMN and CCE, as well as the post-1982 revitalization of the PAN. Organized labor, once a strong actor, was steadily weakened by official practices that, bowing to anti-statist influence, sought to divide and demobilize it. By the time Mexico democratized in the 1990s, the power balance had swung so decisively toward anti-statism that regime change had little impact on the tax burden.

5

Brazil

Moderate Statism and Public Sector Expansion

In recent decades, Brazilian businesspeople and technocrats have often complained about the *custo Brasil*, or "Brazil cost," a concept that expresses the burden that a vast, complex state apparatus and faulty infrastructure place on private businesses. In response, authorities have taken some measures since the mid-2000s to contain tax burden growth, causing revenues to stabilize relative to GDP. Nevertheless, Brazil today remains far more heavily taxed than Chile or Mexico. This chapter attempts to explain why.

One reason Brazil's tax burden is greater than Mexico's is that the state does not receive as large an influx of nontax natural resource revenue. However, as discussed in earlier chapters, this difference falls well short of explaining the vast gap in tax burdens between the two countries. In addition, nontax revenues certainly cannot explain the gap in taxation between Brazil and Chile, given that such revenues are much more modest in Chile than Mexico.

Contemporary analyses of Brazil's tax system tend to emphasize a different theme: the impact of the constitution ratified in 1988, less than three years after civilians retook control of the state (Afonso and Serra 2007; Melo et al. 2010; Afonso 2013). That document saddled the public sector with major new social spending commitments that forced authorities to seek greater revenue. While it raises a legitimate point, this argument cannot account for the fact that Brazil was already the most heavily taxed country in Latin America even before 1988. Nor can it explain why the constitution was so manifestly statist, or why the more than 100 amendments to it have only substantially affected its spending provisions very recently.

The central point of this chapter is that Brazil's heavier tax burden relative to Chile and Mexico must be understood in terms of how historical events have shaped the relative influence of statist and anti-statist actors. In Chile and Mexico, as discussed in previous chapters, episodes of redistributive reform that deeply menaced private property turned economic elites against the state, giving rise to powerful anti-statist actors that subsequently checked tax burden growth by fighting policies that would expand the public sector and by seeking to weaken proponents of such an expansion.

In Brazil, in contrast, elites have faced no comparable threat. Leftist forces have taken power on occasion, but they lacked the will or capacity to implement major reforms. As a result, economic elites have not come to view state expansion as particularly alarming and have not organized intensively to thwart it. Neither encompassing business associations, nor programmatic rightist parties, nor anti-statist research institutions have flourished to the extent they have in Mexico and Chile. Authorities have thus felt relatively free to increase taxes in order to fund existing programs or introduce new ones. In addition, Brazil's relatively state-led development pattern has provided more fertile ground for organized labor to expand and wield influence, aggravating the relative weakness of anti-statist forces. The origins, provisions, and amendment trajectory of the 1988 constitution must be understood within this broader context of statist predominance.

Admittedly, calls to limit taxation have taken on greater force recently, due in part to the unprecedented level the tax burden had reached by the early 2000s, which easily exceeded that of any other Latin American country. The corruption and poor fiscal management of the center-left governments that controlled the presidency from 2003 to 2016 reinforced this trend by providing ammunition for anti-statist assaults. Nevertheless, despite the election of a rightwing president in 2018, it is still not clear that an anti-statist bloc has emerged capable of reversing Brazil's longstanding inclination toward a large public sector.

Given that the argument of this case study emphasizes events that *did not* occur, this chapter is organized somewhat differently from the previous two. The first and second sections each examine a political conjuncture roughly analogous to the ones that put Mexico and Chile, respectively, on paths of light taxation. Specifically, the first focuses on the presidencies of Getúlio Vargas (1930–1945 and 1951–1954), who is often grouped with Cárdenas as one of Latin America's pioneering "populist" leaders, while the second looks at the presidency of João Goulart (1961–1964), who, like Salvador Allende, was widely seen as a leftist and fell victim to a military coup. Each attempts to explain why the episode in question did not give rise to a lasting anti-statist bloc capable of impeding increased taxation. The third section returns to the pattern of earlier chapters by attempting to explain the larger increase in taxation since democratization compared to Chile and Mexico.

5.1 VARGAS AND STATE EXPANSION WITHOUT REDISTRIBUTIVE CONFLICT

An intuitive approach to understanding the roots of a tax system that raises large amounts of revenue would be to focus on periods in which taxation leapt to a higher level. However, the relatively continuous character of tax burden growth in Brazil renders this approach impractical. To be sure, there have been moments of especially rapid expansion. However, there are also periods in which taxation increased steadily over an extended period, resulting in a substantial aggregate rise. Thus, the approach adopted here to comparing Brazil to Chile and Mexico is to focus on those moments in the latter two countries in which a pattern of increasing taxation gave way to one of decline or long-term stagnation and to ask why similar phenomena did not occur in Brazil. Specifically, this section attempts to understand why the Vargas period did not have an effect analogous to that of the Cárdenas presidency, to which it is often compared.

Chapter 4 argued that Cárdenas played a crucial role in establishing Mexico's low-tax trajectory by strengthening anti-statism as a political force. At least on the surface, there are reasons to believe Vargas would have had a similar effect. Both are often viewed as key early examples of Latin American "populism," since they extended new state benefits to working-class people and rhetorically recognized the importance of workers to the nation (Ianni 1973; Conniff 1999). However, neither the first nor the second Vargas presidency was followed by sustained tax burden stagnation or decline. How can we explain this difference?

The argument elaborated here is that the populist label hides crucial differences in how these leaders governed, differences that would have major implications for politics and tax policy far into the future. While Cárdenas advanced reforms that mobilized workers and seemed at times to threaten basic components of the capitalist system, especially property rights, Vargas did not. The latter extended state intervention into many areas but expropriated little property. He also positioned himself clearly as anti-communist and generally discouraged worker engagement in strikes and protests. As a result, he did not engender a strong, sustained counterreaction from economic elites or social conservatives. The lack of a powerful anti-statist political current in Brazil meant that the expansion of the state could occur, both during and after Vargas' periods in government, with relatively little resistance.

5.1.1 State-Led Development and Sustained Tax Burden Growth

In Mexico, as argued previously, a pattern of relatively steady tax burden growth since the revolution was transformed into one of protracted stagnation following the end of the Cárdenas presidency in 1940. Brazil, in contrast, saw no such trend in the wake of either of Vargas' two periods in power. Rather, taxation grew robustly during and after both periods as part of a broader expansion of the public sector. The tax burden did dip somewhat during the late 1950s and early 1960s, but that trend reflected macroeconomic conditions, rather than tax cuts, and was soon decisively reversed.

Brazil's early tax system development resembles those of Chile and Mexico in that an initial dependence on trade taxes was gradually reduced, due at least in

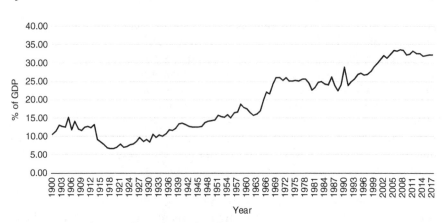

FIGURE 5.1 Evolution of Brazil's tax burden, 1900–2017
Sources: CEPALSTAT/ECLAC; IBGE Estatísticas do Século XX

part to external shocks. In Brazil, as in Chile, relative political stability during the nineteenth century facilitated the construction of a substantial state apparatus.[1] Between 1900 and 1914, tax revenues averaged 12.6 percent of GDP. Problems with GDP estimates make this figure a rough approximation,[2] but Brazil may well have had the heaviest tax burden in Latin America at the time. However, the country's tax system was at least as dependent on trade levies as Chile's (Bowman and Wallerstein 1982, p. 444) so the disruption caused by World War I devastated it. As Figure 5.1 suggests, by 1917 the tax burden had fallen by almost half. To address this vulnerability, Congress approved both a sales tax and an income tax in the early 1920s (Varsano 1996, pp. 2–3). By 1929, the share of import taxes in federal revenues had fallen from as high as 70 percent prior to the war to 46.7 percent (Estatísticas do Século XX). Although revenues rebounded during the 1920s, Brazil's tax burdens during that decade were similar to those of Chile and Mexico, at 7–9 percent of GDP (Estatísticas do Século XX).

Thus, the tax system Vargas would inherit in 1930 was in the midst of a transition from external to domestic sources of revenue. In other respects, however, there was more continuity. In particular, the system retained the decentralized character it had had since at least the 1890s. While the postindependence monarchical regime had been relatively centralized in political and fiscal terms, the republic established in 1889 endowed state

---

[1] After achieving independence peacefully in 1822, Brazil was ruled by an offshoot of the Portuguese monarchy until the establishment of a republic in 1889.

[2] Official GDP estimates were not available until 1947 and there is a debate about the accuracy of unofficial estimates, especially prior to 1920 (Abreu 2006; Tombolo and Sampaio 2013, p. 185). It is possible that GDP is underestimated for all or part of this period, in which case the tax burden would be overestimated.

governments with additional powers and revenue sources (Oliveira 2010, pp. 8–12). The distribution of revenues between national and subnational sources changed little in subsequent decades. Just as they had at the turn of the century, in 1929 federal tax revenues made up about two-thirds of the total, with state governments accounting for essentially all subnational revenues, since municipalities did not yet enjoy tax authority (Estatísticas do Século XX).

During Vargas' first period in power (1930–1945), the trend toward increased domestic taxation was deepened (Oliveira 2010, pp. 17–25; Schneider 2019, p. 125). Limits were placed on export taxation, a previously substantial source of state government revenue, and new domestic levies were created, including a federal fuels tax and (as in Mexico) an excess profits tax. To compensate for restrictions on export taxation, state governments were granted the authority to impose a broad-based Tax on Sales and Consignments (Imposto sobre Vendas e Consignaçoes, IVC). The 1934 constitution granted municipalities the authority to impose certain taxes, including property taxes. Construction of a social security system, which had begun tentatively in the 1920s, also intensified, creating an additional flow of domestic revenue (Malloy 1979). By 1945, the year Vargas was deposed, import taxes accounted for only 19.9 percent of total federal tax revenues (not including social security), less than half their 1920 level (Estatísticas do Século XX).

Because trade taxes were replaced to some extent with direct ones, the tax system probably became somewhat more progressive. The income tax, whose revenues grew especially rapidly in the early 1940s, contributed 31.3 percent of federal tax revenues, while revenues from indirect taxes, including import levies, made up the remaining 69.7 percent.[3] Overall, direct taxes contributed roughly a fifth of total tax revenues, about twice their share in 1920 (IBGE Estatísticas do Século XX).[4] The tax burden, which had stood at 9.2 percent of GDP in 1929, had risen to 12.6 percent by 1945. What did not change much was the distribution of revenues between national and subnational spheres. Municipalities augmented their share from 0 in 1935 to 7.8 percent in 1945, but some of that growth came at the expense of the states. The central government's share in 1945 (67.0 percent) was similar to its share in 1929 (65.8 percent).

Changes in the tax system occurred as part of a more general expansion of the public sector under Vargas, who came to power in 1930 via a military coup, foiling the attempts of São Paulo, the most powerful state, to retain control of the presidency through alleged electoral fraud. Mainly during his dictatorial *Estado Novo* (or "New State") regime (1937–1945), Vargas put in place the

---

[3] Precise breakdowns of subnational tax sources are unavailable for this period, but it is likely that the share of revenue from export taxes fell substantially, given the limitations imposed on them and the creation of the IVC.

[4] It is hard to determine their exact contribution due to the limitations of available tax data, including the lack of precise breakdowns for the subnational level.

rudiments of what would later become a systematic pro-industrialization policy, including state production of crucial inputs (e.g., steel) and subsidized credit (Villela and Suzigan 1973; Fonseca 2011). He also created new development-related agencies and took steps to professionalize the bureaucracy. Concerned about the destabilizing potential of urban social unrest, he extended the social security system and erected a corporatist system of labor relations (Erickson 1977; Malloy 1979).

The *Estado Novo* eventually fell victim to pressures for democratization at the end of World War II. Vargas was forced by the military to resign, a new constitution was drafted, and elections were held, resulting in a relatively democratic regime that would last until 1964.[5] Nevertheless, under the post-*Estado Novo* governments, including Vargas' own stint as an elected president from 1951 until his death in 1954, both taxation and the broader public sector generally continued to expand steadily, consolidating the state-centered, developmentalist thrust of post-1930 policies.

The domestically based tax system forged between the 1920s and 1945 did not undergo structural changes during the next two decades. Nevertheless, many narrower reforms occurred, including the introduction of a federal tax on electric energy and changes in the rates and bases of certain taxes, especially the indirect ones (Varsano 1996, pp. 5–7; Oliveira 2010, pp. 25–31). State governments made increasing use of the IVC sales tax to boost their revenues, causing the tax system to become somewhat more decentralized. As in Chile during the same period, income taxes gradually lost ground to other, probably more regressive, types of levies. Although federal income tax revenues grew relative to GDP, their share in total tax revenues declined from 15.8 percent in 1947 to 11.3 percent in 1963 (Maneschi 1970, p. 50).

Until the end of the 1950s, the tax burden increased rather consistently, rising by a cumulative total of almost 50 percent between 1945 and 1958 (see Figure 5.1). Under both of the immediate post-Vargas governments, those of Eurico Dutra (1946–1951) and Juscelino Kubitschek (1955–1961), the burden grew significantly. In fact, in this period it only failed to grow during Vargas' own abbreviated (1951–1954) final term.

It is true that the late 1950s and the early 1960s brought a significant decline in taxation. After peaking at 18.7 percent of GDP in 1958, the tax burden declined every year thereafter through 1963, bottoming out at 16.1 percent (Estatísticas do Século XX). However, that trend was not due primarily to tax cuts, but rather to a gradually intensifying economic crisis characterized by high inflation, balance of payments problems, and stagnant growth (Varsano 1996, p. 7). Under the free-spending Kubitschek, public outlays outraced even the robust increases in tax revenue, resulting in a ballooning fiscal deficit financed largely through monetary emissions. Neither Kubitschek nor his successors,

---

[5] Unlike the current regime, Brazil's pre-1964 democracy denied the suffrage to illiterates and (in 1948) banned the Communist Party. It also suffered from periodic military interference.

Jânio Quadros (1961) and Goulart (1961–1964), were able to overcome the resulting inflation, which undermined tax collection through the Olivera–Tanzi effect (Barbosa 2018). Moreover, as discussed later, the tax burden decline of this period would be drastically reversed in the second half of the 1960s through a set of reforms that both stabilized the currency and transformed the tax system.

As it had been during Vargas' first period in power, tax burden growth during the late 1940s and 1950s was part and parcel of a more general public sector expansion. Total public spending continued to rise, increasing from 14.7 percent of GDP in 1945 to 21.5 percent in 1958 and stabilizing at about that level thereafter (Estatísticas do Século XX). Vargas created both the National Bank for Economic Development (Banco Nacional de Desenvolvimento Econômico, BNDE), which would become perhaps Latin America's premier development bank, and the state oil company Brazilian Petroleum (Petróleo Brasileiro, PETROBRAS). His protegé Kubitschek built a new national capital, Brasília, from the ground up and instituted an extensive economic planning system (Sikkink 1991). Both presidents used protectionism, public investment, and subsidies of various sorts to aggressively promote industrialization (Leff 1968). Social security spending also grew gradually as the system encompassed new categories of workers and provided enhanced benefits (Rezende 1972; Malloy 1979).

5.1.2 The Limits of *Varguista* Reformism

The reason why the Vargas presidencies were not followed by tax burden stagnation similar to that of post-Cárdenas Mexico can be found in the content of the Brazilian leader's policies, as well as his ideology and relationship to popular sectors. The Vargas era did bring a series of social and labor reforms that extended new rights to workers in the urban formal sector of the economy. In this sense, it bears a substantial resemblance to the Cárdenas years. However, in a number of other ways, *varguismo* differed profoundly from *cardenismo* and represented a far more conservative version of Latin American populism.

Getúlio Vargas is well known for implementing certain pro-worker reforms, including the expansion and legal consolidation of the social security system (Malloy 1979; Santos 1979). The creation of a contributory social insurance scheme providing pensions, health care, and other benefits had begun in the 1920s, but by 1930 it only effectively encompassed railroad workers (Malloy 1979, p. 40). During the 1930s, Vargas extended the system to most wage workers in the urban formal economy. While it was financed largely from taxes on wages, the system was nevertheless billed as a major advance for workers, enhancing their health, security, and dignity (Malloy 1979, ch. 3; Cardoso 2010). Concurrently, he developed a series of legal and judicial reforms strengthening worker rights with regard to issues such as remuneration, working hours, workplace conditions, and unionization (Erickson 1977). These rights were assembled in 1943 into a general labor code called the "Consolidation of Labor Laws" (Consolidação das Leis do Trabalho, CLT). Because of these reforms, Vargas' period at the helm of the state has been viewed as the key historical moment in the political incorporation of labor (Collier and Collier 1991, pp. 169–195).

Nevertheless, the reforms were far more modest than those implemented by Cárdenas in Mexico. Most importantly, they left property relations untouched. With regard to the countryside, Vargas sometimes talked about the need to improve desperate social conditions, which he feared could lead to a massive exodus to the cities (Ribeiro 2008, ch. 1; Cardoso 2010). However, other than some minor frontier colonization projects on public land, he did virtually nothing to address the issue (Camargo 1986, pp. 170–171). In the nonagricultural sector Vargas, again in sharp contrast to Cárdenas, carried out no major expropriations of private firms. As mentioned earlier, Vargas did establish a number of important SOEs, including PETROBRAS and large mining and steel manufacturing enterprises. However, despite being couched in nationalist rhetoric, these actions did not involve significant expropriation of existing companies (Dinius 2010; Triner 2011).

Perhaps because he was not pressing for radical reform, Vargas did not mobilize workers and peasants to the extent that Cárdenas did, especially during the 1930s and 1940s. While the Cárdenas government's relationship to popular sectors involved a blend of mobilization and control, the ones headed by Vargas were much more tilted toward the latter (Malloy 1979; Collier 1982). His labor reforms supported the unionization of urban workers but discouraged industrial conflict and sought to stem communist influence (Werneck Vianna 1976; Weinstein 1996). Their purpose was mainly to "neutralize labor as a source of support for opposition groups that advocated radical change" and to "depoliticize labor organizations as an autonomous source of group demands" (Malloy 1979, p. 56).

Admittedly, Vargas' time as a democratically elected president from 1951 to 1954 did bring some changes (Weinstein 1996, pp. 280–287). Repression of independent unions declined and, partly as a result, strikes intensified. Worker support was courted through minimum wage hikes, social security benefits, and public sector jobs. This late shift leftward notwithstanding, the core aspects of Vargas' previous approach remained largely intact. Private property continued to be essentially inviolate and little effort was made to transform social relations in the countryside (Ribeiro 2008). The highest-profile policy initiatives of this period, including the creation of PETROBRAS and BNDE, were developmentalist rather than social.

A final difference between Vargas and Cárdenas involves their party affiliation and alliances. The Mexican leader did not belong to a party clearly aligned with the left, but he did have informal ties to the Mexican Communist Party. Vargas had no party at all until near the end of the *Estado*

Novo when, facing mounting pressure to step down, he sought to organize a civilian support base. Prior to that time, his relationship to the main left party, the Brazilian Communist Party (Partido Comunista Brasileiro, PCB), had been frankly antagonistic. In 1935 his government had forcefully repressed an armed uprising led in part by PCB leaders. During his final period as president, Vargas was affiliated with the Brazilian Labor Party (Partido Trabalhista Brasileiro, PTB), which he created in 1945 and which had strong ties to labor. However, at almost the same time as the PTB was being created, Vargas allies were founding (with the president's blessing) the Social Democratic Party (Partido Social Democrático, PSD), a more conservative grouping with ties to large landowners, small-town political bosses, and big business. It was on the basis of an alliance between the PTB and PSD, with the latter clearly being the stronger of the two, that Vargas returned to the presidency in 1951.

Why was Vargas so unwilling, compared to Cárdenas, to pursue redistributive change and challenge the power of economic elites? Clearly, there were major contextual differences, especially the greater salience of the agrarian and natural resource questions in Mexico, due to both structural differences and the revolutionary struggle. When Vargas rose to power in 1930, foreign control of natural resource wealth was not a significant political issue, given that large-scale extractivism was not an important element of Brazil's economy, and calls for land reform were only beginning to be heard. To the extent that pressure for land redistribution existed, it came not from peasants themselves but from progressive urban groups, most notably a movement within the armed forces called the *tenentes* (literally, "lieutenants"), which had undertaken a series of uprisings against oligarchic rule during the 1920s.

Still, a satisfying explanation of the divergence between Vargas and Cárdenas must also reserve a place for personal choice. As emphasized in Chapter 4, Cárdenas' bold reformism and victory over Calles represented a surprising outcome for contemporary observers. Vargas' relative conservatism was less remarkable in the sense that it did not mark a sharp break with the past. However, at certain moments, Vargas might have plausibly taken a more confrontational position toward elites and mobilized workers or peasants to support him. Perhaps the best example involves a failed 1932 anti-Vargas military uprising by São Paulo, the richest and most influential state. The government's victory in this nearly three-month conflict could potentially have been used as an opportunity to intensify the land and labor reforms supported by the *tenentes*, some of whom occupied key government positions (Welch 2016, p. 86). Instead, Vargas bowed to the defeated rebels' demand for a constitutional convention (Font 1997, pp. 139–140). While adopting a more confrontational stance toward São Paulo was certainly not without risk, the approach Vargas chose reflected his oft-noted style of governing, marked by conciliation and compromise (Camargo 1999; Fausto 2006).

5.1.3   Relations with Economic Elites and Social Conservatives

Because Vargas' reform project was more modest than that of his Mexican counterpart, it failed to engender as much opposition. Despite having substantially expanded the state's economic role, Vargas enjoyed largely non-conflictual relations with the private sector. Despite some initial concerns, social conservatives also failed to mobilize against him. Vargas' opposition came mainly from urban middle-class groups angered by what they viewed as rampant corruption and authoritarianism. Although they became quite vocal in the early 1950s, anti-Vargas forces had limited electoral success and weak ties to key actors in civil society.

Under Vargas, the relationship between the state and industry, the major beneficiary of interventionist policies, was particularly strong (Leopoldi 2000). The president's pro-worker discourse was initially a source of concern for industrialists, but they were reassured by the limited extent of his labor reforms, his tough crackdown on the left, and the tight control the state exercised over unions (Delgado 2007). By the mid-1930s, the most prominent industrial leader of the era, Roberto Simonsen, had become a vocal Vargas supporter (Weinstein 1996, pp. 82–83). Despite having backed the 1932 São Paulo revolt, Simonsen, the charismatic president of the Industrial Federation of the State of Sao Paulo (Federaçao das Indústrias do Estado de São Paulo, FIESP), came to embrace Vargas' policies and speak eloquently in their defense. The fact that he represented the most industrialized state made his support especially important. Another crucial ally was Euvaldo Lodi, who presided over the officially sanctioned peak industrial association, the National Confederation of Industry (Confederaçao Nacional da Industria, CNI), from its creation in 1938 until 1954 and was a member of the Chamber of Deputies (the lower house of Brazil's Congress) for the PSD from 1947 to 1956.

Vargas' relationship to agriculture was not as close, but he also developed important allies in this sector. The faction most resistant to him was the São Paulo coffee planters, who tended to advocate liberal policies and were organized in the Brazilian Rural Society (Sociedade Rural Brasileira, SRB) (Heinz 2001, p. 98). The *paulista* farm elite backed the 1932 rebellion and remained skeptical of Vargas' statist polices and authoritarian brand of leadership. However, as noted earlier, Vargas went out of his way to assuage them after the conflict and later he intervened forcefully to prop up the sagging price of coffee (Villela and Suzigan 1973, pp. 191–200). The fact that he did not advance land reform and made only symbolic efforts to promote rural unionization further attenuated their opposition. Vargas had closer relations with the National Society of Agriculture (Sociedade Nacional de Agricultura, SNA), which represented agricultural interests outside São Paulo (Ribeiro 2008). Given the relative lack of conflict between Vargas and farm elites, scholars have often described the relationship between them as an implicit "pact" in which the former pledged to leave the latter's core interests unharmed, while the latter agreed not to oppose pro-industrialization policies or otherwise combat the former's leadership (Azevedo 1982; Martins 1994).

As this discussion suggests, oppositional business organizing initiatives akin to those of the Monterrey Group during the 1930s were largely absent under Vargas. To the extent that business organization flourished it was mainly due to the state's own efforts (Schneider 2004, pp. 97–105). Vargas constructed a corporatist representational scheme for business that paralleled the one he set up for labor. After some initial conflicts, corporatism was embraced with considerable enthusiasm, especially among industrialists (Leopoldi 2000, ch. 2; Schneider 2004). Top business leaders like Simonsen and Lodi promoted official entities as a way of influencing and supporting the state's industrialization policies and promoting labor peace. While Cárdenas created a somewhat similar system in the 1930s, it was treated with more skepticism by business elites, given their animosity toward the government (Gauss 2010).

The private sector's relatively benign view of Vargas' policies was illustrated in a multi-sector conference that occurred in 1945, at the end of the *Estado Novo*. The gathering produced a well-known document called the "Economic Charter of Teresópolis," which not only asserted the importance of free enterprise but also conceded a substantial role for the state in terms of economic planning, trade protection, regulation, credit provision, and direct production in sectors in which private businesses lacked sufficient capital or technology (Schmitter 1971, pp. 183–184). It also called for the universalization of social security and even endorsed redistribution of underutilized farmland (Delgado 2007, pp. 148–149).

In addition to enjoying good relations with the private sector, Vargas also generally got along well with social conservatives. The latter were initially concerned about the changes his 1930 "revolution" might bring, given the influence of the reformist *tenentes* and Vargas' own secular positivist background. Early in the decade, conservative clergy sought to mobilize the faithful to demonstrate the force of Catholicism in society (Schwartzman 1986). In 1932, moreover, there arose a quasi-fascist movement called *integralismo* with strong ties to conservative sectors of the Church and a mass following. Over time, however, both the clergy and *integralistas* were reassured by Vargas' moderation. They applauded his repression of the PCB and supported the creation of the *Estado Novo*. Under that regime, Vargas cultivated a close relationship with the Church, conceding it more influence than it had enjoyed since the end of the monarchy (Bruneau 1974, ch. 2). Although he banned *integralismo* (along with other civil society actors), he gave individuals with *integralista* ties influence over certain policy areas, most notably education (Schwartzman 1986).

This is not to say that Vargas and his policies did not face resistance. Their most important opponent was the National Democratic Union (União Democrática Nacional, UDN), a party formed, like both *varguista* parties, at the end of the *Estado Novo*. The UDN was critical of the growing state apparatus, corruption, and what it saw as the manipulation of popular sectors with social benefits and wage hikes (Benevides 1981). One of its key leaders, the combative journalist and legislator Carlos Lacerda, was among Vargas' most potent critics. There was also a substantial anti-Vargas faction within the armed forces. Although the military generally favored industrialization, some officers opposed *varguismo*'s courtship of workers. Finally, the continuation of Vargas' *Estado Novo* policies post-1945 was challenged by Brazil's alignment with the United States. Brazilian military units had fought alongside their US counterparts in Europe and strong relations had been forged between their military establishments. The first government after the war, led by Eurico Dutra (1946–1951), an army officer who had served as Vargas' minister of war, was supportive of US initiatives to isolate communism and reduce barriers to trade and investment among capitalist countries (Bastos 2010).

Nevertheless, these actors never achieved enough influence to derail the *varguista* project. Although it was one of Brazil's three largest parties, the UDN's success was limited. Between its founding and Vargas' death, it was easily defeated by the PTB-PSD coalition in both the 1946 and 1951 presidential elections and managed to control only about a quarter of the seats in the Chamber of Deputies and a fifth in the Senate. The UDN lacked the PTB's connections to organized workers, and its rural clientelist network was not as extensive as the PSD's (Dulci 1986, pp. 33–35). Instead, it relied heavily on the votes of a relatively small urban middle class. Moreover, compared to parties like the PAN and UDI, the UDN did not enjoy a strong base of support among social conservatives, who were not mobilized to oppose Vargas. Dutra's early adherence to the liberal trade policy championed by the United States had threatened to divert the PSD-PTB alliance that backed him from its developmentalist path. However, that policy was soon reversed (Bastos 2010) and the nationalist turn reinforced when Vargas returned to office in 1951. Three years later, military officers allied with the UDN tried to force Vargas to resign, but he dramatically committed suicide instead, a move that, along with a cleverly crafted suicide note, cast himself as a victim and denied his opponents a political victory.[6] After a brief period of instability, his ally Kubitschek was elected.

The common denominator in the failure of these initiatives is that, because of *varguismo*'s essentially moderate character, anti-Vargas figures were never able to convincingly make the case that Vargas and the policies he espoused presented a true threat to Brazil's prosperity, security, or cultural traditions. Thus, although the struggle between pro- and anti-Vargas factions became

---

[6] A key justification for their demand was that Vargas' personal bodyguard had been implicated in a failed plot to assassinate UDN leader Carlos Lacerda.

tumultuous at times, the latter did not develop into a countermovement with enough support to achieve sustained victories.

5.1.4 Post-Vargas Business Organization

Differences in the extent of reformism between Cárdenas and Vargas resulted in distinct political legacies. For the purposes of the argument, the most crucial contrast involves the ideology and organization of economic elites. In Mexico, opposition to *cardenismo* imbued elites with a marked distrust of the state and set in motion a cross-sectoral mobilization process that did not disappear when the presidency changed hands. It was, in other words, a key moment of elite class formation. In contrast, Vargas' tepid social reformism failed to give rise to an anti-statist ideology or a determination to mobilize to defend class-wide capitalist interests. The corporatist organizations he created survived but lacked strong connections to their nominal bases and were never complemented by encompassing voluntary organizations. The analysis here focuses on the period between Vargas' death and the early 1960s, but the private sector characteristics it stresses persist even today, reflecting a path-dependent process in which the initially pro-business character of state intervention fomented a culture of elite collaboration with the state, which in turn facilitated revenue extraction and further public sector expansion.

At least in terms of formal organizations, the private sector that emerged from the Vargas era was far more organized than in the past (Leopoldi 2000; Schneider 2004). Prior to the 1930s, there had been little business organization beyond the state level. Even the influence of nominally national entities, such as the SRB, was in practice confined to particular states. Now, in contrast, there were national confederations representing every major economic sector, each of which formed the apex of a hierarchical network of state federations and local unions. Unlike older associations, which depended on voluntary membership dues, these corporatist organizations received large inflows of revenue from an earmarked tax, as well as an additional tax that funded business-run worker training and social services. As a result, they could afford large staffs and elaborate offices.

Nevertheless, the size and financial might of the corporatist entities masked weaknesses that became increasingly evident over the course of the 1950s, with Vargas' death and the gradual disappearance of the business leaders closely associated with him (Leopoldi 2000, pp. 88–89; Schneider 2004, pp. 103–105). Membership growth and the creation of new local and state entities slackened (Schmitter 1971 pp. 222–223). Major businesses increasingly sought influence through personal contacts or groups representing narrower interests. The latter multiplied as business responded to the growing breadth and sophistication of state intervention by creating voluntary organizations representing specific industries (Schmitter 1971, pp. 198–202; Boschi and Diniz 1978; Schneider 2004, p. 104). Perceiving the weakness of the corporatist entities as representatives of private sector opinion, authorities tended to seek input elsewhere, exacerbating their marginality (Schneider 2004, p. 97).

Despite the growth of non-corporatist groups, no business organization arose that could represent the general interests of the private sector. In the second half of the 1950s, some pre-Vargas commercial associations, rebelling against corporatism, sought to create a broad coalition of employers outside of this system, but ultimately failed (Schmitter 1971, p. 196). Thus, by the early 1960s, Brazilian business was again highly fragmented organizationally. The corporate system failed to inspire loyalty or participation and, in addition, lacked an encompassing, multi-sector association. Voluntary associations, while enjoying greater membership density and participation, represented even narrower interests. Furthermore, and in contrast to the Mexican case, there was little evidence of collaboration between the different business associations, either private or corporatist. Rather, their interactions were indirect, mediated by state institutions (Schmitter 1971, p. 321).

The weakness of business political organization was also reflected in a lack of engagement with parties, despite the robust electoral competition of the era. For example, in a confidential membership survey conducted in the early 1960s by the Rio de Janeiro industrial federation, only 4.8 percent of the 395 respondents reported having participated in a political party at all (Schmitter 1971, pp. 278–279). Moreover, there was no party particularly identified with organized business. While the heads of commercial associations tended to support the liberal UDN, those of both the industrial and agricultural associations were more likely to favor the *varguista* PSD (Schmitter 1971, p. 275).

Scholars have argued that the weak engagement of major businesses in the corporatist system reflected a state-imposed decision-making structure that did not give them a weight proportional to their role in the economy, thereby motivating them to use alternative channels to influence public authorities (Schneider 2004, p. 104–105). While convincing as far as it goes, this argument cannot explain why large businesses did not band together in voluntary peak associations outside the corporatist structure. In other words, why did no entity emerge in the Brazilian case analogous to COPARMEX, CMN, or CCE?

The answer would seem to lie in the nonthreatening character of the Brazilian state. Encompassing organization requires ongoing investments of time and money and necessarily involves complicated compromises between sectors with differing interests. Business leaders need a compelling reason to engage in it. In Mexico, the postrevolutionary state gave them that reason by expropriating property and engaging in other menacing actions. Vargas did not. Expanding the public sector in incremental ways that provided at least some benefit to all major sectors, and deeply threatening none, Vargas helped forge a culture of elite acceptance of state intervention. It was not until Goulart that the state would take on (albeit briefly and ineffectually, as discussed later) a more threatening appearance.

Studies of private sector associative and political activity during this period consistently remark on the business elite's accepting attitude toward state intervention. In his classic study of Brazilian interest groups, Schmitter (1971, p. 350) argues that industrialists responded to the nonthreatening character of statist policies under Vargas by assuming the "conciliatory, non-dogmatic" attitude originally propagated by FIESP's Simonsen. Referring to the early 1960s, he argues that "Ideologically, Brazilian industrialists had long since made their peace with direct public intervention" (Schmitter 1971, p. 349). While strongest in industry, this attitude was broadly shared by the private sector, including agriculture and commerce, despite their more critical positions on some issues (Schmitter 1971, p. 376).

Sikkink (1991) elaborates a similar view in her study of developmentalism in Brazil and Argentina during the late 1950s and early 1960s. She argues that developmentalist policies were adopted with greater consistency in Brazil because there existed a broad ideological consensus spanning the public and private sectors about the beneficial character of state intervention. Brazilian elites disagreed on the role of foreign investment, but they concurred on the need for state leadership of the development process. Such a consensus (as will be discussed in Chapter 6) was lacking in Argentina, where many elites had strong liberal convictions. In Brazil, "liberalism never took root ... the way it did in Argentina. The real debate in Brazil was not between the liberal model and the planning model, but within the developmentalist camp between cosmopolitan and national developmentalists" (Sikkink 1991, p. 67).

Thus, while the Cárdenas years left a legacy of private sector mistrust of the state, the Vargas era did not. By gradually expanding the public sector's role in the economy without threatening vitalelite interests, Vargas assuaged the fears of business elites and helped accustom them to living with an intrusive state. The result was a business community focused less on the broad goal of defending itself against statism than on advancing firm-, subsector-, or region-specific demands best represented by relatively narrow organizations. Such an approach tended to promote public sector growth.

5.1.5 Private Sector Quiescence and Rising Taxation

The Brazilian private sector's relatively accepting attitude toward state economic intervention facilitated the upward trajectory of the tax burden between 1930 and the end of the 1950s (when, as discussed earlier, deteriorating economic conditions began to erode the system's efficacy), helping to separate Brazil from low-tax Mexico.

Although Brazil's tax burden roughly doubled during this period, existing scholarship on taxation, business, and general politics from the 1930s through the early 1960s barely mentions state-private sector conflict regarding taxation

(Skidmore 1967; Leff 1968; Schmitter 1971; Varsano 1996; Leopoldi 2000; Oliveira 2010; Bastos 2011). A wide-ranging proposal made by the Vargas government in 1953 to reorganize the tax system to make it simpler and less distortive did get bogged down in Congress and ultimately died there (Oliveira 2010, p. 29). However, the most important source of resistance to it appears to have come not from business, but from government officials (at all three levels), who were fearful that its attempts to rationalize the system would impede their ongoing efforts to raise additional revenue by inventing new taxes or modifying old ones (Varsano 1996, p. 25).

To be sure, Brazilian economic elites and their organizations did not welcome or encourage heavier taxation. In particular, there was resistance to direct taxes. That resistance grew in the face of the substantial increase in federal income tax revenues during the *Estado Novo* and the introduction of the Excess Profits Tax in 1943 (Delgado 2007, pp. 146–147; Bastos 2011, p. 449). A number of documents published by business associations during the mid-1940s, including the Economic Charter of Teresópolis, expressed opposition to "excessive" direct taxation, which in a poor country like Brazil, they alleged, would slow capital formation and discourage foreign investment (Delgado 2001, p. 122).

Nevertheless, compared to the Mexican case, there appears to have been little resistance to indirect or social security taxes. During the 1930s, concerns were expressed about the impact of indirect taxes on consumer prices (Delgado 2007, p. 142), but there is little evidence of the kind of pressure encountered, for example, by the Alemán government in its efforts to introduce and enforce a federal sales tax. Furthermore, in the 1940s Brazilian business elites, in contrast to their Mexican counterparts, endorsed the universalization of social security coverage along the lines of the Beveridge Report, an influential study commissioned in 1942 by the British government (Delgado 2001, p. 135). Although it is not clear what funding mechanism they envisioned (other than the fact that it would not lean heavily on direct taxes), they must have realized that such a reform would require additional public revenue. In the 1950s, with social security benefits expanding rapidly and the system's reserves declining, business adopted a more defensive position (Delgado 2001, pp. 151–166). Overall, however, elite attitudes toward social security were clearly more accepting in Brazil than in Mexico.

5.2 GOULART, MILITARY RULE, AND DEEPENING STATISM

Just as there are at least superficial parallels between the populist Vargas and Cárdenas experiences, so there are frequent comparisons between the military coups d'état experienced by Brazil in 1964 and Chile in 1973, as well as between the "bureaucratic authoritarian" regimes that emerged from them (O'Donnell 1978; Collier 1979; Remmer and Merkx 1982). In both cases, a left-leaning government attempting to implement redistributive reforms was overthrown by the armed forces with support from business and other conservative actors. In both, furthermore, the coup was followed by the establishment of a long-lasting authoritarian regime. However, in the Chilean case, those events led to the consolidation of a low-tax system, while in Brazil they did not. In fact, the Brazilian regime substantially increased taxation as part of a broader program of state-led development. This section seeks to explain these contrasting outcomes.

The argument it develops is that Brazil's military rulers pursued a more statist, high-tax path than Pinochet because the country's previous experiences suggested to both the military itself and its civilian supporters, especially economic elites, that such a path could bring sustainable growth without undue threats to property and other aspects of the capitalist system. Like Salvador Allende's, Goulart's government highlighted the threats that could potentially arise from state-led development. Nevertheless, his government was simply too vacillating, brief, and ineffectual to seriously undermine the strong preexisting consensus on this question (Ondetti 2015, p. 770; Ondetti 2019).

5.2.1   Rising Taxation under the Military Regime

In stark contrast to Chile's, Brazil's military regime increased taxation rather substantially as part of a development strategy that deepened the state-led approach initially adopted under Vargas. Although the tax burden did not increase significantly after 1970, and actually deteriorated some in the early 1980s, the increase during the second half of the 1960s was so large that for the 1964–1985 period as a whole the rate of increase of the tax burden was similar to the more democratic period that preceded it.

While Brazil's military regime was fiercely anti-communist and repressive toward left-leaning groups, it was statist in economic policy matters (Evans 1979; Schneider 2015). State banks provided huge volumes of subsidized credit to private firms, and the state also increased its own productive role by expanding existing SOEs and establishing new ones in areas such as aircraft and nuclear power. Authorities sought to boost exports, but the economy remained highly protected. Despite its generally conservative outlook, the regime even increased social spending, continuing the expansion of the contributory social security system and creating a noncontributory one for poor rural workers (Malloy 1979, pp. 130–133; Houtzager 1998). Until the 1980s, its state-led economic program was relatively successful, generating easily the largest increase in per capita GDP in the region (Astorga et al. 2005, p. 788).

The regime's 1966 tax reform has been viewed as one of its key policy achievements (Varsano 1981; Oliveira 1991). It simplified the system by eliminating a large number of unproductive levies, transformed the cumulative character of the ICV by shifting to a value-added approach, took steps to reduce income tax evasion, and raised many rates. Brazil became the first country in Latin America to adopt a VAT, although, unusually for a VAT, the tax did not bear that name and operated at the state (rather than national) level. Some of these changes had been introduced in 1964 and 1965, but they were consolidated in the 1966 law. Tax reform, combined with currency stabilization, brought a sharp increase in revenues and helped close the large fiscal deficit that had opened in the early 1960s. The tax burden rose from 16.1 percent in 1963 to 25.9 percent in 1969, a major change by any standard (Estatísticas do Século XX).

During the 1970s and early 1980s, revenues stagnated at about 25 percent of GDP, in part because of liberal use of tax incentives to stimulate investment (Varsano 1996, pp. 10–11). It dropped to 23–24 percent of GDP late in the military regime due to the effects of the debt crisis, including high inflation. Tax incentives had a regressive impact, but authorities made efforts in the 1970s to increase income taxation, both by reducing incentives and by raising rates, causing revenues from this source to rise to their highest level since the 1940s (Gomes 1986, p. 318). To reinforce their control over the state and fuel their development policies, authorities also centralized tax collection, causing the federal share of revenues to rise to more than 75 percent, the highest level since at least 1900 (Estatísticas do Século XX).

5.2.2 Late, Ineffectual Radicalization

Chapter 3 argued that the UP government's radical statism, especially its restructuring of property rights, played a fundamental part in bringing about the Pinochet regime's subsequent reforms because it legitimized profoundly anti-statist views and conferred upon authorities wide latitude to chart a new economic course. Thus, to understand why Brazil's military regime pursued a very different approach to managing the economy, it is important to compare the two pre-coup governments.

There are ways in which the events of Goulart's presidency resembled the process that led to Chile's 1973 coup. In both instances, democratic procedures brought to the presidency a politician whose leftism caused concern among wide sectors of the political elite, armed forces, and the upper and middle classes. Although Goulart was a Vargas disciple and had served as Kubitschek's vice president, he clearly represented *varguismo*'s left wing. Unlike Kubitschek, who was a member of the PSD, Goulart was from the PTB and had built his career on ties to organized labor. He had served briefly as Minister of Labor under Vargas, pushing for a controversial 100 percent minimum wage hike. He supported land reform and restrictions on foreign investment. As occurred with Allende, there was considerable resistance to allowing Goulart to assume the presidency in 1961, when Jânio Quadros (an independent supported by the UDN) abruptly resigned. In the end, a compromise was struck in which Goulart was allowed to take office under a semi-presidential arrangement, sharing power with a prime minister subject to legislative confidence (Stepan 1978, pp. 118–119). Full presidentialism was restored in January 1963 following a popular referendum, but the fact that institutions were restructured to begin with demonstrates the depth of concern among some groups.

Like Allende, Goulart attempted to carry out significant reforms, ones that, had they been approved, would have eroded the *varguista* tradition of limited redistribution and collaborative relations with business (Camargo 1986; Figueiredo 1993). His endorsement of land reform was the most significant, since it called into question the sanctity of property rights. Although Brazil's 1946 constitution had empowered the state to expropriate landed property not serving the "social interest," it required prior compensation in cash, which rendered reform unviable. Goulart sought an amendment allowing compensation in bonds, as well as a statute outlining a land reform program (Ondetti 2016, p. 31). The government also sought to enfranchise illiterates, extend the right to unionize to rural workers, limit profit remittances by MNCs, and establish a state monopoly on coffee exports, among other reforms (Ferreira 2010, p. 275). These initiatives threatened the traditional "oligarchic pact" underpinning the heterogeneous *varguista* alliance (Camargo 1986, p. 229).

In addition, Goulart's term, like Allende's, was characterized by unusually intense popular mobilization, some of it provoked by the government itself. Perhaps the most striking transformation occurred in the previously quiescent countryside, where land invasions and wage worker strikes multiplied (Azevedo 1982; Houtzager 1998). College students and urban workers were also among the mobilized groups (Skidmore 1967, pp. 253–256). These changes in civil society encouraged the growth of left-leaning actors in the electoral arena (Ferreira 2010). The PTB made significant gains in the 1962 legislative elections, although the PSD remained the largest party in Congress. Within the PTB, a leftist sector led by the firebrand Leonel Brizola attained greater prominence. Although banned, the PCB had a significant presence in the labor movement and was involved in efforts to unionize rural workers. Brizola and other left actors urged Goulart to use mass mobilization to force a reluctant Congress to approve his reforms (Ferreira 2010, p. 283). Despite initially resisting this strategy, in early 1964 Goulart embraced it. It backfired in spectacular fashion, leading to a coup d'état and the establishment of a military-led authoritarian regime.

Despite certain rough parallels to the situation that led to Chile's 1973 coup, there were crucial differences. Perhaps the most fundamental is that Goulart achieved little actual reform. His most important accomplishment was arguably the legalization of rural unionism in 1963. Although effective in spurring a unionization drive, this move merely extended Vargas' control-oriented corporatism to the countryside. Rather than rolling it back, the conservative military regime would later exploit it to strengthen its political grip in rural areas (Houtzager 1998). Also significant was a law passed in 1962 that limited profit remittances by foreign corporations, which was applauded by leftists and denounced by the US government. Beyond these two measures, few major policy or institutional changes occurred under Goulart. He failed to implement land reform or expand the suffrage. Unlike Allende, he also did not undertake significant expropriation of urban businesses, or other measures that would strongly impinge upon property rights or domestic markets.

To a large extent, the paucity of reform reflected Goulart's political weakness. While the traditional PSD-PTB alliance gave the president a working legislative majority, in practice the more conservative *varguista* party joined the UDN in rejecting most of his reforms (Skidmore 1967, p. 260). In addition, compared to Allende, Goulart lacked a strong base of popular support. Labor unionism, while growing, was still weaker than in Chile (Ondetti 2015, p. 21). Chile's rural workers were also better organized, in part because of the organizational campaigns initiated under Frei (Houtzager and Kurtz 2000, p. 395). Goulart's last-ditch attempt to use popular mobilization to bludgeon Congress into submission only underscored his weakness. Rather than triggering a wave of pro-government protest, it provoked a military coup that ousted the president with little resistance. In contrast, Chile's coup was bloodier and the initial post-coup repression more intense because military leaders understood that the UP government had enough civilian support to resist the action if it were not undertaken decisively (Remmer and Merkx 1982, p. 12).

There were also important ideological and programmatic differences between the two governments. Allende's UP was a coalition of mainly Marxist parties seeking a socialist transition. In contrast, although it called for nationalist and redistributive policies, Goulart's PTB was not for the most part anti-capitalist. Scholars have characterized it as a party with middle-class or petit bourgeois leadership and a stronger commitment to state-led development than defense of working-class interests (Erickson 1977; Weffort 1978). Leaders of the leftist "new union" movement that arose in the late 1970s would criticize the party's pre-1964 relations with labor as manipulative and self-serving (Benevides 1989, p. 136). Although Goulart represented a leftist current within the PTB, he was not outside the party mainstream. Moreover, at least until the final few months of his presidency, his approach to governing was moderate. Even the land reform measures he pursued were similar to what a number of other Latin American countries adopted during the 1960s under the influence of the US-sponsored Alliance for Progress (Lapp 2004). In fact, soon after the coup, authorities would adopt legal provisions similar to those Congress had rejected under Goulart. Just as importantly, Goulart sought to achieve reform through the traditional PTB-PSD alliance (Ferreira 2010). Even if it had been successful, this approach guaranteed that change would be incremental.

The semi-presidential arrangement adopted in 1961 may seem like an extreme reaction to such a politician taking office, but it must be understood in terms of the Brazilian military's longstanding tradition of political meddling (Stepan 1971). For example, in 1954, as discussed earlier, the armed forces had pressured Vargas to resign, helping precipitate his suicide. A year later, a moderate military faction had executed a preemptive coup against an interim president suspected of conspiring with hardliners to block president-elect Kubitschek's inauguration. Somewhat similarly, the semi-presidential system was a response by civilian leaders to attempts by some officers to veto Goulart's assumption of power (Skidmore 1967, pp. 205–215).

Finally, Goulart's impact was attenuated by the historical context. In Chile, the fact that the UP government followed a center-left Christian Democratic government with a strong reformist bent made it hard to dismiss it as a fluke. Rather, it made that government seem like the culmination of a secular process of state expansion and radicalization requiring a structural solution. In contrast, Goulart followed a series of presidents who had implemented virtually no major redistributive reforms other than the incremental expansion of social security. Moreover, Goulart himself had come to the presidency not through popular election, but a quirk of fate: the unexpected resignation of the relatively conservative Quadros. It was thus easier to interpret the Goulart experience as more of a conjunctural crisis than a reflection of the inherent dangers of a state-driven development model.

5.2.3 Fleeting Countermobilization and Statist Reaffirmation

Because of the differences highlighted in the previous section, Goulart's presidency was far less consequential than Allende's in terms of forging a coalition of anti-statist forces. While economic elites and other conservatives mobilized to oppose Goulart, these efforts did not give rise to enduring anti-statist political actors. Almost as soon as the military assumed power, business political action returned to the fragmented, particularistic pattern that had characterized it before Goulart. Nor were there strong nuclei of anti-statism in other parts of society or the state apparatus. As a result, after taking measures to stabilize the economy, Brazil's new authorities returned to the *varguista* strategy of building a large developmental state.

That the Goulart presidency did not fundamentally alter economic elites' relatively benign view of the state is suggested by the trajectory of business organization during and after this period. To be sure, Goulart's rise did trigger efforts to protect capitalists' basic class interests. The most prominent of these was the Institute for Economic and Social Research (Instituto de Pesquisa Econômica e Social, IPES), which produced studies and propaganda defending private property and free enterprise and warning that Goulart could open the door to communism. It was allied with another entity, the Brazilian Institute for Democratic Action (Instituto Brasileiro de Açao

Democrática, IBAD), which promoted conservative election candidates. Although created in 1959, IBAD came into its own in the 1962 elections, making large campaign donations. Both groups, but especially IPES, were supported by prominent businesspeople. Some scholars have argued that IPES and IBAD played crucial roles in coordinating civilian backing for the 1964 coup (Dreifuss 1981).

Nevertheless, neither developed into a broadly representative or enduring organization. IPES was mainly associated with firms partly or wholly controlled by foreign capital and had an ambivalent relationship with the major industrial interest groups, especially FIESP and CNI, in which national capital was strongly represented. For example, while IPES emerged partly in response to the proposal to limit profit remittances, important sectors of FIESP and CNI actually pressured for the bill's approval (Loureiro 2016). Both IPES and IBAD had close ties to the US government and the latter is often believed to have received much of its funding from the Central Intelligence Agency (Loureiro 2012, p. 223). IBAD was extinguished in 1963 following a congressional investigation that revealed that it had illegally channeled foreign funds into electoral campaigns. IPES quickly lost prominence in the years after the coup, since its basic reason for being, to oppose the Goulart government, had become irrelevant (Schneider 2004, pp. 105–108). In 1972 it ceased to exist even on paper.

Once the anti-Goulart mobilization had subsided, previous trends in business organization reappeared. The political impotence of corporatist entities deepened, and narrower voluntary associations multiplied and, at least in part because they tended to represent the largest businesses, increasingly became the main interlocutors with regime officials (Diniz and Boschi 1978, p. 120; Diniz and Boschi 2003, p. 22–23; Schneider 2004, pp. 111–112). As in the past, there was no organization, either corporatist or voluntary, that could speak for Brazilian capitalists as a class and address broad, cross-sectoral issues of property and free enterprise. While some associations may have been highly effective in lobbying authorities, as a broad check on state action the private sector was weak.

In his influential study of Latin American business organizations, Schneider (2004, p. 114) argues that the lack of encompassing business association in Brazil during this era reflected in part the unwillingness of authorities to grant such entities access to policymaking. This situation, he suggests, differentiated Brazil from Chile and Mexico. However, Brazilian elites never actually created peak associations truly comparable to the CPC, COPARMEX, CMN, or CCE, so on this point Schneider's analysis is unconvincing. Rather, the contrast would seem to be better explained by another factor he discusses: the lack of threats to fundamental private sector interests (Schneider 2004, p. 86). Neither the military regime nor any prior government, including Goulart's, had engaged in the kinds of reform that spurred intense countermobilization in Chile and Mexico. Without a compelling reason to invest money, time, and energy in building cross-sectoral associations capable of representing capitalists as a class, Brazilian economic elites preferred to rely on personal contacts or more specific organizations to advance their interests. In contrast to their Chilean and Mexican counterparts, Brazilian capitalists had developed less wariness about the state and a weaker sense of being a potential target of redistributive policies.

In the mid-1970s, in the context of slowing economic growth, criticisms did emerge about the expanding role of SOEs, which some business leaders complained was undercutting the private sector. However, this campaign was as much about lack of access to decision makers as policy content (Diniz and Boschi 1978, p. 191) and was defused with modest concessions attenuating advantages enjoyed by SOEs (Graham 1982, p. 36). Graham, as discussed in Chapter 4, compares this conflict to the one that erupted in Mexico under Echeverría, emphasizing the greater intensity and impact of business mobilization in the latter case. Drawing on interviews with industrialists during the 1970s, two scholars of Brazilian business reach a similar conclusion. Demands for limiting SOE advantages notwithstanding, they argue, "our research did not reveal an industrial elite opposed to state intervention in the economy. In some cases [this elite] even justified that intervention by the necessity of the state filling gaps the private sector could not" (Diniz and Boschi 1978, p. 191).

Strong resistance to state intervention was also lacking elsewhere in Brazilian society. There were no Brazilian counterparts to Chile's Chicago Boy network or *gremialista* movement. As discussed earlier, the most influential critic of statism from 1945 to 1964 had been the UDN. However, the UDN was, along with other parties, abolished by military fiat in 1965. Many UDN members continued to be active in politics through the officially sanctioned pro-regime party, initially called the "National Renewal Alliance" (Aliança Renovadora Nacional, ARENA) and later the "Democratic Social Party" (Partido Democrático Social, PDS). However, some prominent *udenistas* rejected long-term authoritarian rule and refused to join. More importantly, since ARENA also included former members of the PSD, as well as other parties (even the PTB), it lacked the UDN's liberal identity. Despite military authorities' condemnation of the previous regime's clientelism, in practice ARENA and PDS functioned as loose clientelist networks that supported the government in return for patronage (Mainwaring 1995, 1999; Hagopian 1996). They had relatively little say in major decisions and what influence they did have was not used to defend free-market principles.

The leaders of the regime were also by no means orthodox economic liberals. While official discourse sometimes (especially in the early years) exalted free enterprise, there was broad agreement on continuing the state-led economic strategy of previous decades (Evans 1979; Barros de Castro 1993). This was true of both the military leadership, which had long backed the developmentalist project in general terms, and civilian technocrats. The regime's relative internal unity regarding the importance of an assertive state economic role approximated it to the Kubitschek government, which was probably the most systematically statist of the pre-1964 governments. In fact, there is considerable continuity in economic strategy among all Brazilian governments between the 1930s and the outbreak of the debt crisis in the 1980s, despite occasional economic downturns that might have invited a change of course (Barros de Castro 1993, p. 184).

The substantial consensus in favor of state intervention makes it easier to understand the extraordinary increase in the tax burden during the second half of the 1960s, amounting to some 8 percent of GDP. Studies of the tax reform itself and business-state relations during this period provide hardly any evidence of resistance from either the private sector or other social groups, even though it raised revenues from all types of taxes, including income taxes (Schmitter 1971; Diniz and Boschi 1978; Evans 1979; Varsano 1981; Oliveira 1991). To some extent, the lack of opposition was probably due to the authoritarian character of the regime, as well as widespread recognition that the very large fiscal deficit, a major cause of Brazil's economic woes, needed to be reduced. Nevertheless, it stands to reason that the persistence of a broadly benevolent view of the state's role in the development process also facilitated this change. Key actors in Brazilian society were less resistant to providing revenue to a state whose role in development was widely viewed as positive, if not essential, to continued economic expansion.

In sum, João Goulart's abbreviated government, in sharp contrast to Allende's, failed to provoke the rise of a strongly anti-statist political bloc both because of the solidity of the preexisting statist consensus and the vacillating and ineffective character of his reformism. As a result, the military regime installed in 1964 ended up deepening rather than reversing the country's statist development path and putting it on a firmer fiscal footing by implementing a major, revenue-raising reform of the tax system.

5.3 DEMOCRACY, SOCIAL SPENDING, AND HEAVY TAXATION

Although Brazil entered its current democratic period with the heaviest tax burden in the region, subsequent decades brought an additional large boost. This increase contrasts with the experiences of Chile and Mexico, where the post-democratic transition increment has been smaller, despite the initial burden being far lighter. Explanations of rising taxation in contemporary Brazil usually attribute it to the effects of the constitution drafted soon after the return to civilian rule (Afonso and Serra 2007; Melo et al. 2010; 2015 interviews: Hauly, Maciel). That document, as discussed earlier, mandated increased social spending in several areas, especially pensions, and created mechanisms to fund it.

Although this point is valid, the constitution's fiscal impact must be understood within the broader context of a power balance that favors statism. Compared to its Chilean and Mexican counterparts, Brazilian democracy inherited a dearth of strong actors committed to maintaining a small state. In addition, actors with an explicit commitment to statist policies, most notably organized labor and the leftist Workers Party (Partido dos Trabalhadores, PT), have until recently tended to expand their influence, generating pressure for social spending and thus taxation. Both the original constitutional provisions and the ways in which they have subsequently evolved and been implemented reflect this statist-leaning power balance.

5.3.1 Democratization and Renewed Tax Burden Growth

Beginning in the latter half of the 1970s, Brazil underwent a gradual regime transition. Following an initial expansion of civil liberties, state governors were elected in 1982, a civilian president was indirectly elected (by a special electoral college) in 1985, a new constitution was drafted in 1987–1988, and, finally, a president was chosen by direct popular election in 1989. Although Brazil began its current democratic regime already having the heaviest tax burden in Latin America, revenues nonetheless increased by an additional 7–8 percent of GDP during roughly the first two decades (see Figure 5.1). The tax take has stabilized since then, but at a level that remains about 60 percent higher than the regional average and far above those of Chile and Mexico.

Tax policymaking in the 1980s and early 1990s was influenced by the deep economic problems Brazil had faced since the outbreak of the regional debt crisis, including slow or negative growth, large fiscal deficits, and inflation that at some points reached 2,000 percent per year. Stabilizing prices and returning to sustained growth were central preoccupations of the first four post-military presidents, José Sarney (1985–1989), Fernando Collor (1990–2003), Itamar Franco (1993–1994), and Fernando Henrique Cardoso (1995–2002), all of whom led centrist or right-leaning governments. Inflation was finally brought to heel in 1994 through a stabilization program called the "Real Plan," due to the new currency it introduced. Collor and Cardoso also implemented structural reforms, including trade liberalization and privatization of many SOEs. Liberalization did not go as far as in Chile or Mexico. For example, the pension system remained wholly public and import tariffs continued to be considerably higher. However, it was still an important change, whose impact was reflected in declines in the manufacturing and SOE shares of GDP and employment (Diniz and Boschi 2003, pp. 16–21).

Since fiscal deficits had long been a key source of inflation (Tullio and Ronci 1996), a central challenge facing these governments was to limit the gap between revenues and spending. The difficulties were compounded by the 1988 constitution, which created new social spending commitments in the areas of social assistance, health care, and pensions. Fiscally speaking, the last of these was easily the most important. Among other measures, the constitution set the legal minimum wage as the floor for all pension payments, increased pensions for rural workers, and integrated a large number of state employees into the pension system for civil servants, where they would receive generous benefits. By the early 1990s, pension spending was rising at an alarming pace. Spending controls, privatization revenues, and incremental pension reform all played roles in deficit containment, but authorities also relied heavily on increased taxation (Afonso and Serra 2007; Schneider 2019, pp. 134–135).

As with spending, the approach taken to raising revenue was influenced by constitutional provisions (Afonso and Serra 2007; Melo et al. 2010; Afonso 2013). The 1988 constitution increased the percentage of revenue from the federal income tax and consumption taxes transferred to subnational governments. At the same time, it consolidated a new class of federal taxes called "social contributions" whose revenues remain wholly at the federal level but are earmarked for social programs. The constitution also further broadened the base of the state-level VAT, now dubbed the Tax on the Circulation of Goods and Services (Imposto sobre Circulação de Mercadorias e Prestação de Serviço, ICMS), and gave authorities more freedom to set rates, increasing the potential for interstate tax competition (Mendes 2013).[7]

Because this framework effectively penalized the federal government for raising revenue through traditional taxes while making it possible to create social contributions, authorities relied mainly on the latter to raise revenue (Afonso and Serra 2007; Melo et al. 2010). During the late 1980s and 1990s, they created the Social Contribution on Net Profits (Contribuição Social sobre o Lucro Líquido, CSLL), essentially an additional corporate income tax; the Contribution for the Financing of Social Security (Contribuição para o Financiamento da Seguridade Social, COFINS), a sales tax; and the Provisional Contribution on Financial Movements (Contribuição Provisória sobre Movimentação Financeira, CPMF), a tax on bank transactions. Although temporary, the CPMF was renewed four times and lasted until 2007 (Afonso et al. 2013, p. 63). While these taxes could in principle only be used to finance certain social programs, Cardoso gained approval in 1994 of a constitutional amendment allowing part of the revenue to be diverted for other purposes. Like the CPMF, this measure was nominally provisional, but has repeatedly been extended in various forms.

As a result of these policies, as well as the positive impact of lower inflation on tax collection, reducing the Olivera–Tanzi effect (Varsano 1996, p. 18), tax revenues increased from 24.0 percent of GDP in 1984, the last full year of military control of the federal executive branch, to 32.0 percent in 2002, Cardoso's last year in office (CEPALSTAT). Thus, somewhat ironically, Brazil's supposedly "neoliberal" governments, led by Cardoso's centrist Party of Brazilian Social Democracy (Partido da Social Democracia Brasileira, PSDB), ended up presiding over an impressive increase in the tax burden.

In most other respects, the tax system remained largely the same. Relative to the mid-1980s, the share of revenues contributed by direct taxation increased,

---

[7] The constitution refers to the need for coordination between the states in setting ICMS rates and exemptions, but this has been hard to achieve in practice (Tostes 2015, interview).

in part due to the creation of the CPMF and CSLL, both categorized as direct taxes (CEPALSTAT). However, the change was modest and probably did not substantially increase progressivity. The federal share of tax revenues in 2002 was lower than in 1984, but the decline was not dramatic, from 73.6 to 69.2 percent (Varsano et al. 1998, p. 43; CEPALSTAT). Other than the increased tax burden, the most significant change was the rising complexity of the system, given the creation of new federal levies, the establishment of various special regimes for specific economic subsectors, and the use by state governments of ICMS tax breaks to compete for investment, a phenomenon referred to as the "fiscal war."

The 2002 elections ended the PSDB's reign, bringing to power the PT, a leftist party that had been created in 1981 and expanded gradually thereafter, becoming the key rival of the PSDB-led center-right coalition. Its best-known leader, former trade union activist Luiz Inácio Lula da Silva (known simply as Lula), had come in second in every presidential election since 1989. The PT would dominate the presidency for the next thirteen years under Lula (2003–2011) and Dilma Rousseff (2011–2016), both of whom led coalitions in which centrist forces, especially the Party of the Brazilian Democratic Movement (Partido do Movimento Democrático Brasileiro, PMDB), played a major role.

The PT-led governments were statist in outlook but generally did not bring dramatic policy changes. More extreme proposals traditionally endorsed by the party, such as massive land reform and renationalization of privatized SOEs, fell by the wayside. Instead, the PT focused mainly on fighting poverty through social spending and minimum wage hikes and encouraging economic growth by increasing the resources of the national development bank, now called "BNDES" ("social" was added to its name in the 1980s) (Hochstetler and Montero 2013). With regard to taxes, the changes wrought by PT governments were quite modest. As Cardoso had before him, Lula launched reform initiatives aimed at attenuating the distortions and complexities of the tax system, which discourage investment and impose extraordinary compliance costs on business (2015 interviews: Appy, Lisboa, Palocci). However, these proposals did not seek to alter the tax burden, and also did not substantially address concerns about regressivity.[8] In addition, like Cardoso's proposals, they were eventually largely abandoned by the government itself, resulting in little change.

Perhaps the two most significant tax policy changes during the PT years both tended to reduce the burden, which by the start of Lula's term was more than 7 percent of GDP higher than in any other Latin American country. The first occurred despite, rather than because of, the PT government. In 2007 Congress failed to renew the CPMF, depriving the state of about 1.5 percent of GDP in revenue. Although Lula was able to raise the rates of some other taxes to

---

[8] The PT did reduce federal taxes on staple foods (2015 interviews: Palocci, Pimentel), but most of the burden on these items involves the state-level ICMS, which was not significantly altered.

partially offset this loss, the CPMF's elimination was not a trivial blow. Taxation had continued its upward trajectory during Lula's first term, but largely because of the loss of CMPF revenues, it declined slightly after 2007 (CEPALSTAT). The second change began in 2011, when Rousseff started reducing employer social security contributions with the goal of maintaining high employment in the face of negative economic trends (Souza et al. 2016). Although the revenue loss was compensated by a tax on firms' gross receipts, that compensation was far from complete. By increasing the fiscal deficit, this policy contributed to the prolonged recession that began in the second half of 2014.[9]

The 2016 removal of President Rousseff by Congress brought unprecedented measures to control federal spending (which spiked upward during Rousseff's presidency), but still no clear sign of tax system change. Rousseff was impeached amid a massive corruption scandal involving PETROBRAS. The official investigation did not accuse her personally of wrongdoing, but opponents seized on fiscal irregularities, as well as a climate of public disgust with economic crisis and corruption, to secure her removal and replacement by Vice President Michel Temer of the PMDB. Temer pushed through Congress a draconian constitutional amendment freezing federal expenditure in real terms for twenty years, but failed to pass pension reform, which is essential for controlling spending. In 2018 Brazilian voters elected conservative populist Jair Bolsonaro as president. Although Bolsonaro's economic views had previously been rather statist, he chose a prominent liberal as finance minister and pledged to revive the quest for pension reform. After much debate, Congress approved a law in late 2019 that promises to reduce future pension spending significantly. Nevertheless, the reduction is likely to be insufficient to meet the spending cap (Borges 2019). Moreover, with public debt at an all-time high, there is little discussion of reducing the tax burden.[10]

5.3.2   The Persistent Weakness of Anti-Statism in Democratic Brazil

Previous sections of this chapter have emphasized the relative weakness of anti-statist forces in Brazil. Admittedly, recent years have brought an upsurge of anti-statist sentiment, driven by corruption, recession, and, perhaps, a middle-class backlash against PT efforts to channel more spending toward marginalized groups. Nevertheless, considering the democratic period as a whole, what is most impressive is the persistent lack of strong actors committed to anti-statism. While it has sometimes applauded efforts to reduce the size and inefficiency of the sprawling public sector, business has remained pragmatically accepting of intervention, organizationally fragmented, and focused on extracting narrow

---

[9] By 2014, the state was losing 0.5 percent of GDP in revenues from this policy (Ministério da Fazenda 2015, p. 2).

[10] *Estadão*, September 30, 2019.

benefits from the state. Anti-statism is also lacking in the party system. Non-leftist parties have dominated electoral politics, at least in Congress and at subnational levels, but they have not been programmatic right parties strongly committed to market-oriented policies.

It is true, as scholars have noted, that the private sector was broadly supportive of the liberalizing reforms adopted under Collor and Cardoso during the 1990s (Kingstone 1999, pp. 56–61; Diniz and Boschi 2003, p. 25). Brazil's protracted economic crisis, the constitution's strong focus on labor rights and social policy, and the pro-liberalization pressure exerted by multilateral institutions all helped sway business in favor of reform. While initial business support for Collor's reforms evaporated in the face of skyrocketing inflation and a major corruption scandal that eventually led to his resignation, Cardoso retained strong business backing, especially during his first term, a period of low inflation and solid growth. Business viewed itself as a "strategic ally" of the PSDB-led government in the process of building a more stable, competitive economy (Ferreira 2002, p. 12).

Beneath the apparent pro-market consensus, however, was a reality not so different from previous eras. Support for liberalization reflected discontent with the chaos that had afflicted Brazil since the early 1980s more than it did an ideological sea change. In the face of prolonged crisis, "industrialists who had prospered under state guidance and protection for sixty years came to support neoliberalism, but only because it offered to solve particular concrete problems. They were in no way ideologically committed to neoliberalism" (Kingstone 1999, p. 61). As the reform process advanced, many firms began to suffer the effects of greater competition, high interest rates, and reduced subsidies. When growth faltered in the late 1990s, due mainly to the effects of the "Asian flu" financial crisis, pressures for policy change grew (Diniz and Boschi 2003; Bresser-Pereira and Diniz 2009). Criticism of existing policies, which had until then been muffled, began to be aired publicly. The trend started with the Institute of Industrial Development Studies (IEDI), a think tank with statist leanings, but eventually found echo in FIESP and CNI, as well (Bresser-Pereira and Diniz 2009, pp. 94–96).

The prospect of a PT victory in the 2002 election panicked many economic elites, given the party's historic association with radical policies like suspension of foreign debt payments and massive land reform. However, Lula's rejection of such policies assuaged them and cemented a solid working relationship between business and the PT government (Diniz and Galli 2011). Moreover, an industrial sector that had long depended on state protection and subsidies supported the gradual shift to a more active industrial promotion policy, spearheaded by the increasingly resource-rich BNDES (Bresser-Pereira and Diniz 2009, pp. 94–95). At least until the economy entered a protracted recession in late 2014, even business criticism of PT social policy initiatives, including the CCT program Bolsa Família and steady increases in the real minimum wage, was muted. In other words, the private sector made a relatively fluid transition from Cardoso's market reformism to the PT's more explicit interventionism, reflecting its acceptance of a strong state role in the economy.

The traditional political fragmentation of Brazilian business has also not changed significantly (Schneider 2004; Doctor 2016). In the late 1980s and early 1990s, a number of voluntary organizations were created that sought to express dissent from the corporatist entities and forge a broader, cross-sectoral unity (Kingstone 1999; Schneider 2004; Doctor 2016). Some were attempts to influence the 1987–1988 constituent assembly or the 1993–1994 constitutional "revision," an exercise (foreseen in the constitution) in which reforms could be passed with a simple majority in each legislative chamber, rather than the normal 3/5 majority. By the second half of the 1990s, however, these entities had either disappeared or faded politically and the private sector was as fragmented as ever (Kingstone 1999, p. 225). The initiatives that survived, most notably the aforementioned IEDI, tended to have a statist orientation.

To be sure, democracy has brought changes in how business seeks to influence policy. Business has become more adept at lobbying Congress, which was largely irrelevant under military rule (Mancuso 2007). It has also registered some successes in forming coalitions to address specific issues of broad concern, like multilateral trade negotiations and improvement of the country's seaports (Mancuso and Oliveira 2006; Doctor 2016). Certain individual leaders, including steel magnate Jorge Gerdau, have striven to articulate the interests of various sectors to pressure for reduction of the *custo Brasil* (2015 interviews: Ferreira, Gerdau). However, nothing like the permanent peak associations found in Chile and Mexico has arisen. Brazilian business remains organized mainly to lobby for relatively narrow advantages, rather than to oppose state encroachment on free enterprise (Bresser-Pereira and Diniz 2009; 2015 interviews: Ferreira, Lisboa).

Determined advocacy of economic liberalism has not been a prominent characteristic of Brazil's parties, either. It is true that parties generally viewed as conservative have played an important role under the current democratic regime, especially during the years of neoliberal reformism (Hagopian 1996; Power 2000). Between 1990 and 2002, such parties controlled an average of 43.8 percent of the seats in the Chamber of Deputies and 36.6 percent in the Senate (Montero 2014, p. 301). Most important was the Party of the Liberal Front (Partido da Frente Liberal, PFL), a more or less lineal descendent of the military-era PDS. The PFL, which since 2007 has called itself Democratas (or DEM), averaged 17.8 and 21.5 percent of the seats, respectively, of deputies and senators. It held the vice presidency during both of Cardoso's presidential terms and at times was the largest party in the lower chamber.

Nevertheless, the PFL/DEM and the other Brazilian conservative parties lack the consistent adherence to economic liberalism that characterizes parties like Chile's RN and UDI or Mexico's PAN (Montero 2014; Nicolau 2017, p. 91). As Montero points out, the conventional understanding of such parties as strongly favoring market-oriented policies does not fit Brazil very well. "Although supportive of market-oriented reforms the right has not embraced these policies to the exclusion of developmentalist approaches, including industrial policy. Brazil's conservatives were latecomers to the Washington Consensus and they never adopted it wholly" (Montero 2014, p. 313). In addition, while generally opposed to policies that endanger property rights, Brazil's more conservative parties have not expressed doctrinaire opposition to social programs (Weyland 1996; Montero 2014).

More than ideological or programmatic coherence, what characterizes Brazil's conservative parties is their reliance on clientelism (Mainwaring 1999; Montero 2014). The PFL/DEM, for example, has traditionally drawn strength from a patronage network extending from top federal ministerial positions, which it has used to dole out jobs and access to spending programs, down to small cities and towns. The party has been most successful in poorer, more rural, and less educated regions, where there are fewer obstacles to using patronage to curry support. While even Chile's hyper-liberal UDI engages in clientelism, this strategy is balanced by clear programmatic appeals to more educated voters based on defense of the market economy. That is much less true of the PFL/DEM. In fact, the Brazilian party most consistently identified with support for market-oriented policies is actually the PSDB, which is generally characterized as centrist because of the social democratic orientation of its founders and its support for certain equity-enhancing programs.

In addition to not embodying a consistent demand for a smaller state, the major right-leaning parties have demonstrated important weaknesses in electoral competition. At least since the fall of Collor (an anti-party maverick supported mainly by right-leaning forces), conservative parties have not won a presidential election. In fact, probably sensing their inability to gain support in more developed regions, they have usually not even presented their own candidates, preferring to ally themselves with the centrist PSDB. The major conservative parties have also lost ground since the Cardoso era (Montero 2014; Nicolau 2017). The PFL/DEM, in particular, suffered enormous losses in recent national elections. In the 2014–2018 Congress, it held only 4.1 percent of the Chamber of Deputies seats and 6.2 percent of the Senate. By no means all these votes have flowed to the left, of course, but they have generally gone to parties with an even weaker rightist image. Bolsonaro's victory in the 2018 elections is not really an exception to this trend, since he represented a virtually unknown party that had never won more than a single seat in Congress. Even more than that of Mexico's López Obrador, Bolsonaro's victory was a result of personal charisma rather than the support of a party organization.

Finally, Brazil lacks strong market-oriented centers of intellectual production, at least compared to Chile and Mexico. There are some economically liberal think tanks, including the Rio de Janeiro-based Millennium Institute (Instituto Millenium). However, they are relatively new, possess limited resources, and lack the prestige of Chile's Liberty and

Development or CEP.[11] Nor does Brazil possess prestigious private universities with a strong market orientation comparable to Mexico's Tec de Monterrey or ITAM. The Pontifical Catholic University of Rio de Janeiro has an economic research center formed in 2003 that has a strong liberal orientation. It brings together some of the same researchers associated with the Instituto Millennium, several of whom have ties to the PSDB. Nevertheless, it is a relatively isolated voice within the broader intellectual community.

That anti-statism continues to be a weak force in Brazil reflects continuity in another area: the absence of an episode of state-led redistribution capable of galvanizing social forces into determined opposition to state intervention. While the nominally leftist PT held the presidency from 2003 to 2016, it failed to implement any reform that involved seizing private property, other than scattered land expropriations. Business was undoubtedly upset by the fiscal mismanagement of the Rousseff years, especially in the run-up to the 2014 election, but there is little sign that they viewed the PT's presence in office as a major threat to their core interests.

The notion that the moderation of post-military governments has encouraged the continued weakness of anti-statism is supported, ironically, by a significant exception, involving the farm sector. Agriculture enjoys a level of organization and unity that exceeds other economic sectors (2015 interviews: Castello Branco, Ferreira). During the mid-1980s, it developed a voluntary association, the Democratic Rural Union (União Democrática Ruralista, UDR), which mobilized large landowners across the country. Although the UDR faded in the 1990s, coordination among legislators representing large farm interests persisted and became increasingly institutionalized. Known as the *bancada ruralista*, the commercial agriculture caucus is more cohesive than most Brazilian parties and acts on a range of issues, including environmental protection, labor rights, and land rights. It typically includes 20–30 percent of the Chamber of Deputies and 15–20 percent of the Senate (Vigna de Oliveira 2007; Silva Lima 2017). No other business area has a legislative bloc of comparable size or cohesion (Castello Branco 2015, interview).

What explains agriculture's exceptionalism are threats to property that exceed those faced by other sectors. Goulart's drive for land reform, as discussed earlier, was a key reason behind the 1964 coup. With the democratic transition, pressures again mounted to alter Brazil's extraordinarily unequal landholding structure. President Sarney announced an ambitious reform based largely on expropriating underutilized private estates. Progressive actors mobilized to demand its

---

[11] *Forbes*, March 6, 2013. Instituto Millenium was launched in 2006. While it organizes events and posts articles by well-known economic liberals on its website, the Instituto Millenium has little in-house research production (Alexandre 2017, p. 51) and its annual revenues in recent years have averaged only about US $500,000 (see www.institutomillenium.org.br/institucional/pre-stacao-de-contas/). In comparison, CEP's revenues have averaged US $2.7 million since 2013 (see www.cepchile.cl/estados-financieros/cep/2016–05-12/134328.html).

implementation and ensure that the constituent assembly adopted provisions facilitating expropriation, while landowners mobilized to counter them (Gomes da Silva 1989). Conservative forces prevailed for the most part, but their victories were not definitive and land redistribution continued. Responding to recurrent land seizures, many of them organized by the Movement of Landless Rural Workers (Movimento dos Trabalhadores Rurais Sem Terra, MST), subsequent governments expropriated millions of hectares of land, albeit most of it of limited value. Somewhat surprisingly, the president who seized the most land was the centrist Cardoso, rather than those of the leftist PT (Ondetti 2016, p. 32).

Both the initial scare caused by Sarney's reform plan and the spurts of expropriation activity under subsequent governments have contributed mightily to the growth of a unified, politically mobilized commercial farm sector. Thus, as noted, agriculture is the exception that proves the rule with regard to the relationship between property redistribution and the emergence of strong anti-statist forces. However, the threat to property has not mobilized the private sector as a whole, due to both the limited character of land reform and the fact it occurred mainly under a government whose center-right coalition and generally market-oriented policies immunized it from accusations of being hostile to private property and capitalism.

5.3.3 The Growing Strength of Statist Forces

The persistent weakness of anti-statism in Brazil's democracy has been compounded by the rise of new actors committed to building a more redistributive public sector. The democratic transition witnessed the resurgence of popular mobilization, spearheaded by a stronger, more leftist labor movement than had existed during the earlier democratic interlude. That process also gave rise to the PT, which steadily became a major power contender and would win the presidency four consecutive times beginning in 2002. Both labor and the PT grew considerably more moderate over time and the power of PT presidents was tempered by their legislative dependence on non-left parties. Nevertheless, overall, the left has been a more significant force than during the 1945–1964 democratic regime.

Brazilian labor was not immune to the liberalizing economic trends that undercut unions in Chile, Mexico, and other Latin American countries (Cardoso 2003; Antunes et al. 2014). However, that phenomenon followed a period of rapid union growth in the late 1970s and 1980s with no parallel in the other two countries. The "New Unionism" that emerged during that period of rapid industrial expansion was better organized, more leftist, and more independent from political elites than its pre-1964 counterpart (Sader 1988). Deindustrialization and privatization in the 1990s hurt manufacturing and SOE unions, but those impacts were counterbalanced by the growth of unionism in the rural sector and among public employees outside the privatized SOEs (Jard da Silva 2015). Consequently, overall union density remained relatively stable (Cardoso 2014, p. 23; Cardoso and Gindin 2017).

Compared to Chile and Mexico, Brazil's contemporary labor force is better organized. Estimates of union density vary, but consistently show that Brazil's is greater than in either of the other countries (Confederación Sindical de Trabajadores/as de las Américas 2010; Bensusán 2016, p. 157). Unlike Brazil's private sector, labor has national confederations which unite unions from different sectors, as well as regions. Leadership of the movement is divided between five different confederations. However, the largest, the Unified Workers' Central (Central Única dos Trabalhadores, CUT), has close to three times as many affiliated unions as the next (Cardoso and Gindin 2017, p. 25). In addition, the movement's cohesion and influence are bolstered by organizations that provide support to unions across the confederations, particularly the Inter-Union Department of Statistics and Socioeconomic Studies (Departamento Inter-Sindical de Estatística e Estudos Socioeconômicos, DIEESE), a highly regarded advisory and research institute with no real analogue in Chile or Mexico.

Ideologically, Brazil's labor movement is more left-leaning than those of Chile and Mexico. The CUT grew out of the New Union movement, which had strong socialist leanings (Sader 1988; Keck 1992). Although the CUT became more moderate during the 1990s and early 2000s, it continues to have a center-left orientation. Of the other major union confederations, three are politically centrist and a fourth is to the left of the CUT. Together, the two leftist confederations comprise roughly half the country's unions (Cardoso and Gindin 2017, p. 25). It is harder to quantify the presence of the left in Chilean and Mexican labor movements, but contemporary studies of unions in these countries emphasize their generally moderate or depoliticized character (De la Garza 2014; Bensusán 2016).

Largely the same grassroots organizing drive that gave rise to the CUT also spawned the PT, a party whose ideological and programmatic leftism distinguished it from the pre-1964 PTB, as well as (with relatively minor exceptions) other parties of the current democratic era (Meneguello 1989; Keck 1992; Hunter 2010). Founded in 1980, the PT has had close ties to labor, progressive Catholics, intellectuals, and a variety of social movements. Between the 1980s and early 2000s, the PT's support gradually expanded, giving it an important presence in the Congress and local governments (Samuels 2004; Hunter 2010). It failed to win the presidency but, as noted earlier, came in second in the 1989, 1994, and 1998 elections. Compared to other parties, it was more ideologically coherent and enjoyed a more engaged base of supporters and greater legislative discipline. As can be seen in Table 5.1, the PT's power reached its apex between 2002 and 2014 when it won four straight presidential elections and established a stronger presence in other elected bodies, especially the Chamber of Deputies, where it captured a plurality of seats in all but one election.

Admittedly, the PT's thirteen-year dominance of the presidential office did not mean that the party's original vision became reality. By the time Lula took

TABLE 5.1 *Electoral performance of Brazil's PT, 1985–2016*

Election	Presidency (% first round vote and result)	Congress (% seats won) Chamber of Deputies	Senate	Governors (number elected)	Mayors of state capitals (number elected)
1985	–	–	–	–	1
1986		3.3	0	0	–
1988	–	–	–	–	3
1989–1990	17.2 (2nd round loss)	7.0	3.2	0	–
1992	–	–	–	–	4
1994	27.0 (1st round loss)	9.6	7.4	2	–
1996	–	–	–	–	2
1998	31.7 (1st round loss)	11.3	11.1	3	–
2000	–	–	–	–	6
2002	46.4 (2nd round win)	17.7	18.5	3	–
2004	–	–	–	–	9
2006	48.6 (2nd round win)	16.2	7.4	5	–
2008	–	–	–	–	6
2010	46.9 (2nd round win)	17.2	20.4	5	–
2012	–	–	–	–	5
2014	41.6 (2nd round win)	13.5	7.4	5	–
2016	–	–	–	–	1

Sources: Election Resources on the Internet (www.electionresources.org/); Tribunal Superior Eleitoral (www.justicaeleitoral.jus.br/eleicoes/estatisticas/); Nicolau (1998)
Note: Figures refer only to seats up for election that year.

office, the PT had already moderated its rhetoric and program substantially (Singer 2001; Samuels 2004; Hunter 2010). Change began in the mid-1990s when, following the party's second consecutive defeat in a presidential election, a pragmatic centrist faction led by Lula gained control of the top leadership posts. In an effort to appeal to a broader swath of the electorate, this faction gradually shelved or soft-pedalled the party's more leftist proposals and its goal of achieving socialism. The transformation accelerated during the 2002 campaign, when Lula explicitly promised to prioritize economic growth, maintain fiscal discipline, and honor Brazil's debt obligations.[12] He also took on José Alencar, a prominent industrialist and leader of the small pro-market Liberal Party, as his running mate. Hence, the PT that assumed Brazil's presidency in 2003 was essentially a center-left, social democratic party.

The nature of its governing coalitions, which relied heavily on non-left parties, especially the PMDB, also exerted a moderating impact on the PT. As Table 5.1 suggests, the PT itself never controlled even a fifth of the seats in either chamber of Brazil's highly fragmented Congress. The left as a whole reached roughly 30 percent.[13] At the subnational level, the PT's power was at least equally limited. It never controlled more than five of Brazil's twenty-six state governorships and consistently ran behind the PMDB and PSDB with regard to mayors and city council members. The weakness of PT governments pushed the party not only to moderate its policies but also to use some of the same corrupt tactics as past ruling parties to win elections and maintain legislative support (Pereira et al. 2011), resulting in scandals that undermined its reputation and contributed to its current crisis.

Still, the PT's rise to power represents a significant change in a country that had never before elected a leftist as president. The reasons behind the emergence of a solid leftist bloc in Brazil's contemporary democracy are complex and a full analysis is beyond the scope of this book. One point worth emphasizing, though, is that this process was facilitated in certain ways by the relative weakness of anti-statism. Most importantly, the state-led development drive of the preceding military regime unwittingly created conditions favorable to the rise of both a solid labor movement and a labor-based left party by expanding industry and the state apparatus itself (Keck 1992, pp. 8–12; Ondetti 2015). Both industrial workers and public sector employees would play key roles in the formation and expansion of the CUT and PT. This situation stands in sharp contrast to the Chilean case, in which Pinochet's radical liberalization undercut manufacturing and reduced the public bureaucracy, undermining the structural bases of labor power. Statist development policies were adopted during the 1970s in Mexico but less systematically than in Brazil and with poorer results in terms of industrial growth (Graham 1982).

5.3.4 Statist Predominance, the Constitution, and Taxation

The relatively statist balance of power in Brazil's contemporary democracy shaped both the provisions initially included in the 1988 constitution and the

---

[12] These commitments were articulated in a widely publicized document called the "Letter to the Brazilian People," released in June 2002.

[13] Due the ideological ambiguity of Brazilian parties and the extreme fragmentation of the party system, estimates of leftist strength vary. One scholar views the leftist contingent in the Chamber of Deputies as peaking at 25 percent (Nicolau 2017, p. 91) while another indicates that it reached 36.1 percent as a result of the 2006 elections (Hunter 2010, p. 48).

ways in which that document has subsequently been reformed and implemented, contributing to the creation of a large welfare state and heavy tax burden by developing country standards.

As mentioned earlier, the constitution contained a variety of provisions that put upward pressure on spending. It guaranteed free health care to all citizens, as well as social assistance for the needy, and obligated the various levels of government to dedicate specific minimum percentages of their budgets to education and health care. More importantly, it included a series of guarantees regarding retirement and disability pensions. With regard to pensions for private sector workers, these included setting the legal minimum wage as the floor for pension payments, integrating rural workers into the main pension system (where they would receive higher benefits), and removing restrictions on rural women receiving pensions. The constitution also guaranteed generous pension benefits for public sector workers and made them available to all permanent employees of the federal, state, and municipal governments. While its revenue provisions have been criticized on efficiency grounds, the constitution did provide mechanisms to raise additional funds, including an expanded state-level VAT and the creation of new federal social contributions.

These provisions reflected the rising force of largely the same coalition of labor, grassroots social movements, and middle-class intelligentsia that would eventually turn the CUT and the PT into important political actors and endow the PSDB with the mildly left-leaning character it would have until its embrace of neoliberal reformism in the mid-1990s. Buoyed by hopes of advancing their own agendas and forging a more progressive polity, these actors mobilized energetically to influence the constituent assembly, using a combination of public protests, institutional lobbying, and the submission of dozens of reform proposals (Michiles 1989; Martínez-Lara 1996, pp. 74–87; Hochstetler 2000, pp. 170–171). Their demand for a constitution crafted by and for common citizens resonated strongly with the political conjuncture of democratization and helped make the 1987–1988 constituent assembly a highly participatory exercise in constitution-making (Michiles 1989; Aragão 1996).

The PT and other explicitly leftist parties still lacked strong national organizations and controlled few seats in the constituent assembly, which doubled as Brazil's Congress.[14] Nevertheless, the PMDB, which had functioned as an omnibus opposition party under military rule, harbored many progressives, ranging from communists to the social democrats (e.g., Cardoso) who would form the PSDB in 1988 (Martínez-Lara 1996, pp. 66–69). Because of the PMDB's strong performance in the 1986 elections and the prominent roles played within that party by future PSDB founders, the

---

[14] Together, the PT, the center-left Democratic Workers' Party (Partido Democratico Trabalhista, PDT) and a number of smaller left-leaning parties controlled 9.3 percent of the seats in the constituent assembly. The PMDB alone controlled 54.2 percent (Martínez-Lara 1996, p. 65).

leadership of the assembly was sympathetic to civil society's demands for a socially oriented constitution. Thus, the initial draft ended up containing many new social and labor rights. While some would subsequently be deleted or diluted, the end product was nevertheless a constitution with strong social guarantees (Aragão 1996, p. 153).

Just as important as the forces pushing for statist provisions was the weakness of those resisting them. To be sure, conservative actors eventually mobilized into an interparty coalition, nicknamed the *Centrão* (or, roughly, "Broad Center"), that reversed some of the more left-leaning and pro-labor aspects of the initial constitutional draft. The *Centrão* had solid support from business, which generally shared its concerns. Yet, neither business nor the *Centrão* had a coherent anti-state agenda. Their focus was mainly on defeating a handful of proposals widely seen as especially dangerous, including strong land reform clauses, guaranteed job stability for private sector workers, and a shift to parliamentary government (Martinez-Lara 1996, p. 115; Kingstone 1999, pp. 51–56). Beyond this negative consensus, both were quite divided, and the initiatives they did put forward were in many cases defeated.[15]

Some of the constitutional clauses that have most contributed to rising taxation in democratic Brazil were only lightly contested by conservative forces during the assembly. A crucial example involves the pension programs for public and private sector workers, which were not a particular concern of either the private sector or the *Centrão* (Aragao 1996; Martinez-Lara 1996; Kingstone 1999; Gomes 2006; Lopes 2009). Government researchers had warned that pensions and other social policy commitments would drive federal spending upward and, in combination with increased revenue transfers to states and municipalities, tend to increase the deficit (Rezende and Afonso 1987). As a result, federal authorities would come under pressure to raise existing taxes or create new ones. President Sarney himself spoke publicly of this danger (Gomes 2006, p. 216). However, even among the more conservative parties, the desire for public approbation and patronage resources outweighed fiscal concerns (Weyland 1996, p. 140). Business expressed some misgivings about the impact of the proposed fiscal provisions, but ultimately it did not strongly oppose them.

Brazil's statist-leaning power balance also shaped how the constitution was later revised and implemented. Given the domestic context of hyperinflation and economic stagnation, combined with the international hegemony of neoliberalism, there were reasons to expect Brazilian governments of the early and mid-1990s to prune the constitution's social provisions or find ways to shirk the commitments embedded in them. Both Cardoso and Lula did make efforts to control pension spending on private and public sector workers

---

[15] Indeed, Freitas et al. (2009) suggest that, had the center-left faction that controlled the early phases of the drafting process not overreached by calling for parliamentarism and the shortening of Sarney's presidential term, the *Centrão* might never have arisen.

(Nakahado and Savoia 2008). However, these reforms ended up being relatively minor, especially compared to pension reforms implemented elsewhere in Latin America in the 1990s. Instead, with regard to fiscal policy, policymakers' efforts focused largely on raising enough resources to fulfill the constitution's social commitments (Afonso and Serra 2007; Melo et al. 2010). One of Brazil's top fiscal experts remarked drily that, "It was the first time in history that a fiscal adjustment contributed to increasing social spending" (Rezende 2015, interview).

It might be argued that this focus reflected the immutability of the constitutional clauses on which spending was based. However, the rules for amending Brazil's constitution are not particularly onerous (a 3/5 majority in both chambers in two rounds of voting) and were reduced to a simple majority during the 1993–1994 "revision" exercise. In fact, as of this writing, the 1988 constitution has already been amended 107 times, an average of three and a half amendments per year. Constitutional reform has become almost a routine aspect of Brazilian governance (Arantes and Couto 2009).

Rather than constitutional restrictions, the emphasis on raising revenue rather than cutting spending reflects the fact that pro-spending forces have wielded much influence, while opposition to taxation has been, in general, comparatively weak. Major pension reform, a crucial issue with regard to taxation, has repeatedly been frustrated by a broad alliance of labor unions, parties, professional associations, and pensioners' groups (Weyland 1996, ch. 6; Brooks 2008, pp. 222–236 and 272–295). The PT and CUT have been key members of this alliance, as have certain groups of white-collar federal civil servants who are well organized but unaffiliated with any labor confederation.[16] While the PT was not in power during the period in which pension spending increased most rapidly, Lula's strong performance in presidential elections and the party's growing presence in other elected offices made it crucial for the PSDB-led governments to protect their left flank by portraying themselves as sensitive to social issues. It is true that Lula himself implemented a reform of the pension system for public employees, but that reform was still only an incremental change and caused much strife within the PT and CUT.[17] Although public employees are a powerful lobbying group, this reform affected far fewer people than would a change in the public pension system for private sector workers, which has more than twenty times as many beneficiaries.

Labor and the left have also affected pension spending by pressuring for increases in the minimum wage above the inflation rate. While some observers warned during the constituent assembly that tying pensions to the minimum wage would lead authorities to hold the latter down (Weyland 1996, p. 140),

---

[16] The employees of the federal tax agency are a key example. Their organizations are imposing forces, in part because they can muster expert knowledge to counter official arguments.

[17] A number of PT legislators refused to vote with the government and were expelled from the party. Some unions also left the CUT as a result of its willingness to negotiate a compromise bill.

the reality has been nearly the opposite: consistent real increases in the minimum wage since the mid-1990s, especially under the PT, have tended to raise the values of the lowest pensions and increase public spending (Lavinas et al. 2017, p. 9). Since about 60 percent of pensioners in the system for private sector workers receive the minimum value, this trend has had a large impact on spending and popular welfare.

Meanwhile, the steady rise of taxation during the 1990s and early 2000s met with little in the way of collective resistance. Business associations, especially those representing the manufacturing sector (e.g., CNI and FIESP), issued reports and organized events criticizing taxation's vast contribution to the *custo Brasil*. They even engaged in a degree of interassociational coordination to lobby for reform. The main manifestation of this phenomenon, an initiative dubbed Business Action (Ação Empresarial), was led by industrialist Jorge Gerdau. However, it was informal, episodic, and largely ineffectual (Ferreira 2002; Ferreira 2015, interview). Business Action had no permanent office or staff and little media presence. Furthermore, the group did not call for the tax burden to be reduced, a goal they understood to be out of reach (Ferreira 2015, interview). Rather, their demands focused on simplifying and rationalizing the system in order to reduce distortions, compliance costs, and uncertainty.

Business association leaders and public officials interviewed for this study emphasized that Brazil's private sector is too divided to effectively oppose taxation (2015 interviews: Castello Branco, Ferreira, Hauly). Even within the industrial sector itself, a CNI official argued, the diversity of interests makes it difficult to formulate a common agenda (Castello Branco 2015, interview). Of the major economic sectors, only agriculture, as discussed earlier, demonstrates greater unity. However, farm producers are less concerned about taxation because they face a lower tax burden and thus have not been important actors in this area in recent years (Garret and Rausch 2015, p. 10; Federação das Indústrias do Estado de Rio de Janeiro 2018, p. 4).[18] A veteran PSDB legislator known for his advocacy of tax reform went as far as to dismiss the sectoral confederations as "useless," due to their inability or unwillingness to mobilize their memberships to pressure for change (Hauly 2015, interview).

The very complexity of the tax system, with various special regimes and tax breaks at different levels of government, tends to aggravate the problem of business fragmentation by encouraging firms to pursue individual solutions (2015 interviews: Castello Branco, Mendes). Comparing the system to a cinema, a former top economic policymaker described Brazil as "the country of the half-price ticket" (Lisboa 2015, interview). Rather than seeking global tax reform (i.e., broadly lower ticket prices), interest groups try to improve their own situation by achieving special favors from state authorities in the form of narrow tax breaks or subsidies (i.e., half-price tickets). However,

---

[18] The reasons for this are varied, but probably the most important is that exports of primary and semi-processed products have been exempt from the ICMS since 1996.

this practice only shifts the burden, at least temporarily, to other actors and contributes to making the system as a whole so opaque that no one is ultimately sure how the burden is shared.

CUT, DIEESE, PT, and other left of center forces, for their part, have not expressed opposition to heavy taxation, arguing that it is necessary to provide redistribution and social protection in a highly unequal society (2015 interviews: Huertas, Lucio, Queiroz). They have sometimes held seminars and issued reports calling for greater reliance on direct taxes, but these have been infrequent and low-profile initiatives compared to their advocacy in support of higher wages and opposition to pension reform. For the most part they have kept relatively silent on the tax issue, perhaps for fear of aiding opponents of taxation and endangering the flow of revenues necessary to sustain social programs.

To be sure, tolerance of taxation in Brazil is not unlimited. By the early 2000s, businesses, in particular, were bridling at a tax burden far above that of any other Latin American country and a compliance process that was among the most complex, time consuming, and costly in the world.[19] Although they did not give rise to significant organizational innovations, these concerns did fuel the 2007 revolt against renewal of the CPMF. Spearhead by the PSDB and DEM, with the support of several business associations and media outlets, this effort resulted in one of the most significant opposition victories of the Lula era and may have sensitized the government to the need to avoid further tax increases (2015 interview: Schoueri, Zanotto).[20] President Rousseff's proposal to deal with the mounting budget deficit following her 2014 reelection by reestablishing the CPMF set off another strong reaction among some business organizations, most notably FIESP, which campaigned actively for her removal.[21]

Still, these manifestations of resistance to taxation are notable precisely because they constitute exceptions to the rule and arose only after the tax burden had ascended to very high levels, at least by regional and developing country standards. In fact, politicians and policymakers interviewed for this book regularly asserted that in Brazil it is easier to raise taxes than to contain spending (2015 interviews: Barbosa, Rezende, Villela), an argument that is much harder to make about contemporary Chile or Mexico.

5.4 CONCLUSION

Brazil's heavy tax burden has more than one cause. Economic structures play some role: in particular, the country lacks extractable natural resources from

---

[19] *Paying Taxes*, an annual report on tax compliance processes produced by the World Bank and the accounting firm PwC since 2005, consistently ranks Brazil near the bottom in terms of ease of compliance. The data can be accessed at: www.pwc.com/payingtaxes.

[20] *UOL Notícias*, December 31, 2010.

[21] *Estadão*, December 14, 2015. FIESP attracted attention by using a giant inflatable duck to symbolize its rejection of increased taxation, playing on the popular expression "to pay the duck," which means to bear the costs of someone else's mistakes or misdeeds.

which the state can readily derive nontax revenues. Political institutions are also significant, especially the 1988 Constitution, which created social spending commitments that have pressured democratically elected authorities to increase taxation, while also providing them with certain tools to do so. Nevertheless, as this chapter has argued, the fact that Brazil's tax burden is far heavier than Mexico's or Chile's cannot be adequately understood without appreciating how the relative lack of sharp conflict over property rights in Brazil has shaped societal attitudes toward state intervention, especially at the elite level.

Unlike both Chile and Mexico, Brazil has never experienced a major reform wave that endangered private property. While elites have suffered from the effects of macroeconomic instability, they have never seen a state that effectively challenged their vital interests. As a result, in comparison to elites in the other two countries, Brazil's have not developed either an anti-statist culture or robust organizations devoted to halting public sector expansion. Instead, influenced by the *varguista* tradition of business-friendly statism, they have focused their political energies on deriving particularistic benefits from the state's interventions. The lack of fundamental reforms has also discouraged the political mobilization of social conservatism and the emergence of a strong alliance of social conservatives and economic liberals.

The weakness of anti-statism has affected taxation by depriving Brazil of a strong counterweight to pressures for public sector expansion. Whereas anti-statist forces in Mexico and Chile have generally combatted tax increases fiercely, in Brazil raising taxes has long been seen as the "easy" way to deal with budget deficits, since it encounters less opposition than spending cuts. Facing a challenging situation, the "reflex" of the Brazilian state is to deal with it through intervention, often involving a quest for additional revenues, while in the other countries nearly the opposite is true, since political resistance to an interventionist response is often greater. As a result, state intervention has expanded rather steadily over the years and, in the process, created entrenched interests that resist efforts to prune it, including both a protected manufacturing sector and private and public sector labor unions.

Brazil's contemporary economic and political crisis is putting the traditional tolerance of a large, intrusive state to the test. Anti-statism has flared in response to official corruption and prolonged stagnation and its defenders have secured significant policy victories. However, the analysis developed in this book suggests that the crisis itself may not be enough to turn Brazil away from its statist tradition. Absent existential threats to elite interests, it is difficult to see how the country can develop an anti-statist bloc strong and enduring enough to forge a new, more liberal development model in the long term.

6

Argentina

Populism, Divided Elites, and Heavy Taxation

Today, Argentina has a tax burden similar to Brazil's, at close to a third of GDP. However, the route it has traveled to that outcome is different. In particular, Argentina's tax burden has been far more volatile. Between 1950 and 1990, tax revenues fluctuated between about 11 and 18 percent of GDP, and there were three separate instances in which the tax burden declined by a third or more within a three-year period, only to rebound in subsequent years. While tax revenues appeared to stabilize during the 1990s and early 2000s at around 20 percent of GDP, they subsequently increased by more than half, transforming Argentina from a moderately taxed country into one of the two most heavily taxed in Latin America.

This contrast in trajectories reflects differences in the political forces shaping taxation. In Argentina, there has been greater conflict among economic elites about the proper role of the state. In addition, bottom-up pressures for public sector growth have played a more important role than in Brazil, due to a stronger labor movement and associated populist electoral coalition. While divided elites and an organized popular sector might have led to sustained state growth, that outcome was for decades frustrated by the armed forces, whose repeated interventions generally favored liberal interests but failed to consolidate a stable development model. The stalemate between populism and anti-populism led to extreme instability, reflected in recurrent inflationary surges and an erratic tax burden.

Despite these differences, this chapter argues, Argentina shares with Brazil the fact that the emergence of a heavy tax burden has been facilitated by the lack of a historical episode of redistribution profound enough to spur the rise of a powerful anti-statist coalition. The most significant reform wave in Argentine history occurred during the late 1940s and early 1950s under President Juan Perón. Compared to his contemporary Getúlio Vargas, Perón was more aggressive in mobilizing workers and expanding their rights, which helps explain the unusual strength of Argentina's *peronista*-dominated labor movement. However, Perón resembled the Brazilian leader in sparing private property, positioning himself clearly in opposition to socialism and assiduously courting business. In fact, he was sometimes accused of being a fascist. These traits set him unambiguously apart from Allende and Cárdenas.

As a result, the rise of *peronismo* failed to provoke the emergence of an anti-statist bloc capable of acting as an enduring constraint on public sector growth. While there is a more significant liberal current within Argentina's private sector than Brazil's, its influence has been counterbalanced by others that embrace the interventionist policies championed by Perón. This cleavage has contributed to the political fragmentation of the private sector and the failure to establish competitive conservative parties. It has also helped organized labor to maintain its status as a major actor. While Argentine unions have at times faced repression, private sector divisions have worked to their benefit by allowing them to make common cause with more statist firms. Thus, Argentina, like Brazil, is a case in which historical events have resulted in a balance of power that is relatively statist. The specific components of that balance are somewhat different, but the net result is similar and, at the same time, clearly distinct from Chile and Mexico, where anti-statism is stronger.

The heavy contemporary tax burden in Argentina expresses this balance. For decades, as mentioned earlier, military interventions kept statist forces from wielding power in a sustained fashion. In addition, crippling bouts of hyperinflation and the global ascendancy of neoliberalism pushed even a *peronista* government to adopt IMF-sponsored adjustment policies in the 1990s. Gradually, however, these constraints have fallen away, and the relative superiority of statist forces has come to be reflected in public policies involving heavy taxation and voluminous spending, especially on social programs.

This chapter focuses on explaining the dynamics of four relatively distinct periods in the trajectory of Argentina's tax burden: its rapid growth during Perón's first two presidencies (1946–1955); its marked volatility between Perón's ouster and the beginning of the 1990s; its stabilization at a moderate level for a decade between the early 1990s and early 2000s; and, finally, its sustained upward surge between 2003 and 2015. Unlike the chapters on Chile, Mexico, and Brazil, this one does not have a section focused on the current democratic period as a whole, since that period has seen a great deal of variation in the direction and pace of tax burden growth.

6.1 PERÓN, POPULISM, AND RISING TAXATION

Between the mid-1940s and the early 1950s, Argentina went from having a tax burden about average for the countries analyzed in this book to being clearly the most heavily taxed. While this increase was not consistently sustained thereafter, the episode is worth examining because it set in motion changes that would profoundly affect the country's fiscal development. The proximate cause of the tax increase was Perón's successful effort to forge a new political coalition by redistributing income to workers and promoting industrialization through state intervention. Underlying his success, however, were other factors, including the failure of earlier governments to politically incorporate an expanding working class, the exceptionally favorable economic conditions Argentina enjoyed following World War II, and the concern of many conservatives that workers might embrace revolutionary radicalism.

6.1.1   From Light to Heavy Taxation

In a little over a decade in civilian government positions, Perón profoundly transformed the tax system, increasing all major types of tax revenue relative to GDP and centralizing collection in the national government to a greater extent than before.

Prior to Perón, the development of Argentina's tax system had resembled that of the other case study countries in a number of key respects. Initial heavy dependence on trade levies, especially import tariffs, had gradually given way in the early decades of the twentieth century to a more domestically based system. Customs revenues declined from about two-thirds of total revenues before World War I to about 10 percent in the early 1940s (AFIP). As in the other countries, external shocks, including World War I and the Great Depression, played important roles in this transition (Sánchez Román 2012, chs. 1 and 2). The levels of taxation in Argentina were also roughly in line with the other cases. As Figure 6.1 suggests, Argentina's tax burden pre–World War I averaged about 7–8 percent of GDP, or somewhere between Mexico's and Chile's. At about 10 percent of GDP, its tax burden in the first half of the 1940s was somewhat heavier than Mexico's, somewhat lighter than Brazil's, and similar to Chile's.

Nevertheless, Argentine taxation was comparatively light if one considers that the country was substantially more developed than the others. Due to its exceptional success exporting beef and grains, Argentina had emerged by the early twentieth century as (along with Uruguay) the richest country in Latin America. According to one estimate, its average per capita GDP from 1939 to 1941 was roughly triple Brazil's, double Mexico's, and 50 percent higher than Chile's (Astorga et al. 2005, p. 788). These differences would narrow greatly in the coming decades, but Argentina's wealth at this juncture meant that it was lightly taxed relative to its development level. In substantial measure, this was because its transition to domestic taxation came late. For example, while the other countries adopted the income tax in the first half of the 1920s, Argentina would not do so until 1932 (Sánchez Román 2012, pp. 49–50). The emergence of a broad-based social security program also lagged at least a decade behind Chile and Brazil, occurring in the mid-1940s (Mesa-Lago 1978, ch. 5). It is true that by the early 1940s domestic levies contributed the vast bulk of Argentina's

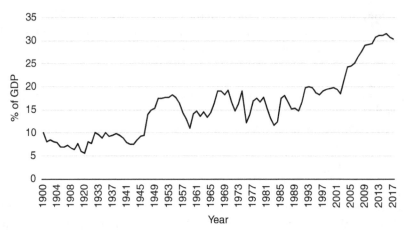

FIGURE 6.1 Evolution of Argentina's tax burden, 1900–2017[2]
Sources: AFIP; CEPALSTAT/ECLAC; Montevideo-Oxford Latin American Economic History Database; Camelo and Itzcovich (1978); Cetrángolo and Gómez Sabaini (2007b)

tax revenues, but this was largely because trade disruptions caused by World War II provoked a 75 percent decline in tariff revenue.[1] Argentina's tax system would undergo a major transformation under Perón's leadership. An army officer, Perón played key roles in the conservative nationalist military regime that ruled from 1943 to 1946, serving as secretary of labor and social security and subsequently adding the titles of secretary of war and vice president. He ran for president in the 1946 election and won a resounding victory. Although reelected in 1951 to a second six-year term, he was removed via a military coup in 1955. During the 1943–1946 regime, Perón had pushed for the expansion of social security, causing the system's revenues to double relative to GDP (AFIP). As president, he deepened this process, incorporating virtually the entire formal sector labor force (Mesa-Lago 1978, p. 164). Since the system ran a large surplus during this period, its revenues were used to support general spending by purchasing public bonds at interest rates below inflation (Cortés Conde 2009, p. 165). In his early years as president, Perón also increased income taxation by raising personal and corporate rates and taxing previously untaxed capital gains (Sánchez Román 2012, pp. 86–88). Beginning in 1948, the emphasis shifted to indirect taxes, mainly in the form of large increases in the federal sales tax rate (Sánchez Román 2012, pp. 93–94).

As a result of these reforms, federal tax revenues rose steadily throughout the latter half of the 1940s (AFIP; Cetrángolo and Gómez Sabaini 2007b, p. 27).

---

[1] Between 1939 and 1945, tariff revenues fell from 2.8 percent of GDP to only 0.7 percent (AFIP).
[2] Data for 1900–1909 and 1932–1949 include only federal taxes. Only selected years are available for 1910–1929.

Revenues from all three major categories grew rapidly, but social security experienced the fastest growth, once again almost doubling relative to GDP (AFIP). During Perón's second term, the system stabilized with regard to both revenue and structure. The overall tax burden during this period averaged 17.8 percent of GDP, the heaviest of any of the countries examined here. While direct tax revenues had increased substantially relative to GDP since the mid-1940s, other types of revenue also grew, so taxation probably did not become more progressive.[3]

Perón's push to increase federal revenues deepened a centralizing trend visible since at least the 1930s. Scattered data from the 1910s and 1920s suggest that provincial governments collected about 25 percent of tax revenues (Herschel and Itzcovich 1957, p. 104). However, reforms undertaken during the 1930s, including the introduction of federal income and sales taxes, had a centralizing impact (Díaz Cayeros 2006, pp. 186–191). Increasingly, the provinces gave up their own taxes in return for fiscal transfers. This system was consolidated under Perón and the federal share of revenues was further boosted by greater social security revenue. From 1952 to 1955, the provincial share was only 10.3 percent, which made the Argentine system more centralized than Brazil's or Mexico's, although less than Chile's. These data do not include municipal revenues, but municipal tax authority in Argentina is limited and the amount of revenue brought in by these governments was undoubtedly small.[4]

In his zeal to raise revenue, Perón also tapped nontax sources. Most importantly, he used a state monopoly on trade to seize part of the income generated by the country's agricultural producers. However, these revenues faded rapidly with the decline in commodity prices in the late 1940s, dropping from a cumulative total of 3.7 percent of GDP between 1946 and 1948 to only 0.5 percent from 1949 to 1955 (Cortés Conde 2009, p. 149). Hence, the sustained increase in fiscal resources under Perón was mainly due to taxation.

6.1.2 Populism and Public Revenue

The rapid increase in tax revenue under Perón was a function of his political strategy, which was to capture the allegiance of workers through redistributive and social protection policies while also spurring industrialization and thus

---

[3] Income taxes comprised 18.5 percent of federal tax revenues in Perón's second term, compared to 18.9 percent in 1940–1945 (AFIP). Indirect taxes contributed 43.8 percent and social security taxes 34.8 percent. Subnational data are not disaggregated by tax type for this period, but since social security was a federal policy, including subnational data would reduce somewhat the weight of social security.

[4] In contrast to Brazil's, Argentina's constitution does not grant municipalities specific authority to levy taxes, but some provincial constitutions have allowed them to impose property taxes. Nevertheless, much of their own-source revenue comes from nontax sources, such as fees for services. Data for selected years between 1961 and 2009 show that municipal revenues hovered around 5 percent of total tax revenue (Cetrángolo and Goldschmidt 2013, p. 40).

further expanding the working class. To be effective, this strategy required much additional revenue.

Without question, the core of *peronismo* was its appeal to labor. Perón's courtship of Argentine workers has been analyzed extensively elsewhere (Germani 1962; Murmis and Portantiero 1971; Torre 1990, 1998) and need only be referred to briefly here. From his position as secretary of labor and social security in the 1943–1946 military regime, Perón built a base of labor support by favoring workers in industrial conflicts, enforcing previously ignored labor laws, strengthening unions vis-à-vis management, and establishing or increasing monetary compensation and non-wage benefits, such as pensions and health care. The pro-labor orientation continued during his first term as president, contributing to a major increase in labor's share of national income. Economic problems during Perón's second term led to fiscal austerity measures, which rolled back some of the previous income gains, but the net result was still positive (Ranis 1992, p. 27).

In addition to material benefits, Perón gave workers a more prominent political role and discursively recognized them as crucial contributors to national greatness (Collier and Collier 1991). Although union leaders lost autonomy relative to the state, the General Confederation of Labor (Confederación General del Trabajo, CGT), their major umbrella organization, grew in size and influence. The material and symbolic gains of this era, combined with the harsh treatment meted out to labor by some later governments, would lead Argentine workers to view Perón's first period in power as a kind of golden age when the state took the side of the common man. *Peronismo*, with its appeal to nationalism and social justice, would become the dominant political identity of Argentina's lower classes (Mora y Araujo 2011, p. 53).

While Perón was pro-worker, he was not anti-capitalist and, in some ways, he aggressively promoted private business. He sought to strengthen domestic industry in order to modernize the economy and increase Argentina's autonomy from rich countries (Brennan 1998; Brennan and Rougier 2009). To this end, he not only strove to limit strike activity but also granted generous trade protection and subsidized credit to industry. Partly to provide inexpensive inputs to domestic firms (as well as consumers), Perón established numerous SOEs in areas such as rail transportation, communications, and electricity (Cortés Conde 2009, p. 171). Perhaps the only sector clearly singled out for hostility were farm exporters, who symbolized the old oligarchical system *peronismo* rejected and whose preference for an open economy clashed with the regime's nationalistic priorities.

Some of Perón's policy measures, such as price controls, foreign exchange controls, and labor regulation, did not require fiscal resources beyond those necessary to establish monitoring and enforcement capacity. However, many others did require copious funding. A key example was the tremendous expansion of the social safety net, which involved payment of pensions and other cash benefits, the construction and staffing of hospitals, and the development of a bureaucratic apparatus to manage the system. Public enterprises were also costly to the federal treasury, not only because of the expenses involved in creating them, but also because many operated at a loss, due to the low prices they charged for their services and their inflated staffs, and thus required subsidies (Cortés Conde 2009, p. 171).

As discussed earlier, prior to Perón Argentina's tax system brought in a modest volume of revenue, in part due to the slow transition to domestic taxation. This situation reflected the lingering influence of the liberal, export-oriented development model, which had brought the country exceptional economic success. However, because the transformations pursued by Perón required greater revenue, they ultimately led to the tax changes outlined earlier, which expanded all major categories of taxation relative to GDP.

6.1.3 Underlying Causes

While a comprehensive analysis of the roots of *peronismo* is not possible here, it is worth making some brief observations about the underlying causes of the major changes in the Argentine state during these years. Undoubtedly, one reason for Perón's relative success was his skill as a political strategist. However, Perón also benefitted from conditions beyond his control. Three such conditions seem especially important: the size and political availability of the working class, the exceptionally positive economic context he enjoyed during his first term, and widespread concern among conservative elites that workers would embrace radical ideologies and become a revolutionary threat.

As Collier and Collier (1991) argue, Perón's impact stems from the comparatively long delay in politically "incorporating" labor. By the 1920s, Argentina's manufacturing sector was the largest in Latin America, and its growth accelerated in the 1930s and early 1940s as a result of the "natural" protection offered by international trade disruptions, as well as incipient state efforts to induce industrialization. Unionization grew alongside industry and, on the eve of the Perón era, Argentina's labor force was already possibly the best organized among the more developed Latin American countries (Collier and Collier 1991, p. 336). In spite of this, no government had yet sought to court labor by offering it truly major inducements. Some appeals had been made during an interlude of democratic governance from 1916 to 1930, but those were cut short by a military coup and the subsequent establishment of a conservative civilian regime sustained by electoral fraud. In this sense, Argentina lagged behind much of the region.

The significance of this delay is that Perón encountered a labor movement that was both large and politically available. Some leftist groups, including the Communist and Socialist parties, had developed ties to unions, but these rather quickly dissolved in the face of the benefits Perón offered to his union allies. To be sure, Perón himself contributed to a major expansion of the unionized population (Ranis 1992, p. 26). However, he also benefitted from being able to draw on the support of a labor movement that was already substantial. Facilitating Perón's efforts further was the favorable economic situation he inherited after winning the 1946 election. For one thing, due to the difficulty of importing manufactured goods during World War II, Argentina had accumulated plentiful foreign exchange reserves (Ferrer 1977, p. 84). In addition, strong external demand for the country's commodity exports in the years immediately after the war buoyed economic growth and exchange earnings (Gerchunoff and Llach, 1998, p. 18). These advantages gave regime authorities a certain freedom from normal concerns about macroeconomic discipline and allowed them to instead focus on boosting living standards through higher wages, greater state benefits, and rapid job creation. While the boom would give way to a bust by the end of the 1940s, the state's largesse during this era cemented Perón's reputation as the Argentine worker's best friend.

A final facilitating factor was the concern among conservatives that the country's growing urban working class would become a source of subversion. Waisman (1987) has argued that resistance to Perón's rise was attenuated by the fear among elites, including officials of the armed forces and Catholic Church, that long-marginalized workers would embrace Marxism. Their fear led them to accept, at least for several years, Perón's ambitious program of labor incorporation and state-led industrialization, which he framed in speeches to elite groups as a way of achieving class harmony. Although perhaps exaggerated in its focus on this factor as the key to Argentina's subsequent economic decline, Waisman's argument helps explain why Perón was able to use his position within the otherwise conservative military regime to cultivate a powerful labor support base.

6.2 POLITICAL CONFLICT AND TAX BURDEN INSTABILITY

One of the more striking aspects of Argentina's tax burden trajectory is its pronounced instability for more than three decades following Peron's ouster. After 1955, the heavy tax burden established by the *peronista* regime was neither sustained nor definitively rolled back. Rather, the country experienced a recurrent cycle of sharp revenue growth and decline, with few if any parallels in the other cases explored in this book.

At bottom, this pattern reflected the peculiar division of Argentine society engendered by Perón. Because he had mobilized workers without threatening property, Perón forged a loose but powerful coalition between labor and domestically oriented businesses, both of which favored state-led development. Anti-statist forces used military intervention to thwart this coalition's bid for dominance but were unable to establish an enduring liberal order of their own. The stalemate resulted in policy instability and periodic economic crises that deeply undermined tax collection. Events of the early 1980s would render military intervention unviable, but Argentina's new democracy inherited economic disequilibria and institutional weaknesses that initially foiled attempts to break with the earlier pattern.

6.2.1 Taxation and Macroeconomic Instability

The exceptional tax revenue volatility of this period was not a reflection of fluctuations in tax policy, which generally sought to increase revenue, even at the cost of marked inefficiencies. Instead, it reflected the country's extraordinary macroeconomic instability, which deeply affected tax collection and over time seriously undermined the state's credibility.

For over thirty-five years after the 1955 coup d'état, Argentina's tax burden surged and declined repeatedly, sometimes rising to a level slightly higher than the peaks reached under Perón and other times falling to one not far above that of the mid-1940s (see Figure 6.1). In three instances (1956–1959, 1974–1975, and 1980–1983), the tax burden declined by a third or more within a period of no more than three years. It was only in the early 1990s that this pattern of periodic collapses was left behind. No other country examined in this book has experienced a period of comparable volatility, at least since 1900.

As mentioned, this pattern cannot readily be ascribed to tax policy, since virtually all governments of the era were engaged in a struggle to extract enough revenue to keep the fiscal deficit manageable (Sánchez Román 2012, chs. 3 and 4). To be sure, there were governments of varying policy preferences during this tumultuous period, which saw numerous political crises and regime transitions. Some, including those of Arturo Frondizi (1958–1962) and Perón, who was elected to a third term in October 1973 but died less than a year later, pursued relatively statist policies. Others, especially the 1976–1983 military regime, embraced a strongly liberal approach. However, even the more economically liberal governments did not set out to substantially reduce taxation. In some cases, they sought to grant key constituencies relief from specific taxes, but, given the strong spending pressures they faced, none could afford to reduce the overall volume of revenue.

Rather, the modal pattern of tax policymaking during these decades was one of frequent tinkering, often involving urgent efforts to raise revenue in the face of a growing deficit. In such cases, there was a tendency to rely on measures that could be deployed quickly but were often criticized as excessively distortive (World Bank 1990, pp. 23–25; Melo 2007). A prime example was the recurrent imposition of export taxes. During the 1940s and 1950s, Perón had extracted revenue from exporters through the state's trade monopoly. Subsequent governments rejected that tool but periodically raised export taxes instead (Cortés Conde 2009, p. 204). At their peak in 1989, they contributed 2 percent of GDP, or 15 percent of the tax burden (Cetrángolo and Gómez Sabaini 2007b, p. 33). Compared to other taxes, these levies had some advantages: they were hard to evade, could be justified by the windfall profits earned by exporters in the wake of repeated currency devaluations, and attenuated inflation by pushing farmers to sell more of their production domestically. At the same time, however, they undercut foreign exchange earnings and discouraged investment in Argentina's most competitive sector.

In contrast, revenues from major domestic taxes, especially the income tax, tended to decline. After hovering at around a fifth of federal tax revenues from the late 1940s until 1960, the contribution of the income tax tended to drop, reaching its nadir in 1984, when it contributed less than 5 percent (AFIP). The income tax's decline did not reflect rates, which actually increased for both individuals and corporations after 1955 (Sánchez Román 2012, p. 145). Rather, it was due to a combination of exceptions and deductions, evasion, repeated amnesties, and the Olivera–Tanzi effect, to which this levy was especially vulnerable because of relatively long lags between taxable events and collection (World Bank 1990, p. 7). The decline of both personal and corporate income taxation probably made the system as a whole more regressive. In addition, it contributed to the modest decentralization of taxation that occurred post-Perón.[5]

A significant exception that should be noted to the growing reliance on relatively inefficient and ad hoc taxes was the 1974 adoption of a VAT with a general rate of 13 percent (Sánchez Román 2012, p. 171). The tax had been debated since the late 1960s but was finally introduced in the context of mounting fiscal problems under Perón. Like those of most other major federal taxes, VAT revenues were to be shared with the provinces. While its revenue contribution was initially modest, during the 1990s, for reasons discussed later, the VAT would become the workhorse of Argentina's tax system.

Instead of efforts to raise or lower taxes, what tax burden volatility reflected was the broader instability of the macroeconomy. Argentina post-1955 was a paradigmatic case of an economy afflicted by recurrent boom-bust cycles. There were periods of solid growth, but these were followed by increasingly devastating crises characterized by inflation, balance of payments problems, and recession. Instability meant that Argentina's regional exceptionalism in terms of wealth was gradually eroded, as countries with more consistent growth increasingly gained ground on it (Astorga et al. 2005, p. 78).

The variable most closely linked to the tax burden was inflation. Rapid price increases became a chronic problem beginning after World War II, but one whose intensity varied over time (Mallon and Sourrouille 1975; Carciofi 1990). As Figure 6.2 suggests, there was a roughly inverse relationship between the inflation rate and the tax burden. In particular, periods of very high inflation, including 1959, 1975–1976, 1983–1984, and 1989, were also ones of light taxation. Inflation undermined revenues because of the Olivera–Tanzi effect, in which the lag between a taxable event and the state's receipt of the

[5] The federal share of revenues dropped from an average of 89.7 percent during the first half of the 1950s to 85.9 percent from 1956 to 1989 (Ctrángolo and Gómez Sabaini 2007b).

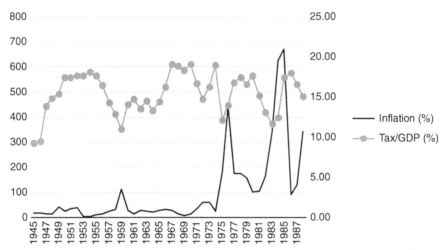

FIGURE 6.2 Annual inflation rate and the tax burden in Argentina, 1945–1988[6]
Sources: AFIP; ECLAC; Cetrángolo and Gómez Sabaini (2007b); Ferreres (2010)

corresponding revenues causes the value of those revenues to be reduced by inflation (Tanzi 1978; Carciofi 1990). Understanding this dynamic, taxpayers often delayed their payments, aggravating its impact (Sánchez Román 2012, pp. 132–133). The declining role of income taxation beginning in the 1960s probably worked to soften this effect somewhat (since, as mentioned earlier, the collection lag tended to be longer for this tax than for others), but the inflationary peaks also grew higher, which had the opposite effect. There is also anecdotal evidence that the tax burden was positively correlated with GDP growth (Carciofi 1990; Cetrángolo and Gómez Sabaini 2007b; Sánchez Román 2012). While this may have simply reflected the negative correlation between growth and inflation, it could also be a consequence of other factors, such as evasion, which has tended to intensify during recessions, as taxpayers seek to limit their financial losses (Bergman 2009, p. 71; Sánchez Román 2012, p. 133).

6.2.2 The Political Roots of Macroeconomic Instability

Underlying Argentina's macroeconomic instability was a struggle over the development model. While post-1955 political cleavages were not free of complexities, scholars have identified two main rival coalitions (Corradi 1974; O'Donnell 1977; Sikkink 1991). One favored a more activist state and policies prioritizing national capital and domestic consumption. Its core

---

[6] The graph excludes 1989 because the rate of inflation was so high (above 3,000 percent) that including it would obscure the pattern of earlier years. However, 1989 does follow the pattern since, despite a major increase in export taxes, the tax burden was relatively light (15.3 percent of GDP).

members were organized labor, *peronista* politicians in the poorer interior provinces, and a segment of business consisting mainly of small and medium-sized manufacturing firms and others highly sensitive to imports, often based outside the Buenos Aires metropolitan area. The other camp favored a small state and an economy open to trade and capital flows. Its core members were export-oriented farm producers and larger and more competitive nonfarm businesses linked to the global economy through ownership or exports. The anti-*peronismo* of these groups was shared by many top military officers and part of the middle class.

The two factions possessed different political resources. Statists enjoyed the advantage of a mass base, which allowed them to disrupt the economy through strikes and win elections. Argentina's labor force continued to be exceptionally well organized and relatively unified, given that the vast majority of union members accepted the ideology and leadership of Perón, who was in exile until 1973 but in close touch with key supporters. The *peronista* CGT was troubled by leadership divisions but had no significant rivals. While marginalizing more ideologically radical currents, this common identity bolstered labor's capacity for collective action, making it an imposing force (James 1988; Torre 1998).

The statist business faction also had a strong peak organization in the General Economic Confederation (Confederación General Económica, CGE), which Perón had promoted after dissolving the Argentine Industrial Union (Unión Industrial Argentina, UIA), the traditional representative of the country's industrial sector. While especially closely associated with manufacturing, the CGE also represented other sectors, including agriculture. What it lacked in terms of the economic weight of individual members, the CGE made up for with its large, nationwide membership. Compared to its chief rival, the free-market-oriented Coordinating Association of Free Business Institutions (Asociación Coordinadora de Instituciones Empresarias Libres, ACIEL), the CGE had roughly three times as many affiliated associations and was particularly dominant outside the Buenos Aires metropolitan area (Smith 1989, p. 92).

In addition, the CGE possessed a strong collective identity rooted in nationalism and pseudo-class distinctions (Brennan 1998; Brennan and Rougier 2009). Its members viewed themselves as scrappy entrepreneurs and patriotic Argentines, in contradistinction to the haughty oligarchs of the agro-export sector and the sold-out heads of large, internationalized businesses. Although similar business factions existed elsewhere in Latin America under ISI, "Argentina's experience with national capitalism was unusually intense and consequential" (Brennan and Rougier 2009, p. 200). CGE members did not necessarily identify as *peronistas*, but they sympathized with Perón's project of building a domestic private sector independent of foreign MNCs and were willing to ally with labor to repel measures that would depress consumption or intensify foreign competition (O'Donnell 1977).

In comparison to the statists, the anti-statist camp lacked a mass base. Argentina never developed a conservative party capable of winning national elections. This characteristic has sometimes been attributed to the absence of a large peasantry, which deprived economic elites of a base of poor, uneducated, and socially conservative voters who could be manipulated with patronage (McGuire 1997, p. 38). Just as important, however, is the fact that Perón, because of his ideological moderation and use of state resources, had developed his own network of political support in the more rural interior provinces, which complemented his metropolitan labor base. This success helped give *peronismo* a dualistic character as a programmatic, labor-based party in urban areas and a somewhat more conservative, clientelist actor in the interior (Mora y Araujo and Llorente 1980; Gibson 1996). In addition, Argentina's large middle class was divided, with one side favoring the liberal, anti-*peronista* camp and the other adopting more statist views and a more conciliatory stance toward *peronismo*. This division was reflected in the Radical Civic Union (Unión Cívica Radical, UCR), the traditional middle-class party, which split in two during the late 1950s and would only reunify in the 1970s.

While weak at the mass level, the anti-statists enjoyed powerful advantages in other respects. First, Argentina's largest businesses and the ones that produced the bulk of its foreign exchange earnings generally backed this position. Second, while the CGE kept them from exercising hegemony over the private sector, anti-statist interests boasted some solid organizations. Large landowners were ably represented by the Argentine Rural Society (Sociedad Rural Argentina, SRA), an entity with deep roots in the upper class and an abiding commitment to free markets. Also influential was the UIA, which was revived after the 1955 coup. While more divided than the SRA, the UIA tended to favor liberal policies and to side with the SRA against the CGE (Schneider 2004, p. 181; Brennan and Rougier 2009, pp. 130–134). The major associations representing commerce and the stock market were also liberal. During periods of perceived threat, these groups joined forces to create umbrella organizations. The most significant was ACIEL, which arose in the late 1950s in response to the renewed influence of *peronismo* and the CGE under President Frondizi (who represented the more statist faction of the UCR) and lasted until about the mid-1970s (Jauregui 2013).

Finally, liberal-oriented elites enjoyed strong ties to the armed forces. While this organization suffered from serious divisions during most of this period, there was much resistance among the officer corps to allowing *peronismo* to exercise influence within the state, and there were close relations between certain military factions and anti-statist business and technocratic elites. Even the 1966–1973 military regime, which pursued somewhat heterodox policies and initially sought a pragmatic accommodation with labor, relied mainly on liberal economists and was deeply opposed by the CGE (Smith 1989, ch. 4). The more resolutely liberal 1976–1983 regime, which implemented a trade and financial opening that led to substantial deindustrialization, was especially close to big agriculture and other internationalized sectors of the economy (Schvarzer 1983).

Despite these differences in the nature of their political resources, the two sides were evenly matched, in the sense that neither could decisively prevail over the other. To be sure, military intervention kept *peronismo* from controlling the state for nearly two decades after Perón's fall. Even when civilians held office, the armed forces effectively imposed a ban on parties associated with Perón.[7] Moreover, after finally permitting *peronismo* to participate in elections in 1973, the armed forces soon overthrew Perón's widow (who had served as vice president until her husband's death) and founded a dictatorship known as the Process of National Reorganization, or simply *Proceso*, that would be the most repressive in Argentine history.

Nevertheless, even military governments had trouble sustaining painful economic reforms, given their lack of popular legitimacy and the ability of statist forces to resist. Military leaders implicitly acknowledged as much in 1973 when, following a period of rising protest and violence, they allowed Perón to return to Argentina and run for president (Torre and De Riz 1993, p. 311). The *Proceso*, which was established at a moment of even greater turmoil following Perón's death and was rooted in a coalition of top military brass, pro-market technocrats, and liberal economic interests, initially appeared capable of delivering a decisive blow to statism. Labor unions were repressed, the CGE dissolved, and major neoliberal reforms set in motion. Argentina seemed to be moving in the same direction as neighboring Chile (Schorr 2012, p. 34). However, even the leaders of the *Proceso*, probably fearing for their political survival, failed to impose tough macroeconomic discipline in a lasting fashion.

This stalemate fed macroeconomic instability by inhibiting the establishment of a reasonably consistent and sustainable economic strategy (O'Donnell 1977). When allowed to wield power, *peronismo*, as well as non-*peronistas* who sought to attract the movement's supporters, tended to pursue expansionist policies that eventually engendered inflation and balance of payments problems, necessitating stabilization measures. However, the latter met with resistance from unions and domestically oriented businesses because of their negative impact on jobs, wages, and consumption. Sensing defeat, even larger manufacturing firms and conglomerates would eventually abandon the liberal coalition, leaving farm exporters isolated and forcing a relaxation of macroeconomic discipline and a renewal of the cycle. The *Proceso* at first seemed to possess the determination and support to stabilize the economy, but it, too, ultimately ran large fiscal deficits and funded them with monetary emissions, leading to triple-digit inflation (Cortés Conde 2009, pp. 266–273).

---

[7] In fact, accusations that they were secretly collaborating with Perón or being too soft on *peronismo* contributed to the military coups against presidents Frondizi and Arturo Illia (1963–1966), who headed rival factions of the UCR.

Had *peronismo* been allowed to compete freely in elections, it might have eventually developed a relatively stable "state capitalist" development model (O'Donnell 1977, p. 552). Likewise, had they been able to forge a broader coalition, anti-statists might have formulated a sustainable Chilean-style growth model. However, given the deep division at the center of Argentine society, neither side was able to establish a stable policy framework and the country drifted from crisis to crisis, each seemingly worse than the last. Over time, moreover, instability and the resort to short-term policy fixes corroded the state's credibility, pushing economic actors to adopt defensive strategies, including tax evasion, dollarization, and indexation of contracts for inflation, which erected additional obstacles to stabilization. The country became a textbook case of institutional weakness and its noxious consequences for economic development (Levitsky and Murillo 2006; Spiller and Tommasi 2009).

Events of the early 1980s offered hope that the *peronista* versus anti-*peronista* division could be left behind and a sustainable, democratic middle ground consolidated. The debt crisis and the armed forces' ignominious defeat in the Malvinas/Falkland Islands War forced the ruling junta to step aside in 1983. Furthermore, in the presidential election of that year the UCR's Raul Alfonsín emerged victorious, marking the first time *peronismo* had been defeated in a free and fair contest. While democracy indeed survived, the toxic legacies the new government inherited, including massive debt, high inflation, a labor movement militantly resistant to austerity, and a population deeply skeptical of the state's ability to manage the economy, overwhelmed it (Smith 1990; Baglini 2014, interview). Authorities implemented a series of stabilization programs, but all failed, culminating in one of the worst crises in Argentine history and Alfonsín's decision to relinquish his position to president-elect Carlos Menem before the end of his term.

6.2.3 Perón and the Roots of Instability

The division of Argentine society between statist and anti-statist camps was in large measure a consequence of the hybrid character of the *peronista* reform wave relative to the ones highlighted in earlier chapters. On the one hand, Perón had encouraged labor organization and provided benefits to workers more boldly than Vargas. In this sense, he was closer to Cárdenas and Allende, although his methods and ideology were different. On the other hand, he approximated Vargas in sparing private property from major attacks, embracing conspicuously anti-communist views, and adopting assertive pro-industrialization policies. This combination had the effect of strengthening labor at the same time it divided economic elites.

As discussed previously, the core of Perón's political strategy was his courtship of the working class. In this sense, his legacy is different from Vargas'. While the Brazilian leader implemented some pro-worker reforms, neither his attempts to organize workers nor his initiatives to redistribute income in labor's favor were as ambitious as Perón's. As a result, Vargas did not develop into nearly as potent a symbol of social justice for lower-class people.

Nevertheless, despite mobilizing workers and handing them a larger share of national income, the Perón governments of the 1940s and 1950s did not stimulate the rise of a broad, enduring anti-statist coalition. As discussed earlier, the Argentine private sector post-Perón was deeply divided between statist and anti-statist factions. This division, which also permeated technocratic sectors and state institutions (Sikkink 1991), arguably helps explain why no conservative party of any significance emerged during this period. As a conservative politician of the 1960s put it, "The Argentine right is fragmented and weak because the Argentine bourgeoisie is as well" (quoted in Mora y Araujo 2011, p. 173).

The most important reason why Peron's reformism did not give rise to such a bloc is that it spared private property. Earlier chapters argued that the key factor provoking the mobilization of a strong ant-statist political coalition in Chile and Mexico was the threat posed to property by state policies under Allende and Cárdenas, respectively. In Brazil, in contrast, the lack of expropriation, even under Vargas, the most important social reformer of the country's history, worked against the rise of a powerful anti-statist coalition. While Perón diverged from Vargas in terms of his labor and social policies, he converged strongly with the Brazilian leader in both eschewing property reforms and rejecting ideologies hostile to private property.

In contrast to Cárdenas and Allende, Perón did not implement an expropriation-based land reform. He talked about such a reform during his 1946 campaign, and subsequently put in place policies to promote land access for sharecroppers and smallholders, but he did not undertake significant land redistribution (Ribeiro 2008). Perón did nationalize several public services, but these actions were less conflictual than Cárdenas' dramatic seizure of the oil industry and far less numerous than Allende's expropriations of banks and industrial firms. Probably the highest-profile nationalization involved the railways, a sector in which British firms were dominant. Although the government cast its takeover as a victory for sovereignty, the British wanted to divest and negotiated a relatively favorable deal (Rock 1987, pp. 279–281). As a well-known analysis of Argentina's postwar instability observes "although in some ways the advent of Perón resembled a leftist revolution, unlike such a revolution it hardly touched legal property rights" (Mallon and Sourrouille 1975, p. 25).

Respect for private property flowed naturally from Perón's ideology and political background. While Allende's UP was explicitly Marxist and Cárdenas' support coalition contained both communists and moderates, Perón, as discussed earlier, rose to power as part of a conservative nationalist military regime and promoted his pro-labor reforms as a way of preventing

Marxism from gaining a foothold in the working class (Torre and De Riz 1993, p. 243). Indeed, for many of its critics, *peronismo*, due to its anti-communism, authoritarianism, and social conservatism, was a creole variant of European fascism (Nállim 2012).

The absence of a threat to property was combined with an appeal to business to participate in a "national capitalist" project that would advance Argentina's industrialization through an alliance of capital and labor (Corradi 1974; Brennan and Rougier 2009). Perón promised that his policies would protect private enterprise by promoting labor peace. These appeals did not prevent much of the private sector from opposing him, but they did attract the sympathy of the owners of many smaller and less internationally competitive firms, who saw little future for themselves in an open, export-oriented economy. Although elites generally applauded Perón's fall, that event did not reflect a broad countermobilization by groups facing what they perceived as an existential threat. Rather, it was a product of his authoritarian and highly personalist leadership style, as well as an avoidable and uncharacteristic conflict with an erstwhile ally, the Catholic Church. As Ranis notes,

Peron was overthrown not because he was a deep-seated economic threat to the agrarian and industrial interests but because he had over time alienated the Catholic Church, elements of the military, and some competing liberal cultural and political institutions and organization that saw his regime as vulgar, pedestrian, personalist, and unpredict-able. (Ranis 1992, p. 27)

As this discussion suggests, *peronismo* was a deeply destabilizing force not only because it mobilized workers to demand more from businesses and the state but also, somewhat paradoxically, because it did not seek more profound change. Like the Cárdenas and Allende governments, the *peronista* regime was a path-changing episode of redistributive reform that would influence politics for decades to come. However, unlike those two governments, its impact was not to prompt the emergence of a dominant anti-statist bloc, but rather to strengthen statism, both by forging a new labor-based populist movement and by aggravating divisions among economic elites. In the near term, this transformation set off a factional conflict that disorganized public policy, making Argentina synonymous with instability and institutional weakness. However, in the longer term, as we shall see, it favored the emergence of a large, redistributive public sector, albeit without entirely erasing the tendency toward unsustainable macroeconomic policies characteristic of the earlier period.

6.3 TAX BURDEN STABILITY UNDER NEOLIBERALISM

For a decade beginning in the early 1990s, the volatility that had characterized Argentina's tax burden post-1955 ceased. Revenues rose to about 20 percent of GDP, a level somewhat higher than the peaks of earlier decades, and remained at roughly that level until 2003, when they began to spike up sharply. Why did taxation increase at the beginning of this period and remain stable for (at least by Argentine standards) so long? The core of the answer to both questions is that the deeply traumatic hyperinflationary surges of the late 1980s and early 1990s introduced important political changes that allowed the country to stabilize its currency more effectively than in the past and implement significant tax reform. At the same time, both the dominance enjoyed by neoliberal thought during that period and the particular method chosen for achieving stabilization worked to marginalize arguments in favor of state activism, helping ensure that revenues would not increase beyond a moderate level.

6.3.1 Neoliberalism, Convertibility, and Tax Burden Stability

This phase in the country's fiscal development largely coincided with a process of macroeconomic stabilization and structural reform launched, surprisingly, by a *peronista*. Carlos Menem (1989–1999) was one of several Latin American presidents during the 1990s who came to office representing a traditionally populist or leftist party but soon adopted IMF-backed neoliberal reforms (Stokes 2001). Mainly during the first of his two terms, Menem substantially restructured the economy, liberalizing trade, privatizing many SOEs, rationalizing the bureaucracy, and adopting a pension reform that offered workers the option of channeling contributions to Chilean-style individual accounts (Teichman 2001, ch. 5).

The most distinctive aspect of Argentina's reform wave was its method for fighting inflation. Given the country's notorious policy instability, Menem opted for an approach whose very rigidity would signal the government's determination to stay the course. The Convertibility Plan, adopted in 1991, mandated a fixed, 1:1 exchange rate between the Argentine peso and the US dollar and placed strong constraints on monetary emissions. The latter had long been a key cause of inflation, which reached hyperinflationary levels (i.e., exceeding 50 percent per month) in 1989 and early 1990. Convertibility brought a drastic reduction in inflation and led to a number of years of solid growth. However, the inability to devalue the currency meant that external shocks (including those provoked by the Mexican and Brazilian devaluations of 1994 and 1999, respectively) had to be addressed mainly through domestic austerity. Argentina entered a recession in 1999 from which it would only emerge after a law was passed ending Convertibility in 2002. During that chaotic period, Argentina experienced massive protests, the resignation of another UCR president (Fernando de la Rúa), and two interim *peronista* presidents.

With regard to taxation, the focus of Convertibility-era governments was on raising enough revenue to keep the fiscal deficit, which could no longer be financed through the "inflation tax" (i.e., printing money), under control (Guidotti 2014, interview). A key instrument was the VAT, which was gradually broadened to include a variety of goods and services previously exempted, and whose general rate rose from 15 to 21 percent (Sanchez 2011, chs. 3 and 4). Numerous modifications were also made to income taxation. Rates, which had been reduced in 1989 to discourage evasion, were gradually raised thereafter to boost revenues (Cortés Conde and Harriague 2010, p. 91). Efforts were also made to expand the base of taxpayers by, for example, introducing a corporate minimum tax and lowering the minimum taxable income for individuals. Export taxes were eliminated in 1991. However, as economic conditions deteriorated in the early 2000s, officials resorted to other measures often frowned upon by economists, including an emergency tax on high incomes, a levy on bank transactions, and a tax amnesty (Cetrángolo and Gómez Sabaini 2007b, p. 28).

The neoliberal period did not significantly alter the relative weight of different levels of government in tax collection. Federal taxes averaged 82.9 percent of the total from 1990 to 2002, compared to 84.3 percent during the 1980s (Cetrángolo and Gómez Sabaini 2007b). However, this period did consolidate a trend that had begun in the 1980s toward decentralization of public spending. The federal share, which had averaged 67.7 percent in 1961, 1970, and 1984, dropped to 52.0 percent in 1993, 2000, and 2002 (Cetrángolo and Jiménez 2004, p. 122). This trend coincided with the shifting of responsibility for some policy areas, especially education, downward to subnational governments (Eaton 2004, ch. 6; Faletti 2010, pp. 81–100).

Propelled by tax policy changes and the economic effects of Convertibility, overall tax revenues rose from 14.8 to 20.0 percent of GDP between 1990 and 1993 (ECLAC). Over the next decade (until 2003), the tax burden essentially stagnated at about that level. Nevertheless, even during the brutal economic crisis of the early 2000s, Argentina did not suffer a revenue collapse comparable to those of earlier decades.

6.3.2 Hyperinflation and Sustained Stabilization

Remarkably, given *peronismo*'s historical association with unsustainable macroeconomic policies, Menem achieved greater success in lowering inflation than any other post-Perón president. After exceeding 3,000 percent in 1989 and 2,300 percent in 1990, inflation dropped to less than 100 percent in 1991, less than 25 percent in 1992, and single digits from 1993 on. The reasons behind this success are complex, but the most important was the impact of the devastating hyperinflationary episodes of 1989 and 1990, which changed the strategic calculus of key political and economic actors, including the labor unions and the president's Justicialista Party (Partido Justicialista, PJ), the lineal descendant of a party created in 1946 by Juan Perón.[8]

---

[8] Perón's party was originally called the Partido *Peronista* but its name was changed to Partido Justicialista in 1971.

Menem came to office in the midst of a profound crisis. Argentines were accustomed to inflation, but the rapidity of the price increases at the end of Alfonsín's term and the beginning of Menem's was wholly unprecedented. Price increases reached hyperinflation levels in mid-1989 and the overall 1989 rate would be some six times the previous high. The peak monthly rate was more than double that of Brazil during the same period (Hanke and Krus 2012, p. 13). After a brief lull, prices surged again in early 1990. GDP declined by 7 percent in 1989 and 1.8 percent in 1990. Riots and looting broke out in many cities in mid-1989 and more than a dozen people were killed in conflicts with police. Unable to contain the situation, Alfonsín handed over the presidency to Menem in July, six months prior to the official inauguration date.

While he faced a challenging economic situation, the new president enjoyed certain political advantages. Some were institutional in nature. Menem had won the election with a solid 47.5 percent of the popular vote and his party coalition, anchored by the PJ, had won an outright Senate majority and enough seats in the Chamber of Deputies to fashion a working majority. *Peronismo* also governed seventeen of Argentina's twenty-three provinces. During the negotiations over the early transfer of power, Alfonsín's UCR had agreed to grant Menem emergency powers to deal with the crisis. Finally, Argentina's constitution gave him significant decree authority, which he would rely on heavily to implement his reforms (Ferreira Rubio and Goretti 1996). In addition to these institutional sources of strength, Menem benefitted from an intolerable economic status quo, which made Argentines more willing to accept solutions that might otherwise have been viewed as excessively costly or risky (Palermo and Torre 1992; Weyland 2002).

Although *peronismo* had traditionally rejected austerity and market reform, the international climate in the early 1990s was frankly hostile to a statist path. By that time, neoliberal ideas had achieved clear hegemony among international financial institutions, developed country governments, and university economics departments. At the same time, deviations from orthodoxy had failed spectacularly both at home and in neighboring Bolivia and Peru, which also experienced hyperinflation during the 1980s.

In the face of these circumstances, Menem advanced a bold policy of austerity and structural reform. When initial measures failed to reduce inflation to a reasonable level, Menem doubled down on his bet, handing over the reins of economic policy to Domingo Cavallo, a well-known Harvard-trained economist. The Convertibility Plan, Cavallo's brainchild, sought to overcome lack of confidence in the state's ability to stick to a stabilization plan by legally binding it to a fixed exchange rate and removing its ability to cover deficits with monetary emissions. It also forbade "indexation" of contracts for inflation, a longstanding practice that some economists saw as a key to the failure of past stabilization programs (Smith 1990, p. 10).[9] The

---

[9] Indexation means that any payments specified in a contract will be adjusted in accordance with changes in the consumer price index, so that inflation does not erode their real value.

sharp drop in inflation and the revival of growth following the implementation of Convertibility in April 1991 provided Menem with enormous political capital, allowing him to deepen the market opening and win reelection in 1995.

Unsurprisingly, Menem's reforms enjoyed strong backing from the longstanding domestic supporters of free-market policies, including farm exporters, multinational corporations, and more internationalized domestic conglomerates (Acuña 1998; Teichman 2001, pp. 123–126). Menem actively cultivated their support by awarding business executives important bureaucratic posts. In return, these actors provided public praise, campaign donations, and (according to some sources) large bribes (Teichman 2001, pp. 125–126).

At the same time, opposition from traditional enemies of market-oriented policies was blunted by a combination of three factors. First, economic trends of previous decades, including deindustrialization and growing workforce informality, had weakened both smaller industrial firms and labor unionism relative to the pre-1976 era (Azpiazu and Schorr 2010; Murillo 2013). For example, union density, though still high by regional standards at roughly 25 percent of the EAP, was below historical peaks (Blanchflower 2006, p. 31; Roberts 2014, p. 100). Second, the president's *peronista* credentials gave him a degree of credibility among working-class Argentines that a non-*peronista* would have lacked. At least for a time, they shielded him from accusations that, by liberalizing the economy, he was selling out to domestic elites and foreign interests. Finally, and most importantly, Menem's success in conquering hyperinflation made his policies popular and difficult to oppose. Few Argentines were willing to risk a return to the bad old days of out-of-control price increases (Teichman 2001, p. 161).

The CGT was initially deeply divided over Menem's reforms and split into two confederations (Murillo 2013). However, most of the labor movement eventually reunified and, in return for a series of important concessions (discussed later), opted to give Menem at least their critical support. Only the Confederation of Argentina Workers (Central de Trabajadores de la Argentina, CTA), whose key members were public sector unions, remained independent and openly opposed the government. During his first term in office, when virtually all the major reforms were implemented, Menem faced only two general strikes, compared to the thirteen suffered by Alfonsín (Bambaci et al. 2002, p. 82). In this period, the president also enjoyed solid cooperation from his PJ-led legislative bloc, which generally approved his economic initiatives and did not resist his frequent use of decrees (Eaton 2002).

Although they suffered from Menem's policies, until the late 1990s the industrial firms traditionally associated with the CGE were also not a major source of opposition. This was partly due to the shrinkage of this sector since the 1970s, but mainly to the larger context of neoliberal hegemony. The CGE itself was no longer a significant actor. It had been relegalized under Alfonsín, but by then many of its members had joined the UIA instead, creating a nationalist current within that organization known as the National Industrial Movement (Movimiento Industrial Nacional, MIN). Instead of trying to revive the CGE, most of these firms opted to continue within the UIA, where they competed with the more liberal Argentine Industrial Movement (Movimiento Industrial Argentino, MIA). While many MIN members undoubtedly objected to liberalization, they were encouraged by the post-1990 economic revival and understood that the societal consensus in favor of Convertibility made outright opposition counterproductive (Schneider 2004; Dossi 2010). Instead, the MIN grudgingly accepted a consensus UIA leadership that supported Menem's reform program but sought to soften its impact on domestic firms. Their influence would only revive under De la Rúa, when a deepening recession cast doubt on the wisdom of continued adherence to existing policies (Dossi 2010, pp. 17–18).

Gaining the acquiescence of traditionally statist forces was not without costs. Large and politically influential ISI firms that could potentially obstruct liberalization were compensated by enlarging their share of the domestic market through various means, including privileged access to privatized assets and selective trade protection (Etchemendy 2011, ch. 4). Perhaps even more costly concessions were made to labor (Teichman 2001; Etchemendy 2011, pp. 161–167). Unions retained control of healthcare funds that provided them with large streams of revenue, and both unions and individual workers in privatized firms were given the opportunity to purchase shares in the firms at low cost. Most importantly, labor market reform was limited and left key sources of union power, including industry-wide contract negotiation, representational monopoly (i.e., only one union per firm), and automatic renewal of existing contracts, intact. The lack of deeper reform was significant because the overvaluation of the peso and the impossibility of devaluing it under Convertibility put a premium on keeping business costs low in tradable sectors (Salvia 2015, p. 327).

In addition, Menem was unable to fully impose fiscal discipline on another key component of the *peronista* coalition, its provincial political machines (Gibson and Calvo 2000; Remmer and Wibbels 2000). The PJ and its allies controlled most of the provinces, including almost all the poorer ones. In many of them, a substantial part of the population was employed in the public sector, making fiscal adjustment a risky proposition.[10] Leveraging their influence over PJ legislators, governors successfully resisted austerity (Eaton 2002). Thus, fiscal transfers to the provinces increased even as the national government imposed upon itself tough spending cuts. The failure to force adjustment on the provinces contributed to persistent deficits and rising indebtedness, which

---

[10] The dangers of enforcing fiscal austerity on the provinces were dramatically demonstrated in 1993 when public employees in Santiago del Estero torched the major public buildings in protest against unpaid wages (Silva 2009, pp. 66–68).

endangered the sustainability of Convertibility by driving up interest rates and inhibiting growth (Fanelli 2002, p. 27; Galiani et al. 2003).

These compromises, combined with external shocks and some political missteps by the De la Rúa government, helped give rise to a punishing recession and the decision to abandon Convertibility (Galiani et al. 2003). However, the collapse of this system did not bring the much-feared return to hyperinflation. Prices spiked up by 40 percent in 2002 but subsequently returned to much lower levels. Even under the Kirchners, inflation would not significantly exceed its 2002 peak. While a full analysis of this phenomenon is beyond the scope of this book, it seems likely that changes implemented under Menem, including trade liberalization and the banning of price indexation, attenuated inflationary pressures. Thus, while Convertibility did not prove to be a sustainable growth model, the Menem years did bring about some lasting changes to Argentina's post–World War II political economy.

6.3.3 Taxation under Convertibility

The forces unleashed by hyperinflation and Menem's audacious reaction to it worked simultaneously to boost the tax burden, avoiding the revenue collapses of earlier periods, and to ensure that it would not rise beyond a moderate level.

Argentina's tax burden rose in the early 1990s for two main reasons. First, the sharp drop in inflation achieved in 1991 eliminated the Olivera–Tanzi effect, increasing the productivity of the existing tax system, and restored economic growth (Dillinger and Webb 1999, p. 16). Second, the political imperative of achieving and preserving stability gave officials leverage to increase taxes. The VAT was broadened in 1990 to include many previously excluded goods (Sanchez 2011, p. 100). Its rate was initially reduced from 15 to 13 percent, but was soon raised again, reaching 18 percent in 1992 (Morisset and Izquierdo 1993, p. 4). The corporate income tax rate also rose, from 20 to 30 percent. Efforts were made to strengthen enforcement, in recognition of the high level of evasion. Menem augmented the human resources and technical capacity of the federal tax-collection agency. The latter also launched a publicity campaign to promote the idea that tax evasion was equivalent to theft and formed an elite group of inspectors tasked with pursuing large-scale evaders (Sanchez 2011, pp. 109–110).

These measures provoked some pushback from the private sector, but the reaction was relatively mild, because of both the political divisions within that sector and, perhaps more importantly, a widespread desire not to return to the chaos of the Alfonsín era. Sanchez (2011, p. 102) points out that, "The hyperinflation experience had been similarly traumatic and economically costly for Argentine entrepreneurs of all sectors of the economy. Thus, they were more than ready to pay the price (i.e., higher taxes) of a program that promised to cast the economic past aside and set the foundations of better economic times."

Following the initial tax increase, a rough balance of pro- and anti-tax influences worked to keep the burden relatively stable. Two factors favored taxation. First, inflation continued to be low throughout the Convertibility period, so the Olivera–Tanzi effect was kept at bay. Second, given their inability to cut provincial spending, authorities found it necessary to ensure a solid revenue flow to control the deficit. This task became challenging in the face of the repeated external shocks, which had negative revenue effects. In both 1994 and 1999, authorities responded to such events by raising taxes. They sought to demonstrate to market actors that the government was determined to maintain Convertibility, even if it meant taking unpalatable measures. In the first case, those measures focused mainly on the VAT, increasing its rate and widening its base. By the late 1990s, however, concerns about the regressive impact of neoliberalism had taken on greater prominence. De la Rúa, who came to power on the basis of a coalition between his centrist UCR and a collection of left-leaning forces (including dissident *peronistas*), was more sensitive to social concerns. His revenue-raising efforts thus focused on direct taxes, especially the personal income tax and the personal wealth tax (Machinea 2014, interview). Later, he would also make recourse to a financial transactions tax.

At the same time, a number of other factors worked against heavier taxation. One was the consequence of a specific feature of Menem's reform program: the partial pension privatization. Undertaken to deepen the domestic capital market and promote long-term fiscal stability, the reform nevertheless had a medium-term fiscal cost, since it deprived the state of a substantial revenue stream (Guidotti 2014, interview). Largely because of the diversion of some worker and employer contributions to private pension funds, social security tax revenues declined by 1.7 percent of GDP between 1995 and 1999, putting upward pressure on the deficit (CEPALSTAT).

Two other factors had a more generalized influence on taxation. One was the basically liberal ideology of the officials directing economy policy. Differences on certain issues notwithstanding, both Cavallo and his successor as Minister of the Economy, Roque Fernández, were US-trained economists who believed Argentina could only thrive under a market-oriented policy regime. They were ideologically averse to expanding the public sector or saddling private actors with a heavier tax burden (2014 interviews: Fernández, Guidotti, Lamberto). De la Rúa's first Minister of Finance, José Luis Machinea, was less orthodox, but he was followed by two others (one of whom was Cavallo, who made a last-ditch effort to save Convertibility) with a liberal orientation. Second, the Convertibility Plan itself discouraged taxation in some ways. In particular, the imperative of lowering production costs to compensate for an unfavorable exchange rate made it difficult to impose additional taxes on the private sector. While officials sometimes raised taxes to close the deficit and boost confidence in the economic model, they were conscious that doing so could dampen growth and aggravate unemployment, as it arguably did in 2000 when De la Rúa implemented his income tax hike (Guidotti 2014, interview).

6.4 KIRCHNERISMO AND RISING TAXATION

Following a decade of comparative stability, Argentina's tax revenues underwent a striking transformation, rising by more than 50 percent relative to GDP between 2003 and 2015. Despite some recent efforts to lighten the burden, they have remained at roughly that level in subsequent years. This extraordinary increase constitutes a crucial step in the emergence of a heavy tax burden in Argentina and thus demands an explanation.

The argument developed below frames it as the product of a combination of conjunctural shifts and longer-term factors. With regard to the former, the account highlights both the traumatic collapse of Convertibility and the subsequent onset of a global commodity boom. Public rejection of neoliberalism, which came to be associated with the punishing recession of the late Convertibility years, created an environment ripe for the rise of politicians promising to use the state to promote social and economic development. Not long after leaving Convertibility behind, Argentina also began feeling the effects of a sharp rise in commodity prices, which fueled growth, aided revenue collection, and legitimized the statist policy turn. This conjunctural account is only part of the story, however. In addition, the sustained increase in taxation reflects the interaction of two more deeply rooted conditions. The first is a statist-leaning balance of political power related to the existence of a strong populist movement and divided economic elite, both legacies of the Perón era. The second is the consolidation of democracy, which has allowed the underlying statist power balance to gradually translate into policy.

6.4.1 Growth and Stabilization of the Tax Burden

Argentina's tax burden began to increase under interim President Eduardo Duhalde (2002–2003), but the surge occurred mainly under fellow *peronistas* Néstor Kirchner (2003–2007) and his wife Cristina Fernández de Kirchner (2007–2015), who led a center-left coalition called "Front for Victory" (Frente para la Victoria, FPV). Mauricio Macri (2015–2019) of the more economically liberal Republican Proposal (Propuesta Republicana, PRO) party sought to attenuate taxation but ultimately failed.

Between 2002 and 2015, Argentina's tax revenues rose from about 19 percent of GDP to almost 32 percent (CEPAL). Revenue from all major categories grew robustly (Cetrángolo et al. 2015, p. 19). However, the largest increases involved trade and social security taxes. Trade tax revenues grew because of the reimposition of export levies, especially on farm commodities. Duhalde initiated this change after devaluing the peso, but Kirchner and Fernández subsequently raised rates. Soybeans, a key source of foreign exchange, were subject to especially high rates. Social security revenues rose because of higher contribution rates, increasing labor formality, and renationalization of pensions. Despite rising less than trade and social security taxation, direct tax revenues also grew. Income taxation surged, not so much because of policy reform, but because the government purposely failed to adjust brackets for inflation. Property tax revenues grew mainly because of the bank transaction tax adopted in 2001, which became a potent revenue-raising tool as the economy expanded. Billed as temporary, it was subsequently renewed a number of times (Cetrángolo et al. 2015, p. 26).

Beyond the increase in revenues, the tax system did not change dramatically. While the overall fiscal system became more redistributive (for reasons discussed later) that does not appear to be true for taxation specifically. Direct tax revenues increased their share only marginally, from 28.8 percent of tax revenues in 2002 to 29.9 percent in 2015 (CEPALSTAT). Moreover, part of this increase came from the tax on bank transactions, whose progressivity is disputed, and rising taxation of individuals with moderate incomes. Tax centralization increased during the Kirchner and first Fernández governments, but the effect eventually faded due to the waning of the commodity boom (which lowered export tax revenues) and increasing subnational revenues.[11] Municipal receipts were relatively stagnant (Agosto 2017, p. 5), but provincial taxation rose, mainly due to a sales tax called the Tax on Gross Receipts (Impuesto sobre los Ingresos Brutos). Many provinces broadened the base of this tax and raised rates, consolidating its role as the major subnational tax (Cetrángolo et al. 2015, p. 30).

The 2015 elections brought a turn toward more market-oriented policies, including efforts to lighten the tax burden. Macri, leader of a coalition called Cambiemos ("let's change"), which included his center-right PRO and the centrist UCR and Civic Coalition (Coalición Cívica), defeated *peronista* candidate Daniel Scioli by a narrow margin. He inherited an economy troubled by a large fiscal deficit, inflation approaching 30 percent, and a legal dispute with holdouts from Kirchner's debt restructuring. Once in office, Macri quickly paid off foreign bondholders, reformed the state statistical institute, cut back consumer subsidies, and dismantled currency controls Fernández had imposed to check capital flight.

The Cambiemos government also attempted to reduce the tax burden but did not succeed. Early on, Macri moved to fulfill campaign promises by initiating a reduction of export taxes and the minimum taxable income for families with children. The tax burden dropped from 31.5 percent of GDP in 2015 to 30.3 percent in 2017 (CEPALSTAT). In December 2017, following a strong Cambiemos showing in mid-term elections, he secured approval of a broader reform that promised to reduce revenues by 1.5 percent of GDP within five years (IMF 2017, p. 23). However, Macri's failure to substantially shrink the fiscal deficit undermined market confidence and contributed to a run on the peso. In mid-2018, Macri was obligated to seek an emergency loan from the IMF, adopt

---

[11] The federal share increased from 82.2 percent in 2000 to 85.8 percent in 2010, then dropped to 83.2 percent in 2015 (OECD 2017, p.224).

more ambitious deficit reduction goals, and suspend planned tax reductions. Fiscal experts predicted that the federal tax burden in 2019, the last year of his term, would be higher than when he took office.[12] Moreover, *peronismo*'s solid victory in the 2019 elections promised a return to unapologetically statist policies.

6.4.2 Anti-Neoliberal Backlash, Commodity-Led Growth, and State Expansion

The direct causes of rising taxation were discontent with the neoliberal policies of the previous decade and favorable international economic conditions. The agonizing decline and ultimate demise of Convertibility gave rise to an ideological climate in which criticism of the policies of the 1990s found a receptive audience. Néstor Kirchner and Cristina Fernández exploited this climate by advancing a statist, redistributive, and nationalist agenda that explicitly rejected Menem's legacy and appealed to both *peronista*s and left-leaning non-*peronista* groups. Like a number of other contemporary leftist or populist Latin American leaders, their success was aided by an unusually long-lasting global commodity boom, which fueled growth and employment and helped enrich the treasury.

Although it did not involve a major inflationary surge, the crisis that brought the end of Convertibility was at least as devastating as the one that had given rise to it. The economy contracted for four straight years beginning in 1999, culminating in a shocking 10.9 percent drop in 2002 (CEPALSTAT). Unemployment, poverty, and inequality escalated to levels significantly exceeding even those of the early 1990s (CEPALSTAT; Ferreres 2010, p. 267). A massive protest wave emerged in late 2001 whose broad rejection of political elites was crystallized in the slogan *que se vayan todos*, or "throw them all out." The protests forced De la Rúa to resign after little more than two years in office. The balance of his term was served out by the *peronistas* Adolfo Rodríguez Saá, who was in office only a week, and Duhalde, who stayed for seventeen months. Both faced the challenge of an ailing economy and grassroots protest movements, including the so-called *piqueteros*, who blocked roads in many areas of the country to force authorities to provide work and social benefits (Svampa and Pereyra 2003; Rossi 2017).

Despite the brevity of their presidencies, Rodríguez Saá and Duhalde made pivotal decisions that moved Argentina away from Menem-era policies. Most importantly, the former suspended payment of the large foreign debt and the latter pushed through Congress a law revoking Convertibility, causing a drastic devaluation of the peso. In addition, Duhalde, a prominent critic of Menem's policies as governor of the Province of Buenos Aires (1991–1999), made some other moves that reflected a more statist logic than the one that had guided

---

[12] *La Nación*, January 5, 2019.

policymaking over the previous decade. In particular, he reinstated taxes on agricultural and hydrocarbon exports, capturing for the state part of the windfall from the devaluation, and used the revenues to pay for major new social programs (Riggirozzi 2008, pp. 135–136). The most important was probably the Unemployed Heads of Household Plan (Plan Jefes y Jefas de Hogar Desocupados) – a workfare program that by the end of 2002 was benefitting about 20 percent of Argentine households (Garay 2016, p. 183).

Néstor Kirchner rose to power in 2003 by joining Duhalde in his condemnation of Menem and the policies he had implemented in office. *Peronismo* was divided by Menem's desire to return to the presidency and ended up fielding three different candidates: Menem, Rodríguez Saá, and Kirchner, the PJ governor of the small province of Santa Cruz. Kirchner ran on a platform of economic interventionism, social justice, and human rights, attempting to appeal to both *peronistas* and left-leaning sectors of the middle class (Levitsky and Murillo 2008). Although little known at the national level, Kirchner benefitted from President Duhalde's personal endorsement. In the first round, Menem won the largest share of votes (24.5 percent) but Kirchner was not far behind (22.3 percent). The UCR, discredited by the De la Rúa government's implosion, was not a factor. As the runoff campaign developed, it became clear that Kirchner would triumph in a landslide. Unwilling to suffer a humiliating defeat, Menem pulled out and Kirchner became president by default.

Once in office, Kirchner acted decisively to define himself in opposition to Menem (Levitsky and Murillo 2008). He substantially expanded the state's presence in the economy by making pensions available to people who had not previously contributed to the system, freezing energy and public transportation prices to the point that the firms supplying them required large public subsidies, supporting unions in collective bargaining, raising the minimum wage, and investing in infrastructure (Cetrángolo et al. 2015; Damill and Frenkel 2015). Although he lacked a well-defined industrial strategy, Kirchner's policies promoted domestic consumption and provided cheap energy to local firms, contributing to a reversal of the deindustrialization trend of earlier decades (Azpiazu and Schorr 2010, ch. 4). He also broke off relations with the IMF, which many Argentines felt was partly to blame for their economic woes, and negotiated a deal with most of the country's creditors involving a large reduction in future debt payments. In addition to these economic and social measures, Kirchner reinitiated prosecution of military officers accused of *Proceso*-era human rights violations, which Menem had abandoned.

When she reached the presidency in 2008 Cristina Fernández de Kirchner pursued statist and nationalist policies just as, or even more, aggressively. She reversed Menem's privatization of the state oil company, re-imposed full state control over pensions, and introduced a major new social assistance program, among other domestic measures. Her foreign policy sought autonomy from the United States and favored closer relations with other Latin American nations.

She also continued the policy, introduced late in Kirchner's presidency and widely criticized both within and outside Argentina, of manipulating official price data to show a lower rate of inflation. Perhaps more than her husband (who died in 2010) Fernández was a polarizing figure who went out of her way to castigate her opponents as elitist, unpatriotic, and uninterested in the welfare of ordinary Argentines.

Although the Kirchners no doubt profited from playing on public disenchantment with neoliberalism, their success also owed much to the commodity boom that began at about the same time they came to power and lasted roughly a decade (Richardson 2009; Calvo and Murillo 2012). That phenomenon propelled the prices of key export commodities, especially soybeans, to exceptionally high levels and helped drive growth and job creation. The economy's expansion, which averaged 8.7 percent from 2003 to 2007 (CEPALSTAT), allowed them to claim that their policies were not only progressive but also pro-growth. The expansion slowed under Fernández but, excluding 2009 (when Argentina was hit by the effects of the US subprime mortgage crisis), it continued at a solid pace during her first term in office. It was only in her second term that growth slowed markedly, turning negative in two years and averaging only 0.4 percent annually (CEPALSTAT). Not coincidentally, the FPV ended up losing the presidency and suffering setbacks in legislative elections (Murillo et al. 2016).

Aided by luck and strategy, the Kirchners gained the support both of traditionally *peronista* sectors and others that did not embrace this identity. Until late 2011, *kirchnerismo* enjoyed the strong support of organized labor (Etchemendy and Collier 2007; Varela 2013). A sector of the CGT that had opposed Menem's reforms, led by truckers' union boss Hugo Moyano, took control of the confederation and allied it closely with the government. Following the 2011 election, Moyano broke with Fernández over a combination of policy disagreements and disputes over the distribution of FPV candidacies. A sector of the CTA also opposed the government. However, unions representing a solid majority of organized workers continued to support it (Etchemendy 2012).[13]

The Kirchners also enjoyed substantial support among the majority of lower-class voters who are not unionized. Their relationship with this group was partly clientelistic in nature. Clientelism had long been an important aspect of *peronismo*'s electoral strength in the interior provinces. However, beginning in the 1990s, it took on greater importance in more developed areas, especially the Province of Buenos Aires, easily the most populous (Auyero 2001; Levitsky 2003). This change responded in large part to economic shifts, including the decline of formal labor and the growth of poverty. At the same time, *kirchnerismo* also appealed to this sector in more programmatic ways, including its initiatives to expand access to social assistance and pensions.

---

[13] *Gestión Sindical*, September 10, 2015.

This combination of clientelism and programmatic appeals helped *kirchnerismo* build strong ties to social movements, including the *piqueteros* (Rossi 2017).

Especially under Néstor Kirchner, *kirchnerismo* was also seen as a "transversal" phenomenon that cut across party lines. In addition to attracting support from a variety of small left and center-left groups, it built an alliance with some leaders of the UCR, particularly in the interior. In fact, Fernández's running mate in the 2007 election was Julio Cobos, the former UCR governor of the Province of Mendoza. However, a major conflict between the government and the agricultural sector (discussed below) led many of the so-called K Radicals, to distance themselves from the government.[14]

This shifting coalition of forces allowed the Kirchners to largely dominate Argentine elections for a dozen years. Although Menem had denied Kirchner a broad popular mandate in 2003 by withdrawing, Fernández triumphed easily in the 2007 and 2011 elections. The FPV generally did not control a majority of its own in both chambers of Congress (see Table 6.1), but with the exception of the 2009–2011 period, its success was sufficient to allow it to cobble together working majorities by negotiating support from Radicals, small provincial and leftist parties, independent legislators, and individual members of non-FPV *peronista* factions (Zelaznik 2011, 2014). On issues central to their respective governing agendas, the Kirchners achieved considerably stronger legislative support than Menem had (Zelaznik 2014). Kirchner allies also controlled most governorships, including those of a large majority of the poorer provinces and Buenos Aires (Gervasoni 2010). The Kirchners were unable to entirely subjugate *peronismo* to their leadership. Duhalde broke with them in 2005 and he and Rodríguez Saá continued to oppose them throughout their time in power. However, whether out of affinity or realism, most other major *peronista* leaders ended up aligning with them.

6.4.3   Taxation under the Kirchners

Expanding state action in a sustained manner required increased revenue. Néstor Kirchner, in particular, was strongly committed to ensuring that tax revenues rose rapidly enough to support a high level of spending and thus the ability to provide benefits to actual or potential supporters. According to Alberto Abad, who directed the federal tax agency from 2002 to 2008, Kirchner "recognized that tax collection has strong political implications and that a comfortable fiscal situation generates political power. He followed collection almost daily" (Abad 2014, interview). Facing a weaker economy, Fernández allowed a large fiscal deficit to emerge, but she also took strong measures to raise additional revenue, and the tax burden continued to grow steadily during her terms in office.

---

[14] "Radical" here refers to their membership in the Radical Civic Union, not their ideology.

TABLE 6.1 *Distribution of seats in the Argentine Congress by term and chamber, 2003–2015 (percentages)*

Party	2003–2005 COD[b]	2003–2005 Sen	2005–2007 COD	2005–2007 Sen	2007–2009 COD	2007–2009 Sen	2009–2011 COD	2009–2011 Sen	2011–2013 COD	2011–2013 Sen	2013–2015 COD	2013–2015 Sen
PJ	50.2	56.9	–	–	–	–	–	–	–	–	–	–
FPV	–	–	45.5	56.9	54.1	59.7	37.7	47.2	46.3	48.6	47.9	44.4
Non-FPV PJ	–	–	7.0	6.9	3.5	6.9	12.5	9.7	3.5	9.7	2.7	11.1
UCR	17.1	20.8	14.0	18.1	9.3	11.1	16.7	19.4	14.9	19.4	14	15.3
CC-ARI[a]	4.3	0	5.4	0	7.0	5.6	5.8	2.8	2.3	5.6	1.2	0
PRO	–	–	4.3	0	3.5	0	4.3	0	4.3	0	7.0	2.3
Others	28.4	22.3	23.8	18.1	22.6	16.7	23	20.9	28.7	16.7	27.2	26.9
	100	100	100	100	100	100	100	100	100	100	100	100

Sources: Directorio Legislativo (https://en.directoriolegislativo.org/)
Party acronyms: Civic Coalition-Affirmation of an Egalitarian Republic (CC-ARI), Front for Victory (FPV), Justicialista Party (PJ), Republican Proposal (PRO).
[a] Includes both ARI, which was originally a separate party, and CC-ARI, which was created in 2007.
[b] "COD" stands for Chamber of Deputies and "Sen" for Senate.

With the exception of the 2008 pension renationalization, which redirected a large stream of payroll contributions back to the public sector, neither president advanced a major tax reform (Lavagna 2014, interview; Cetrángolo et al. 2015). Nevertheless, they took several other decisions that contributed greatly to rising taxation. Early on, the Federal Administration for Public Revenue (Administración Federal de Ingresos Públicos, AFIP), which collects all federal taxes, was strengthened, mainly by incorporating new information technology. Abad claimed that evasion declined significantly as a result (Abad 2014, interview). Few studies track Argentine tax evasion over time, but the findings that do exist are consistent with this argument. In particular, estimates of VAT evasion between 2001 and 2007 show a steady decline beginning in 2003, resulting in an overall drop of more than a third (Gómez Sabaini and Moran 2016, p. 41).[15] Even critics of *kirchnerismo* acknowledged that computerization had improved tax administration (2014 interviews: Baglini, Machinea).

In addition, the Kirchners took measures to raise revenues from some specific taxes. A key area was export taxation. The Kirchners not only failed to revoke Duhalde's post-devaluation export levies but also increased their rates quite significantly. Although a wide variety of exports were taxed, soybeans, whose prices rose dramatically during the 2000s, faced the highest rates. Kirchner kept Duhalde's 20 percent rate until early 2007 but raised it to 27.5 percent in February of that year and 35 percent in November, only a few weeks before Fernández's inauguration. Surprisingly, the new president promptly raised it again, to 44 percent. In addition, she introduced a system of marginal rates that would vary with international prices, potentially reaching 95 percent (Fairfield 2011, p. 439). The new regime was ultimately rolled back in mid-2008 in the face of prolonged protests by farmers, who blocked highways and refused to deliver staple foods to market. Nevertheless, export taxes remained at a high level. Due overwhelmingly to export taxation, Argentina's trade taxes from 2003 to 2015 generated revenues averaging 2.9 percent of GDP, a level only exceeded in Latin America by Haiti – a country with exceptionally low domestic tax capacity (CEPALSTAT).

The Kirchners also benefitted fiscally from their decision to perpetuate the tax on bank transactions introduced in 2001. Acknowledging its distortive character, Cavallo had proposed the tax as an emergency measure that would last six months.[16] However, as in the case of Brazil's CPMF (a similar levy), it was renewed a number of times. Unlike the CPMF, it continues to exist today. Although the rate was not increased after 2001, revenues rose with the revival of the economy, reaching a level of 1.5 percent of GDP that persisted throughout the *kirchnerista* period. While often criticized for discouraging use of the banking system, it is appealing to federal authorities because, much like

---

[15] The upturn in economic growth most likely contributed to this trend, as well.
[16] Ámbito.com, September 27, 2013.

export taxes, it is easy to collect and only a small portion of the revenue is shared with provincial governments.

The sharp rise in income taxation reflected a somewhat different set of decisions. De la Rúa's 1999 personal income tax reform, which reduced deductions, raised some rates and lowered the minimum taxable income, laid part of the groundwork (Machinea 2014, interview). As growth revived, this structure helped boost revenue. However, the full extent of the increase cannot be understood without appreciating how authorities responded to inflation (Lavagna 2014, interview; Cetrángolo et al. 2015, pp. 21–24), which began to surge in 2007 and peaked at about 40 percent in 2014 (Cavallo and Bertolotto, 2016). With regard to corporations, they suspended legal provisions for inflation adjustment in calculating profits, thus increasing tax liabilities. An even larger increase occurred in personal income tax revenues due to the failure to adjust brackets upward, which caused many people previously exempt from the tax to begin paying it and others to pay higher rates despite a constant rate structure.[17] Eventually, pressure mounted for tax relief. The fact that some unionized workers began to pay this tax created friction between Fernández and the CGT, contributing to the break with Moyano and subsequent labor protests (2014 interviews: Cortina, Recalde). In response, Fernández raised the minimum taxable income incrementally in 2012, 2013, and 2014.[18] Despite these changes, personal income tax revenues continued to rise, increasing from 1.5 percent of GDP her first year in office to 3.2 percent in 2015 (CEPALSTAT). Overall, the income tax burden rose 65 percent under *kirchnerismo*, going from 4.0 percent of GDP in 2003 to 6.6 percent in 2015 (CEPALSTAT).

As mentioned earlier, the most significant structural reform of the tax system was Fernández's reversion of the 1994 pension reform. This change, which occurred in the wake of her failed bid to boost export taxation and obeyed at least partly fiscal motives, meant that the payroll contributions that previously flowed to private pension funds would now go to the state, boosting revenues (Datz and Dansci 2013). Social security revenues had already increased from 2.6 to 4.6 percent of GDP between 2003 and 2008 (CEPALSTAT) because of rate increases and growing formalization of the economy. With renationalization they experienced an additional upward surge, reaching 7.1 percent of GDP in 2015. The state also inherited the balances previously held by private pension funds, equivalent to 8 percent of GDP. These were used to pay for investments in energy and infrastructure and provide subsidized credit for housing construction and purchases (Cetrángolo et al. 2015, pp.

---

[17] Of course, the fact that inflation enhanced taxation was ironic, since in the past it had often had the opposite effect. This relationship, it should be noted, does not contradict the Olivera–Tanzi effect, because inflation, though rising, was never high enough during these years to substantially undermine the value of tax receipts.

[18] Rate changes normally require legislative approval, but in 2012 Congress passed a measure delegating to the president the ability to change the minimum taxable income.

48–51). As in the Perón years, social security taxes became an important tool for funding other types of spending.

The large rise in federal taxes was compounded by increases in provincial taxation, especially the Tax on Gross Receipts. Two factors interacted to drive this trend. First, the fact that most key sources of federal revenue growth during this period were not shared, or only minimally shared, with the provinces meant that the latter gained relatively little from them. This was particularly true for provinces whose governments were not part of the national ruling coalition, since the president enjoys some discretion in distributing revenues and the Kirchners were not shy about using it to reward friends and punish enemies (Gervasoni 2011; Abad 2014, interview). Second, certain federal decisions drove up provincial spending without providing a proportionate revenue transfer (Lodola 2011, p. 225; Vaquié 2014, interview). This was especially true in education, where a 2005 law committed both national and provincial governments to increased spending and established a system by which federal authorities and the national teachers' union engage in centralized wage bargaining (Cetrángolo and Goldschmidt 2013, pp. 27–28). To make matters worse, raises won by teachers inspired other provincial employees to pressure for concessions of their own. Caught between rising spending commitments and an inadequate flow of federal transfers, many provincial governments sought to boost their own revenues (2014 interviews: Baglini, Lavagna, Vaquié).

6.4.4   The Statist Power Balance and Public Sector Growth

Given the traditional volatility of Argentina's tax burden, it is tempting to view the increase of recent decades as a purely conjunctural phenomenon driven by the short-term changes highlighted earlier. Nevertheless, the exceptionally high level of taxation reached in the last two decades also reflects more deeply rooted conditions. One of these is the relative superiority of statist forces, an enduring legacy of the Perón era.

As argued earlier, the Kirchners exploited both disillusionment with neoliberalism and surging demand for Argentine exports. However, the extent and duration of their control of the state, as well as the content of their policies, also owe much to the presence of a large segment of society that embraces *peronismo*, an identity that rests on the idea of an activist, redistributive, and nationalist public sector. A key component of this segment is organized labor. Just as importantly, *kirchnerismo*'s success in advancing a statist agenda was related to political and ideological divisions within the private sector and the inexistence of a party willing and able to defend pro-market policies in the electoral arena. Together, these conditions comprised a statist-leaning power balance potentially favorable to public sector expansion.

Although much was sometimes made of the "transversal" character of *kirchnerismo*, its electoral base and legislative coalition were essentially *peronista*. The Kirchners enjoyed their highest levels of support among poorer and less educated voters (Murillo 2015, pp. 60–61), the same social sectors that have traditionally been loyal to *peronismo* and endowed it with its impressive ability to win elections (Mora y Araujo 2011, p. 34). Their legislative coalitions, though diverse, were anchored by the PJ and provincial *peronista* parties (Zelaznik 2011, 2014). The Kirchners did suffer from the resistance of certain *peronista* politicians to accept their leadership, the most prominent case being that of Duhalde in the Province of Buenos Aires. However, *kirchnerismo* defeated *duhaldismo* in 2005 and was the dominant force in the province's politics until 2015. Other defections occurred in 2008–2009 due to the rural protests and poor state of the economy, but later some dissidents returned to the FPV fold.

Kirchnerismo was also typical of *peronista* governments in that, for the most part, it enjoyed the support of organized labor. The CGT, as mentioned, was aligned with the government until late 2011. After that, the confederation split, but the pro-government CGT unions had far more members, and a majority sector of the CTA was also sympathetic to the government (Etchemendy 2012). Union support was no small matter. Although market reforms and repeated economic crises since the 1970s have taken their toll on unions, Argentina's labor force remains unusually well organized by regional standards (Cook 2007; Niedzwiecki 2014, 2015). Its union density is the highest in Latin America and at least double Chile's and Mexico's (Bensusan 2016, p. 157). While labor leaders are not very popular among the general population, their electoral endorsements have an impact, since a significant portion of the electorate is unionized. Perhaps more importantly, Argentine unions can make life very difficult for authorities they oppose through strikes and other protests. It is thus quite significant that the Kirchners benefitted from the longest period (2003–2012) without a general strike since 1955 (Cardoso and Gindin 2017, p. 24).

With regard to the state's role in the economy, the *peronista* character of the Kirchner governments was not neutral. To be sure, *peronismo* is not anti-capitalist and it harbors groups with diverse views about the state's role. Its flexibility compared to leftist parties arguably contributed to Menem's successes in advancing neoliberal reform. Nevertheless, *peronismo* is still basically statist in its economic ideology and policy preferences. Juan Perón articulated a governing philosophy based on a paternalistic state able to promote economic growth while at the same time redistributing resources in favor of workers. Support for Menem's reforms reflected a response to acute crisis, rather than a fundamental transformation of *peronismo*. While public sympathy for market-based policies surged in the late 1980s and early 1990s, the effect was temporary. By the late 1990s, it was already in frank decline (Mora y Araujo 2011, p. 29). Moreover, among the lower-class people that comprise *peronismo*'s core constituency, support for market reformism was always weaker than among higher-income groups (Mora y Araujo 2011, p. 34). Argentina's *peronista* unions share this perspective. Although they are more apt to focus narrowly on wage and benefit issues than, for example, those of Brazil's leftist CUT, they nevertheless believe in the virtues of a strong state (Recalde 2014, interview).

Less apparent but no less important to the success of *kirchnerismo*'s statist project was the weakness of anti-statist forces in Argentine society. The economic elite the Kirchners encountered was politically and ideologically fragmented (Schneider 2004, ch. 7; Fairfield 2015, pp. 136–137). There was no cross-sectoral association of any real consequence. Perhaps the closest thing was the Argentine Business Association (Asociación Empresaria Argentina, AEA), an entity created following the end of Convertibility in 2002. Like Mexico's CMN it is composed of individual executives from many of the largest firms. However, it lacks the cohesion, tradition, and prestige of its Mexican counterpart. While some members are outspoken advocates of economic liberalism, others are dependent on state largesse and thus disinclined to criticize authorities. The AEA was invigorated to some extent by Fernández's aggressive statism, but it never developed into a highly visible opponent of the government and its divisions reappeared under Macri.[19]

Important divisions also exist at the sectoral level and, to a substantial extent, they obey the traditional statist versus anti-statist logic. This is true, for example, of industry. The UIA's two internal factions changed names in 2003, but they continue to exist and defend similar interests and views (Dossi 2010). Industriales, which descends from the MIN, has more small and medium-sized firms and more firms (both small and large) oriented toward the domestic market, rather than exports. Import-sensitive industries such as textiles, appliances, and steel are well represented. Although weakened by the liberalizing policies applied intermittently since the mid-1970s, such firms play a larger role in Argentina than in countries with more open economies, such as Chile and Mexico. Like those of the MIA, the firms that comprise Celeste y Blanca tend to be larger and more export-oriented and have stronger ties to foreign capital. Food producers are particularly prominent.[20] Although their differences are less profound than those that separated the CGE from the UIA and ACIEL, Industriales favors an activist industrial policy while Celeste y Blanca prefers a more laissez-faire approach. The UIA has managed this division by rotating its presidency among the factions every two years. However, factionalism no doubt hinders its ability to speak with a single voice.

Even agriculture, which is probably the most liberal sector of the economy overall, is by no means entirely homogeneous. The key rivalry is between the SRA, the major representative of big agriculture, and the Argentine Agricultural Federation (Federación Agrária Argentina, FAA), which represents smaller producers. Although the two share some common interests, they have traditionally been divided over others, including land rights and regulation of tenant farming contracts (2014 interviews: De Freijo, Miguens). The FAA,

---

[19] *La Nación*, August 17, 2018.   [20] *La Nación*, February 13, 2011.

which was at one time part of the CGE, has tended to embrace a more activist state and had better relations with *peronismo*. The divisions within the private sector are mirrored in intellectual and research institutions. Given Argentina's stronger liberal tradition, it is unsurprising that anti-statist think tanks have a greater presence than in Brazil. They include the Foundation for Latin American Economic Research (Fundación de Investigaciones Económicas Latinoamericanas, FIEL), the Mediterranean Foundation (Fundación Mediterránea), and the Liberty Foundation (Fundación Libertad). FIEL is among the oldest think tanks in Latin America and all three have business connections and significant capabilities (McGann 2017). However, they exist within a larger think tank community than in the other countries discussed here, which dilutes their influence.[21] While *peronismo* has a weak presence in this area, most of Argentina's top think tanks have a centrist or center-left perspective.[22] Hence, anti-statist institutions do not enjoy the influence of Chile's CEP and Freedom and Development. In addition, although there are some more conservative universities in Argentina, there is arguably no institution of higher education that is both clearly market-oriented and possesses the prestige of Mexico's top private universities.[23]

Private sector fragmentation and the presence of important statist actors meant that resistance to the Kirchners' project of public sector expansion was, for the most part, limited. Important segments of business, including the UIA's Industriales faction, were openly supportive during most of the Kirchner era (Peirano 2014, interview). Even those that were less enthusiastic hesitated to criticize official policies, partly out of fear of retribution. Business association leaders and others interviewed for this study noted that the Kirchners acted aggressively against their detractors, even to the point of ordering tax audits or lawsuits against them (2014 interviews: Abad, IDEA, Lamberto). In explaining his organization's hesitance to publicly oppose Fernández's policies, the president of the Argentine Chamber of Commerce and Services (Cámara Argentina de Comercio y Servicios, CAC) said that, "This is not the United States or Great Britain where you can say anything you want. I can say something negative about the government, but then I can't go to them and ask them to fix a problem. One thing is to disagree with them, which we do, but another is to openly criticize" (De la Vega 2014, interview).

[21] In 2016 Argentina had 138 think tanks (the seventh highest total in the world), Brazil 89, Mexico 61, and Chile 44 (McGann 2017, p. 27–29).
[22] Examples include the Center for the Study of State and Society (Centro de Estudios de Estado y Sociedad, CEDES) and the Center for the Implementation of Public Policies for Equity and Growth (Centro de Implementación de Políticas Públicas para la Equidad y el Crecimiento, CIPPEC).
[23] The Universidad del CEMA, founded in 1978 as a think tank by scholars with ties to the University of Chicago, is probably the university with the clearest liberal orientation.

Some interviewees attributed the Kirchners' willingness to punish businesses that crossed them to the culture of *peronismo* (2014 interviews: Baglini, Machinea). However, in comparative perspective, it was also clearly a function of preexisting divisions within the private sector, which facilitate a divide-and-conquer strategy. In Chile and Mexico, where the private sector enjoys a certain organizational and political unity, the politicized use of tax audits, fines, or lawsuits against large firms would likely draw a strong collective response. In Argentina, in contrast, governments can wield such tactics with relative impunity, not only because the rule of law is weaker (at least compared to Chile) but also because solidarity across firms and sectors is low (2014 interviews: IDEA, Miguens). A business association or firm that comes out publicly against some official decision cannot expect to be defended by other associations or firms or some larger organization with the influence to stand up to authorities.[24] As one veteran association official complained, "the business world is too atomized. There is a lot of individualism, a lot of every man for himself" (IDEA 2014, interview).

Private sector divisions and the Kirchners' exploitation of them help explain why mobilization against rising taxation was limited. With the important exception of the 2008 farm protests, there was little in the way of collective resistance to taxation (Fairfield 2015). In the wake of that event, criticism of the tax burden grew, but attempts to mold it into a broad private sector front had little effect. Probably the most significant effort in this sense began in 2013, when representatives of some 40 associations drafted a manifesto calling for extensive institutional and policy reforms, including tax relief. Their collaboration, dubbed the Forum for Business Convergence, generated significant media coverage. However, some key associations stayed away,[25] and government pressure led others, including the UIA, to distance themselves from the initiative (IDEA 2014, interview). Moreover, after issuing its initial document, the Forum largely disappeared from public view.

To be sure, the 2008 protests against Fernández's export tax hike constitute a major exception to the lack of anti-tax collective action. They unified the farm sector, divided the governing coalition, and inflicted an embarrassing defeat on the president. However, the uprising responded to exceptional circumstances, especially the imposition of a "mobile" rate scheme in which rates rose in conjunction with prices and could potentially reach nearly confiscatory levels (Fairfield 2011; Fairfield 2015, pp. 210–218). In practice, producers complained, the new policy constituted a virtual "ceiling" on profits (De Freijo 2014, interview). This measure was deeply offensive to them and led to

---

[24] Firms that dared stand up to the Kirchners could face harsh sanctions. A paradigmatic case was Shell Argentina, which resisted efforts to regulate the domestic hydrocarbons market. The government called for a consumer boycott of the company, levied dozens of fines against it, and at one point requested that its CEO be jailed. See *Apertura*, November 25, 2015.

[25] *Télam*, November 27, 2014.

an unprecedented collaboration between rival organizations, especially the SRA and FAA. The SRA president during that period claimed that representatives of the four entities that coordinated the campaign had never before engaged in any collective initiative (Miguens 2014, interview).

In addition, the campaign did not elicit anything close to unified support from other private sector associations. The UIA, then led by a member of Industriales, backed the government's position, only adopting a more critical stance as the conflict dragged on and began to negatively affect the economy (Arreseygor 2012; Peirano 2014, interview). A similar trajectory was followed by a number of other organizations with good relations with the government, including the CAC and the Argentine Chamber of Construction (Cámara Argentina de la Construcción, CAMARCO) (Arreseygor 2012, p. 44). Even when they assumed more critical postures, these groups did not openly make common cause with farm producers. Rather, they urged both sides to negotiate a pragmatic solution. According to former SRA president Luciano Miguens, some business leaders "congratulated us privately but didn't want to publicly embrace the protests" due to the risk involved (Miguens 2014 interview).

Public sector growth was also facilitated by the weakness of the electoral right. Even when the FPV lacked a legislative majority of its own, it was usually able to muster a working majority. A key reason is that few legislators embraced a clear anti-statist agenda. Argentina, in contrast to Chile and Mexico, has traditionally not had a programmatic rightwing party capable of competing successfully in national elections (Gibson 1996; Morresi and Vommaro 2014). The closest thing during the Kirchner years was Macri's PRO, created to contest the 2005 elections. Although strong in the capital city, until the 2015 elections it had little presence in most provinces and (as Table 6.1 indicates) was a minor actor in Congress. In a country where provincial governors can exercise substantial power, the PRO controlled not one governorship. The FPV's competitors were mainly centrist and center-left groups, including the UCR, the Civic Coalition-Affirmation of an Egalitarian Republic (Coalición Cívica-Afirmación de un República Igualitaria, CC-ARI), the Socialist Party, and dissident *peronistas*. At different times, the FPV was able to negotiate support from factions or individual legislators from virtually all of them, especially the UCR.

As previous sections of this chapter suggest, Argentina's contemporary statist-leaning balance of power is a path-dependent legacy of the cultural and institutional impacts of Perón's period in power during the 1940s and 1950s. By providing workers with material benefits and symbolic recognition, Perón forged a movement that has retained a stubbornly tight grip on Argentina's lower classes, due to both its normative appeal and its organizational grounding in the powerful labor unions (McGuire 1997; Mora y Araujo 2011). Although Perón himself died more than four decades ago and the *peronista* versus anti-*peronista* cleavage is not as stark as it once was, the movement he created continues to be meaningful to many Argentines, embodying a desire for social justice, national sovereignty, and a strong state.

The contemporary divisions among Argentina's economic elites can also be explained as at least partly a consequence of the eruption of *peronismo*, which, rather than uniting the private sector, set different business leaders against each other (Schneider 2004, pp. 194–196). Although the CGE is no longer a major actor, the interventionist and nationalist sentiments it embodied are still alive to a considerable extent within the UIA's Industriales faction, the FAA, and other entities representing smaller and more domestically oriented businesses. The divisions Perón helped to foster, furthermore, have contributed to the repeated frustration of attempts to form a competitive conservative party, since elites have lacked any semblance of a common political project (Mora y Araujo 2011, p. 173). In addition, Perón's relative conservatism inhibited the political fusion of economic liberalism and Catholic social conservatism that has helped buoy rightist parties like Chile's UDI and Mexico's PAN.

6.4.5   The Role of Democracy

The second long-term factor behind Argentina's tax increase is democracy, which has over time allowed the statist power balance to influence policymaking in a more sustained way and thus transform the public sector in the direction of greater intervention.

Of course, the statist-leaning balance of power highlighted in the previous subsection has existed for several decades. However, it did not lead to sustained state expansion until the Kirchner era. A key reason, as argued earlier in this chapter, is that civilian anti-statist forces were able to secure the military's assistance in keeping *peronismo* out of power or removing it from power once it got there. This civil-military coalition lacked the private sector support and mass legitimacy to construct a coherent, enduring liberal model, but it was able to impede the statist faction from doing the opposite. The result was pronounced policymaking instability, institutional decay, and, ultimately, hyperinflation.

Beginning in the 1980s, however, the military strategy became unviable. The traumatic events of the 1976–1983 *Proceso*, particularly its gross human rights violations and its decision to launch the tragic invasion of the Falkland/Malvinas Islands, discredited military rule in the eyes of many Argentines (Mainwaring and Pérez-Liñan 2013, ch. 5). Argentina's deep economic problems during the early 1980s only aggravated the armed forces' disrepute. This domestic transformation was reinforced by a growing wave of democratization in Latin America and beyond. Argentina did experience some brief military uprisings under Alfonsín, but they were protests against the government's efforts to prosecute human rights abuses, rather than attempts to seize power. Even during the hyperinflationary crisis that ended his presidency, a military coup was never a real possibility. In short, by the 1990s democracy had become something close to the "only game in town" (Przeworski 1991).

The interaction of a statist-leaning power balance and a democratic regime did not immediately lead to a major increase in taxation because in the 1990s Argentine society was preoccupied with overcoming the scourge of inflation. The mantra of "defending stability" was used to justify liberalizing reforms and to ignore issues of equity or social protection, or at least defer them to a later date. As long as *peronismo*'s statist preferences were neutralized by the perceived need to sustain Convertibility, the inability of anti-statist forces to resort to the military veto was irrelevant. Traditionally anti-*peronista* groups had little reason to challenge Menem, who adopted some of their most cherished policies.

However, once the neoliberal edifice crumbled in the early 2000s, the lack of a military card became quite relevant. In some key aspects, the *kirchnerista* governments bore more than a passing resemblance to Perón's. Policymaking veered in a statist and nationalist direction and, eventually, important macroeconomic problems emerged, including inflation. Authorities also adopted an intolerant attitude toward dissent, seeking to isolate or punish those who opposed them and taking a confrontational stance toward press critics (Kitzberger 2011; Catterberg and Palanza 2012, pp. 8–10). Business, as mentioned earlier, was not exempt from harsh treatment. In an earlier era, the opposition would have had strong incentives to resort to military intervention to change the political leadership or at least alter its behavior.

Yet, intervention was never even rumored. Fernández and her associates did sometimes accuse their conservative opponents, especially the leaders of the 2008 rural protests, of being "coup mongers," but that was a rhetorical tactic meant to associate them with earlier interventions, especially the brutal *Proceso*. There is no evidence that they actually sought military support for their demands, much less a coup. Moreover, despite the revival of human rights trials, civil-military relations were non-conflictual during the entire *kirchnerista* period. Civilian control was reinforced and measures taken to limit the military's mission to defense against external threats (Battaglino 2011). Military interference in civilian politics was essentially a nonissue and officers were seldom mentioned in the media.

Thus, although it was largely taken for granted by the press and scholars, Argentina had passed an important milestone. A succession of *peronista* governments advancing policies broadly reminiscent of Perón's had governed without any military interference whatsoever. In the process, they had substantially expanded the public sector, raising taxes, broadening the social safety net, hiring thousands of new employees, and redistributing resources from agriculture to urban workers and businesses. The *peronista* project of state-led capitalist development with redistribution had in a sense become a sustained reality.

That the Cambiemos government was unable to substantially roll back the Kirchners' tax increase is partly a result of the inherent difficulty of retracting spending commitments. Welfare state scholars have noted that there is a "ratchet effect" in social spending: once a program has been introduced or expanded, it is often hard to reverse, since beneficiaries resist losing what they have gained (Huber and Stephens 2001, ch. 2). Given that he inherited a large fiscal deficit, Macri would have had to make major spending cuts to permit a large tax reduction. Since much of the increased spending under the Kirchners went to social programs, these would presumably have had to suffer important cuts.

However, the specific balance of power in the Argentine case reinforces this dilemma. In the 2015 elections Cambiemos won only 26.5 percent of the seats in the Chamber of Deputies and 27.8 percent in the Senate, making it dependent on *peronismo* to pass legislation. It increased its strength in the 2017 midterm elections, but still fell well short of a majority in either chamber. Labor and popular movement militancy posed additional obstacles, since the government could expect proposed spending cuts to face intense protest. The problem was illustrated in December 2017, when Macri proposed an adjustment to the formula for calculating pension benefits. The proposal was met with a general strike and violent demonstrations that left more than 160 people injured. Although the measure passed, the conflict was politically damaging to the president.[26] Macri received pledges of support from business leaders glad to be rid of *kirchnerismo*, but private sector fragmentation meant that there was no entity with which the government could form a strong partnership to promote investment and contain inflation.

6.5   CONCLUSION

Argentina took a more winding road than Brazil to heavy taxation due to the deep and enduring conflict that emerged during the mid-twentieth century between *peronismo* and its opponents. That struggle, which would dominate the country's politics for decades and has still not entirely subsided, was reflected in a tax burden that fluctuated markedly, sometimes rising to well above the regional average and other times falling to a level similar to that of Mexico, consistently one of the most lightly taxed Latin American countries. Only since 1990 has the tendency toward periodic revenue collapses been left behind.

Despite this difference, Argentina's contemporary tax burden is the product of causal dynamics similar to those of high-tax Brazil and distinct from those of lower-tax Chile and Mexico. Because Argentine economic elites never experienced an episode of profound redistribution that menaced their property, they failed to mobilize into a cohesive anti-statist bloc capable of mounting effective resistance to interventionism and decisively domesticating labor. Instead, they remained divided and organizationally fragmented. While the weakness of anti-statist forces, combined with the abiding strength of

---

[26] *World Politics Review*, January 9, 2018.

peronismo, favored the emergence of a large public sector, that outcome would be delayed for decades because liberals exploited the anti-*peronismo* of the armed forces to thwart sustained implementation of statist policies. Eventually, however, society's rejection of authoritarianism rendered that strategy unusable, opening the door to the large tax increase the country has seen in recent decades, which seems unlikely to be significantly reversed in the foreseeable future.

Thus, although Argentina's political system contrasts starkly with Brazil's in some important respects, the Argentine case strongly reinforces the idea that the historical absence of profound property rights redistribution can facilitate taxation by discouraging the mobilization of economic elites into a broad anti-statist coalition and the consolidation of a potent political alliance between economic liberals and social conservatives. Together, these two cases provide a telling counterpoint to the Chilean and Mexican experiences of strong property rights threats, enduring conservative backlash and light taxation.

7

Conclusions

The preceding chapters have advanced an argument about the origins of tax burden variance among four relatively prosperous Latin American democracies that emphasizes the impact of episodes of redistributive reform that deeply menaced, but did not extinguish, private property. Where such episodes occurred, namely in Mexico and Chile, they triggered backlashes that became institutionalized in organizations dedicated to limiting state economic intervention in the name of preserving property and free enterprise. These actors have checked tax burden growth by opposing tax reforms and other public sector-expanding policies, as well as by combatting initiatives that could strengthen labor. In essence, efforts to redistribute property had the unanticipated effect of making it more difficult to extract revenue from society by fomenting a distrustful attitude toward the state, especially among elites, and forging stronger alliances between economic liberals and social conservatives.

In contrast, the lack of analogous reform waves in Argentina and Brazil has facilitated heavier taxation by discouraging the formation of a strong, enduring anti-statist bloc. Although the political systems of these two countries (like those of Chile and Mexico) differ in important ways, they share the fact that neither has experienced a government that threatened property rights on a large scale. As a result, both lack the kinds of anti-statist actors that have hindered public sector growth in Chile and Mexico, especially encompassing business associations, competitive rightist parties, and intellectual institutions committed to market-based policies. The relative absence of such actors has facilitated tax increases both directly, by attenuating opposition to public sector expansion, and indirectly, by aiding the growth of organized labor, which puts upward pressure on the tax burden through demands for public spending and support for statist parties.

This closing chapter extends the scope of the book in three ways. First, it explores the relevance of the central argument for other Latin American countries. Second, it examines how well the argument travels outside this region. Finally, since the book's argument would seem to reflect negatively on the possibility of attenuating Latin America's profound social divisions, it closes by discussing the argument's implications for this issue and pondering the way forward for advocates of equality. This chapter demonstrates that the causal account developed to explain tax burden differences among the core cases also sheds much light on at least some other Latin American countries. While its grounding in the distinctive socioeconomic and political context of Latin America means that this account does not perform as well elsewhere, it nevertheless holds implications for theoretical discussions that transcend this region. With regard to the equality question, this chapter finds that a strategy based on gradual reform centered on the fiscal system represents the least bad of the available alternatives.

7.1 BROADER RELEVANCE FOR LATIN AMERICA

This book seeks to explain tax burden variance among four countries. Whether its arguments are useful beyond these countries is a question left mainly for future scholarship. Nevertheless, it would seem worthwhile in this conclusion to at least tentatively address the question of external validity, both for its own sake and because demonstrating that the argument holds in other countries can lend additional credence to the causal inferences made with regard to the core cases. In particular, this section focuses on Latin America, where the argument would a priori seem most likely to apply.

Specifically, the analysis focuses on Guatemala and Ecuador. The reason for limiting it to only two countries is that demonstrating that the contemporary tax burden is a function of the occurrence or nonoccurrence of earlier episodes of redistribution necessarily involves space-intensive historical process tracing. Even dealing with two countries in a single chapter is challenging. There are other Latin American countries that could be used to illustrate the broader relevance of the argument. For example, El Salvador and Peru are both cases in which major reform episodes involving property threats helped give rise to enduring anti-statist actors that have resisted taxation. In contrast, Uruguay is a clear example of how the lack of property threats can facilitate taxation by inhibiting the formation of such actors. Nevertheless, contrasting Guatemala and Ecuador offers advantages. Most importantly, because both countries are relatively poor, the comparison demonstrates that the argument is valid for societies at lower levels of economic development than the core case study countries.

Admittedly, Guatemala and Ecuador possess characteristics that distinguish them from the other cases of light and heavy contemporary taxation, respectively. In the former, the key difference involves parties. While in Mexico and Chile instances of sharp redistributive reform gave rise to highly institutionalized rightist parties, in Guatemala that was not the case. The party system in general remains deeply inchoate. With regard to Ecuador, the main distinguishing characteristic involves labor. Unlike Argentina and Brazil, Ecuador has weak labor unions. This difference is compensated to some degree by an unusually strong and centralized indigenous movement, but popular organization cannot easily be seen as a key factor in the country's heavy tax burden. These differences notwithstanding, Guatemala and Ecuador offer excellent illustrations of the broader validity of the core argument regarding the impact of major redistributive reform episodes on taxation.

7.1.1   Reform, Backlash, and Light Taxation in Guatemala

In recent years, Guatemala has had the lightest tax burden in Latin America, averaging 12.6 percent of GDP between 2013 and 2017 (CEPALSTAT). Unlike its Mexican counterpart, the Guatemalan state does not enjoy significant nontax revenues since the country lacks substantial mineral or hydrocarbon resources. While Guatemala does receive more foreign aid than any of the core case study countries relative to the size of its economy, aid has amounted to only about 0.6 percent of GDP annually in recent years, so it also fails to explain the country's light taxation (OECD International Development Statistics, https://stats.oecd.org/qwids/; World Bank Database). Due to its exceptionally low public revenues, Guatemala also ranks below other Latin American countries at similar levels of economic development, such as Bolivia, Honduras, and Paraguay, with regard to public spending (CEPALSTAT; Cabrera et al. 2015).

Guatemala was not always at the bottom of the regional tax burden ranking, however. In the late 1940s and early 1950s, Guatemala's burden was comparable to those of other lower-income Latin American countries (ECLAC 1956, p. 132). However, by 1970 Guatemala had the single lightest tax burden in the region, as well as the lowest current expenditures (ECLAC 1979, pp. 99 and 104). Despite some fluctuations, public sector growth would remain largely stagnant over the next three decades (United Nations Development Program, UNDP, 2008, pp. 446–448). In fact, Guatemala's central government tax revenues in 1953 were remarkably similar relative to GDP (10 percent) to what they would be in 2013 (11.1 percent), six decades later. In contrast, in Latin America as a whole, tax burdens increased by roughly 50 percent during that period (ECLAC 1956; CEPALSTAT).

As these figures imply, Guatemala's transition to civilian rule in 1985, after three decades of almost unbroken military domination, did little to alter the reality of extremely light taxation. Even an internationally brokered peace agreement that ended the country's long-running (1960–1996) leftist insurgency and explicitly committed the state to raising its revenues failed to significantly disturb the low-tax equilibrium. Government negotiators pledged during the 1996 talks to increase the tax burden (not including social security contributions) from 9 percent of GDP to 12 percent, as one of a series of measures meant to address poverty and inequality (Sanchez 2009, pp. 115). That level was supposed to be reached by 2000, but as of 2016 it had still not been attained (OECD 2017, p. 153).

Several works have attempted to explain Guatemala's persistently light taxation. Some have identified institutional factors, including the lack of stable, programmatic parties (Schneider 2012; Schneider and Cabrera 2015). Guatemalan parties are notoriously ephemeral, factionalized, and ideologically ambiguous (Sanchez 2008; Jones 2011). For some scholars, these characteristics have made it difficult for presidents, even ones seemingly committed to tax reform, to pilot reform bills through Congress (Sanchez 2009). The effects of party weakness were on display, for example, in the failure of an effort in 2000 to belatedly fulfill the tax commitments assumed by the state under the 1996 peace agreement. President Alfonso Portillo of the heterogenous Guatemalan Republican Front (FRG) spearheaded the negotiation of a "Fiscal Pact" among a broad set of actors. Conditions for achieving tax reform seemed favorable, but ultimately only minor change occurred. While the reasons are multiple, one was that the FRG was divided into two rival factions, one of which ultimately opposed the government's bill (Sanchez 2009, pp. 118–123).

Another institutional factor often viewed as hindering taxation consists of provisions in the current constitution, written in 1985, that facilitate judicial challenges to tax laws (Fuentes and Cabrera 2005; Sanchez 2009). The constitution imposes strong limits on taxation, including a vague prohibition on "confiscatory taxes" and a ban on levying multiple taxes on the same source. The latter has been interpreted by the courts as meaning that payments of indirect taxes by businesses are deductible from income tax liabilities. Moreover, the constitution allows individual citizens and firms to challenge the constitutionality of tax laws before the Constitutional Court. If the challenge is successful, the measure in question is struck down.

These provisions are somewhat similar to the one in Mexico that permits the use of *amparos*, but they are stronger since the Mexican constitution does not place such strict limits on taxation and the *amparo* system only results in generalized relief from a tax provision if five different challenges are successful (Elizondo 2009). During its first twenty years of existence, the Guatemalan Constitutional Court heard slightly over one hundred such challenges and agreed with no less than eighty-five of them (Schneider and Cabrera 2015, p. 132). This instrument caused significant declines in revenue, especially in the early 2000s, when the Portillo government's imposition of a tax reform despite the collapse of the Fiscal Pact inflamed resistance to the measures approved (Sanchez 2009, pp. 118–123).

These institutional factors notwithstanding, the scholarship on Guatemala's tax system makes clear that the key to understanding the country's light taxation lies in the overwhelming dominance of political forces committed to maintaining a small, unobtrusive state (Valdez and Palencia 1998; Fuentes and Cabrera 2005; UNDP 2008; Sanchez 2009; Schneider 2012). To a large extent, the institutional barriers to reform described in the preceding discussion reflect the influence of this underlying balance.

In particular, analysts have consistently put great weight on the role of the peak business association known as the "Coordinating Committee of Agricultural, Commercial, Industrial and Financial Associations" (Comité Coordinador de Asociaciones Agrícolas, Comerciales, Industriales y Financieras, CACIF). Among the most encompassing business organizations in Latin America, CACIF includes both large and medium-sized firms and its member associations together reportedly represent upward of 80 percent of the country's GDP (UNDP 2008, p. 477). Although not immune to factionalism (especially between agriculture and industry), CACIF is in general quite unified and thus relatively insusceptible to efforts to neutralize it by dividing its members (Jonas 1991, p. 92; Sanchez 2009, p. 109).

As in Chile and Mexico, centralized business organization reflects the private sector's longstanding mistrust of the state and its readiness to go on the offensive against measures that would increase public sector capabilities. Scholars have long noted this characteristic of the country's economic elite. For example, a history of Guatemala's industrialists (who have been less consistently anti-statist than agricultural elites) notes that a "belligerent economic liberalism ... remains their salient ideological characteristic" (Dosal 1995, pp. 123–124). Similarly, a study of tax reform in post-authoritarian Guatemala argues that business's reflexively anti-interventionist culture is a key to understanding the failure of such efforts. According to the author, "Thus, the virulently anti-statist attitudes of the Guatemalan oligarchy cannot be ignored in this study of tax non-reform" (Sanchez 2009, p. 110).

For decades, CACIF has played a crucial role in blocking or gutting proposals to increase public revenues (Valdez and Palencia 1998; Fuentes and Cabrera 2005; Sánchez 2009). Sometimes it has done so through private channels, using its privileged access to public officials, especially under business-friendly governments. Other times it has engaged in public displays of contention, including disinformation campaigns disseminated through the media, national producer strikes, and threats to provoke military intervention. With CACIF's support and encouragement, businesses have also pursued, as mentioned earlier, numerous lawsuits meant to strike down reforms intended to increase public revenue. Even military governments, which generally benefitted from considerable goodwill among business leaders, were affected by these pressures. In fact, the efforts of certain military leaders during the 1970s to follow a more statist and redistributive development path were blunted by business's refusal to accept heavier taxation (Dosal 1995, ch. 7).

While Guatemala resembles Chile and Mexico in having a highly organized and anti-statist business community, it differs from them in lacking a strongly institutionalized rightwing party or coalition. Almost all the parties that have controlled the presidency or held a substantial number of legislative seats since 1985 have been composed mainly of politicians with relatively conservative views. These parties have also received funding from business (Torres-Rivas and Aguilar 1998; Sanchez 2008). However, none has lasted as a significant force for more than two election cycles. They have risen and declined according to the fortunes of individual leaders and failed to develop either a clear platform or strong ties to any social group, including business (Sanchez 2008; Jones 2011).

In a sense, this characteristic is not surprising, since Guatemala is a substantially less developed country than Mexico or Chile and there is a strong correlation between economic development and party system institutionalization in general (Mainwaring and Torcal 2006). However, since this relationship is neither absolute nor well understood, it is worth thinking about the specific causes of the lack of a strong right party in Guatemala. Two, in particular, would seem to be most significant.

One is that, until the 1980s, Guatemala had had little experience of competitive elections (Yashar 1997). Peak business organization emerged at the outset of a long period of authoritarian rule. Between CACIF's founding in early 1957 and the transition to civilian rule in 1985, Guatemala experienced a succession of governments that were either outright military dictatorships or civilian-led governments dominated by the armed forces. Even during the early years of democracy, moreover, elected authorities labored under the chronic threat of military intervention (Williams and Ruhl 2013, pp. 229–230). In this context, there was little reason for business elites to invest in constructing a party organization.

Second, democratization has not given rise to anything close to a substantial left. As this book has suggested, the strength of anti-statist actors is not a simple function of the degree of threat experienced by elites at a particular point in time. Traumatic events can have an enduring, path-dependent impact. Still, the fact that the left in Guatemala has been especially weak is not irrelevant to the persistent electoral disorganization of the right. Unlike in neighboring El Salvador, where the major guerrilla organization of the 1980s registered important victories and made a successful transition to a leftist political party, in Guatemala the rebels were never a true threat to take power and the party they established, the Guatemalan National Revolutionary Union (Unidad Revolucionaria Nacional Guatemalteca, URNG), has not been a significant contender (Allison 2016). Collectively, moreover, left parties have never held more than 10 percent of the seats in Congress. A center-left party called "National Union of Hope" (Unión Nacional de la Esperanza, UNE) has had more success, holding the presidency from 2008 to 2011 and winning roughly a fifth of the seats in Congress on average since 2003. However, the UNE government's attempts to advance mild progressive reforms were frustrated by the lack of a legislative majority (Perla et al. 2013, p. 345). Among the reasons why the partisan left is weak is that labor organization is also negligible. Union members represent only 3 percent of the wage-earning population, the lowest figure in Latin America (Confederación Sindical de Trabajadores y Trabajadoras de las Américas 2016, p. 200).

In other words, the evolution of Guatemalan politics since the democratic transition has not given economic elites a strong reason to invest in party-building (Sanchez 2009). The policy outcomes that have resulted from the country's fluid, fragmented party system, though arguably bad for Guatemalan society as a whole, have protected what they perceive to be their vital interest in keeping state intervention at bay.

Guatemala's light taxation thus reflects an extreme power imbalance favoring anti-statist forces. Indeed, there is perhaps no other Latin American country where the power structure so unambiguously favors anti-statism (Sanchez 2009). The institutional impediments to taxation mentioned earlier reflect this dominance. Party disorganization is at least partly a function of the weakness of popular civil society, which impedes the creation of a competitive leftist party and affords more conservative actors the luxury of focusing on clientelism and pursuit of personal gain, rather than investing in a strong rightist party. The constitutional provisions that allow business to nullify tax increases approved by Congress reflect the fact that the 1985 constitution was created in a context of high elite organization and a popular sector fragmented and intimidated by decades of repression (Brett and Delgado 2005). In contrast to Brazil's 1988 constitution, also crafted during a period of democratic transition but in the context of very different power relations, it severely restrains state action by instituting exceptionally strong taxpayer protections (ECLAC 1996).

The origins of this imbalance do not lie in a single factor. Certain social structural conditions, including stronger ethnic divisions than in most Latin American countries and low levels of urbanization and industrialization, have probably contributed to the weakness of statism. Nevertheless, it must be underscored that, despite these obstacles, Guatemala did experience a period of strong popular movements and progressive government from 1945 to 1954. During this period, often known as the "Guatemalan revolution," two left-leaning politicians rose to the presidency through democratic elections (Gleijeses 1991; Handy 1994). Capitalizing on legislative majorities and popular mobilization, they implemented extensive redistributive labor, social, and property reforms.

To understand why Guatemala subsequently became an extreme case of anti-statist dominance, we must appreciate the impact these presidencies, particularly the second, had on economic elites and social conservatives. Much as in Chile and Mexico, in Guatemala the attempt to redistribute societal resources, especially property, provoked a conservative countermobilization whose anti-statist thrust would become institutionalized in key political organizations, most importantly CACIF.

Guatemala's "revolution" began in a relatively cautious way. President Juan José Arevalo (1945–1951), who was elected to office after the overthrow of longtime dictator Jorge Ubico, implemented a pro-union labor code reform, passed a social security law, and spearheaded a constitutional reform that expanded the suffrage and banned the traditional practice of forced labor. These were important changes, which provoked considerable resistance from elites and some military officers (Dosal 1995). However, Arevalo left the deeply unequal rural landholding structure intact. Furthermore, he kept his distance from communist groups, which had a significant presence in Guatemala.

President Jacobo Arbenz (1951–1954) departed from Arevalo's approach in two important ways. First, he legalized Guatemala's version of the Communist Party and employed some communists in his government. Second, and more important, he undertook one of the most ambitious land reforms in Latin America up to that time. In only eighteen months, the state expropriated about a quarter of Guatemala's arable land (Gleijeses 1991, p. 155). Had it been fully implemented, the decree authorizing the reform would have resulted in the seizure of more than half the country's private land. Expropriated landowners, including the mighty US-based United Fruit Corporation, were compensated. However, indemnities were based on land values reported for tax purposes, which were typically far below market value. To make matters worse, from the perspective of domestic elites and the US government, the program was directed by the secretary general of Guatemala's Communist Party, José Manuel Fortuny.

While Arbenz portrayed his land reform program as pro-industrialization, it did not enjoy significant support from industrialists. As soon as the reform was launched, a tentative alliance with industrialists collapsed. "Few of them," one scholar argues of the industrialists, "failed to recognize that a government that nationalized private land could also expropriate industrial plants" (Dosal 1995, p. 101). What they perceived as a growing threat to core aspects of capitalism prompted industrialists to forge "an internal cohesiveness and ideological consensus" they had previously lacked (Dosal 1995, p. 103). Moreover, far from taking the government's side against agrarian elites, industrialists made common cause with this traditionally dominant sector to halt what both perceived as a mortal threat (Yashar 1997, ch. 6).

In their opposition to the government, economic elites were joined by the Catholic Church, which was panicked by the specter of communism (Gleijeses 1991, pp. 211–214; Harms 2011). Mariano Rossell y Arellano, Archbishop of Guatemala, became an outspoken critic of the government and especially its land reform, which he viewed as portending a slide into totalitarianism. Although these attacks exaggerated the role of communism in the government, they helped propel a growing wave of anti-communist sentiment among middle- and upper-class Guatemalans (Yashar 1997, pp. 196–200).

The armed forces initially stood by Arbenz, but their loyalty eventually wilted in the face of a US-organized invasion of the country manned by Guatemalan exiles and mercenaries and supported with propaganda and airpower. When the military leadership demanded his resignation, Arbenz was forced to comply and leave the country. His reforms, including land redistribution, were quickly rolled back and many of his supporters killed, jailed, or exiled.

Like the Allende and Cárdenas reform periods, Guatemala's revolutionary years left a deep mark on business owners and the upper class (Dosal 1995; Yashar 1997). Although the military regime installed after Arbenz's fall reversed his reforms, elites felt they had dodged a bullet and became determined to avoid exposing themselves to such risks in the future. CACIF's creation in January 1957 reflected this wariness. Evolving out of a council created to advise the military regime, it was formed to provide a unified voice on issues of importance to the capitalist class as a whole. Rather than fading after the "communist threat" had passed, it gained further strength in the 1960s and 1970s by spearheading business resistance to the efforts of reformist military leaders to forge a state apparatus that would more proactively address problems of social and economic underdevelopment. Although far from radical, these moves only seemed to confirm the fears and resentments of "a private sector still haunted by the memory the two revolutionary governments" and reinforce the need to hang together despite recurrent intersectoral disagreements (Dosal 1995, p. 34).

Elite unity also helped weaken the labor movement. While the armed forces were a somewhat ambivalent ally, business continued to support military rule because it provided protection against threats from below. The primary target of repression was armed guerrillas, but anyone seeking to defend social justice and workers' rights was fair game (Jonas 1991). Repression peaked in the early 1980s, when the military reacted to a growing insurgency with massive violence against anyone who supported, or even just tolerated, the rebels. It was only when international pressures began to mount that business leaders decided that the costs of military rule outweighed its benefits and engineered a transition to some semblance of democracy. By then popular organizations had been decimated. Moreover, since that transition, CACIF and friendly politicians have largely ignored the frequent use of private violence against workers, which has made Guatemala among the most dangerous places to be a union leader (International Trade Union Confederation 2013).

Thus, while some of the specifics of the Guatemalan case are different, the basic causal dynamics of light taxation closely parallel those highlighted in the Chilean and Mexican cases. In all three countries, a redistributive reform wave that menaced property rights in the context of left-leaning governance and widespread mobilization led to a conservative backlash institutionalized in organizations that have posed enduring obstacles to heavier taxation. Moreover, the ways in which Guatemala differs from these other cases largely reflect the fact that it is a more extreme case of the same causal process. In particular, Guatemala lacks a programmatic anti-statist party not because elites are divided by longstanding cleavages or fundamental issues, but because their dominance is so great that they have little incentive to come together to forge a united conservative party.

7.1.2 Mild Reformism, Elite Fragmentation, and Heavy Taxation in Ecuador

Ecuador has a heavy tax burden for a country whose per capita GDP has historically been in the bottom third of Latin America and whose public sector receives large inflows of nontax revenue. During the 2013–2017 period, tax revenues averaged 21.4 percent of GDP (OECD 2018, p. 149). Nontax revenues from the state oil company, Petroecuador, meanwhile, averaged 8.6 percent of GDP from 2013 to 2016 (OECD 2016, 2017, 2018), meaning that the Ecuadorian state enjoyed total fiscal revenues of roughly 30 percent of GDP, considerably more than Chile or Mexico and vastly more than Guatemala.

Ecuador's tax burden has increased rapidly in the last two decades, especially under the left-leaning governments of Rafael Correa (2007–2017). However, historically its public sector has tended to be substantial by the standards of poorer Latin American countries. Data from the 1960s and early 1970s suggest that Ecuador had a heavier tax burden than any of the Central American countries, Paraguay or Bolivia (ECLAC 1979, p. 99). Taxation deteriorated during the post-1973 oil boom, but that was because nontax revenues surged, giving Ecuador a level of fiscal resources similar to recent years, at 26–28 percent of GDP (World Bank 1984, p. 24). Ecuador's tax revenues by the 1990s were only about 8 percent of GDP, but its oil revenues gave it fiscal income of 20–22 percent of GDP, lower than during the oil boom but still substantial for a poorer country (World Bank 2005, p. 14).

While the post-2000 governments have increased direct taxes substantially, such taxes only accounted for 22.3 percent of total tax revenues on average between 2012 and 2016, a smaller share than in Guatemala (30.9 percent) (OECD 2018, pp. 190 and 194). That is in large part because social security taxes contribute substantially more than in Guatemala. Thus, as in the core cases, in Guatemala and Ecuador there is an inverse correlation between the tax burden magnitude and the degree of reliance on direct taxation.

How do we explain the current high level of taxation in Ecuador? Clearly, any satisfactory explanation must account for the tremendous increase during the Correa period. However, it must also be consistent with the fact that, prior to the mid-1970s oil boom, Ecuador was a country with a substantial tax burden, at least relative to other Latin American countries at similar levels of development.

Correa's impressive electoral support and his determination to use it to strengthen the state were the driving forces behind the tax burden increases of recent decades. Coming to office in 2006 with a nationalist, anti-neoliberal, and anti-party discourse, Correa promised to reconstruct the state and put it at the service of the citizenry (De la Torre 2010). He soon moved to consolidate power by holding a constituent assembly in which his Proud and Sovereign Fatherland Alliance (Alianza Patria Altiva y Soberana, or Alianza PAIS) party won a large majority. The 2008 constitution boosted executive power and paved the way for new elections in 2009, which Correa and his party won handily. They duplicated that feat in 2013, capturing 71 percent of the seats in the unicameral legislature.

Under the Alianza PAIS governments both revenue and spending grew rapidly. High oil prices meant increased revenues for Petroecuador, the state-owned oil company, and the government also sought to force private oil companies to turn over a larger share of their own revenues (Lyall and Valdivia 2019). In addition, between 2007 and 2011, the government approved a series of reforms to the general tax code meant both to increase revenues and make the tax structure more equitable (Schützhofer 2016, pp. 19–21). The national tax authority also underwent organizational, staffing, and technical changes to bolster enforcement and expand the taxpayer base (Servicio de Rentas Internas 2012, pp. 367–384). These reforms helped tax revenues increase by about 50 percent relative to GDP between 2007 and 2015 (OECD 2017, p. 151). Armed with greater revenues, the national government increased social spending by an annual average of 15 percent between 2007 and 2012 (Naranjo 2014, p. 23).

President Correa's success in expanding the public sector cannot easily be attributed to the influence of preexisting statist forces. Ecuador does have one of the region's strongest indigenous movements, which, in addition to demanding recognition of the country's ethnic diversity, has also supported a more interventionist state in certain areas, such as agriculture and environmental protection (Becker 2008). However, labor unions are weak and organizationally fragmented (Herrera 2016). Ecuador's union density, while more than double that of Guatemala (at 8 percent of the wage labor force), is among the lowest in the region (Confederación Sindical de Trabajadores y Trabajadoras de las Américas 2016, p. 200). While left-of-center forces have sometimes enjoyed significant electoral success, their victories have been fleeting and left little organizational trace. There have been many socialist parties, but none has emerged as an important national contender.

Furthermore, Correa was generally not close to leftist groups other than his own party. Much of the preexisting left initially supported him, but he soon developed antagonistic relationships with some of its key organizations, including the Confederation of Indigenous Nationalities of Ecuador (Confederación de las Nacionalidades Indígenas del Ecuador, CONAIE). The reasons for this conflict were diverse but include Correa's general hostility to what he perceived as self-interested lobbying by organized groups and his determination to develop large-scale mining, which CONAIE opposes because mining projects often encroach on indigenous territory (De la Torre 2010).

Thus, Correa's electoral success and the large legislative majorities eventually captured by Alianza PAIS cannot be attributed to the mobilizational capacity of the organized left. Rather, they were due largely to his skill in channeling diffuse public discontent with the extraordinary instability of the preceding decade, including the removal of three successive presidents before their terms had expired and a financial meltdown that led to the controversial decision to adopt the US dollar as Ecuador's official currency (De la Torre 2011). Of course, the high international price of oil was also beneficial.

Nevertheless, the literature on Ecuador is also rather clear in stating that a key facilitating condition in both Correa's electoral rise and, especially, the implementation of his statist reform agenda was the pronounced weakness of anti-statist forces.

As with the left, programmatic parties of the right have not enjoyed sustained success in Ecuador (Conaghan 1995; Bowen 2015). The Social Christian Party (Partido Social Cristiano, PSC) has been the closest thing to such a party. It has generally endorsed pro-market policies and one of its leaders, León Febres Cordero, was president from 1984 to 1988, initiating a number of liberalizing reforms in a context of deep economic crisis. However, the PSC's commitment to liberalism has been tempered by personalism and clientelism. Febres Corderos' reform program, for example, quickly lost steam in the face of criticism from within and outside his party, leaving the degree of state intervention virtually unchanged (Montúfar 2000; Roberts 2014, p. 157). Moreover, since the 2006 elections the PSC's electoral fortunes have declined precipitously. In recent years, its victories have been limited essentially to its regional bastion in Guayas province (Bowen 2014).

Just as important for understanding the rapid public sector growth under Correa is the weakness of private sector resistance to his initiatives. While there were certainly many business leaders who expressed doubts about the president's policies, most did so in measured tones and there was little in the way of an orchestrated campaign to block the reforms. A study of contemporary business-state relations in Ecuador and Bolivia points out that "Ecuadorian business groups never adopted an openly confrontation stance and were, in fact, always willing to enter into dialogue with the Correa government" (Wolff 2016, pp. 138). Similarly, a work on the right in the same two countries argues that, while Ecuador's conservative parties assumed a confrontational stance toward the Alianza PAIS government, business's approach was "far more diverse and strategically more pragmatic" (Bowen 2014, p. 107).

This cautious response stems from both organizational weakness and the lack of strong anti-statist current among Ecuadorian business leaders. Correa encountered a business community that was highly fragmented politically (Eaton 2011; Bowen 2014; Wolff 2016). In stark contrast to the cases of light taxation examined in this book, Ecuador has no significant national, cross-sectoral business associations. Even in Guayas, the key stronghold of conservative politics, there is no entity that can effectively aggregate business interests across sectors (Eaton 2011, p. 303). The lack of major business associations is so pronounced that even studies focused on business-state relations barely mention specific organizations (Conaghan and Malloy 1994; Montúfar 2000; Wolff 2016).

In addition, the economic elite Correa faced did not have a tradition of steadfast opposition to state intervention. To be sure, there had been times when business had mobilized to oppose policies they found threatening. This was the case, perhaps most notably, under the military government headed by Guillermo Rodríguez Lara (1972–1976), which, fueled by rising oil revenues, increased spending, nationalized some businesses, and implemented a land reform involving some (albeit very limited) expropriation of private estates (Conaghan 1988). However, even this episode did not prompt, for reasons discussed later, an enduring shift from fragmented rent seeking to more confrontational class politics. As Montúfar (2000) has argued, Ecuador's private sector has historically been more concerned with exploiting the potential benefits of state intervention than limiting its extent.

The weakness of anti-statism within the Ecuadorian business community helps explain the limited extent of state retrenchment achieved under presidents Febres Cordero and Sixto Duran Ballén (1992–1996), who also promised liberalizing reform (Eaton 2011; Bowen 2014). An important reflection of these failures, since it directly affects tax revenues, is Ecuador's refusal to embrace the regional trend toward pension privatization. Like Brazil, Ecuador is one of the relatively few countries in Latin America with a significant public pension system where no privatization occurred. Although a law that would have proceeded down this road was passed in 2001, it was blocked by the judiciary and the project was subsequently abandoned.

Why are elites in Ecuador so little disposed to battle the state, particularly in comparison to Guatemala, a country that is in some ways rather similar? In the case of the Correa government, it is likely that the sheer level of popular support the president attained intimidated some business leaders. However, as the preceding discussion emphasized, the lack of strong business-state conflict under Correa also reflects a preexisting pattern of weak organization and collective action within Ecuador's private sector. This, in turn, would seem to be rooted in the lack of an episode of deep redistributive reform of the kind that occurred under Arbenz in Guatemala, as well as in Mexico and Chile.

Ecuador has a long history of mild, incremental social reformism. Civilian governments have generally made little progress in this area, but some of the country's many military regimes have advanced further. The "July Revolution" of 1925 initiated a number of reforms that were precocious relative to Ecuador's development level, including the creation of a pension system and an income tax, as well as the introduction of a constitutional clause subjecting private property rights to the collective interest. From 1963 to 1966 another military government, following the cautious guidelines of the US-sponsored Alliance for Progress, implemented the country's first significant land reform (Blankstein and Zuvekas 1973). During the 1970s, Rodríguez Lara revived land redistribution and channeled some of the oil revenue windfall into social policies like education and health care (North 2004, p. 195).

Ecuador's reformist tradition helps us understand why the country has long had an extensive public sector and, before the oil boom led to deterioration of the tax system, a substantial tax burden for a poor country. Along with the developmentalist economic policies adopted beginning in the 1950s, these reforms helped created a political and economic "state-centered matrix" into which both popular and elite groups were inserted (Montúfar 2000).

Nevertheless, even the most significant of these military-led reform episodes resulted in only superficial redistribution that did not seriously threaten property. The land reforms implemented under military rule were minor compared to those undertaken in several other Latin American countries, including Chile, Guatemala, and Mexico (Sobhan 1993, pp. 8–11). They distributed a significant quantity of land, but did so overwhelmingly through colonization of public areas, rather than expropriation of private holdings, which was the method of choice in the other three countries (Albertus 2015, p. 132). Rodriguez Lara's nonagricultural expropriations were limited to industries often considered natural monopolies (e.g., electricity generation) and relatively small and unprofitable industries, such as the national airline. In the crucial oil sector, the government moved to reap a larger share of the profits, but its reforms fell well short of full nationalization (Brogan 1984).

Importantly, Rodríguez Lara's reforms were also implemented by an ideologically moderate government and in the context of very limited popular mobilization, both characteristics that attenuated the threat felt by economic elites. While elites did mobilize to oppose these initiatives, the experience was far less traumatic than the Arbenz period in Guatemala, or the analogous reform episodes in Mexico and Chile. In all three of the latter cases, major property restructuring occurred in tandem with a government influenced or, in the Chilean case, led by Marxist forces and supported by mass mobilization in the cities and countryside. In Ecuador none of these factors was present, at least to the same degree.

Thus, as in Argentina and Brazil, in Ecuador economic elites have lacked a strong impetus to engage in broad political mobilization to defend themselves against the state. Their lack of organization and class-wide solidarity made it easier for Correa to elevate taxes to unprecedented levels, even though he did not enjoy the support of strong statist groups in civil society. In other words, the Ecuadorian case could hardly be more different than that of Guatemala, in which an episode of pronounced redistribution forged a highly unified elite deeply committed to limiting public sector expansion.

While Guatemala and Ecuador differ in some important respects from the other low- and high-tax countries, respectively, analyzed in this book, they nevertheless illustrate the central argument quite clearly. Like Chile and Mexico, Guatemala is a case in which light taxation reflects the indirect impact of an episode of sharp redistributive change that had the long-term effect of tilting the power balance in favor of anti-statist forces. Ecuador, meanwhile, resembles the Argentine and Brazilian cases in that the lack of any major redistributive reform episode facilitated the construction of a heavy tax burden by depriving economic elites and social conservatives of the stimulus necessary to engage in broad mobilization and organization-building aimed at combatting statism.

Because it confirms the argument advanced in earlier chapters, this comparison underscores the importance of paying more attention to the long-term political impacts of attempts to restructure property rights in Latin America. Of course, there are significant literatures on land reform (Grindle 1986; Thiesenhusen 1995; Albertus 2015) and the nationalization of nonfarm assets (Moran 1974; Sigmund 1980; Berrios et al. 2011). However, they tend to focus either on why reforms did or did not occur, or their welfare outcomes. The question of how attempts to alter property relations have shaped subsequent political patterns has been neglected, at least in broadly comparative studies. This book contributes to our understanding of this question, but there is more work to be done.

7.2 RELEVANCE BEYOND LATIN AMERICA

Having established that the book's argument applies to at least some Latin American societies other than the core cases, the logical next step is to ask whether it can shed light on tax burden variance beyond this region. While it would be appealing to assert that it can, a preliminary examination suggests otherwise. Redistributive episodes of the kind highlighted in the cases of Chile, Mexico, and Guatemala appear to be rare outside Latin America. Moreover, even among cases that approximate this model, taxation does not appear to be especially light. The argument's regional specificity would seem to be rooted in a combination of traits, including extreme inequality, limited industrialization, US political dominance, and early independence from colonial rule, that distinguishes Latin America from other regions. Although its empirical relevance may be restricted to Latin America, the argument nevertheless holds implications for theoretical debates extending well beyond this region, including ones pertaining to path dependence, preference formation, and backlash processes. The section begins by highlighting the difficulties of applying the book's argument beyond Latin America, then analyzes the reasons behind them. It ends by discussing the argument's theoretical implications.

7.2.1 The Difficulties of Applying the Argument Outside Latin America

There are two key obstacles to applying the argument of this study beyond Latin America. First, the type of redistributive reform episode it emphasizes in the low-tax Latin American cases appears to be rare outside this region. Second, even in those countries in which similar episodes have occurred, subsequent taxation levels do not seem to be consistently low, at least after other influences on the tax burden are taken into consideration.

As previous chapters have suggested, what distinguishes the low-tax cases in this study is the occurrence at some point in their histories of a reform episode possessing three characteristics: (1) the existence of a left-leaning government with ties to radical groups; (2) strong popular mobilization in favor of the reform project; and, most importantly, (3) the implementation of reforms that involve widespread expropriation of private property but do not actually liquidate the economic elite and consolidate socialism.

This combination appears to be quite uncommon outside Latin America, at least among larger and better-studied countries. The majority of countries, much like Argentina, Brazil, and Ecuador, have simply never experienced in their modern histories a reform wave that posed a major threat to property. They may have never witnessed the rise of a leftist government, or the leftist governments that did come to power did not propose major property reforms, or those property reforms that were proposed were never substantially implemented. Countries such as Germany, India, Nigeria, Turkey, and the United States, just to name a few from different regions, fall into this category.

Among the countries that have undergone important episodes of property redistribution, a good many consolidated socialist transitions that essentially destroyed the private sector, thus preventing a backlash of the kind discussed in the cases of Chile, Mexico, and Guatemala. Most of these are in either Eastern Europe or East Asia. In the former, socialism began in Russia and its Central Asian republics but spread widely after World War II to include most of the region. In the latter, it triumphed first in China and North Korea (with Soviet assistance) in the late 1940s and later in parts of southeast Asia, including Vietnam.

Of the relatively few episodes of major property reform that did not bring socialism, several were undertaken by conservative governments or did not involve significant popular mobilization or (most commonly) both. This category includes post-World War II governments in Japan, South Korea, and Taiwan which, under strong US influence, undertook major land reforms to impede the spread of communism. It also includes extensive programs of nonagricultural nationalization implemented in France and Great Britain after World War II, at least partly in response to problems created by the war. Of the episodes mentioned here, only the British one involved a left-leaning government. However, this reform wave has often been viewed as part of a "post-war consensus" that spanned the party system (Addison 1994), and it did not involve widespread popular mobilization.

Outside Latin America the cases that can most readily be likened to the Chilean, Guatemalan, and Mexican ones are found mainly in the Middle East and North Africa (MENA). They consist of countries that implemented major reform waves during the mid-twentieth century following the end of European colonial rule. The reforms involved land redistribution and nationalization of key sectors of the nonfarm economy and they were implemented by nominally socialist governments seeking to mobilize broad popular support for nationalist and redistributive political projects. The transformations wrought by these governments varied in magnitude, but arguably in all cases fell short of eliminating private sector businesses as important contributors to the economy. The clearest examples are probably Algeria, Egypt, Iraq, Libya, and Syria.

Nevertheless, it is not clear that taxation in these cases tends to be lighter than in MENA countries that did not undergo such reforms. Iraq and Libya have extremely light tax burdens (about 2 percent of GDP) but that is a common phenomenon in the region and can be explained by extraordinarily high nontax revenues from oil. Between 2013 and 2017, their average total fiscal revenues, at 34.2 and 57.4 percent of GDP, respectively, substantially exceeded the regional average of 30.5 percent (IMF World Economic Outlook Database). Algeria has not only lower natural resource revenues, but also a heavier tax burden at around 13 percent of GDP (IMF 2018, p. 27). Thus, like Iraq and Libya, its total fiscal revenues, at 32.2 percent of GDP, are above the MENA average (IMF World Economic Outlook Database).

It is true that both Egypt and Syria have tax burdens that are lighter than some non-oil exporting MENA countries (e.g., Morocco) and that this difference is not entirely compensated by nontax revenue. However, Egypt's total fiscal revenues, at 22.0 percent of GDP, are greater than some countries that did not undergo major property reforms (e.g., Lebanon) and only moderately below others.[1] Syria's contemporary fiscal revenues are quite low, but that is mainly because of its long-running civil war. It is also crucial to note that for roughly two decades following its property reforms, Egypt had one of the largest public sectors in the MENA region. For example, in 1982–1983 its tax revenues equaled 23 percent of GDP and its total revenues 42 percent (World Bank 1986, p. 13). Its public spending was the highest in the region (Cammett et al. 2015, p. 62). It was only with the adoption of neoliberal reforms, partly in response to external pressure, that the state began to contract. Syria's public sector was smaller, but in the early 1980s it had fiscal revenues of roughly 27 percent of GDP (World Bank 1982, p. 8) and spending comparable to the MENA average (Cammett et al. 2015, p. 62). Hence, although their current tax burdens are modest, neither Egypt nor Syria parallels the pattern of Chile, Guatemala, and Mexico, in which major property threats were followed by chronically light taxation and small public sectors.

7.2.2 Explaining the Argument's Regional Specificity

The difficulty of applying this book's argument outside Latin America reflects the fact that this region possesses a constellation of socioeconomic and political

---

[1] In addition, Egypt's true fiscal revenues may well be higher than this figure suggests, since its large military apparatus has important off-budget revenue sources (Sayigh 2019).

characteristics not found elsewhere. In elaborating this view, it is important to separate these characteristics into two categories. The first consists of ones that have promoted the occurrence of episodes of major property reform by left-leaning governments that nonetheless fell short of full socialist transition. They explain why such episodes have occurred more frequently in Latin America than elsewhere. The second consists of one major characteristic, early independence from colonial rule, that facilitated the translation of property threats into strong anti-statist blocs and thus light taxation. Its relative absence in the MENA region helps explain why seemingly similar threats did not have the same impact on taxes as in Latin America.

As noted earlier, reform waves akin to those that occurred in Chile, Guatemala, and Mexico have been uncommon outside Latin America. That is because they reflect a combination of three characteristics relatively unique to this region. One is extreme socioeconomic inequality. Latin America's income inequality has often been described as the highest of any region (Deininger and Squire 1996; Ortiz and Cummins 2011; Lustig 2015). In 2010, for example, its average Gini coefficient was substantially higher (0.50 versus 0.44) than that of the next most unequal region, sub-Saharan Africa, and far above the global average of 0.38 (Lustig 2015, p. 22). Latin America's exceptionalism with regard to land inequality is even more pronounced. Global data sets have long shown that no region even comes close to Latin America on this variable (Russett 1964; Oxfam 2016).[2] The significance of Latin America's exceptional inequality is that it has contributed to chronic calls for redistribution (Dornbusch and Edwards 1991; De Ferranti et al. 2004; UNDP 2013). Of course, deep inequality does not guarantee the rise of radical demands, much less drastic reform, but it does make them more likely, other things being equal.

Aggravating the effects of inequality in land is an economy that, compared to the early developing countries, such as those of Western Europe and North America, gave rise to a delayed and limited process of industrialization.[3] Control over farmland has remained highly salient in Latin America in part because the industrial sector failed to provide a viable alternative for much of the rural population. The same can be said of other natural resources, such as petroleum and hard minerals, which have played a bigger role in Latin American economies than they would have if the region had experienced a stronger push toward industrialization. Limited industrialization has thus increased the chances that political conflicts would center on ownership of natural resources.

---

[2] For example, data from the 1990s show that Latin America's average Gini coefficient for land was 0.79. Europe, Africa, and Asia had much lower, and strikingly similar, coefficients, at 0.57, 0.56, and 0.55, respectively (Oxfam 2016, p. 21).

[3] Of course, this condition does not separate Latin America from other developing regions, which generally suffer from the same problem.

The third condition is a regional political context particularly hostile to the translation of demands for redistribution into revolutionary change. In Eastern Europe and East Asia, the two regions in which true socialist regimes arose in largest numbers, the diffusion of this system was aided by its early adoption by a major power. The Soviet Union, created in 1917, played a fundamental role in implanting socialism throughout Eastern Europe after World War II (Applebaum 2013). Likewise, China's revolutionary regime, founded in 1949, contributed to the consolidation of socialism in North Korea, Vietnam, Laos, and Cambodia (Zhai 2000; Sheng 2014). In contrast, socialism has had no such ally in the Americas. The only socialist regime in the hemisphere emerged late (1959) and did so in a country, Cuba, lacking anywhere near the economic and military resources of China or the Soviet Union. Moreover, the dominant regional power, the United States, has generally been an implacable foe of redistribution. Given the enormous resources wielded by US governments, it is likely that no other world region has been as resistant to revolutionary change.

This combination of an unusually strong structural predisposition to demands for profound change and a regional context exceptionally averse to such change has meant that Latin America has experienced many instances of equalizing reform that either fell short of revolution or were quickly rolled back, or both. Because they harmed and frightened the economic elite without destroying it, these processes of reform and reaction could end up bolstering the organization of that class and its determination to nip future threats in the bud. Chile, Guatemala, and Mexico are prime examples.

While such episodes have been especially common in Latin America, they have not been wholly absent elsewhere. As discussed earlier, most of the examples outside Latin America appear to have occurred in the MENA region following independence from European domination. However, these reform waves did not lead to long-term trajectories of light taxation. How can we explain this difference? The argument developed here is that the MENA region's much later emergence from colonial rule meant that its capitalist classes at the time of the reforms lacked domestic legitimacy and allies. As a result, they were unable to respond by forging strong anti-statist political blocs of the kind that arose in Latin America.

Latin American countries are sometimes grouped with those of other developing regions as "post-colonial" societies, but this characterization blurs a fundamental difference: Latin America was both colonized and gained its independence far earlier. Many of today's developing countries were colonized in the nineteenth or early twentieth centuries and achieved their independence in the wake of World War II. In contrast, the Latin American countries came under colonial control in the sixteenth century and, with only two exceptions (Cuba and Puerto Rico), gained their independence from European powers by the mid-1820s.

This difference is important because of its effects on the character of the private sector at the time of the major challenge to property. Even in Mexico, where this challenge arose earliest, more than a century had passed since independence from Spain. This period, especially the relatively peaceful decades of the *porfiriato* (1876–1911), helped give rise to a substantial indigenous landowning, merchant, and industrial capitalist class. Like their counterparts in Guatemala and Chile, Mexican capitalists were connected to the broader society through dense social, economic, and political networks. These ties often included the Catholic Church, which at that point exercised virtually a monopoly on institutional religion. Although perhaps not loved by the broader public, Latin American economic elites were neither politically isolated nor tainted by association with the former colonial rulers, who were by that time a distant memory.

This situation contrasts markedly with that of the MENA region at the time of its major redistributive reform waves. In the societies that experienced these waves, many elites were either Europeans themselves or had obtained or increased their wealth due to their relationships with colonial authorities (Ahsan 1984; Hartnett 2019). Although some countries, including Egypt and Iraq, had achieved nominal independence decades earlier, the colonial power often continued to exercise great influence over domestic politics and business until the rise of Arab socialism and other nationalist currents after World War II. The royal families of Iraq, Egypt, and some other MENA countries were closely associated with the former colonial powers and they held vast quantities of land and other assets.

As this discussion suggests, the MENA countries that experienced substantial property reforms differed from their Latin American counterparts in that they lacked a strong class of indigenous economic elites with deep roots in society. Thus, when the reforms came, there was little resistance against them. Property relations were restructured in the name of rolling back colonial legacies, and the defenders of the old order, lacking political legitimacy or strong allies in civil society, were unable to stop them (Cammett et al. 2015, pp. 235–236). The robust anti-statist countermobilizations seen in Chile, Guatemala, and Mexico failed to materialize and the state was able to achieve lasting hegemony over the private sector and civil society as a whole.

Out of this situation came societies that, while preserving substantial private property, were thoroughly dominated by interventionist states. Studies of the MENA region as a whole have underscored the political fragmentation and lack of autonomy of the private sector (Hertog 2013; Cammett et al. 2015). The countries that experienced major property reforms are no exception. While there is little research on business politics in Iraq and Libya, studies of Egypt (Sfakianakis 2004; Springborg 2013), Syria (Haddad 2011), and Algeria (Ghanem-Yazbeck 2018) describe situations in which private sector collective action is extremely limited. Inasmuch as it exists, business influence within the authoritarian regimes that have usually controlled these countries is exercised by individual elites who use personal connections to extract rents for their own firms. Programmatic anti-statist parties also do not appear to have been a substantial phenomenon, even during periods with some electoral competition (Hinnebusch 2017). The economic liberalization of recent decades was widely expected to bring a more politically assertive capitalist class but has not done so (Hertog 2013).

Egypt provides a good illustration of the argument. While nominal independence from Great Britain was achieved in 1932, the British retained a strong military, political, and commercial presence in Egypt until 1952, when Gamel Abdel Nasser and his Free Officers movement overthrew King Farouk. Property reforms gradually deepened after the coup. Land reform began immediately, targeting especially the enormous holdings of the royal family (Margold 1957, p. 9). It would ultimately redistribute about 13 percent of Egypt's cultivated land (Waterbury 1983, p. 267). Following a conflict with Great Britain, France, and Israel triggered by Nasser's nationalization of the Suez Canal, the regime expropriated most large British- and French-owned businesses. Beginning in 1961, Nasser deepened his commitment to Arab socialism and nationalized the banks, much of the manufacturing sector, and a variety of other large industries. These moves completed the takeover of foreign holdings and delivered a harsh blow to local elites, although private capital continued to play an important economic role (Waterbury 1983, pp. 159–171). It was only in the second half of the 1960s, after more than a decade of transformations, that the reform tide slackened.

Elite resistance to these changes was modest. Until its humbling defeat in the 1967 Arab–Israeli war, the Nasserist regime enjoyed great popularity, and many economic elites simply chose to follow King Farouk into exile (Springborg 2013, p. 252). Existing parties and civil society organizations were repressed, and the private sector came under tight state control. The pre-1952 commercial and industrial federations lost political autonomy and were transformed into quasi-state entities for the purpose of implementing regulatory policies (Bianchi 1985, p. 148). There was nothing, for example, like the fierce opposition organized business had offered, when its privileges were threatened, to governments of the dominant-party PRI regime in Mexico during the 1960s and 1970s.

The halting process of economic liberalization that began under President Anwar El Sadat (1970–1981) helped give rise to new business associations, such as the Egyptian Businessmen's Association and the Egyptian-American Chamber of Commerce. However, these apparent manifestations of business assertiveness developed neither wide support within the private sector nor significant autonomy from the state. Instead, they remained closely tied to particular regime cronies and their networks (Springborg 2013, p. 257). As economic reform proceeded under Sadat and Hosni Mubarak (1981–2011), authorities built clientelist links to a small group of businessmen, but the private sector did not acquire greater organizational density or broader representative structures (Sfakianakis 2004; Cammett et al. 2015, p. 263). Pro-market right parties arose, but never achieved much real influence (Hinnebusch 2017, pp. 166–168).

As a result, business has played little role in the dramatic events that have shaken Egypt in recent years, including the protest movement that toppled Mubarak in 2011, the election of an Islamist government later that year, and the coup that removed that government from office in 2013 and restored secular authoritarian rule. Its lack of influence "suggests that whatever power business exercised under Sadat and Mubarak was almost exclusively through 'informal networks of privilege' rather than being consolidated through state institutions or civil society organizations, or even in a widespread popular consensus on liberalism, whether economic or political" (Springborg 2013, pp. 247–248).

Thus, as in other MENA countries that underwent major reform waves, late independence in Egypt meant that economic elites could not serve as the core of an anti-statist coalition capable of resisting reform and forging a more liberal economic order. Although this analysis of the relevance of the book's argument beyond Latin America is quite preliminary, it suggests that this region is unusual in terms of both the conditions that give rise to such reform waves and the ones that translate them into an anti-statist bloc. If the goal of political science is to formulate general covering laws, then the regional specificity of the argument is a major limitation. However, as Tilly and Goodin (2006) argue, the quest for such laws has not necessarily generated impressive results, and many scholars favor more context-specific arguments. Studies that provide a compelling explanation of variance on a given dependent variable within a specific regional setting may be just as valuable as ones that seek greater universality but account for only a small share of the variance or provide less insight into the causal mechanisms at work.

7.2.3 Theoretical Implications

Although this book's empirical argument may not travel well outside Latin America, it nevertheless holds implications for general theoretical discussions extending far beyond this region. Three seem especially noteworthy. First, and most obviously, it reinforces the value of the concept of path dependence. Although many studies employ this concept, it has sometimes been used merely to express the vague idea that "history matters" (Pierson 2000; Jackson and Kollman 2012). Even when they adopt a more specific definition, scholars have not always acknowledged the diverse and sometimes contradictory conceptualizations proposed by path-dependence theorists. In contrast, this book has employed a relatively precise definition of path dependence constructed explicitly in reference to theoretical divergences and applied it in a way that, hopefully, sheds considerable light on the empirical puzzle at hand. In particular, the analysis developed here highlights the role of mechanisms of path reproduction involving the interaction between ideas and organizations.

Second, the book's argument underscores the risks involved in assuming that an actor's economic or class position dictates their political and policy preferences. Commonly found in both rational choice and Marxist scholarship (albeit for different reasons), this assumption contradicts a central finding of this book – that economic elite attitudes toward state intervention differ greatly across the case study countries due to their specific historical trajectories. Rather, this study, like some others in the historical institutionalist tradition (Fioretos 2011), emphasizes that preferences are constructed through partly contingent historical processes, ones in which conflict with the state may play an important role.

Finally, this book contributes to a small but growing literature on the phenomenon of political backlash. Although this term is used frequently in both scholarly and non-scholarly discussions of politics, there have been few efforts to develop a theory of backlash and most are relatively recent (Lipset and Rabb 1978; Mansbridge and Shames 2008; Alter and Zürn forthcoming). While differing in some respects, these works generally define backlash as consisting of collective efforts by groups that feel threatened by some process of change to halt or reverse it, an understanding that parallels the way the term is used here.

This book makes two main contributions to the backlash literature. First, and most clearly, it underscores a key point made by Alter and Zürn (forthcoming): that backlash movements can have long-term effects on the polity by establishing new cleavages and reshaping institutions. In fact, that idea is central to the book's explanation of the determinants of tax burden variance. Second, it goes beyond this point by suggesting that one condition for having such impacts may be that the change that triggers the backlash effectively threatens the vital interests of economic elites and thus mobilizes this group to oppose it. When that condition is present, the backlash movement may possess the political resources needed not only to effectively resist change but also to alter state institutions and policies in ways that hinder future threats from arising.

7.3   IMPLICATIONS FOR EQUITY-ENHANCING CHANGE

At least at first glance, the arguments elaborated here do not paint an optimistic picture of the possibilities of achieving reforms that revert Latin America's notorious inequalities. Rather, they portray an unappealing set of choices. On the one hand, it is precisely in those countries in which the farthest-reaching reforms were launched that forces contrary to state activism have attained the greatest strength and success. On the other, where reformism was more cautious, anti-statist forces are weaker and there is more income redistribution, but redistribution is still quite limited, due to regressive tax systems and social programs that channel many of their benefits to relatively well-off people.

Given the centrality of inequality to scholarly and political debates on Latin America, it seems fitting to close this book by exploring more explicitly the implications of the argument for equity-enhancing reform and, based on those implications, to reflect briefly on the most favorable pathways to change. The discussion advances three main points. First, achieving major property redistribution through peaceful means is a risky proposition because of the inherent power of property holders and the potential for a backlash that makes them even more resistant to progressive change. Second, although violent revolution addresses a key weakness of this strategy, it has its own risks and shortcomings that make it an undesirable path under most circumstances. Finally, while admittedly slow and unreliable, democratic social reformism through the fiscal system, combined with incremental property reform, offers the best prospects for achieving sustainable gains in socioeconomic equality. Or, to put it another way, it is the worst path to equality in Latin America, except for all the others.

Of course, the first point flows logically from the argument developed in the rest of the book. The three countries in which governments tried to undertake major property redistribution through peaceful and relatively democratic means ended up spurring counterreactions that rolled back the reforms in two of the cases and set the country on a highly conservative development path in all three. In fact, the more democratic the context, the worse the effects of the backlash. In Mexico, where the ruling party enjoyed certain authoritarian control mechanisms, the backlash halted the reform wave but did not immediately reverse what had been achieved. In the more democratic contexts of Chile and Guatemala, in contrast, it not only unseated the government but also largely wiped out its reforms.

It is not simply that radical redistribution is difficult to achieve under democratic conditions, a point made in earlier works (Harms and Zink 2003; Albertus 2015). It is that the attempts to carry out such reforms can leave a lasting legacy of mistrust and defensiveness toward the state among the elite groups targeted for redistribution of their property, as well as others who suspect they could be next. By poisoning the relationship between such groups and the state, these attempts subsequently make it difficult for the latter to obtain the former's acquiescence to its efforts to raise revenue and expand intervention in the social and economic spheres. Public sector growth becomes a more conflictive and difficult process.

In a sense, the underlying problem with the peaceful approach to restructuring property rights is that it leaves property-owning elites with the capacity to organize themselves and fight back, both during the reform wave and after it. An alternative strategy that addresses this problem directly is violent socialist revolution. By transferring control of the means of production to the state and liquidating the capitalist class and its institutions, revolutions make it impossible for elites to recuperate their strength and exercise effective opposition to equity-enhancing change. It is partly for this reason that Latin American leftists have often concluded that violent revolution is the only viable path to substantive change (Grandin and Joseph 2010).

In Latin America, only Cuba has successfully followed this path. Although the 26th of July Movement had originally portrayed itself as a democratic actor, once Fidel Castro, Che Guevara, and their colleagues secured power they summarily jailed, executed, or exiled the old regime officials who remained in Cuba and within about three years had expropriated all landholdings and businesses of substantial size. Many (if not most) economic elites fled the country, leaving much of their wealth behind. To defend the new regime against subversion, authorities reconstructed the armed forces and established a secret police force and local vigilance committees. Through these means they consolidated the only true socialist regime in the western hemisphere, one that has survived six decades and registered impressive gains in areas like health care, literacy, and racial equality (Brundenius 2009; Mesa-Lago 2009).

Nevertheless, the revolutionary socialist approach suffers from some grave and well-known maladies. First, it rarely works. In his manual for guerrillas, Guevara argued that the Cuban struggle had shown that even a small, ill-armed movement could defeat a professional military, and that it was not necessary to wait until economic development had created the objective conditions for proletarian revolution (Guevara 1961). While his interpretation of the Cuban case may have been accurate, the guerrilla strategy encountered little success elsewhere in the region. Of the dozens of Latin American guerrilla groups that sprang up in the wake of the Cuban Revolution only one, Nicaragua's Sandinista movement, actually defeated the armed forces and came to power (Wickham-Crowley 1992). Moreover, unlike their Cuban counterparts, the Sandinistas were unable to consolidate revolutionary change.

Second, whether it ultimately succeeds or not, armed insurgency typically results in massive suffering among civilians. More often than not, the victims are precisely the people the guerrillas are seeking to help – the poor and downtrodden. In Guatemala, for example, the civil war took the lives of some 200,000 unarmed civilians, most of them indigenous people from the country's impoverished highland regions (Jonas 1996, p. 146). To be sure, the armed forces and rightwing paramilitaries are usually directly responsible for most of the violence (Grandin 2010). Still, the guerrillas cannot wholly evade responsibility for these acts since they would not have happened had the state and its allies not been responding to an insurgency.

Finally, socialist regimes have suffered from serious defects in areas other than equality. Economically, they lack sustained dynamism. Despite early gains that result mainly from mobilizing savings and manpower, these regimes have proven unable to maintain solid rates of growth. A lack of individual incentives for work, innovation, and entrepreneurship eventually causes stagnation to set in. For example, Cuba's ranking among Latin American countries with regard to per capita GDP has declined dramatically since the revolution (Mesa-Lago 2009, p. 379). True socialist regimes also suffer from a deficit of political freedom, including the right to criticize authorities and vote in elections offering real choice. Cuba, again, is a good example. Although the Cuban state has been far less violent in recent decades than those of many other countries, its Communist Party-dominated regime is quite authoritarian, as reflected in all major regime indices.[4]

Undoubtedly, there are situations in which armed struggle against the state is justified by the oppressiveness and injustice of the status quo. However, as a practical strategy for improving the welfare of the bulk of a country's population in the long term, the revolutionary path is hard to recommend.

Essentially by a process of elimination, this discussion has left us with one broad option for achieving equity: democratic reformism driven mainly by taxation and spending. Admittedly, this strategy is far from having a sterling record in Latin America. The expansion of welfare states in the region has generally not been very favorable to the poor (Mesa-Lago 1978; de Ferranti et al. 2004). Latin American tax systems have typically derived most of their revenues from levies on consumption and wages, rather than income and property. Social programs have delivered their benefits mainly to white-collar workers and people who, despite performing manual labor, have incomes placing them in the middle class. Informal workers, who comprise the bulk of the population in some countries, have traditionally been largely excluded (Haggard and Kaufman 2008). Thus, Latin American welfare states have often been described as reinforcing, rather than diminishing inequality. While developed country fiscal systems generally do not have dramatic leveling effects either, on average they offer greater protection from socioeconomic risks and redistribute far more income (Goñi et al. 2011).

Nevertheless, there are sound reasons to view a fiscally based strategy as the most likely to deliver greater equity in the long term. Most obviously, such an approach avoids the pitfalls of the alternatives discussed earlier. It goes without saying that a strategy of fiscal redistribution skirts most of the practical and ethical problems associated with violent revolution. However, it also avoids the risks associated with trying to restructure property ownership without resort to violence. Elites may bridle at increased taxation, but tax reform alone (or even in combination with spending measures) does not generate the enduring, organized backlash caused by initiatives to restructure property ownership. While potentially controversial, this assertion is supported by the cases examined here. For example, the major tax hikes seen in recent decades in Brazil, Argentina, and Ecuador, despite boosting the tax burden by 50 percent or more in the latter two cases, have not substantially increased the political organization of business. As a result of this quality, gains in redistribution achieved through fiscal policy are likely to be more sustainable.

In addition, recent decades have provided tentative signs that Latin American fiscal systems can increase their redistributive impact through incremental

---

[4] For example, in the Polity V database, Cuba has had the lowest democracy scores in Latin America since the "third wave" of democratization in the 1980s and 1990s. The data can be accessed at: www.systemicpeace.org/inscrdata.html.

reform (López-Calvo and Lustig 2010; Huber and Stephens 2012). On the tax side, as noted in the introduction, there have been robust increases in revenue across much of the region, thus providing greater resources for social programs. The average tax burden in 2017 was 4.8 percent of GDP above its level in 2000 and 8.0 percent above its 1990 level (OECD 2019, p. 135). There has also been an increase in the proportion of revenues coming from direct taxes, from 20.6 percent in 1990 to 22.3 percent in 2000 to 30.9 percent in 2017 (OECD 2019, pp. 139 and 142).[5] The share of tax revenues contributed by the personal income tax, probably the most progressive major tax, increased at an even faster rate, but remains small, at 8.1 percent.[6] Given the lack of systematic tax incidence data, as well as the many design variables affecting the distributive impact of taxation, it cannot be safely concluded that tax systems on the whole have become more progressive. However, based on the available tax structure data, it seems likely that they at least have not gotten more regressive.

More progress has occurred on the spending side, which is where the bulk of the redistribution occurs in most fiscal systems (Huber and Stephens 2012, p. 67). There have been clear trends toward both greater social outlays and ones that are more targeted at the poor. Total public spending region-wide increased from an average of 20.2 percent of GDP in 1990 to 22.6 percent in 2000 to 27.2 percent in 2016 (IMF World Economic Outlook Database). The available data on social spending suggest that it has increased at an even faster rate. For example, one ECLAC study calculates that the share of total spending devoted to social policies increased from 49.3 percent in 1991–1992 to 61.7 percent in 2001–2002 to 65.7 percent in 2011–2012 (ECLAC 2015, p. 83). A more recent one suggests that the share of central government spending going to social programs increased from 48 percent in 2000 to 53 percent in 2015 (ECLAC 2017b, p. 103).

With regard to the immediate reduction of poverty and inequality, the most important changes have been in pensions and social assistance. Until fairly recently, people who worked in the informal economy had little or no access to a public pension in all but a few Latin American countries. Pension coverage was consequently highly restricted and those excluded tended to be the poorest citizens (Mesa-Lago 1978; Rofman 2006). During the last two decades, however, non-contributory pension programs, most of which are also means-tested, have been adopted by all but four countries (ECLAC 2018, p. 145). The share of the elderly population covered by them increased from 14.2 to 33.7 percent between 2000 and 2015. Growth in non-contributory pensions was the major factor behind an increase in overall pension coverage from 53.6 to 70.8 percent between 2002 and 2015 (ECLAC 2018, p. 55). While non-

---

[5] The 2017 figure excludes Venezuela, for which there are no data.
[6] It increased from 4.1 percent in 1990 to 6.2 percent in 2000 to 8.1 percent in 2017 (CEPALSTAT; OECD 2018). These figures are based on ten countries for which income tax revenues are disaggregated for all three years.

contributory pensions have been criticized for encouraging informality, there is substantial evidence that they attenuate poverty and inequality (ECLAC 2018, pp. 62–63).

A type of social assistance program called "conditional cash transfers" (CCTs) has also spread rapidly across the region (Borges 2018). Although the design of these programs varies, they all provide modest cash payments to poor families on the condition that they comply with certain behavioral requisites, generally involving the use of preventive healthcare services and school attendance. Almost every country in the region has at least one such program, although the extent of investment in CCTs varies greatly (Cecchini and Atuesta 2017). In a region where social assistance was previously limited largely to scattered food distribution programs and other in-kind benefits, the diffusion of CCTs has changed the character of the welfare state. While evidence regarding their long-term effects on education and labor-market outcomes is inconclusive, studies have consistently shown a significant short-term impact on poverty and income inequality, at least among the programs that enjoy substantial funding (Fiszbein and Schady 2009; Amarante and Brun 2016).

There have also been advances in public education and health care, which can have long-term equity-enhancing effects by strengthening human capital (Huber and Stephens 2012, pp. 3–4). Average public spending on education in Latin America and the Caribbean increased from roughly 2.5 percent of GDP in 1990 to 3.0 percent in 2000 to 4.5 percent in 2013 (Busso et al. 2017, p. 103). In addition, there are indications of increasing efficiency in resource use in this area (Dufrechou 2016). Access to education has expanded steadily, helping to reduce the wage premium associated with higher levels of it and thus promoting greater equity (Busso et al. 2017). Latin America still performs poorly on international skills tests, and there continue to be major concerns with quality and efficiency, but trends in education are at least modestly positive (Fiszbein and Stanton 2018, p. 10). Changes in public health provision are also encouraging. Public spending on health care in Latin America rose from 2.5 percent of GDP in 2000 to 4.1 percent in 2016 (World Bank Database). Albeit with important national variations, the basic thrust of policy reform during this period was to broaden access to health services to traditionally underserved populations (Báscolo et al. 2018).

Social policy reforms have played an important role in the declines in poverty and income inequality seen across the region since the early 2000s (ECLAC 2018, pp. 42–50). For example, the Gini coefficient for income declined in every country in the region between 2002 and 2016 (ECLAC 2018, p. 44). These changes have not usually been dramatic, and their occurrence can be traced in part to conjunctural events, including the global commodity boom of the 2000s, which boosted growth and public revenue in many countries. Since the boom ended, around 2014, poverty rates have tended to rise, albeit at a slow pace (ECLAC 2019, p. 17). Nonetheless, the progress registered during the 2000s and early 2010s suggests that it is possible to significantly enhance the redistributive impact of state action in Latin America through a combination of revenue and spending policies.

This emphasis on fiscal redistribution does not mean that policies aimed at changing patterns of property ownership cannot play a role in enhancing equity. While far-reaching property redistribution is, as this book has argued, fraught with risk, more moderate policies can make a positive contribution in both the countryside and the cities.

Admittedly, rural land reform programs have frequently fallen short of expectations in Latin America. Not only have they generally been small in scale relative to the rural population, but their beneficiaries have often failed to develop into economically solid, market-integrated family farmers (Thiesenhusen 1995). However, to a large extent those failures can be traced to insufficient public investment in infrastructure, extension services, and credit, as well as distribution of land with poor soils (De Janvry and Sadoulet 1989). After implementing land redistribution, Latin American states tended to prioritize investment in the commercial, non-reform sector rather than helping reform beneficiaries consolidate themselves (Grindle 1986). These and other deficiencies can be attenuated if there is a political will to do so (Binswanger-Mkhize et al. 2009; Ondetti 2016).

Moreover, expropriation-based reform can be complemented by newer, market-assisted approaches that work mainly by providing subsidized credit to poor farmers seeking to purchase private land (Binswanger-Mkhize et al. 2009). The latter have already been implemented to some extent in Brazil. Although criticized by advocates of traditional land reform, preliminary assessments of their impact are cautiously optimistic (Fitz 2018; Sarshar and Helfand 2019). While the market-assisted approach in theory has a smaller redistributive impact, since the recipient is paying for the land they receive, the difference is not necessarily large, since the state subsidy can be significant. In addition, this method avoids the high costs often associated with expropriation, due to large indemnities, drawn-out court battles, and the need for extensive bureaucracies (Deininger and Binswanger 1999).

Policies aimed at changing property ownership patterns can also have positive effects in urban areas (Azuela 2011; UN Habitat 2011). Expropriation of urban land for redistributive purposes has been rare in Latin America. Even in Brazil, which has some of the most progressive urban policies and where the "social function" of property is extensively incorporated into law, this approach has made little headway (Ondetti 2016). However, there are some countries where unused lots have been expropriated to provide housing space for the urban poor (Galiani and Schargrodsky 2010; Azuela 2017). Moreover, the state can promote more equitable urban land distribution using other tools, such as titling informal settlements, providing subsidies for home purchases, and promoting housing microcredit. There are examples of all these approaches among the countries of the region (UN Habitat 2011). Hence, even if states foreswear major, expropriation-based property redistribution that does not necessarily mean that they are accepting the existing division of property as immutable.

These observations are not meant to dispel or substantially dilute the idea that Latin American societies face a difficult dilemma in pursuing socioeconomic equality. That dilemma, implied by the book's analysis of the causes of tax burden variance, is quite real and unlikely to be substantially attenuated in the future. Fiscally centered redistribution is far from being a panacea. If it structurally transforms Latin American societies at all, it will most likely do so only in the long term, over the course of several generations. Its virtue lies not so much in its own advantages, as in the shortcomings of alternative approaches.

Appendix: Interviews

This section lists the individuals interviewed for this book, along with their professional position and the date of the interview. Unless otherwise noted, the position description reflects the position held at the time of the interview. Only the positions most relevant to the subject matter of this book are listed. Interviewees who requested anonymity are listed according to the organization they worked for. As noted in the list, one interview was conducted via email and one via telephone. The rest were conducted in person, usually in the subject's professional office.

ARGENTINA

Argentine Institute for Business Development (IDEA). Senior official. July 21, 2014.

Artana, Daniel. Chief Economist at the Foundation for Latin American Economic Research (FIEL). August 6, 2014.

Abad, Alberto. Former Executive Director of the Federal Public Revenue Administration (AFIP) (2002–2008). July 30, 2014.

Baglini, Raúl. Former Radical Civic Union (UCR) Deputy (1983–1993) and Senator (2001–2003). July 24, 2014.

Argentine Chamber of Commerce (CAC). Senior official in charge of tax policy. July 13, 2014.

Cortina, Rubén. Secretary for International Affairs of the Argentine Federation of Commerce and Services Employees (FAECYS). August 11, 2014.

De Freijo, Ezequiel. Chief Economist at the Argentine Rural Society (SRA). August 1, 2014.

De la Vega, Juan Carlos. President of CAC. August 4, 2014.

Fernández, Roque. Former President of the Central Bank (1991–1996) and Minister of the Economy (1996–1999). August 11, 2014.

González Fraga, Javier. Former President of the Central Bank (1989 and 1990–1991). July 22, 2014.

Guidotti, Pablo. Former Deputy Minister of the Economy and Secretary of the Treasury (1996–1999). August 1, 2014.

Lago, Fernando. Director of Strategic Thinking, Argentine Chamber of Construction (CAMARCO). July 28, 2014.

Lamberto, Oscar. Auditor General of the Nation and former Justicialista Party (PJ) Deputy (1985–2001 and 2003–2007) and Senator (2001–2003). July 17, 2014.

Lavagna, Roberto. Former Minister of the Economy (2002–2005). August 14, 2014.

Machinea, José Luis. Former President of the Central Bank (1986–1989) and Minister of the Economy (1999–2001). July 24, 2014.

Miguens, Luciano. Former President of the SRA (2002–2008). August 6, 2014.

Peirano, Miguel. Former Chief Economist at the Argentine Industrial Union (UIA) (1990s and early 2000s) and Minister of the Economy (2007). August 15, 2014.

Pesce, Miguel. Vice-president of the Central Bank. July 18, 2014.

Paulón, Victorio. International Affairs Secretary of the Argentine Workers' Central (CTA). August 14, 2014.

Recalde, Héctor. Lawyer for the General Labor Confederation (CGT) and PJ Deputy. August 8, 2014.

Remes Lenicov, Jorge. Former Minister of the Economy of the Province of Buenos Aires (1989–1997), PJ Deputy (1997–2002) and Minister of the Economy (2002). July 22, 2014.

Rodríguez Córdoba, Jorge. Tax lawyer with Razzetto, López, Rodríguez Córdoba. July 23, 2014.

Vaquié, Enrique. UCR Deputy and former Minister of Finance of the Province of Mendoza (2000–2003). August 8, 2014.

BRAZIL

Appy, Bernard. Former senior official in the Ministry of Finance (2003–2009). July 6, 2015.

Castelo Branco, Flavio. Chief economist, National Confederation of Industry (CNI). June 16, 2015.

Cardoso, Paulo Ricardo. Assistant Secretary of the Federal Revenue Service. June 24, 2015.

Damasceno, Cláudio. President of National Union of Fiscal Auditors of the Federal Revenue Service of Brazil (SINDIFISCO). June 26, 2015.

Gama, Benito. Brazilian Labor Party (PTB) Deputy. June 17, 2015.

Ganz Lúcio, Clemente. Technical Director of the Inter-Union Department of Statistics and Socioeconomic Studies (DIEESE). July 3, 2015.

Gerdau, Jorge. Chairman and CEO of Gerdau Group and former coordinator of Brazilian Business Action (1990s and 2000s). July 14, 2015.

Godoy, Tarcísio. Executive Secretary of the Ministry of Finance. June 18, 2015.

Hauly, Luiz Carlos. Party of Brazilian Social Democracy (PSDB) Deputy. June 19, 2015.

Huertas, Miguel. Advisor to the president of the Unified Workers' Central (CUT). July 1, 2015.

Lisboa, Marcos. Former Secretary for Economic Policy in the Ministry of Finance (2003–2005). July 8, 2015.

Maciel, Everardo. Former Secretary of the Federal Revenue Service (1994–2002). June 18, 2015.

Mendes, Marcos. Legislative advisor to the Senate. June 16, 2015.

Nogueira Ferreira, Roberto. Advisor to the president of the National Confederation of Commerce (CNC). June 19, 2015.

Palocci, Antônio. Former Minister of Finance (2003–2006). July 27, 2015.

Pimentel, José. Workers' Party (PT) Senator and former Deputy (1995–2011). June 29, 2015.

Queiroz, Antônio. Director of the Inter-Union Legislative Advisory Department (DIAP), June 24, 2015.

Rezende, Fernando. Economist at the Getúlio Vargas Foundation and former president, Institute for Applied Economic Research (IPEA) (1996–1999). June 25, 2015.

Sardenberg, Rubens. Chief Economist of the Brazilian Federation of Banks (FEBRABAN). July 6, 2015.

Sato, Hiroyuki. Director of Tax Affairs, Labor Relations and Finance, Brazilian Association of the Machines and Equipment Industry (ABIMAQ). July 7, 2015.

Schoueri, Luis Eduardo. Tax lawyer with Lacaz Martins, Pereira Neto, Gurevich and Schoueri Advogados. July 22, 2015.

Tostes, José. Secretary of Finance, State of Pará and former coordinator of National Council of Finance Policy (CONFAZ) (2013–2015). June 23, 2015.

Villela, Renato. Secretary of Finance, State of São Paulo. July 8, 2015.

Yazbek, Cristiano. Tax lawyer with Amaral Yazbek Advogados. July 13, 2015.

Zanotto, Thomaz. Director of the Department of International Relations and Foreign Trade, Industrial Federation of the State of São Paulo (FIESP). July 7, 2015.

CHILE

Aninat, Eduardo. Former Minister of Finance (1994–1999). July 27, 2014 (via email).

Brzovic, Franco. Tax lawyer with Brzovic y Cía Avogados. June 17, 2014.

Central Bank. Senior official. July 2, 2014.

Budget Department. Senior official. June 12, 2014.

Dittborn, Julio. Former President of the Independent Democratic Union (UDI) (1990–1992), UDI Deputy (1998–2010) and Sub-Secretary of Finance (2011–2014). June 13, 2014.

Insunza, Carlos. Member of the Board of the Unitary Workers' Central (CUT). July 11, 2014.

Lagos, Felipe. Director of the Economics Program at Liberty and Development. June 10, 2014.

Larroulet, Cristián. Co-founder of Liberty and Development and former Minister of the General Secretariat of the Presidency (2011–2014). June 25, 2014.

Lizana, Pedro. Former president of the Society for Industrial Promotion (SOFOFA) (1993–1997). June 18, 2014.

Marfán, Manuel. Former Minister of Finance (1999–2000) and Member of the Board of the Central Bank (2003–2013). June 12, 2014.

Ominami, Carlos. Former Minister of the Economy (1990–1992) and Socialist Party (PS) Senator (1994–2011). July 2, 2014.

Ortiz, José Miguel. Christian Democratic Party (PDC) Deputy. July 8, 2014.

Rivera Urrutia, Eugenio. Director of Economic Program at Chile 21. June 16, 2014.

SOFOFA. Senior official. June 19, 2014.

UDI. Former Senator (2006–2011). July 10, 2014.

MEXICO

Aguilar, Julio Cesar. Tax advisor and former Chief of the Revenue Policy Unit, Secretariat of Finance and Public Credit (SHCP) (2005–2007). October 6, 2014.

Alonso Raya, Miguel. Party of the Democratic Revolution (PRD) Deputy. November 4, 2014.

Becerra Pocoroba, Mario Alberto. Former National Action Party (PAN) Deputy (2009–2012). October 14, 2014.

Coordinating Business Council (CCE) and Mexican Business Council (CMN). Senior tax advisor. October 10, 2014.

Delgado Carrillo, Mario. National Regeneration Movement (MORENA) Senator. October 23, 2014.

Foncerrada Pascal, Luis. Director general of the CCE's Center for Private Sector Economic Studies (CEESP). October 7, 2014.

Hernández Juárez, Francisco. Secretary General of the Union of Telephone Workers of the Mexican Republic (STRM), president of National Union of Workers (UNT), and former PRD Deputy (2009–2012). November 10, 2014.

Kurczyn Bañuelos, Sergio. Director of Economic Studies, Banamex. October 20, 2014.

Madero Muñoz, Gustavo. Former PAN Deputy (2003–2006) and Senator (2006–2012), as well as president of the PAN (2010–2015). November 22, 2014.

Molinar Horcasitas, Juan. Former PAN Deputy (2003–2006) and Director of Mexican Institute of Social Security (2006–2009). October 15, 2014.

Moreno, Alma Rosa. Deputy Director of Corporate Finance at PEMEX and former president of the Tax Administration Service (SAT) (1999–2000). October 22, 2014.

Núñez Esteva, Alberto. Former President of the Mexican Employers' Confederation (COPARMEX) (2004–2006). October 17, 2014.

Paredes, Armando. Former President of the National Agricultural Council (CNA) (2002–2004) and the CCE (2007–2009). October 16, 2014.

Penchyna Grub, David. Institutional Revolutionary Party (PRI) Senator and former Deputy (2000–2003 and 2009–2012). November 6, 2014.

Pérez Góngora, Juan Carlos. Tax accountant with Pérez Góngora y Asociados, Vice President of the National Confederation of Chambers of Commerce, Services and Tourism (CONCANACO) and former PRI Deputy (2003–2006). October 21, 2014.

Real Benítez, Alberto. Tax lawyer with Solis Cámara y Cía and various senior posts in the SAT. October 22, 2014.

Ramírez de la O, Rogelio. Former economic advisor to Andrés Manuel López Obrador. December 6, 2014 (by telephone).

Revilla, Eduardo. Tax lawyer with Revilla y Alvarez Alcalá and various senior posts in SHCP. October 20, 2014.

Salinas Narváez, Javier. PRD Deputy. October 29, 2014.

Sánchez Ugarte, Fernando. Former Sub-Secretary for Revenues at SHCP (2005–2007). October 21, 2014.

SHCP1. Senior post under Peña Nieto. November 13, 2014.

SHCP2. Various posts between the 1970s and early 2000s, including Secretary of Finance. November 5, 2014.

Tello, Carlos. Former Secretary of Planning and Budget (1976–1977) and Director General of the Central Bank (1982). November 6, 2014.

References

Aboites Aguilar, Luis. 2005. "Imposición directa, combate a la anarquía y cambios en la relación federación-estados. Una caracterización general de los impuestos internos en México 1920–1972." In Luis Aboites Aguilar and Luis Jáuregui, eds., *Penuria Sin Fin: Historia de los Impuestos en México Siglos XVIII–XX*. Mexico City: Instituto Mora.
   2003. *Excepciones y Privilegios: Modernización Tributaria y Centralización en México 1922–1972*. Mexico City: El Colegio de México.
Aboites Aguilar, Luis and Mónica Unda Gutiérrez. 2011. *El Fracaso de la Reforma Fiscal de 1961*. Mexico City: El Colegio de México.
Abreu, Marcelo de Paiva. 2006. "O Brasil no século XX: A economia." In *Estatísticas do Século XX*. Rio de Janeiro: IBGE.
Acuña, Carlos. 1998. "Political Struggle and Business Peak Associations: Theoretical Reflections on the Argentine Case." In Francisco Durand and Eduardo Silva, eds. *Organized Business, Economic Change, and Democracy in Latin America*. Miami: North-South Center Press.
Addison, Paul. 1994. *The Road to 1945: British Politics and the Second World War*. London: Pimlico.
Afonso, José Roberto R. 2013. "A economia política da reforma tributária: o caso brasileiro." Washington, DC: Wilson Center.
   2013. "Brasil: Nuevos acuerdos fiscales." In Jorge Rodríguez Cabello and Francisco Javier Díaz, eds., *Caminos para la Reforma. Estrategia Política de un Acuerdo Fiscal*. Santiago: CIEPLAN.
Afonso, José Roberto R. and José Serra. 2007. "Tributação, seguridade e coesão social no Brasil." Serie Políticas Sociales No. 133. Santiago: ECLAC.
Afonso, José Roberto R., Julia Morais Soares, and Kleber Pacheco Castro. 2013. "Evaluation of the Structure and Performance of the Brazilian Tax System: White Paper on Taxation in Brazil." Discussion Paper No. IDB-DP-265. Washington, DC: IDB.
Agosín, Manuel R. and Ricardo Ffrench-Davis. 1995. "Trade Liberalization and Growth: Recent Experiences in Latin America." *Journal of Interamerican Studies and World Affairs* 37 (3): 9–58.
Agostini, Claudio A. 2012. "Financiamiento de la política en Chile: Campañas electorales 2009–2010." Working Paper 26. Santiago: Escuela de Gobierno, Universidad Adolfo Ibañez.

Agosto, Walter. 2017. "El ABC del sistema tributario argentino." Documento de Políticas Públicas/Análisis No. 188. Buenos Aires: CIPPEC.

Ahsan, Syed Aziz-al. 1984. "Economic Policy and Class Structure in Syria: 1958–1980." *International Journal of Middle East Studies* 16 (3): 301–323.

Alaimo, Veronica, Mariano Bosch, Melany Gualavisi, and Juan Miguel Villa. 2017. "Measuring the Cost of Salaried Labor in Latin America and the Caribbean." Technical Note no. 1291. Washington, DC: IDB.

Albertus, Michael. 2015. *Autocracy and Redistribution: The Politics of Land Reform.* New York: Cambridge University Press.

Alexandre, Thiago de Andrade Romeu. 2017. "O Instituto Millenium e os intelectuais da 'Nova Direita' no Brasil." Working Paper, Universidade Federal de Juiz de Fora, Instituto de Ciências Humanas.

Allison, Michael E. 2016. "The Guatemalan National Revolutionary Unit: The Long Collapse." *Democratization* 23 (6): 1042–1058.

Alm, James and Jorge Martinez-Vazquez. 2007. "Tax Morale and Tax Evasion in Latin America." International Studies Program Working Paper 07-32. Andrew Young School of Policy Studies, Georgia State University.

Alter, Karen and Michael Zürn. Forthcoming. "Backlash Politics: An Introduction to a Symposium on Backlash Politics in Comparison." *British Journal of Politics and International Relations* 22, special edition.

Amarante, Verónica and Martín Brun. 2016. "Cash Transfers in Latin America: Effects on Poverty and Redistribution." *Economía* 19 (1): 1–31.

Angell, Alan. 1972. *Politics and the Labour Movement in Chile.* Oxford: Oxford University Press.

Anguiano, Arturo. 1984. *El Estado y la Política Obrera del Cardenismo.* Mexico City: Ediciones Era.

Ankersen, Thomas T. and Thomas Ruppert. 2006. "Tierra y Libertad: The Social Function Doctrine and Land Reform in Latin America." *Tulane Environmental Law Journal* 19: 69–120.

Antunes, Ricardo, Marco Aurélio Santana, and Luis Alberto Hernández. 2014. "The Dilemmas of the New Unionism in Brazil: Breaks and Continuities." *Latin American Perspectives* 41 (5): 10–21.

Applebaum, Anne. 2013. *Iron Curtain: The Crushing of Eastern Europe, 1944–1956.* New York: Anchor.

Aragão, Murillo de. 1996. "A ação dos grupos de pressão nos processos constitucionais recentes no Brasil." *Revista de Sociologia e Política* (6-7): 149–165.

Arantes, Rogério Bastos and Cláudio Gonçalves Couto. 2009. "Uma constituição incomum." In Maria Alice Rezende de Carvalho, Cícero Araújo, and Júlio Assis Simões, eds., *A Constituição de 1988: Passado e Futuro.* São Paulo: ANPOCS.

Ard, Michael J. 2003. *An Eternal Struggle: How the National Action Party Transformed Mexican Politics.* Westport: Praeger.

Arellano, José-Pablo 1985. "Social Policies in Chile: An Historical Review." *Journal of Latin American Studies* 17 (2): 397–418.

Arreseygor, Ignacio. 2012. "El Papel de la UIA en el Conflicto del Campo (Marzo- Julio 2008)." *Licenciatura* thesis, Sociology, Universidad Nacional de La Plata.

Arriagada, Genaro. 2004. *Los Empresarios y la Política.* Santiago: LOM Ediciones.

Arriola, Carlos. 1988. *Los Empresarios y el Estado, 1970–1982.* Mexico City: National Autonomous University of Mexico.

1976. "Los grupos empresariales frente al estado (1973–1975)." *Foro Internacional* 16 (4): 449–495.

Arthur, W. Brian. 1989. "Competing Technologies, Increasing Returns, and Lock-In by Historical Events." *The Economic Journal* 99 (394): 116–131.

Arza, Camila. 2017. "The Expansion of Economic Protection for Older Adults in Latin America: Key Design Features of Non-Contributory Pensions." Working Paper 2017/29. Helsinki: UNU-WIDER.

Astorga, Pablo, Ame R. Berges, and Valpy Fitzgerald. 2005. "The Standard of Living in Latin America during the Twentieth Century." *Economic History Review* 58 (4): 765–796.

Auyero, Javier. 2001. *Poor People's Politics: Peronist Survival Networks and the Legacy of Evita*. Durham: Duke University Press.

Azevedo, Fernando Antônio. 1982. *As Ligas Camponesas*. Rio de Janeiro: Paz e Terra.

Azpiazu, Daniel and Martín Schorr. 2010. *Hecho en Argentina: Industria y Economía, 1976–2007*. Buenos Aires: Siglo Veintiuno Editores.

Azuela, Antonio. 2017. *Eminent Domain and Social Conflict in Five Latin American Metropolitan Areas*. Cambridge: Lincoln Institute of Land Policy.

Babb, Sarah. 2001. *Managing Mexico: Economists from Nationalism to Neoliberalism*. Princeton: Princeton University Press.

Bambaci, Juliana, Tamara Saront, and Mariano Tommasi. 2002. "The Political Economy of Economic Reforms." *Policy Reform* 5 (2): 75–88.

Barbosa, Fernando de Holanda. 2018. "Experiences of Inflation and Stabilization, 1960–1990." In Edmund Amman, Carlos Azzoni and Werner Baer, eds., *The Oxford Handbook of the Brazilian Economy*. New York: Oxford University Press.

Barros de Castro, Antônio. 1993. "Renegade Development: Rise and Demise of State-Led Development in Brazil." In William C. Smith, Carlos H. Acuña, and Eduardo A. Gamarra, eds., *Democracy, Markets, and Structural Reform in Latin America*. Miami: North-South Center.

Basañez, Miguel. 1999. *La Lucha Por la Hegemona en México 1968–1980*. Mexico City: Siglo XXI.

Báscolo, Ernesto, Natalia Houghton, and Amalia Del Riego. 2018. "Lógicas de transformación de los sistemas de salud en América Latina y resultados en acceso y cobertura de salud." *Revista Panamericana de Salud Pública* 42. Accessed May 2019. http://iris.paho.org/xmlui/bitstream/handle/123456789/49472/v42e1262018. pdf?sequence=1&isAllowed=y.

Bastos, Pedro Paulo Zahluth. 2011. "Ascensão e crise do projeto nacional-desenvolvimentista de Getúlio Vargas." In Pedro Paulo Zahluth Bastos and Pedro Cezar Dutra Fonseca, eds., *A Era Vargas: Desenvolvimentismo, Economia e Sociedade*. São Paulo: Editora UNESP.

2010. "Liberal esclarecido ou aliado fiel? Sobre a natureza da política econômica externa brasileira no governo Dutra (1946–1951)." *Economia* 11 (4): 285–320.

Battaglino, Jorge. 2011. "Política de defensa y política militar durante el Kirchnerismo." In Andrés Malamud and Miguel De Luca, eds., *La Política en Tiempos de los Kirchner*. Buenos Aires: Eudeba.

Bazdresch, Carlos and Santiago Levy. 1991. "El populismo y la política económica de México, 1970–1982." In Rudiger Dornbusch and Sebastian Edwards, eds., *Macroeconomía del Populismo en la América Latina*. Chicago: University of Chicago Press.

Becker, Marc. 2008. *Indians and Leftists in the Making of Ecuador's Modern Indigenous Movements.* Durham: Duke University Press.

Benarroch, Michael and Manish Pandey. 2012. "The Relationship between Trade Openness and Government Size: Does Disaggregating Government Expenditure Matter?" *Journal of Macroeconomics* 34 (1): 239–252.

Benevides, Maria Victoria. 1989. "O velho PTB paulista (Partido, sindicato e governo em São Paulo – 1945/1964)." *Lua Nova* 89 (17): 133–161.

1981. *A UDN e o Udenismo: Ambiguidades do Liberalismo Brasileiro (1945–1965).* Rio de Janeiro: Paz e Terra.

Bensusán, Graciela. 2016. "Organizing Workers in Argentina, Brazil, Chile and Mexico: The Authoritarian-Corporatist Legacy and Old Institutional Designs in a New Context." *Theoretical Inquiries in Law* 17 (1): 131–161.

Bensusán, Graciela and Kevin J. Middlebrook. 2012. "El sindicalismo y la democratización en México." *Foro Internacional* 52 (4): 796–835.

Beramendi, Pablo and David Rueda. 2007. "Social Democracy Constrained: Indirect Taxation in Industrialized Democracies." *British Journal of Political Science* 37 (4): 619–641.

Bergman, Marcelo. 2009. *Tax Evasion and the Rule of Law in Latin America: The Political Culture of Cheating and Compliance in Argentina and Chile.* University Park: Pennsylvania State University Press.

Bernal, Federico. 2005. *Petróleo, Estado y Soberanía: Hacia la Empresa Multiestatal Latinoamericana de Hidrocarburos.* Buenos Aires: Biblos.

Berrios, Ruben, Andrae Marak, and Scott Morgenstern. 2011. "Explaining Hydrocarbon Nationalization in Latin America: Economics and Political Ideology." *Review of International Political Economy* 18 (5): 673–697.

Besley, Timothy J. and Torsten Persson. 2013. "Taxation and Development." Discussion Paper No. DP9307. Washington, DC: Center for Economic and Policy Research.

Beteta, Ramón. 1951. *Tres Años (1947–1948–1949) de Política Hacendaria: Perspectiva y Acción.* Mexico City: Secretaría de Hacienda y Crédito Público.

Bianchi, Robert. 1985. "Businessmen's Associations in Egypt and Turkey." *The Annals of the American Academy of Political and Social Science* 482: 147–159.

Bird, Richard M. 2003. "Taxation in Latin America: Reflections on Sustainability and the Balance between Equity and Efficiency." Working paper. Washington, DC: World Bank.

1992. "Tax Reform in Latin America: A Review of Some Recent Experiences." *Latin American Research Review* 27 (1): 7–36.

Bird, Richard M. and Luc Henry De Wulf. 1973. "Taxation and Income Distribution in Latin America: A Critical Review of Empirical Studies." *IMF Staff Papers* 20 (3): 639–682.

Bird, Richard M., Jorge Martinez-Vazquez, and Benno Torgler. 2014. "Societal Institutions and Tax Effort in Developing Countries." *Annals of Economics and Finance* 15 (1): 1–51.

Bizberg, Ilán. 1990. *Estado y Sindicalismo en México.* Mexico City: El Colegio de México.

Blanchflower, David. 2006. "A Cross-Country Study of Union Membership." IZA Discussion Paper no. 2016. Amsterdam: Elsevier.

Blankstein, Charles S. and Clarence Zuvekas Jr. 1973. "Agrarian Reform in Ecuador: An Evaluation of Past Efforts and the Development of a New Approach." *Economic Development and Cultural Change* 22 (1): 73–94.

Bogliaccini, Juan Ariel. 2013. "Trade Liberalization, Deindustrialization, and Inequality: Evidence from Middle-Income Latin American Countries." *Latin American Research Review* 48 (2): 80–105.

Boix, Carles. 2001. "Democracy, Development, and the Public Sector." *American Journal of Political Science* 45 (1): 1–17.

Borges, Bráulio. 2019. "Quão factível é o cumprimento do teto de gastos após a reforma da Previdência?" Blog do IBRE, Fundação Getulio Vargas. Accessed March 2020. https://blogdoibre.fgv.br/posts/quao-factivel-e-o-cumprimento-do-teto-de-gastos-apos-reforma-da-previdencia.

Borges, Fabian. 2018. "Neoliberalism with a Human Face? Ideology and the Diffusion of Latin America's Conditional Cash Transfers." *Comparative Politics* 50 (2): 147–169.

Borzutzky, Silvia and Mark Hyde. 2016. "Chile's Private Pension System at 35: Impact and Lessons." *Journal of International and Comparative Social Policy* 32 (1): 57–73.

Bowen, James David. 2015. "Rethinking Democratic Governance: State Building, Autonomy, and Accountability in Correa's Ecuador." *Journal of Politics in Latin America* 7 (1): 83–110.

2014. "The Right and Nonparty Forms of Representation and Participation: Bolivia and Ecuador Compared." In Juan Pablo Luna and Cristóbal Rovira Kaltwasser, eds., *The Resilience of the Latin American Right*. Baltimore: Johns Hopkins University Press.

Bowman, John R. and Michael Wallerstein. 1982. "The Fall of Balmaceda and Public Finance in Chile: New Data for an Old Debate." *Journal of Interamerican Studies and World Affairs* 24 (4): 421–460.

Boylan, Delia M. 1996. "Taxation and Transition: The Politics of the 1990 Chilean Tax Reform." *Latin American Research Review* 31 (1): 7–31.

Brady, Henry E. and David Collier. 2010. *Rethinking Social Inquiry: Diverse Tools, Shared Standards*. Second edition. Lanham: Rowman and Littlefield.

Braun-Llona, Juan, Matías Braun-Llona, Ignacio Briones, José Díaz, Rolf Lüders, and Gert Wagner. 1998. "Economía Chilena 1810–1995: Estadísticas Históricas." Documentos de Trabajos 187, Instituto de Economía, Universidad Católica de Chile. www.economia.uc.cl/docs/dt_187.pdf

Bravo Mena, Luis Felipe. 1987. "COPARMEX and Mexican Politics." In Sylvia Maxfield and Ricardo Anzaldúa, eds., *Government and Private Sector in Contemporary Mexico*. University of California, San Diego: Center for U.S.-Mexican Studies.

Brennan, Geoffrey and James M. Buchanan. 1980. *The Power to Tax: Analytical Foundations of a Fiscal Constitution*. New York: Cambridge University Press.

Brennan, James P. 1998. "Industrialists and *Bolicheros*: Business and the Peronist Populist Alliance, 1943–1976." In James P. Brennan, ed., *Peronism and Argentina*. Wilmington: Scholarly Resources.

Brennan, James P. and Marcelo Rougier. 2009. *The Politics of National Capitalism: Peronism and the Argentine Bourgeoisie, 1946–1976*. University Park: Pennsylvania State University Press.

Bresser–Pereira, Luiz Carlos, and Eli Diniz. 2009. "Empresariado industrial, democracia e poder político." *Novos Estudos CEBRAP* 84: 83–99.

Brett, Roddy, and Antonio Delgado. 2005. "The Role of Constitution-Building Processes in Democratization: Case Study of Guatemala." Working Paper.

Stockholm: International IDEA. http://constitutionnet.org/sites/default/files/CBP-Guatemala.pdf

Brogan, Christopher. 1984. "The Retreat from Oil Nationalism in Ecuador 1976–1983." Working Paper 13. London: University of London, Institute of Latin American Studies.

Brooks, Sarah M. 2008. *Social Protection and the Market in Latin America: The Transformation of Social Security Institutions.* New York: Cambridge University Press.

Brown, Jonathan C. 1993. *Oil and Revolution in Mexico.* Berkeley: University of California Press.

Bruhn, Kathleen. 1996. *Taking on Goliath: The Emergence of a New Left Party and the Struggle for Democracy in Mexico.* University Park: The Pennsylvania State University Press.

Brundenius, Claes. 2009. "Revolutionary Cuba at 50: Growth with Equity Revisited." *Latin American Perspectives* 36 (2): 31–48.

Bruneau, Thomas C. 1974. *The Political Transformation of the Brazilian Catholic Church.* New York: Cambridge University Press.

Burgess, Katrina. 1999. "Loyalty Dilemmas and Market Reform: Party-Union Alliances under Stress in Mexico, Spain, and Venezuela." *World Politics* 52 (1): 105–134.

Busso, Matías, Julián Cristia, Diana Hincapié, Julián Messina and Laura Ripani. 2017. *Aprender Mejor: Políticas Públicas para el Desarrollo de Habilidades.* Washington, DC: Inter-American Develoment Bank.

Cabrera, Maynor, Nora Lustig, and Hilcías E. Morán. 2015. "Fiscal Policy, Inequality, and the Ethnic Divide in Guatemala." Working Paper 397. Washington, DC: Center for Global Development.

Cademartori, Juan, Carlos Paez, and Juan Daniel Soto D. 2014. "Tasas óptimas para el impuesto a la minería del cobre en Chile." *Polis* 13 (37): 299–316.

Calvo, Ernesto and María Victoria Murillo. 2012. "Argentina: The Persistence of Peronism." *Journal of Democracy* 23 (2): 148–161.

Camargo, Aspásia. 1999. "Carisma e personalidade política: Vargas, da conciliação ao maquiavelismo." In Maria Celina D'Araújo, ed., *As Instituições na Era Vargas.* Rio de Janeiro: EdUERJ.

1986. "A questão agrária: Crise de poder e reforma de base (1930–1964)" In Boris Fausto, ed., *História Geral da Civilização Brasileira. Vol. III, Tomo III.* São Paulo: Difel.

Camelo, Heber and Samuel Itzcovich. 1978. "Algunas consideraciones sobre el financiamiento del sector público en América Latina." Working Paper. Buenos Aires: ECLAC.

Cameron, David R. 1978. "The Expansion of the Public Economy: A Comparative Analysis." *The American Political Science Review* 72 (4): 1243–1261.

Cammett, Melani, Ishac Diwan, Alan Richards, and John Waterbury. 2015. *A Political Economy of the Middle East.* Fourth Edition. London: Routledge.

Camp, Roderic A. 1989. *Entrepreneurs and Politics in Twentieth Century Mexico.* New York: Oxford University Press.

Campero, Guillermo. 2003. "La relación entre el gobierno y los grupos de presión: el proceso de la acción de bloques a la acción segmentada." *Revista de Ciencia Política* 23 (2): 159–176.

1984. *Los Gremios Empresariales en el Período 1970–83: Comportamiento Sociopolítico y Orientaciones Ideológicas.* Santiago: ILET.

Capoccia, Giovanni. 2015. "Critical Junctures and Institutional Change." In James Mahoney and Kathleen Thelen, eds., *Advances in Comparative-Historical Analysis*. New York: Cambridge University Press.

Capoccia, Giovanni and R. Daniel Kelemen. 2007. "The Study of Critical Junctures: Theory, Narrative, and Counterfactuals in Historical Institutionalism." *World Politics* 59 (3): 341–369.

Caraway, Teri L., Maria Lorena Cook, and Stephen Crowley. 2015. *Working through the Past: Labor and Authoritarian Legacies in Comparative Perspective*. Ithaca: Cornell University Press.

Carciofi, Ricardo. 1990. "La desarticulación del pacto fiscal: Una interpretación sobre la evolución del sector público argentino en las dos últimas décadas." *Documento de Trabajo 36*. Buenos Aires: ECLAC.

Cárdenas Tomažič, and Camilo Navarro Oyarzún. 2013. *Redefiniendo Límites, Acortando Distancias: El Movimiento Estudiantil en Chile*. Santiago: Heinrich Böll Stiftung and ICSO/Universidad Diego Portales.

Cardoso, Adalberto. 2014. "Os Sindicatos no Brasil." Nota Técnica 56, Mercado de Trabalho. Rio de Janeiro: IPEA.

2010. "Uma utopia brasileira: Vargas e a construção do estado de bem-estar numa sociedade estruturalmente desigual." *Dados* 53 (4): 775–819.

2003. *A Década Neoliberal e a Crise dos Sindicatos no Brasil*. São Paulo: Boitempo.

Cardoso, Adalberto and Julián Gindin. 2017. "O movimento sindical na Argentina e no Brasil (2002–2014)." *Revista Sociedade e Estado* 32 (1): 13–37.

Carey, John M. 2006. "Las virtudes del sistema binominal." *Revista de Ciencia Política* 26 (1): 226–235.

Carmagnani, Marcello. 1994. *Estado y Mercado: La Economía Pública del Liberalismo Mexicano, 1850–1911*. Mexico City: Fondo de Cultura Económica.

Castillo Soto, Sandra. 2010. "Sociabilidad y organización política popular: cordón industrial Cerrillos-Maipú (Santiago 1972)." *Cuadernos de Historia* 32: 99–121.

Catterberg, Gabriela and Valeria Palanza. 2012. "Argentina: dispersión de la oposición y el auge de Cristina Fernández de Kirchner." *Revista de Ciencia Política* 32 (1): 3–30.

Cavallo, Alberto and Manuel Bertolotto. 2016. "Filling the Gap in Argentina's Inflation Data." Unpublished manuscript.

Cavallo, Ascanio, Oscar Sepúlveda, and Manuel de Jesús Salazar Tetzagüic. 1997. *La Historia Oculta del Régimen Militar: Chile, 1973–1988*. Santiago: Grijalbo.

Cavarozzi, Marcelo. 1992. "Beyond Transitions to Democracy in Latin America." *Journal of Latin American Studies* 24 (3): 665–684.

1975. *The Government and the Industrial Bourgeoisie in Chile, 1938–1964*. PhD Dissertation, University of California, Berkeley.

Cecchini, Simone and Bernardo Atuesta. 2017. "Conditional Cash Transfer Programmes in Latin America and the Caribbean: Coverage and Investment Trends." Social Policy Series no. 224. Santiago: ECLAC.

Centeno, Miguel Angel. 2002. *Blood and Debt: War and the Nation-State in Latin America*. University Park: Pennsylvania State University Press.

Centro Interamericano de Administraciones Tributarias (CIAT). 2016. "Los sistemas tributarios de América Latina: Breve repaso de la legislación." Serie Comparativa no.1. Panama City: CIAT.

Cetrángolo, Oscar and Ariela Goldschmit. 2013. "La descentralización y el financiamiento de políticas sociales eficaces: Impactos, desafíos y reformas: el caso de la Argentina." Serie Macroeconomía del Desarrollo No. 144. Santiago: ECLAC.

Cetrángolo, Oscar and Juan Pablo Jiménez. 2004. "Las relaciones entre niveles de gobierno en Argentina." *Revista de la CEPAL* 84: 117–134.

Cetrángolo, Oscar and Juan Carlos Gómez Sabaini. 2007a. "La tributación directa en América Latina y los desafíos a la imposición sobre la renta." Serie Macroeconomía del Desarrollo No. 60. Santiago: ECLAC.

2007b. "Política tributaria en Argentina: Entre la solvencia y la emergencia." Serie Estudios y Perspectivas No. 38. Buenos Aires: ECLAC.

Cetrángolo, Oscar, Juan Carlos Gómez Sabaini, and Dalmiro Morán. 2015. "Argentina: reformas fiscales, crecimiento e inversión (2000–2014)." Serie Macroeconomía del Desarrollo No. 165. Santiago: ECLAC.

Chávez, Marcos. 2005. "Las finanzas públicas en México, 1970–2000. Crónica del fracaso de la política fiscal." In Luis Aboites Aguilar and Luis Jáuregui, eds., *Penuria Sin Fin: Historia de los Impuestos en México Siglos XVIII–XX*. Mexico City: Instituto Mora.

Cheyre, Hernán. 1986. "Análisis de las reformas tributarias en la década 1974–1983." *Estudios Públicos* 21: 1–45.

Collier, David. 1979. *The New Authoritarianism in Latin America*. Princeton: Princeton University Press.

Collier, Ruth Berins. 1982. "Popular Sector Incorporation and Political Supremacy: Regime Evolution in Brazil and Mexico." In Sylvia Ann Hewlett and Richard S. Weinert, eds., *Brazil and Mexico: Patterns in Late Development*. Philadelphia: Institute for the Study of Human Issues.

Collier, Ruth Berins and David Collier. 1991. *Shaping the Political Arena*. Princeton: Princeton University Press.

Conaghan, Catherine. 1995. "Politicians Against Parties: Discord and Disconnection in Ecuador's Party System." In Scott Mainwaring and Timothy Scully, eds., *Building Democratic Institutions*. Stanford: Stanford University Press.

1988. *Restructuring Domination Industrialists and the State in Ecuador*. Pittsburgh: University of Pittsburgh Press.

Conaghan, Catherine and James M. Malloy. 1994. *Unsettling Statecraft: Democracy and Neoliberalism in the Central Andes*. Pittsburgh: University of Pittsburgh Press.

Confederación Sindical de Trabajadores y Trabajadoras de las Américas (CSA). 2016. *Panorama Laboral Normativo: En Materia de Libertad Sindical y Negociación Colectiva en América Latina y el Caribe*. São Paulo: Pigma Limitada.

Conniff, Michael L. 1999. "Brazil's Populist Republic and Beyond." In Michael L. Conniff, ed., *Populism in Latin America*. Tuscaloosa: University of Alabama Press.

Consejo Coordinador Empresarial (CCE). 2010. "*Informe APAL 2007–2010*." Mexico City: CCE.

Contreras, Ariel José. 1989. *México 1940: Industrialización y Crisis Política*. Mexico City: Siglo Veintiuno Editores.

Cook, Maria Lorena. 2007. *Politics of Labor Reform in Latin America: Between Flexibility and Rights*. University Park: Pennsylvania State University Press.

Corbacho, Ana, Vicente Fretes Cibils, and Eduardo Lora. 2013. *More than Revenue: Taxation as A Development Tool*. New York: Palgrave Macmillan.

Córdova, Arnaldo. 1974. *La Política de Masas del Cardenismo.* Mexico City: Ediciones Era.

Corradi, Juan Eugenio. 1974. "Argentina and Peronism: Fragments of the Puzzle." *Latin American Perspectives* 1 (3): 3–20.

Cortés Conde, Roberto. 2009. *The Political Economy of Argentina in the Twentieth Century.* New York: Cambridge University Press.

Cortés Conde, Roberto and María Marcela Harriague. 2010. "Evolución del Sistema Tributario Argentino." Working Paper IR06. Argentina: AFIP.

Costanzi, Rogério Nagamine. 2015. "Estrutura demográfica e despesa com previdência: Comparação do Brasil com o cenário internacional." *Boletim Informações Fipe* (December): 11–16.

Cristi, Renato. 2000. *El Pensamiento Político de Jaime Guzmán.* Santiago: LOM Ediciones.

Crivelli, Ernesto and Sanjeev Gupta. 2014. "Resource Blessing, Revenue Curse? Domestic Revenue Effort in Resource-Rich Countries." Working Paper No. 14/5. Washington, DC: IMF.

Cypher, James M. 1990. *State and Capital in Mexico: Development Policy Since 1940.* Boulder: Westview Press.

Damill, Mario and Roberto Frenkel. 2015. "Macroeconomic Policy in Argentina during 2002–2013." *Comparative Economic Studies* 57 (3): 369–400.

Datz, Giselle and Katalin Dansci. 2013. "The Politics of Pension Reform Reversal: A Comparative Analysis of Hungary and Argentina." *East European Politics* 29 (1): 83–100.

David, Paul A. 1985. "Clio and the Economics of QWERTY." *The American Economic Review* 75 (2): 332–337.

De Castro, Sergio. 1992. *"El Ladrillo": Bases de la Política Economica del Gobierno Militar Chileno.* Santiago: CEP.

De Ferranti, David, Guillermo Perry, Francisco Ferreira, and Michael Walton. 2004. *Inequality in Latin America: Breaking with History?* Washington, DC: World Bank.

Deininger, Klaus and Hans Binswanger. 1999. "The Evolution of the World Bank's Land Policy: Principles, Experience, and Future Challenges." *The World Bank Research Observer* 14 (2): 247–276.

Deininger, Klaus and Lyn Squire. 1996. "Measuring Income Inequality: A New Database." *World Bank Economic Review* 10 (3): 565–591.

De Janvry, Alain and Elisabeth Sadoulet. 1989. "A Study in Resistance to Institutional Change: The Lost Game of Latin American Land Reform." *World Development* 17 (9): 1397–1407.

De la Garza Toledo, Enrique. 2014. "Reflexiones Acerca de la Reforma Laboral." Unpublished manuscript.

De la Torre, Carlos. 2011. "Rafael Correa: Un Populista del Siglo XXI." Unpublished manuscript.

    2010. "Rafael Correa's Government: Post-Neoliberalism, Confrontation with Social Movements and Plebiscite Democracy." *Temas y Debates* 20: 157–172.

Delgado, Ignacio Godinho. 2007. "O empresariado industrial e a gênese das políticas sociais modernas no Brasil." *Locus: Revista de História* 13 (2): 135–160.

    2001. *Previdência Social e Mercado no Brasil.* São Paulo: Editora LTr.

Diaz-Cayeros, Alberto. 2006. *Federalism, Fiscal Authority, and Centralization in Latin America*. New York: Cambridge University Press.

Díaz Pérez, Miguel Ángel. 2012. "Evaluación de la política tributaria en México, 2007–2012." *Finanzas Públicas* 4 (7): 17–47.

Dillinger, William and Steven B. Webb. 1999. "Fiscal Management in Federal Democracies: Argentina and Brazil." *Policy Research Working Paper 2121*. Washington, DC: World Bank.

Dinius, Oliver. 2010. *Brazil's Steel City: Developmentalism, Strategic Power, and Industrial Relations in Volta Redonda, 1941–1964*. Stanford: Stanford University Press.

Diniz, Eli and Renato Raul Boschi. 2003. "Empresariado e estratégias de desenvolvimento." *Revista Brasileira de Ciências Sociais* 18 (52): 15–33.

1978. *Empresariado Nacional e Estado no Brasil*. Rio de Janeiro: Forense-Universitária.

Diniz, Eli and Rosemary Galli. 2011. "Democracy, State, and Industry: Continuity and Change between the Cardoso and Lula Administrations." *Latin American Perspectives* 38 (3): 59–77.

Dioda, Luca. 2012. *Structural Determinants of Tax Revenue in Latin America and the Caribbean, 1990–2009*. Mexico City: ECLAC.

Dion, Michelle. 2010. *Workers and Welfare: Comparative Institutional Change in Twentieth-Century Mexico*. Pittsburgh: University of Pittsburgh Press.

Doctor, Mahruk. 2016. "From Neo-Corporatism to Policy Networks in Brazil: The Case of Lobbying for Port Reform." *Revista Agenda Política* 4 (1): 175–185.

Donoso, Sofia. 2016. "When Social Movements Become a Democratizing Force: The Political Impact of the Student Movement in Chile." In Thomas Davies, Holly Eva Ryan and Alejandro Milcíades Peña, eds., *Protest, Social Movements and Global Democracy Since 2011: New Perspectives*. London: Emerald Group.

Dornbusch, Rudiger and Sebastian Edwards. 1991. *The Macroeconomics of Populism in Latin America*. Chicago: University of Chicago Press.

Dorner, Peter. 1992. *Latin American Land Reforms in Theory and Practice: A Retrospective Analysis*. Madison: University of Wisconsin Press.

Dosal, Paul J. 1995. *Power in Transition: The Rise of Guatemala's Industrial Oligarchy, 1871–1994*. Westport: Praeger Publishers.

Dossi, Marina Virginia. 2010. "La acción colectiva de la Unión Industrial Argentina en el período 1989–2002: Un análisis desde su dinámica organizativa-institucional." Documentos de Investigación Social, No. 10. Instituto de Altos Estudios Sociales, Universidad Nacional de San Martín. www.unsam.edu.ar/institutos/idaes/docs/DocIS_10_Dossi.pdf

Dreifuss, René. 1981. *1964: A Conquista do Estado*. São Paulo: Vozes.

Dufrechou, Paola Azar. 2016. "The Efficiency of Public Education Spending in Latin America: A Comparison to High-Income Countries." *International Journal of Educational Development* 49: 188–203.

Dulci, Otávio. 1986. *A UDN e o Anti-Populismo no Brasil*. Belo Horizonte: Editora UFMG/PROED.

Durán, Gonzalo and Marco Kremerman. 2015. "Sindicatos y negociación colectiva: panorama estadístico nacional y evidencia comparada." Documento de trabajo, área Sindicatos y Negociación Colectiva. Santiago: Fundación Sol.

Eaton, Kent. 2011. "Conservative Autonomy Movements: Territorial Dimensions of Ideological Conflict in Bolivia and Ecuador." *Comparative Politics* 43 (3): 291–310.

2004. *Politics Beyond the Capital: The Design of Subnational Institutions in South America*. Stanford: Stanford University Press.

2002. *Politicians and Economic Reform in New Democracies: Argentina and the Philippines in the 1990s*. University Park: Pennsylvania State University Press.

Eckstein, Shlomo, Gordon Donal, Douglas Horton, and Thomas Carroll. 1978. "Land Reform in Latin America: Bolivia, Chile, Mexico, Peru and Venezuela." Working Paper 275. Washington, DC: World Bank.

Economic Commission for Latin America and the Caribbean (ECLAC). 2019. "*Panorama social de América Latina*." Santiago: United Nations.

2018. "Social Panorama of Latin America."

2017a. "Panorama fiscal de América Latina y el Caribe."

2017b. "Panorama social de América Latina."

2015. "Panorama fiscal de América Latina y el Caribe 2015: Dilemas y espacios de políticas."

1996. "Economía política de las reformas tributarias en Costa Rica, El Salvador y Guatemala, 1980–1994." Mexico City: ECLAC.

1979. "Statistical Yearbook for Latin America."

1956. "Economic Survey of Latin America 1955."

Elizondo Mayer-Serra, Carlos. 2014. "Progresividad y eficacia del gasto público en México: precondición para una política recaudatoria efectiva." Working Paper, Latin American Program. Washington, DC: Wilson Center. www.wilsoncenter.org/sites/default/files/media/documents/publication/Politica%20Fiscal%20en%20Mexico.pdf.

2009. "La industria del amparo fiscal." *Política y Gobierno* 16 (2): 349–383.

1994. "In Search of Revenue: Tax Reform in Mexico under the Administrations of Echeverría and Salinas." *Journal of Latin American Studies* 26 (1): 159–190.

Ensignia, Jaime. 2017. "Chile: a reforma trabalhista de Bachelet e o papel do sindicalismo." *Teoria e Debate* 161. Accessed April 2018. https://teoriaedebate.org.br/2017/06/07/%EF%BB%BFchile-a-reforma-trabalhista-de-bachelet-e-o-papel-do-sindicalismo/.

Erickson, Kenneth Paul. 1977. *The Brazilian Corporative State and Working-Class Politics*. Berkeley: University of California Press.

Ernst & Young. 2017. *Strategically Managing Indirect Taxes in Latin America*. London: Ernst & Young Global Limited.

Escalona Caba, Esteban. 2014. "Historia de los impuestos al consumo en Chile desde 1920 y al valor agregado." *Revista de Estudios Tributarios* 10: 9–49.

Espinoza, José and Mario Marcel. 1994. "Descentralización fiscal: el caso de Chile." Serie Política Fiscal, No. 57. Santiago: ECLAC.

Etchemendy, Sebastián. 2012. "El sindicalismo argentino en la era pos-liberal (2003–2011)." In Andrés Malamud and Miguel De Luca, eds., *La Política en Tiempos de los Kirchner*. Buenos Aires: Eudeba.

2011. *Models of Economic Liberalization: Business, Workers, and Compensation in Latin America, Spain, and Portugal*. New York: Cambridge University Press.

Etchemendy, Sebastián and Ruth Berins Collier. 2007. "Down but Not Out: Union Resurgence and Segmented Neocorporatism in Argentina (2003–2007)." *Politics & Society* 35 (3): 363–401.

Evans, Peter. 1979. *Dependent Development: The Alliance of Multinational, State, and Local Capital in Brazil.* Princeton: Princeton University Press.

Fairfield, Tasha. 2015. *Private Wealth and Public Revenue in Latin America: Business Power and Tax Politics.* New York: Cambridge University Press.

2014. "The Political Economy of Progressive Tax Reform in Chile." Washington, DC: Wilson Center.

2011. "Business Power and Protest: Argentina's Agricultural Producers Protest in Comparative Context." *Studies in Comparative International Development* 46 (4): 424–453.

2010. "Business Power and Tax Reform: Taxing Income and Profits in Chile and Argentina." *Latin American Politics and Society* 52 (2): 37–71.

Fairfield, Tasha and Candelaria Garay. 2017. "Redistribution Under the Right in Latin America: Electoral Competition and Organized Actors in Policymaking." *Comparative Political Studies* 50 (14): 1871–1906.

Falleti, Tulia G. 2010. *Decentralization and Subnational Politics in Latin America.* Cambridge: Cambridge University Press.

Fanelli, José María. 2002. "Growth, Instability and the Convertibility Crisis in Argentina." *CEPAL Review* 77: 25–43.

Farfán-Mares, Gabriel. 2011. "La economía política del estado rentista mexicano (1970–2010)." *Foro Internacional* 51 (3): 541–577.

Farhad, Mohammad and Michael Jetter. 2019. "On the Relationship between Trade Openness and Government Size." Working Paper No. 7832. Munich: CESifo.

Fatehi, Kamal. 1994. "Capital Flight from Latin America as a Barometer of Political Instability." *Journal of Business Research* 30 (2): 187–195.

Fausto, Boris. 2006. *História do Brasil.* São Paulo: Editora Universidade de São Paulo.

Fazio Vengoa, Hugo. 1996. "Chile: Modelo de desarrollo e inserción internacional." *Historia Crítica* 13: 68–89.

Fazio Vengoa, Hugo and Magaly Parada. 2010. *Veinte Años de Política Económica de la Concertación.* Santiago: LOM Ediciones.

Federação das Indústrias do Estado de Rio de Janeiro. 2018. "A carga tributária para a indústria da transformação." Rio de Janeiro: FIRJAN.

Ferrer, Aldo. 1977. *Crisis y Alternativas de la Política Económica Argentina.* Buenos Aires: Fondo de Cultura Económica.

Ferreira, Jorge. 2010. "História e biografia: as escolhas de João Goulart." *Cadernos Arquivo Edgard Leuenroth (UNICAMP)* 17: 267–291.

Ferreira, Roberto Nogueira. 2002. *A Reforma Essencial: Uma Análise, sob a Ótica Empresarial, das Propostas e dos Bastidores da Reforma Tributária.* São Paulo: Geração Editorial.

Ferreira Rubio, Delia and Matteo Goretti. 1996. "Cuando el presidente gobierna solo: Menem y los decretos de necesidad y urgencia hasta la reforma constitucional (julio 1989 - agosto 1994)." *Desarrollo Económico* 36 (141): 443–474.

Ferreira de Mendonça, Helder and Ana Jordânia de Oliveira. 2019. "Openness and Government Size: A New Empirical Assessment." *Economics Bulletin* 39 (2): 982–995.

Ferreres, Orlando J. 2010. *Dos Siglos de Economía Argentina: Edición Bicentenario.* Buenos Aires: El Ateneo.

Ffrench-Davis, Ricardo. 2010. *Economic Reforms in Chile: From Dictatorship to Democracy.* Second Edition. New York: Palgrave Macmillan.

2002. *Economic Reforms in Chile: From Dictatorship to Democracy*. Ann Arbor: University of Michigan Press.

1973. *Políticas Económicas en Chile, 1952–1970*. Santiago: Ediciones Nueva Universidad.

Figueiredo, Argelina. 1993. *Democracia ou Reformas? Alternativas Democráticas à Crise Política: 1961–1964*. São Paulo: Paz e Terra.

Fioretos, Orfeo. 2011. "Historical Institutionalism in International Relations." *International Organization* 65 (2): 367–399.

Fiszbein, Ariel and Norbert R. Schady. 2009. *Conditional Cash Transfers: Reducing Present and Future Poverty*. Washington DC: World Bank.

Fiszbein, Ariel and Sarah Stanton. 2018. *Education in Latin America and the Caribbean: Possibilities for United States Investment and Engagement*. Washington, DC: Inter-American Dialogue.

Fitz, Dylan. 2018. "Evaluating the Impact of Market-Assisted Land Reform in Brazil." *World Development* 103: 255–267.

Fitzgerald, E.V.K. 1978. "The Fiscal Crisis of the Latin American State." In John Toye, ed., *Taxation and Economic Development: Twelve Critical Studies*. Totowa: Frank Cass & Co.

Fleet, Michael. 1985. *The Rise and Fall of Chilean Christian Democracy*. Princeton: Princeton University Press.

Flisfisch, Ángel, Maximiliano Prieto, and Alejandro Siebert. 2013. "Potenciando universidades y think tanks en América Latina: El caso de Chile." Santiago: FLACSO. www.flacsochile.org/wp-content/uploads/2014/04/Potenciando-universidades-y-think-tanks-en-Am%C3%A9rica-Latina-El-caso-de-Chile1.pdf

Flores-Macías, Gustavo A. 2019. "Introduction: The Political Economy of Taxation in Latin America." In Flores-Macías, ed., *The Political Economy of Taxation in Latin America*. New York: Cambridge University Press.

2018. "Building Support for Taxation in Developing Countries: Experimental Evidence from Mexico." *World Development* 105: 15–24.

2014. "Financing Security through Elite Taxation: The Case of Colombia's Democratic Security Taxes." *Studies in Comparative International Development* 49 (4): 477–500.

Fonseca, Pedro Cezar Dutra. 2011. "Instituições e política econômica: crise e crescimento do Brasil na década de 1930." In Pedro Paulo Zahluth Bastos and Pedro Cezar Dutra Fonseca, eds., *A Era Vargas: Desenvolvimentismo, Economia e Sociedade*. São Paulo: Editora UNESP.

Font, Mauricio A. 1997. "Failed Democratization: Region, Class, and Political Change in Brazil, 1930–1937." In Fernando J. Devoto and Torcuato S. Di Tella, eds., *Political Culture, Social Movements, and Democratic Transitions in South America in the Twentieth Century*. Milan: Fondazione Giangiacomo Feltrinelli.

Frank, Volker. 2015. "Living in the Past or Living with the Past? Reflections on Chilean Labor Unions Twenty Years into Democracy." In Teri L. Caraway, Maria Lorena Cook and Stephen Crowley, eds., *Working through the Past: Labor and Authoritarian Legacies in Comparative Perspective*. Ithaca: Cornell University Press.

Freitas, Rafael, Samuel Moura, and Danilo Medeiros. 2009. "Procurando o Centrão: Direita e esquerda na Assembléia Nacional Constituinte 1987–88." Concurso

ANPOCS-FUNDAÇÃO FORD. Melhores trabalhos sobre a Constituição de 1988. http://neci.fflch.usp.br/sites/neci.fflch.usp.br/files/freitas-moura-medeiros_2009.pdf

Fuentes, Aldo Casali. 2011. "Reforma universitaria en Chile, 1967–1973: Pre-balance histórico de una experiencia frustrada." *Intus-Legere Historia* 5 (1): 81–101.

Fuentes, Claudio. 2015. "Shifting the Status Quo: Constitutional Reforms in Chile." *Latin American Politics and Society* 57 (1): 99–122.

Fuentes, Juan Alberto and Maynor Cabrera. 2005. "El pacto fiscal de Guatemala: Una oportunidad perdida." CEPAL Regional Seminar on Fiscal Policy. Santiago.

Galiani, Sebastián, Daniel Heymann, Mariano Tommasi, Luis Servén, and María Cristina Terra. 2003. "Great Expectations and Hard Times: The Argentine Convertibility Plan." *Economía* 3 (2): 109–160.

Galiani, Sebastián and Ernesto Schargrodsky. 2010. "Property Rights for the Poor: Effects of Land Titling." *Journal of Public Economics* 94: 700–729.

Gárate, Manuel. 2012. *La Revolución Capitalista de Chile (1973–2003).* Santiago: Ediciones Universidad Alberto Hurtado.

Garay, Candelaria. 2016. *Social Policy Expansion in Latin America.* New York: Cambridge University Press.

Gargarella, Roberto. 2014. *Latin American Constitutionalism, 1810–2010: The Engine Room of the Constitution.* Oxford: Oxford University Press.

Garretón, Manuel Antonio. 2012. *Neoliberalismo Corregido y Progresismo Limitado: Los Gobiernos de la Concertación en Chile, 1990–2010.* Santiago: Editorial ARCIS.

1995. "Redemocratization in Chile." *Journal of Democracy* 6 (1): 146–158.

Garrett, Rachael D. and Lisa L. Rausch. 2015. "Green for Gold: Social and Ecological Tradeoffs Influencing the Sustainability of the Brazilian Soy Industry." *Journal of Peasant Studies* 43 (2): 461–493.

Gaudichaud, Franck. 2004. *Poder Popular y Cordones Industriales: Testimonios Sobre el Movimiento Popular Urbano, 1970–1973.* Santiago: Ediciones LOM.

Gauss, Susan M. 2010. *Made in Mexico: Regions, Nation, and the State in the Rise of Mexican Industrialism, 1920s–1940s.* University Park: Pennsylvania State University Press.

George, Alexander L. and Andrew Bennett. 2005. *Case Studies and Theory Development in the Social Sciences.* Cambridge: MIT Press.

Gerchunoff, Pablo and Lucas Llach. 1998. *El Ciclo de la Ilusión y el Desencanto: Un Siglo de Políticas Económicas Argentinas.* Buenos Aires: Ariel Sociedad Económica.

Germani, Gino. 1962. *Política y Sociedad en una Época de Transición: De la Sociedad Tradicional a la Sociedad de Masas.* Buenos Aires: Paidos.

Gervasoni, Carlos. 2011. "La política provincial es política nacional: Cambios y continuidades subnacionales del menemismo al kirchnerismo." In Andrés Malamud and Miguel De Luca, eds., *La Política en Tiempos de los Kirchner.* Buenos Aires: Eudeba.

2010. "A Rentier Theory of Subnational Regimes: Fiscal Federalism, Democracy, and Authoritarianism in the Argentine Provinces." *World Politics* 62 (2): 302–340.

Ghanem-Yazbeck, Dalia. 2018. "Limiting Change through Change: The Key to the Algerian Regime's Longevity." Washington, DC: Carnegie Endowment.

Gibson, Edward L. 1996. *Class and Conservative Parties: Argentina in Comparative Perspective.* Baltimore: Johns Hopkins University Press.

Gibson, Edward L. and Ernesto Calvo. 2000. "Federalism and Low-Maintenance Constituencies: Territorial Dimensions of Economic Reform in Argentina." *Studies in Comparative International Development* 35 (3): 32–55.

Gil-Díaz, Francisco and Wayne Thirsk. 1997. "Mexico's Protracted Tax Reform." In Thirsk, ed., *Tax Reform in Developing Countries.* Washington, DC: World Bank.

Gilly, Adolfo. 2013. *El Cardenismo: Una Utopía Mexicana.* Mexico City: Ediciones Era.

Gleijeses, Piero. 1991. *Shattered Hope: The Guatemalan Revolution and the United States, 1944–1954.* Princeton: Princeton University Press.

Gomes, Angela de Castro. 1989. *A Invenção do Trabalhismo.* Rio de Janeiro: Vértice.

Gomes, Gustavo Maia. 1986. *The Roots of State Intervention in the Brazilian Economy.* New York: Praeger Publishers.

Gomes, Sandra. 2006. "O impacto das regras de organização do processo legislativo no comportamento dos parlamentares: Um estudo de caso da Assembléia Nacional Constituinte (1987–1988)." *Revista de Ciências Sociais* 49 (1): 193–224.

Gomes da Silva, José. 1989. *Buraco Negro: A Reforma Agrária na Constituinte de 1987–1988.* Rio de Janeiro: Paz e Terra.

Gómez Sabaini, Juan Carlos. 2006. "Evolución y situación tributaria actual en América Latin: Una serie de temas para la discusión." In Oscar Cetrángolo and Juan Carlos Gómez Sabaini, eds., *Tributación en América Latina: En Busca de una Nueva Agenda de Reformas.* Santiago: ECLAC

Gómez Sabaini, Juan Carlos and Dalmiro Morán. 2016. "Evasión tributaria en América Latina: Nuevos y antiguos desafíos en la cuantificación del fenómeno en los países de la región." Serie Macroeconomía del Desarrollo No. 172. Santiago: ECLAC

2012. "Informalidad y tributación en América Latina: Explorando los nexos para mejorar la equidad." Serie Macroeconomía del Desarrollo No. 124. Santiago: ECLAC.

Gómez Valle, José de Jesús. 2008. "El cabildeo al poder legislativo en México: Origen y evolución." *Espiral* 14 (42): 97–124.

Goñi, Edwin, J. Humberto López, and Luis Servén. 2011. "Fiscal Redistribution and Income Inequality in Latin America." *World Development* 39 (9): 1558–1569.

Graham, Douglas H. 1982. "Mexican and Brazilian Economic Development: Legacies, Patterns, and Performance." In Sylvia Ann Hewlett and Richard S. Weinert, eds., *Brazil and Mexico: Patterns in Late Development.* Philadelphia: Institute for the Study of Human Issues.

Gramsci, Antonio. 2000. *The Antonio Gramsci Reader: Selected Writings 1916–1935.* Edited by David Forgacs and Eric Hobsbawm. New York: New York University Press.

Grandin, Greg. 2010. *The Blood of Guatemala: A History of Race and Nation.* Durham: Duke University Press.

Grandin, Greg and Gilbert M. Joseph. 2010. *A Century of Revolution: Insurgent and Counterinsurgent Violence during Latin America's Long Cold War.* Durham: Duke University Press.

Grindle, Merilee S. 1986. *State and Countryside: Development Policy and Agrarian Politics in Latin America.* Baltimore: Johns Hopkins University Press.

Guevara, Che. 1961. *Guerrilla Warfare.* Havana: Centro de Estudios Che Guevara.

Gupta, Abhijit Sen. 2007. "Determinants of Tax Revenue Efforts in Developing Countries." Working Paper 07/184. Washington, DC: IMF.

Gutiérrez, Silvia. 2007. "La construcción de la imagen de López Obrador en los spots de sus adversarios." *Cultura y Representaciones Sociales* 26: 31–54.

Haber, Stephen. 1989. *Industry and Underdevelopment: The Industrialization of Mexico, 1890–1940*. Stanford: Stanford University Press.

Haddad, Bassam. 2011. *Business Networks in Syria: The Political Economy of Authoritarian Resilience*. Stanford: Stanford University Press.

Haggard, Stephan and Robert R. Kaufman. 2008. *Development, Democracy, and Welfare States: Latin America, East Asia, and Eastern Europe*. Princeton: Princeton University Press.

Hagopian, Frances. 1996. *Traditional Politics and Regime Change in Brazil*. New York: Cambridge University Press.

Hamilton, Nora. 1982. *The Limits of State Autonomy: Post-Revolutionary Mexico*. Princeton: Princeton University Press.

Handy, Jim. 1994. *Revolution in the Countryside: Rural Conflict and Agrarian Reform in Guatemala, 1944–1954*. Chapel Hill: University of North Carolina Press

Hanke, Steve H. and Nicholas E. Krus. 2012. "World Hyperinflations." Cato Working Paper No. 8. Washington, DC: CATO Institute.

Hanni, Michael, Ricardo Martner Fanta, and Andrea Podestá. 2015. "El potencial redistributivo de la fiscalidad en América Latina." *Revista CEPAL* 116: 7–26.

Hansen, Roger D. 1971. *The Politics of Mexican Development*. Baltimore: Johns Hopkins University Press.

Harms, Patricia. 2011. "'God Doesn't Like the Revolution': The Archbishop, the Market Women, and the Economy of Gender in Guatemala, 1944–1954." *Frontiers: A Journal of Women Studies* 32 (2): 111–139.

Harms, Philipp and Stefan Zink. 2003. "Limits to Redistribution in a Democracy: A Survey." *European Journal of Political Economy* 19 (4): 651–668.

Hartnett, Allison Spencer. 2019. "Redistributive Authoritarianism: Land Reform and Leader Tenure in the Middle East." PhD Dissertation, University of Oxford.

Heinz, Flavio M. 2001. "Elites rurais: Representação profissional e política no Brasil, 1930–1960." *Anuario IEHS* 16: 93–94.

Heiss, Claudia and Patricio Navia. 2007. "You Win Some, You Lose Some: Constitutional Reform in Chile's Transition to Democracy." *Latin American Politics and Society* 49 (3): 163–190.

Helfand, Steven M., Vilma H. Sielawa and Deepak Singhania. 2019. "A Matter of Time: An Impact Evaluation of the Brazilian National Land Credit Program." *Journal of Development Economics* 141. www.sciencedirect.com/science/article/abs/pii/S0304387818304346

Heredia, Blanca. 1995. "Mexican Business and the State: The Political Economy of a Muddled Transition." In Ernest Bartell and Leigh Payne, eds., *Business and Democracy in Latin America*. Pittsburgh: University of Pittsburgh Press.

Herrera, Stalin Gonzalo. 2016. "Situación, estrategia y contexto de los sindicatos en el Ecuador." In Emilce Cuda, ed., *Nuevos Estilos Sindicales en América Latina y el Caribe*. Buenos Aires: CLACSO.

Herschel, Federico and Samuel Itzcovich. 1957. "Fiscal Policy in Argentina." *Public Finance* 12 (2): 97–115.

Hertog, Steffen. 2013. "Introduction: The Role of MENA Business in Policy-Making and Political Transitions." In Steffen Hertog, Giacomo Luciani and Marc Valeri, eds., *Business Politics in the Middle East*. London: Hurst.

Hinnebusch, Raymond A. 2017. "Political Parties in MENA: Their Functions and Development." *British Journal of Middle Eastern Studies* 44 (2): 159–175.

Hintze, Otto. 1975. *The Historical Essays of Otto Hintze, 1861–1940*. New York: Oxford University Press.

Hochstetler, Kathryn. 2000. "Democratizing Pressures from Below? Social Movements in the New Brazilian Democracy." In Peter R. Kingstone and Timothy J. Power, eds., *Democratic Brazil: Actors, Institutions, and Processes*. Pittsburgh: University of Pittsburgh Press.

Hochstetler, Kathryn and Alfred P. Montero. 2013. "The Renewed Developmental State: The National Development Bank and the Brazil Model." *The Journal of Development Studies* 49 (11): 1484–1499.

Houtzager, Peter P. 1998. "State and Unions in the Transformation of the Brazilian Countryside, 1964–1979." *Latin American Research Review* 33 (2): 103–42.

Houtzager, Peter P. and Marcus Kurtz. 2000. "The Institutional Roots of Popular Mobilization: State Transformation and Rural Politics in Brazil and Chile, 1960–1995." *Comparative Studies in Society and History* 42 (2): 394–424.

Hsieh, Chang-Tai and Jonathan A. Parker. 2006. "Taxes and Growth in a Financially Underdeveloped Country: Evidence from the Chilean Investment Boom." NBER Working Paper 12104. Cambridge: National Bureau of Economic Research.

Huber, Evelyne and John D. Stephens. 2012. *Democracy and the Left: Social Policy and Inequality in Latin America*. Chicago: University of Chicago Press.

2001. *Development and Crisis of the Welfare State: Parties and Policies in Global Markets*. Chicago: University of Chicago Press.

Huneeus, Carlos. 2001. "La derecha en Chile después de Pinochet: El caso de la Unión Demócrata Independiente." Working Paper No. 285. Notre Dame: Kellogg Institute.

Hunter, Wendy. 2010. *The Transformation of the Workers' Party in Brazil, 1989–2009*. New York: Cambridge University Press.

Ianni, Octavio. 1973. "Populismo y relaciones de clase." In Gino Germani, Torcuato S. di Tella, and Octavio Ianni, eds., *Populismo y Contradicciones de Clase en Latinoamérica*. Mexico City: Serie Popular Era.

INEGI (Instituto Nacional de Estadística y Geografía). 2015. "Estadísticas Históricas de México 2014." Aguascalientes: INEGI.

Inter-American Development Bank. 1998. *Facing Up to Inequality in Latin America: Economic and Social Progress in Latin America, 1998–1999*. Baltimore: The Johns Hopkins University Press.

IMF (International Monetary Fund). 2018. "Algeria: 2018 Article IV Consultation." Country Report No. 18/168. Washington, DC: IMF.

2017. "Argentina: 2017 Article IV Consultation." Country Report No. 17/409.

2014. "Chile: Selected Issues." Country Report No. 14/219.

International Trade Union Confederation (ITUC). 2013. *Countries at Risk: 2013 Report on Violations of Trade Union Rights*. Brussels: ITUC.

Iversen, Torben and David Soskice. 2006. "Electoral Institutions and the Politics of Coalitions: Why Some Democracies Redistribute More than Others." *The American Political Science Review* 100 (2): 165–181.

Izquierdo, Rafael. 1995. *Política Hacendaria del Desarrollo Estabilizador, 1958–1970*. Mexico City: El Colegio de México.

Jackson, John E. and Ken Kollman. 2012. "Modeling, Measuring, and Distinguishing Path Dependence, Outcome Dependence, and Outcome Independence." *Political Analysis* 20 (2): 157–174.

James, Daniel. 1988. *Resistance and Integration: Peronism and the Argentine Working Class, 1946–1976*. New York: Cambridge University Press.

Jard da Silva, Sidney. 2015. *Companheiros Servidores: O Sindicalismo do Setor Público na CUT*. São Bernardo do Campo: EdUFABC.

Jauregui, Aníbal. 2013. "The Argentinean Industrial Organizations in the 'Age of Development' (1955–1976)." *Revista de Sociologia e Política* 21 (47): 55–68.

Jonas, Susanne. 1996. "Dangerous Liaisons: The U. S. in Guatemala." *Foreign Policy* 103: 144–160.

1991. *The Battle for Guatemala: Rebels, Death Squads, and U.S. Power*. Boulder: Westview Press.

Jones, Mark P. 2011. "Weakly Institutionalized Party Systems and Presidential Democracy: Evidence from Guatemala." *International Area Studies Review* 14 (4): 3–30.

Joumard, Isabelle, Mauro Pisu, and Debbie Bloch. 2012. "Tackling Income Inequality: The Role of Taxes and Transfers." *OECD Journal: Economic Studies* 2012 (1): 37–70.

Kato, Junko. 2003. *Regressive Taxation and the Welfare State: Path Dependence and Policy Diffusion*. New York: Cambridge University Press.

Katz, Friedrich. 1996. "The Agrarian Policies and Ideas of the Revolutionary Mexican Factions Led by Emiliano Zapata, Pancho Villa, and Venustiano Carranza." In Laura Randall, ed., *Reforming Mexico's Agrarian Reform*. Armonk: Sharpe.

Kaufman Purcell, Susan. 1981. "Business-Government Relations in Mexico: The Case of the Sugar Industry." *Comparative Politics* 13 (2): 211–233.

1975. *The Mexican Profit-Sharing Decision: Politics in an Authoritarian Regime*. Berkeley: University of California Press.

Kaufman, Robert R. 1972. *The Politics of Land Reform in Chile, 1950–1970: Public Policy, Political Institutions and Social Change*. Cambridge: Harvard University Press.

Keck, Margaret E. 1992. *The Workers' Party and Democratization in Brazil*. New Haven: Yale University Press.

Kenworthy, Lane. 2001. "Wage-Setting Measures: A Survey and Assessment." *World Politics* 54 (1): 57–98.

Kerevel, Yann. 2010. "The Legislative Consequences of Mexico's Mixed-Member Electoral System, 2000–2009." *Electoral Studies* 29 (4): 691–703.

King, Gary, Robert O. Keohane, and Sidney Verba. 1994. *Designing Social Inquiry: Scientific Inference in Qualitative Research*. Princeton: Princeton University Press.

Kingstone, Peter R. 1999. *Crafting Coalitions for Reform: Business Preferences, Political Institutions, and Neoliberal Reform in Brazil*. University Park: Pennsylvania State University.

Kitzberger, Phillip. 2011. "'La madre de todas las batallas': el kirchnerismo y los medios de comunicación." In Andrés Malamud and Miguel de Luca, eds., *La Política en Tiempos de Kirchner*. Buenos Aires: Eudeba.

Knight, Alan. 2016. *The Mexican Revolution: A Very Short Introduction*. New York: Oxford University Press.

1994. "Cardenismo: Juggernaut or Jalopy?" *Journal Latin American Studies* 26 (1): 73–107.

Kolbeck, Gustavo Romero and Víctor L. Urquidi. 1952. *La Exención Fiscal en el Distrito Federal como Instrumento de Atracción de Industrias.* Mexico City: Departamento del Distrito Federal.

Kornbluh, Peter. 2003. *The Pinochet File: A Declassified Dossier on Atrocity and Accountability.* New York: The New Press.

Korpi, Walter. 1983. *The Democratic Class Struggle.* London: Routledge.

KPMG. 2016. Americas Indirect Tax Country Guide.

Kritzer, Barbara E. 1996. "Privatizing Social Security: The Chilean Experience." *Social Security Bulletin* 59 (3): 45–55.

Kurtz, Marcus J. 2013. *Latin American State Building in Comparative Perspective: Social Foundations of Institutional Order.* New York: Cambridge University Press.

   1999. "Free Markets and Democratic Consolidation in Chile: The National Politics of Rural Transformation." *Politics & Society* 27 (2): 275–301.

Landerretche Moreno, Óscar. 2013. "Economic Policy and the Ideology of Stability." In Peter M. Siavelis and Kirsten Sehnbruch, eds., *Democratic Chile: The Politics and Policies of a Historic Coalition, 1990–2010.* Boulder: Lynne Rienner.

Lapp, Nancy D. 2004. *Landing Votes: Representation and Land Reform in Latin America.* New York: Palgrave Macmillan.

Larraín, Felipe and Patricio Meller. 1991. "The Socialist-Populist Chilean Experience, 1970–1973." In Rudiger Dornbusch and Sebastian Edwards, eds., *The Macroeconomics of Populism in Latin America.* Chicago: University of Chicago Press.

Larraín B., Felipe and Rodrigo Vergara M. 2001. "Un cuarto de siglo de reformas fiscales." In Larraín and Vergara, eds., *La Transformación Económica de Chile.* Santiago: Andros.

Lavinas, Lena, Denise Gentil, and Barbara Cobo. 2017. "The Controversial Brazilian Welfare Regime." Working Paper 2017-10. Geneva: UNRISD.

Leff, Nathaniel. 1968. *Economic Policy Making and Development in Brazil, 1947–1964.* New York: John Wiley.

Leopoldi, Maria Antonieta. 2000. *Política e Interesses na Industrialização Brasileira: As Associações Industriais, a Política Econômica e o Estado.* São Paulo: Paz e Terra.

Levi, Margaret. 1988. *Of Rule and Revenue.* Los Angeles: University of California Press.

Levitsky, Steven. 2003. *Transforming Labor-Based Parties in Latin America: Argentine Peronism in Comparative Perspective.* New York: Cambridge University Press

Levitsky, Steven and María Victoria Murillo. 2008. "Argentina: From Kirchner to Kirchner." *Journal of Democracy* 19 (2): 16–30.

   2006. *Argentine Democracy: The Politics of Institutional Weakness.* University Park: Pennsylvania State University Press.

Lieberman, Evan S. 2003. *Race and Regionalism in the Politics of Taxation in Brazil and South Africa.* New York: Cambridge University Press.

Lipset, Seymour Martin and Earl Raab. 1978. *The Politics of Unreason: Right-Wing Extremism in America, 1790–1970.* Chicago: University of Chicago Press.

Lindert, Peter H. 2004. *Growing Public: Social Spending and Economic Growth Since the Eighteenth Century.* New York: Cambridge University Press.

Loaeza, Soledad. 2003. "The National Action Party (PAN): From the Fringes of the Political System to the Heart of Change." In Scott Mainwaring and Timothy R. Scully, eds., *Christian Democracy in Latin America: Electoral Competition and Regime Conflicts.* Stanford: Stanford University Press.

1987. "El Partido Acción Nacional: De la oposición leal a la impaciencia electoral." In Loaeza and Rafael Segovia, eds., *La Vida Política Mexicana en la Crisis*. Mexico City: El Colegio de México.

1974. "El Partido Acción Nacional: La oposición leal en México." *Foro Internacional* 14 (3): 352–374.

Lodola, Germán. 2011. "Gobierno nacional, gobernadores e intendentes en el período kirchnerista." In Andrés Malamud and Miguel De Luca, eds., *La Política en Tiempos de los Kirchner*. Buenos Aires: Eudeba.

Lopes, Júlio Aurélio Vianna. 2009. "O consórcio político da ordem de 1988." In Maria Alice Rezende de Carvalho, Cícero Araújo, and Júlio Assis Simões, eds., *A Constituição de 1988: Passado e Futuro*. São Paulo: ANPOCS.

López, Ramón. 2013. "Fiscal Policy: Promoting Faustian Growth." In Peter M. Siavelis and Kirsten Sehnbruch, eds., *Democratic Chile: The Politics and Policies of a Historic Coalition, 1990–2010*. Boulder: Lynne Rienner.

López-Calva, Luis F. and Nora Claudia Lustig. 2010. *Declining Inequality in Latin America: A Decade of Progress*. Washington, DC: Brookings Institution.

López Portillo, Felícitas. 1995. *Estado e Ideología Empresarial en el Gobierno Alemanista*. Mexico City: UNAM.

Lotz, Joergen R. and Elliott R. Morss. 1970. "A Theory of Tax Level Determinants for Developing Countries." *Economic Development and Cultural Change* 18 (3): 328–341.

Loureiro, Felipe Pereira. 2016. "The Passing of the Profit Remittance Limitation Law during the Goulart Administration and Brazilian and Foreign Entrepreneurs (1961–1964)." *Revista Brasileira de História* 36 (71): 155–177.

2012. "Empresários, Trabalhadores e Grupos de Interesse: a Política Econômica nos Governos Jânio Quadros e João Goulart, 1961–1964." PhD Dissertation, Universidade São Paulo.

Loxton, James. 2014. "The Authoritarian Roots of New Right Party Success in Latin America." In Juan Pablo Luna and Cristóbal Rovira Kaltwasser, eds., *The Resilience of the Latin American Right*. Baltimore: Johns Hopkins University Press.

Lüders, Rolf and Gert Wagner. 2003. "The Great Depression: A Definining Moment in Chile's Development?" *Cuadernos de Economía* 4 (121): 786–791.

Luna, Juan Pablo. 2014. *Segmented Representation: Political Party Strategies in Unequal Democracies*. New York: Oxford University Press.

Luna, Juan Pablo and Cristóbal Rovira Kaltwasser. 2014. "The Right in Contemporary Latin America: A Framework for Analysis." In Luna and Rovira Kaltwasser, eds., *The Resilience of the Latin American Right*. Baltimore: Johns Hopkins University Press.

Luna Ledesma, Matilde. 1992. *Los Empresarios y el Cambio Político: México, 1970–1987*. Mexico City: Ediciones Era.

Lustig, Nora. 2017. "El impacto del sistema tributario y el gasto social en la distribución del ingreso y la pobreza en América Latina. Una aplicación del marco metodológico del proyecto Compromiso con la Equidad." *El Trimestre Económico* 84 (3): 493–568.

2016. "El Impacto del Sistema Tributario y el Gasto Social en la Distribución del Ingreso y la Pobreza en América Latina: Argentina, Bolivia, Brasil, Chile, Colombia, Costa Rica, Ecuador, El Salvador, Guatemala, Honduras, México, Perú y Uruguay." Documento de Trabajo no. 37, Commitment to Equity Institute, Tulane University.

2015. "Inequality and Fiscal Redistribution in Middle-Income Countries: Brazil, Chile, Colombia, Indonesia, Mexico, Peru and South Africa." Working Paper 410, Center Global for Development.

Lustig, Nora, Carola Pessino, and John Scott. 2014. "The Impact of Taxes and Social Spending on Inequality and Poverty in Argentina, Bolivia, Brazil, Mexico, Peru, and Uruguay: Introduction to the Special Issue." *Public Finance Review* 42 (3): 287–303.

Lyall, Angus and Gabriela Valdivia. 2019. "The Speculative Petro-State: Volatile Oil Prices and Resource Populism in Ecuador." *Annals of the American Association of Geographers* 109 (2): 349–360.

Madrid, Raúl L. 2003. *Retiring the State: The Politics of Pension Privatization in Latin America and Beyond.* Stanford: Stanford University Press.

Mahon, James E. 2019. "Weak Liberalism and Weak Property Taxation in Latin America." In Gustavo Flores-Macías, ed., *The Political Economy of Taxation in Latin America.* New York: Cambridge University Press.

2004. "Causes of Tax Reform in Latin America, 1977–95." *Latin American Research Review* 39 (1): 3–30.

1996. *Mobile Capital and Latin American Development.* University Park: Pennsylvania State University Press.

Mahoney, James. 2000. "Path Dependence in Historical Sociology." *Theory and Society* 29 (4): 507–548.

Mahoney, James and Daniel Schensul. 2006. "Historical Context and Path Dependence." In Robert E. Goodin and Charles Tilly, eds., *The Oxford Handbook of Contextual Political Analysis.* New York: Oxford University Press.

Mahoney, James and Kathleen Thelen. 2015. *Advances in Comparative-Historical Analysis.* New York: Cambridge University Press.

Mainwaring, Scott. 1999. *Rethinking Party Systems in the Third Wave of Democratization: The Case of Brazil.* Stanford: Stanford University Press.

1995. "Brazil: Weak Parties, Feckless Democracy." In Mainwaring and Timothy R. Scully, eds., *Building Democratic Institutions: Party Systems in Latin America.* Stanford: Stanford University Press.

Mainwaring, Scott and Aníbal Pérez-Liñán. 2013. *Democracies and Dictatorships in Latin America: Emergence, Survival, and Fall.* New York: Cambridge University Press.

Mainwaring, Scott and Mariano Torcal. 2006. "Party System Institutionalization and Party System Theory After the Third Wave of Democratization." In Richard S. Katz, and William Crotty, eds., *Handbook of Party Politics.* London: SAGE.

Mallon, Richard D. and Juan V. Sourrouille. 1975. *Economic Policymaking in a Conflict Society: The Argentine Case.* Cambridge: Harvard University Press.

Malloy, James M. 1979. *The Politics of Social Security in Brazil.* Pittsburgh: University of Pittsburgh Press.

Mancuso, Wagner Pralon. 2007. "O empresariado como ator político no Brasil: Balanço da literatura e agenda de pesquisa." *Revista de Sociologia e Política* 28: 131–146.

Mancuso, Wagner Pralon and Amâncio Jorge de Oliveira. 2006. "Abertura econômica, empresariado e política: Os planos doméstico e internacional." *Lua Nova* 69: 147–172.

Maneschi, Andrea. 1970. "Aspectos quantitativos do setor público do Brasil de 1939 a 1968." Instituto de Pesquisas Econômicas, Universidade de São Paulo.

Mansbridge, Jane and Shauna L. Shames. 2008. "Toward a Theory of Backlash: Dynamic Resistance and the Central Role of Power." *Politics & Gender* 4 (4): 623–634.

Marcel, Mario. 1997. "Políticas Públicas en Democracia: el Caso de la Reforma Tributaria de 1990 en Chile." Estudios CIEPLAN No. 45. Santiago: CIEPLAN.

Margold, Stella. 1957. "Agrarian Land Reform in Egypt." *The American Journal of Economics and Sociology* 17 (1): 9–19.

Márquez, Graciela. 2005. "Aranceles a la importación y finanzas públicas: Del Porfiriato a la crisis de 1929." In Luis Aboites Aguilar and Luis Jáuregui, eds., *Penuria Sin Fin: Historia de los Impuestos en México Siglos XVIII–XX*. Mexico City: Instituto Mora.

Martín-Mayoral, Fernando and Carlos Andrés Uribe. 2010. "Determinantes económicos e institucionales del esfuerzo fiscal en América Latina." *Investigación Económica* 69 (273): 85–113.

Martínez de Navarrete, Ifigenia. 1973. "La evolución del sistema tributario de México y las reformas 1972–73." *Revista de Análisis Económico y Social* 23 (1): 48–55.

1967. *Los Incentivos Fiscales y el Desarrollo Económico de México*. Mexico City: Instituto de Investigaciones Económicas, UNAM.

Martínez-Lara, Javier. 1996. *Building Democracy in Brazil: The Politics of Constitutional Change, 1985–95*. London: Palgrave Macmillan.

Martínez Nava, Juan M. 1984. *Conflicto Estado-Empresarios en los Gobiernos de Cárdenas, López Mateos y Echeverría*. Mexico City: Editorial Nueva Imagen.

Martínez-Vazquez, Jorge. 2001. "Mexico: An Evaluation of the Main Features of the Tax System." Working Paper 01–12, International Studies Program, School of Policy Studies, Georgia State University.

Martins, José de Souza. 1994. *O Poder do Atraso: Ensaios de Sociologia da História Lenta*. São Paulo: Hucitec.

Mayol, Alberto and Carla Azocar. 2011. "Politización del malestar, movilización social y transformación ideológica: el caso 'Chile 2011'." *Polis* 10 (30): 163–184.

McGann, James G. 2017. "2016 Global Go-To Think Tank Index Report." Think Tanks and Civil Societies Program. Philadelphia: University of Pennsylvania. https://repository.upenn.edu/cgi/viewcontent.cgi?article=1011&context=think_tanks

McGuire, James W. 1997. *Peronism Without Perón: Unions, Parties, and Democracy in Argentina*. Stanford: Stanford University Press.

1995. "Political Parties and Democracy in Argentina." In Scott Mainwaring and Timothy R. Scully, eds., *Building Democratic Institutions: Party Systems in Latin America*. Stanford: Stanford University Press.

Medin, Tzvi. 1971. "Cárdenas: Del Maximato al presidencialismo." *Revista de la Universidad de México* 9: 13–17.

Meller, Patricio. 1998. *Un Siglo de Economía Política Chilena (1890–1990)*. Santiago: Andrés Bello.

Melo, Marcus André. 2007. "Institutional Weakness and the Puzzle of Argentina's Low Taxation." *Latin American Politics and Society* 49 (4): 115–148.

Melo, Marcus André, Carlos Pereira, and Saulo Souza. 2010. "The Political Economy of Fiscal Reform in Brazil: The Rationale for the Suboptimal Equilibrium." Working Paper No. 117. Washington, D.C.: IDB.

Meltzer, Allan H. and Scott F. Richard. 1981. "A Rational Theory of the Size of Government." *Journal of Political Economy* 89 (5): 914–927.

Mendes, Marcos. 2013. "Transformações e impasses da estrutura fiscal e tributária de 1988 a 2013." Texto para Discussão No. 136. Brasília: Núcleo de Estudos e Pesquisas/CONLEG/Senado.

Meneguello, Rachel. 1989. *PT: A Formação de um Partido, 1979–1982*. São Paulo: Paz e Terra.

Mesa-Lago, Carmelo. 2009. "Balance económico-social de 50 años de Revolución en Cuba." *América Latina Hoy* 52: 41–61.

1978. *Social Security in Latin America: Pressure Groups, Stratification, and Inequality*. Pittsburgh: University of Pittsburgh Press.

Michiles, Carlos. 1989. *Cidadão Constituinte: A Saga das Emendas Populares*. Rio de Janeiro: Paz e Terra.

Middlebrook, Kevin J. 1995. *The Paradox of Revolution: Labor, the State, and Authoritarianism in Mexico*. Baltimore: Johns Hopkins University Press.

Ministério da Fazenda. 2015. "Nota de Análise Sobre a Desoneração da Folha." Brasília: Secretaria de Política Econômica, Ministério da Fazenda.

Ministerio de Hacienda. 2014. "Ministro de Hacienda: Esta es una reforma tributaria consistente con los objetivos de recuperar la senda del crecimiento." Press reléase. Accessed March 2018. www.hacienda.cl/sala-de-prensa/archivo-2014-2018/noticias/ministro-de-hacienda-esta-es-una.html.

Mirow, Matthew C. 2011. "Origins of the Social Function of Property in Chile." *Fordham Law Review* 80 (3): 1183–1217.

Mizrahi, Yemile. 2003. *From Martyrdom to Power: The Partido Acción Nacional in Mexico*. Notre Dame: University of Notre Dame Press.

Moctezuma Barragán, Pablo. 1997. *Los Orígenes del PAN*. Mexico City: Ehecatl Ediciones.

Monckeberg, María Olivia. 2017. *El Poder de la UDI: 50 Años de Gremialismo en Chile*. Santiago: Debate.

Montero, Alfred P. 2014. "Brazil: Explaining the Rise and Decline of the Conservatives." In Juan Pablo Luna and Cristóbal Rovira Kaltwasser, eds., *The Resilience of the Latin American Right*. Baltimore: Johns Hopkins University Press.

Montúfar, César. 2000. *La Reconstrucción Neoliberal: Febres Cordero o la Estatización del Neoliberalismo en el Ecuador, 1984–1988*. Albuquerque: New Mexico University Press.

Moore, Mick. 2008. "Between Coercion and Contract: Competing Narratives on Taxation and Governance." In Deborah Brautigam, Odd-Helge Fjelstad and Moore, eds., *Taxation and State-Building in Developing Countries: Capacity and Consent*. Cambridge: Cambridge University Press.

Morales Quiroga, Mauricio. 2014. "Congruencia programática entre partidos y votantes en Chile." *Perfiles Latinoamericanos* 22 (44): 59–90.

Moran, Theodore H. 1974. *Multinational Corporations and the Politics of Dependence: Copper in Chile*. Princeton: Princeton University Press.

Mora y Araujo, Manuel. 2011. *La Argentina Bipolar: Los Vaivenes de la Opinión Pública (1983–2011)*. Buenos Aires: Sudamericana.

Mora y Araujo, Manuel and Ignacio Llorente. 1980. *El Voto Peronista: Ensayos de Sociología Electoral Argentina*. Buenos Aires: Sudamericana.

Morresi, Sergio and Gabriel Vommaro. 2014. "Argentina: The Difficulties of the Partisan Right and the Case of Propuesta Republicana." In Juan Pablo Luna and

Cristóbal Rovira Kaltwasser, eds., *The Resilience of the Latin American Right*. Baltimore: Johns Hopkins University Press.

Morett Sánchez, Jesús Carlos. 2003. *Reforma Agraria: Del Latifundio al Neoliberalismo*. Mexico City: Plaza y Valdes.

Morisset, Jacques and Alejandro Izquierdo. 1993. "Effects of Tax Reform on Argentina's Revenues." Working Paper 1192. Washington, DC: World Bank.

Moulian, Tomás. 1997. *Chile Actual: Anatomía de un Mito*. Santiago: LOM-ARCIS.

Moulian, Tomás and Isabel Torres Dujisin. 1988. "La reorganización de los partidos de la derecha entre 1983 y 1988." Documento de Trabajo, FLACSO-Chile No. 388. Santiago: FLACSO.

Moulian, Tomás and Pilar Vergara. 1980 "Estado, ideologia y politicas economicas en Chile: 1973–1978." Colección Estudios CIEPLAN, No. 3. Santiago: CIEPLAN.

Mueller, Dennis C. 2003. *Public Choice III*. Cambridge: Cambridge University Press.

Muñoz, María L.O. 2016. *Stand Up and Fight: Participatory Indigenismo, Populism, and Mobilization in Mexico, 1970–1984*. Tucson: University of Arizona Press.

Murillo, Maria Victoria. 2015. "Curtains for Argentina's Kirchner Era." *Current History* 114 (769): 56–61.

2013. "Cambio y continuidad del sindicalismo en democracia." *Revista SAAP: Sociedad Argentina de Análisis Político* 7 (2): 339–348.

Murillo, María Victoria, Julia María Rubio, and Jorge Mangonnet. 2016. "Argentina: El protagonismo de los votantes y la alternancia electoral." *Revista de Ciencia Política* 36 (1): 3–26.

Murmis, Miguel and Juan Carlos Portantiero. 1971. *Estudios Sobre los Orígenes del Peronismo*. Buenos Aires: Siglo Veintiuno.

Musacchio, Aldo and Sergio G. Lazzarini. 2014. *Reinventing State Capitalism: Leviathan in Business, Brazil and Beyond*. Cambridge: Harvard University Press.

Nakahado, Sidney and José Roberto Savoia. 2008. "A reforma da previdência no Brasil: estudo comparativo dos governos Fernando Henrique Cardoso e Lula." *Revista Brasileira de Ciências Sociais* 23 (66): 43–56.

Nállim, Jorge A. 2012. *Transformation and Crisis of Liberalism in Argentina, 1930–1955*. Pittsburgh: Pittsburgh University Press.

Naranjo, Mariana. 2014. "Social Protection Systems in Latin America and the Caribbean: Ecuador." Project Document 552. Santiago: ECLAC.

Niblo, Stephen R. 2000. *Mexico in the 1940s: Modernity, Politics, and Corruption*. Lanham: Rowman & Littlefield.

Nicolau, Jairo. 2017. "Os quatro fundamentos da competição política no Brasil (1994–2014)." *Journal of Democracy em Português* 6 (1): 83–106.

1998. *Dados Eleitorais do Brasil (1982–1996)*. Rio de Janeiro: Editora Revan.

Niedzwiecki, Sara. 2015. "Social Policy Commitment in South America. The Effect of Organized Labor on Social Spending from 1980 to 2010." *Journal of Politics in Latin America* 7 (2): 3–42.

2014. "The Effect of Unions and Organized Civil Society on Social Policy: Pension and Health Reforms in Argentina and Brazil, 1988–2008." *Latin American Politics and Society* 56 (4): 1–27.

North, Douglass C. 1990. *Institutions, Institutional Change and Economic Performance*. New York: Cambridge University Press.

North, Liisa L. 2004. "State Building, State Dismantling, and Financial Crises in Ecuador." In Jo-Marie Burt, ed., *Politics in the Andes: Identity, Conflict, Reform*. Pittsburgh: University of Pittsburgh Press.

O'Donnell, Guillermo. 1978. "Reflections on the Patterns of Change in the Bureaucratic-Authoritarian State." *Latin American Research Review* 13: 3–38.

    1977. "Estado y alianzas en la Argentina, 1956–1976." *Desarrollo Económico* 16 (64): 523–554.

Oliveira, Fabrício Augusto de. 2010. "A evolução da estrutura tributária e do fisco brasileiro: 1889–2009." Texto para Discussão No. 1469. Rio de Janeiro: IPEA.

    1991. *A Reforma Tributária de 1966 e a Acumulação de Capital no Brasil*. Rio de Janeiro: Oficina de Livros.

Olivera, Gabriela. 2004. "La Federación Agraria Argentina y la cuestión del cooperativismo en la Argentina peronista." *Ciclos* 14 (27): 99–122.

Ondetti, Gabriel. 2019. "Once Bitten, Twice Shy: Path Dependence, Power Resources, and the Magnitude of the Tax Burden in Latin America." In Gustavo Flores-Macías, ed., *The Political Economy of Taxation in Latin America*. New York: Cambridge University Press.

    2017. "The Power of Preferences: Economic Elites and Light Taxation in Mexico." *Revista Mexicana de Ciencias Políticas y Sociales* 62 (231): 47–76.

    2016. "The Social Function of Property, Land Rights and Social Welfare in Brazil." *Land Use Policy* 50: 29–37.

    2015. "The Roots of Brazil's Heavy Taxation." *Journal of Latin American Studies* 47 (4): 749–779.

Organisation for Economic Co-operation and Development (OECD). 2015–2019. *Revenue Statistics in Latin America and the Caribbean*. Paris: OECD.

Ortiz Mena, Antonio. 1998. *El Desarrollo Estabilizador: Reflexiones Sobre una Época*. Mexico City: Fondo de Cultura Económica.

Ortiz, Isabel and Matthew Cummins. 2011. "Global Inequality: Beyond the Bottom Billion – A Rapid Review of Income Distribution in 141 Countries." Social and Economic Policy Working Paper. New York: UNICEF.

Owens, Daniel Scott. 2017. *Fight or Flight? Democratic Consolidation and Capital Flight in Latin America*. PhD Dissertation, University of Maryland.

Oxfam. 2016. *Unearthed: Land, Power and Inequality in Latin America*. Washington, DC: Oxfam America.

Palacios-Valladares, Indira and Gabriel Ondetti. 2019. "Student Protest and the Nueva Mayoría Reforms in Chile." *Bulletin of Latin American Research* 38 (5): 638–653.

Palermo, Vincente and Juan Carlos Torre. 1992. "A la sombra de la hiperinflación: La política de reformas estructurales en Argentina." Working Paper. Santiago: ECLAC. https://repositorio.cepal.org/bitstream/handle/11362/33817/S9200602_es.pdf?seque nce=1&isAllowed=y

Pastor, Manuel Jr. 1990. "Capital Flight from Latin America." *World Development* 18 (1): 1–18.

Pastor, Manuel Jr. and Carol Wise. 2005. "Policy Issues: The Lost Sexenio: Vicente Fox and the New Politics of Economic Reform in Mexico." *Latin American Politics and Society* 47 (4): 135–160.

Patrucchi, Leticia and Leonardo Grottola. 2011. "Estructura tributaria, ingresos rentísticos y regresividad en América Latina: Un análisis de la situación actual." *Leviathan* 2: 96–122.

Perdigão, Francinete and Luiz Bassegio. 1992. *Migrantes Amazônicos: Rondônia – a Trajetória da Ilusão*. São Paulo: Edições Loyola.

Pereira, Carlos, Lucio Rennó, and David Samuels. 2011. "Corruption, Campaign Finance, and Reelection." In Timothy J. Power and Matthew Taylor, eds., *Corruption and Democracy in Brazil. The Struggle for Accountability*. Notre Dame: University of Notre Dame Press.

Perla, Héctor, Marco Mojica, and Jared Bibler. 2013. "From Guerrillas to Government: The Continued Relevance of the Central American Left." In Jeffery R. Webber and Barry Carr, eds., *The New Latin American Left: Cracks in the Empire*. Lanham: Rowman and Littlefield.

Persson, Torsten and Guido Tabellini. 2003. *The Economic Effects of Constitutions*. Cambridge: The MIT Press.

Pessino, Carola and Ricardo Fenochietto. 2010. "Determining Countries' Tax Effort." *Hacienda Pública Española/Revista de Economía Pública* 195 (4): 65–87.

Piancastelli, Marcelo. 2001. "Measuring the Tax Effort of Developed and Developing Countries: Cross Country Panel Data Analysis - 1985/95." Working Paper No. 818. Rio de Janeiro: IPEA.

Pierson, Paul. 2015. "Power and Path Dependence." In James Mahoney and Kathleen Thelen, eds., *Advances in Comparative-Historical Analysis*. New York: Cambridge University Press.

2004. *Politics in Time: History, Institutions, and Social Analysis*. Princeton: Princeton University Press.

2000. "Increasing Returns, Path Dependence, and the Study of Politics." *The American Political Science Review* 94 (2): 251–267.

Polga-Hecimovich, John and Peter M. Siavelis. 2015. "Here's the Bias! A (Re-) Reassessment of the Chilean Electoral System." *Electoral Studies* 40: 268–279.

Pollack, Marcelo. 1999. *The New Right in Chile, 1973–97*. New York: St. Martin.

Ponce de Leon, Zoila. 2018. "Policy Reform, Political Parties and Organized Interests: Universalization of Healthcare in Latin America." PhD Dissertation, University of North Carolina, Chapel Hill.

Posner, Paul W. 2017. "Labor Market Flexibility, Employment and Inequality: Lessons from Chile." *New Political Economy* 22 (2): 237–256.

Power, Timothy J. 2000. *The Political Right in Postauthoritarian Brazil: Elites, Institutions, and Democratization*. University Park: Penn State University Press.

Przeworski, Adam. 1991. *Democracy and the Market*. New York: Cambridge University Press.

Przeworski, Adam and Henry Teune. 1970. *The Logic of Comparative Social Inquiry*. New York: Wiley-Interscience.

Przeworski, Adam and Michael Wallerstein. 1988. "Structural Dependence of the State on Capital." *American Political Science Review* 82 (1): 11–29.

Raby, David L. 1981. "La 'educación socialista' en México." *Cuadernos Políticos* 29: 75–82.

Ram, Rati. 2009. "Openness, Country Size and Government Size: Additional Evidence from a Large Cross-Country Panel." *Journal of Public Economics* 93 (1–2): 213–218.

Ramírez-Cendrero, Juan M. and María J. Paz. 2017. "Oil Fiscal Regimes and National Oil Companies: A Comparison between Pemex and Petrobras." *Energy Policy* 101: 473–483.

Ramírez Cedillo, Eduardo. 2013. "La generalización del Impuesto al Valor Agregado: ¿Una opción para México?" *Revista Mexicana de Ciencias Políticas y Sociales* 58 (219): 75–101.

Ramos, Joseph. 1986. *Neoconservative Economics in the Southern Cone of Latin America, 1973–1983*. Baltimore: Johns Hopkins University Press.

Ranis, Peter. 1992. *Argentine Workers: Peronism and Contemporary Class Consciousness*. Pittsburgh: University of Pittsburgh Press.

Remmer, Karen L. and Gilbert W. Merkx. 1982. "Bureaucratic-Authoritarianism Revisited." *Latin American Research Review* 17 (2): 3–40.

Remmer, Karen L. and Erik Wibbels. 2000. "The Subnational Politics of Economic Adjustment: Provincial Politics and Fiscal Performance in Argentina." *Comparative Political Studies* 33 (4): 419–451.

Reynolds, Clark M. 1970. *The Mexican Economy: Twentieth-Century Structure and Growth*. New Haven: Yale University Press.

Rezende, Fernando. 1972. *Avaliação do Setor Público na Economia Brasileira: Estrutura Funcional da Despesa*. São Paulo: IPEA/INPES.

Rezende, Fernando and José Roberto R. Afonso. 1987. "A reforma fiscal no processo de elaboração da nova constituição." Working Paper 121. Rio de Janeiro: IPEA.

Ribeiro, Vanderlei Vazelesk. 2008. *Cuestiones Agrarias en el Varguismo y el Peronismo: Una Mirada Histórica*. Buenos Aires: Universidad Nacional de Quilmes.

Richardson, Neal P. 2009. "Export-Oriented Populism: Commodities and Coalitions in Argentina." *Studies in Comparative International Development* 44 (3): 228–255.

Riesco Larraín, Manuel. 2007. *Se Derrumba un Mito: Chile Reforma sus Sistemas Privatizados de Educación y Previsión*. Santiago: CENDA.

Riggirozzi, Maria Pia. 2008. "Argentina: State Capacity and Leverage in External Negotiations." In Justin Roberson, ed., *Power and Politics After Financial Crises*. Basingstoke: Palgrave Macmillan.

Riguizzi, Paolo. 2009. "From Globalisation to Revolution? The Porfirian Political Economy: An Essay on Issues and Interpretations." *Journal of Latin American Studies* 41 (2): 347–368.

Roberts, Kenneth M. 2014. *Changing Course: Party Systems in Latin America's Neoliberal Era*. New York: Cambridge University Press.

——— 2012. "The Politics of Inequality and Redistribution in Latin America's Post-Adjustment Era." Working Paper No. 2012/08. Helsinki: UNU-WIDER.

Rock, David. 1987. *Argentina, 1516–1987: From Spanish Colonization to Alfonsín*. Berkeley: University of California Press

Rodden, Jonathan. 2003. "Reviving Leviathan: Fiscal Federalism and the Growth of Government." *International Organization* 57 (4): 695–729.

Rodrigues Neto, João. 2005. "A gênese da Petrobrás: um debate entre Nacionalistas e Liberais." *H-industri@* 6 (10). Accessed June 2019. http://ojs.econ.uba.ar/ojs/index.php/H-ind/article/view/377/691.

Rodrik, Dani. 1998. "Why Do More Open Countries Have Bigger Governments?" *Journal of Political Economy* 106 (5): 997–1032.

Rofman, Rafael. 2006. "Sistema de pensiones: Las reformas de la reforma." In Marcelo M. Giugale, Connie Luff, and Vicente Fretes-Cibils, eds., *Bolivia: Por el Bienestar de Todos*. Washington, DC: World Bank.

Romero, Vidal. 2015. "The Political Economy of Progressive Tax Reforms in Mexico." In James E. Mahon Jr., Marcelo Bergman, and Cynthia Arnson, eds., *Progressive Tax Reform and Equality in Latin America*. Washington, DC: Wilson Center.

Romero Sotelo, Maria Eugenia. 2011. "Las raíces de la ortodoxia en México." *Economía UNAM* 8 (24): 23–50.

Ros, Jaime. 1993. "Mexico's Trade and Industrialization Experience Since 1960: A Reconsideration of Past Policies and Assessment of Current Reforms." Working Paper 186. Notre Dame: Kellogg Institute.

Rossi, Federico M. 2017. *The Poor's Struggle for Political Incorporation: The Piquetero Movement in Argentina*. New York: Cambridge University Press.

Rubio, Mar. 2003. "Oil and Economy in Mexico, 1900–1930s." Working Paper 690. Department of Economics and Business, Universitat Pompeu Fabra.

Russett, Bruce. 1964. "Inequality and Instability: The Relation of Land Tenure and Politics." *World Politics* 16: 442–54.

Sader, Eder. 1988. *Quando Novos Personagens Entraram em Cena: Experiências e Lutas dos Trabalhadores da Grande São Paulo 1970–1980*. Rio de Janeiro: Paz e Terra.

Salvia, Sebastían Pedro. 2015. "The Boom and Crisis of the Convertibility Plan in Argentina." *Revista de Economía Política* 35 (2): 325–342.

Samuels, David. 2004. "From Socialism to Social Democracy: Party Organization and the Transformation of the Workers' Party in Brazil." *Comparative Political Studies* 37 (9): 999–1024.

Sanchez, Omar. 2011. *Mobilizing Resources in Latin America: The Political Economy of Tax Reform in Chile and Argentina*. New York: Palgrave Macmillan.

2009. "Tax Reform Paralysis in Post-Conflict Guatemala." *New Political Economy* 14 (1): 101–131.

2008. "Guatemala's Party Universe: A Case Study in Underinstitutionalization." *Latin American Politics and Society* 50 (1): 123–151.

Sánchez Román, José Antonio. 2012. *Taxation and Society in Twentieth-Century Argentina*. New York: Palgrave Macmillan.

Santos, Wanderley Guilherme dos. 1979. *Cidadania e Justiça: A Política Social na Ordem Brasileira*. Rio de Janeiro: Campus.

Saragoza, Alex M. 1988. *The Monterrey Elite and the Mexican State, 1880–1940*. Austin: University of Texas Press.

Sarigil, Zeki. 2015. "Showing the Path to Path Dependence: The Habitual Path." *European Political Science Review* 7 (2): 221–242.

Sayigh, Yezid. 2019. *Owners of the Republic: An Anatomy of Egypt's Military Economy*. Washington, DC: Carnegie Endowment.

Schmitter, Philippe C. 1971. *Interest Conflict and Political Change in Brazil*. Stanford: Stanford University Press.

Schneider, Aaron. 2019. "Federalism and Taxation: Periods of Brazilian International Insertion." In Gustavo Flores-Macías, ed., *The Political Economy of Taxation in Latin America*. New York: Cambridge University Press.

2012. *State-Building and Tax Regimes in Central America*. New York: Cambridge University Press.

Schneider, Aaron and Maynor Cabrera. 2015. "Institutions, Inequality, and Taxes in Guatemala." In James E. Mahon Jr., Marcelo Bergman, and Cynthia Arnson, eds.,

Progressive Tax Reform and Equality in Latin America. Washington, DC: Wilson Center.

Schneider, Ben Ross. 2004. *Business Politics and the State in Twentieth-Century Latin America*. New York: Cambridge University Press.

2002. "Why is Mexican Business so Organized?" *Latin American Research Review* 37 (1): 77–118.

Schorr, Martín. 2012. "La desindustrialización como eje del proyecto refundacional de la economía y la sociedad en Argentina, 1976–1983." *América Latina en la História Económica* 19 (3): 31–56.

Schützhofer, Tim B. 2016. "Ecuador's Fiscal Policies in the Context of the Citizens' Revolution A 'Virtuous Cycle' and its Limits." Discussion Paper 15/2016. Bonn: Deutsches Institut für Entwicklungspolitik.

Schvarzer, Jorge. 1983. *Martínez de Hoz: La Lógica Política de la Política Económica*. Buenos Aires: Centro de Investigaciones Sociales Sobre el Estado y la Administración.

Schwartzman, Simon. 1986. "A política da Igreja e a educação: O sentido de um pacto." *Religião e Sociedade* 13 (1): 108–127.

Seawright, Jason. 2016. *Multi-Method Social Science: Combining Qualitative and Quantitative Tools*. New York: Cambridge University Press.

Sehnbruch, Kirsten. 2012. "Unable to Shape the Political Arena: The Impact of Poor-Quality Employment on Unions in Post-Transition Chile." Working Paper No. 4. Santiago: Centre for New Development Thinking.

2006. *The Chilean Labor Market: A Key to Understanding Latin American Labor Markets*. New York: Palgrave Macmillan.

Sehnbruch, Kirsten and Peter M. Siavelis. 2014. "Political and Economic Life under the Rainbow." In Sehnbruch and Siavelis, eds., *Democratic Chile: The Politics and Policies of a Historic Coalition, 1990–2010*. Boulder: Lynne Rienner.

Semo, Enrique. 1989. *México, un Pueblo en la Historia 6: El Ocaso de los Mitos (1958–1968)*. Mexico City: Alianza Editorial.

Servicio de Rentas Internas. 2012. *Una Nueva Política Fiscal para el Buen Vivir: La Equidad como Soporte del Pacto Fiscal*. Quito: Servicio de Rentas Internas.

Sfakianakis, John. 2004. "The Whales of the Nile: Networks, Businessmen, and Bureaucrats During the Era of Privatization in Egypt." In Steven Heydemann, ed., *Networks of Privilege in the Middle East: The Politics of Economic Reform Revisited*. New York: Palgrave Macmillan.

Shadlen, Kenneth C. 2004. *Democratization Without Representation: The Politics of Small Industry in Mexico*. University Park: Pennsylvania State University Press.

Shafer, Robert Jones. 1973. *Mexican Business Organizations: History and Analysis*. Syracuse: Syracuse University Press.

Sheng, Michael. 2014. "Mao's Role in the Korean Conflict: A Revision." *Twentieth-Century China* 39 (3): 269–290.

Siavelis, Peter M. 2016. "Crisis of Representation in Chile? The Institutional Connection." *Journal of Politics in Latin America* 8 (3): 61–93.

2009. "Elite-Mass Congruence, Partidocracia and the Quality of Chilean Democracy." *Journal of Politics in Latin America* 1 (3): 3–31.

Sigmund, Paul E. 1980. *Multinationals in Latin America: The Politics of Nationalization*. Madison: University of Wisconsin Press.

Sikkink, Kathryn. 1991. *Ideas and Institutions: Developmentalism in Brazil and Argentina*. Ithaca: Cornell University Press.

Silva, Eduardo. 2009. *Challenging Neoliberalism in Latin America*. New York: Cambridge University Press.

1996. *The State and Capital in Chile: Business Elites, Technocrats, and Market Economics*. Boulder: Westview Press.

Silva, Patricio. 1995. "Empresarios, neoliberalismo y transición democrática en Chile." *Revista Mexicana de Sociología* 57 (4): 3–25.

1991. "Technocrats and Politics in Chile: From the Chicago Boys to the CIEPLAN Monks." *Journal of Latin American Studies* 23 (2): 385–410.

Silva Lima, Mayrá. 2017. "O ruralismo enquanto elite política no Brasil: Atuação parlamentar e limites à democracia." Prepared for the Ninth Congress of the Latin American Political Science Association, Montevideo, Uruguay.

Singer, André. 2001. *O PT*. São Paulo: Publifolha.

Skidmore, Thomas E. 1967. *Politics in Brazil, 1930–1964: An Experiment in Democracy*. New York: Oxford University Press.

Slater, Dan and Erica Simmons. 2010. "Informative Regress: Critical Antecedents in Comparative Politics." *Comparative Political Studies* 43 (7): 886–917.

Smith, William C. 1990. "Democracy, Distributive Conflict and Macroeconomic Policymaking in Argentina, 1983–1989". *Journal of Interamerican Studies and World Affairs* 32 (2): 1–42.

1989. *Authoritarianism and the Crisis of the Argentine Political Economy*. Stanford: Stanford University Press.

Sobhan, Rehman. 1993. *Agrarian Reform and Social Transformation: Precondition for Development*. New Brunswick: Zed Books.

Soifer, Hillel David. 2012. "The Causal Logic of Critical Junctures." *Comparative Political Studies* 45 (12): 1572–1597.

Solís, Leopoldo. 1988. *Intento de la Reforma Económica de México*. Mexico City: El Colegio Nacional.

Souza, Kênia Barreiro de, Débora Freire Cardoso, and Edson Paulo Domingues. 2016. "Medidas recentes de desoneração tributária no Brasil: Uma análise de equilíbrio computável." *Revista Brasileira de Economia* 70 (1): 99–125.

Spenser, Daniela. 2007. *Unidad a Toda Costa: La Tercera Internacional en México durante la Presidencia de Lázaro Cárdenas*. Mexico City: CIESAS.

Spiller, Pablo T. and Mariano Tommasi. 2009. *The Institutional Foundations of Public Policy in Argentina: A Transactions Cost Approach*. New York: Cambridge University Press.

Springborg, Robert. 2013. "The Hound that Did Not Bark: Solving the Mystery of Business without Voice in Egypt." In Steffen Hertog, Giacomo Luciani and Marc Valeri, eds., *Business Politics in the Middle East*. London: Hurst.

Stallings, Barbara. 1978. *Class Conflict and Economic Development in Chile, 1958–1973*. Stanford: Stanford University Press.

Stein, Ernesto. 1999. "Fiscal Decentralization and Government Size in Latin America." *Journal of Applied Economics* 2: 357–391.

Stein, Ernesto and Lorena Caro. 2013. "Ideology and Tax Revenues in Latin America." IDB Working Paper 407. Washington, DC: IDB.

Steinmo, Sven. 1993. *Taxation and Democracy: Swedish, British, and American Approaches to Financing the Modern State*. New Haven: Yale University Press.

Steinmo, Sven and Caroline J. Tolbert. 1998. "Do Institutions Really Matter? Taxation in Industrialized Democracies." *Comparative Political Studies* 31 (2): 165–187.

Stepan, Alfred. 1978. "Political Leadership and Regime Breakdown: Brazil." In Juan J. Linz and Stepan, eds., *The Breakdown of Democratic Regimes: Latin America*. Baltimore: Johns Hopkins University Press.

1971. *The Military in Politics: Changing Patterns in Brazil*. Princeton: Princeton University Press.

Stephens, John D. 1979. *The Transition from Capitalism to Socialism*. Champaign: University of Illinois Press.

Stevens, Mitchell L. 2002. "The Organizational Vitality of Conservative Protestantism." In Michael Lounsbury and Marc J. Ventresca, eds., *Social Structure and Organizations Revisited*. London: Emerald Group Publishing.

Stinchcombe, Arthur L. 1968. *Constructing Social Theories*. Chicago: University of Chicago Press.

1965. "Social Structure and Organizations." In James G. March, ed., *Handbook of Organizations*. Chicago: Rand McNally.

Stokes, Susan C. 2001. *Mandates and Democracy: Neoliberalism by Surprise in Latin America*. New York: Cambridge University Press.

Story, Dale. 1986. *Industry, the State, and Public Policy in Mexico*. Austin: University of Texas Press.

Suárez Dávila, Francisco. 2006. "Desarrollismo y ortodoxia monetaria (1927–1952): El debate entre dos visiones de política financiera mexicana." In María Eugenia Romero Sotelo and Leonor Ludlow, eds., *Temas a Debate Moneda y Banca en México 1884–1954*. Mexico City: UNAM.

Svampa, Maristella and Sebastián Pereyra. 2003. *Entre la Ruta y el Barrio. La Experiencia de las Organizaciones Piqueteros*. Buenos Aires: Editorial Biblos.

Tacuba, Angélica and Luis Augusto Chávez. 2018. "Gestión de Pemex como empresa productiva del estado." *Problemas del Desarrollo* 49 (193): 119–144.

Tai, Hung-Chao. 1974. *Land Reform and Politics: A Comparative Analysis*. Berkeley: University of California.

Tanzi, Vito. 2000. "Taxation in Latin America in the Last Decade." Working Paper No. 76. Stanford: Stanford Center for International Development.

1978. "Inflation, Real Tax Revenue, and the Case for Inflationary Finance: Theory with an Application to Argentina." *IMF Staff Papers* 25 (3): 417–451.

1977. "Inflation, Lags in Collection, and the Real Value of Tax Revenue." *IMF Staff Papers* 24 (1): 154–167.

Teichman, Judith A. 2001. *The Politics of Freeing Markets in Latin America: Chile, Argentina, and Mexico*. Chapel Hill: University of North Carolina Press.

Tejeda Ávila, Roberto. 2005. "Amigos de Fox, breve historia de un 'partido' efímero." *Espiral* 12 (34): 67–92.

Tello, Carlos. 2010. *Estado y Desarrollo Económico: México 1920–2006*. Mexico City: UNAM.

1979. *La Política Económica en México 1970–1976*. México: Siglo Veintiuno.

Tello, Carlos and Domingo Hernández. 2010. "Sobre la Reforma Tributaria en México." *Economía UNAM* 7 (21): 37–56.

Ten Kate, Adriaan and Robert Bruce Wallace. 1980. *Protection and Economic Development in Mexico*. London: Palgrave Macmillan.

Tenenbaum, Barbara A. 1986. *The Politics of Penury: Debt and Taxes in Mexico, 1821–1856*. Albuquerque: University of New Mexico Press.

Thacker, Strom C. 2012. "Big Business, Democracy, and the Politics of Competition." In Roderic A. Camp, ed., *The Oxford Handbook of Mexican Politics*. Oxford: Oxford University Press.

2006. *Big Business, the State, and Free Trade: Constructing Coalitions in Mexico*. New York: Cambridge University Press.

Thiesenhusen, William C. 1995. *Broken Promises: Agrarian Reform and the Latin American Campesino*. Boulder: Westview Press.

Tilly, Charles. 1990. *Coercion, Capital, and European States, A.D. 990–1990*. Oxford: Basil Blackwell.

Tilly, Charles and Robert E. Goodin. 2006. "It Depends." In Tilly and Goodin, eds., *The Oxford Handbook of Contextual Political Analysis*. New York: Oxford University Press.

Timmons, Jeffrey F. 2005. "The Fiscal Contract: States, Taxes, and Public Services." *World Politics* 57 (4): 530–567.

Tirado, Ricardo. 1985. "Los empresarios y la derecha en México." *Revista Mexicana de Sociología* 47 (1): 105–123.

Tirado, Ricardo and Matilde Luna. 1992. "El Consejo Coordinador Empresarial: Una radiografía." *Proyecto Organizaciones Empresariales en México, Cuaderno 1*. Mexico City: UNAM.

1986. "La politización de los empresarios (1970–1982)." In Julio Labastida, ed., *Grupos Económicos y Organizaciones Empresariales en México*. Mexico City: Alianza Editorial Mexicana.

Tombolo, Guilherme and Armando Vaz Sampaio. 2013. "O PIB brasileiro nos séculos XIX e XX: Duzentos anos de flutuações econômicas." *Revista de Economia* 39 (3): 181–216.

Torre, Juan Carlos. 1998. "The Ambivalent Giant: The Peronist Labor Movement, 1945–1995." In James P. Brennan, ed., *Peronism and Argentina*. Wilmington: Scholarly Resources.

1990. *La Vieja Guardia Sindical y Perón: Sobre los Orígenes del Peronismo*. Buenos Aires: Sudamericana.

Torre, Juan Carlos and Liliana de Riz. 1993. "Argentina since 1946." In Leslie Bethell, ed., *Argentina since Independence*. New York: Cambridge University Press.

Torres-Rivas, Edelberto and Carla Aguilar. 1998. "Financiación de partidos y campañas electorales. El caso guatemalteco." In Pilar del Castillo and Daniel Zovatto, eds., *La Financiación de la Política en Iberoamérica*. San José: IIDH-CAPEL

Trevizo, Dolores. 2011. *Rural Protest and the Making of Democracy in Mexico, 1968–2000*. University Park: Pennsylvania State University Press.

Triner, Gail D. 2011. *Mining and the State in Brazilian Development*. London: Pickering & Chatto.

Tullio, Giuseppe and Marcio Ronci. 1996. "Brazilian Inflation from 1980 to 1993: Causes, Consequences and Dynamics." *Journal of Latin American Studies* 28 (3): 635–666.

Unda Gutiérrez, Mónica. 2015. "La reforma tributaria de 2013: Los problemas de la hacienda pública y la desigualdad en México." *Espiral* 22 (64): 69–99.

2010. "The Building of a Poor Tax State: The Political Economy of Income Tax in Mexico, 1925–1964." PhD Thesis, University of London.

Undurraga, Tomás. 2015. "Neoliberalism in Argentina and Chile: Common Antecedents, Divergent Paths." *Revista de Sociologia e Política* 23 (55): 11–34.

UNDP (United Nations Development Program). 2013. "Understanding Social Conflict in Latin America." Working Paper. La Paz: UNDP/Fundación UNIR Bolivia. www .undp.org/content/undp/en/home/librarypage/crisis-prevention-and-recovery/Under standing-Social-Conflict-in-Latin-America.html

2008. *Guatemala: ¿Una Economía al Servicio del Desarrollo Humano? Informe Nacional de Desarrollo Humano 2007/2008.* Guatemala City: UNPD.

UN-Habitat (United Nations-Habitat). 2011. "Affordable Land and Housing in Latin America and the Caribbean." Adequate Housing Series, Volume I. Nairobi: UN-Habitat.

Urzúa, Carlos M. 1993. "Tax Reform and Macroeconomic Policy in Mexico." Documento de Trabajo 10. Mexico City: Centro de Estudios Económicos, El Colegio de México.

Valdés, Alberto and William Foster. 2014. "The Agrarian Reform Experiment in Chile: History, Impact, and Implications." IFPRI Discussion Paper 1368. Washington, DC: International Food Policy Research Institute.

Valdés, Juan Gabriel. 1995. *Pinochet's Economists: The Chicago School of Economics in Chile.* New York: Cambridge University Press.

Valdés Ugalde, Francisco. 1997. *Autonomía y Legitimidad: Los Empresarios, la Política y el Estado en México.* Mexico City: Siglo XXI.

Valdez, J. Fernando and Mayra Palencia. 1998. *Los Dominios del Poder: La Encrucijada Tributaria.* Guatemala City: FLACSO.

Valdivia Ortiz de Zárate, Verónica. 2008. *Nacionales y Gremialistas: El "Parto" de la Nueva Derecha Política Chilena, 1964–1973.* Santiago: LOM Ediciones.

Valenzuela, Arturo. 1978. *The Breakdown of Democratic Regimes: Chile.* Baltimore: Johns Hopkins University Press.

Valenzuela, J. Samuel. 1995. "The Origins and Transformations of the Chilean Party System." Working Paper No. 215. Notre Dame: Kellogg Institute.

Varela, Paula. 2013. "Los sindicatos en la Argentina kirchnerista: Entre la herencia de los ´90 y la emergencia de un nuevo sindicalismo de base." *Archivos de Historia del Movimiento Obrero y la Izquierda* 2 (3): 77–100.

Varsano, Ricardo. 1996. "A evolução do sistema tributário brasileiro ao longo do século: anotações e reflexões para futuras reformas." Working Paper 405. Brasília: IPEA.

1981. "O sistema tributário de 1967: Adequado ao Brasil de 80?" *Pesquisa e Planejamento Econômico* 11 (1): 203–228.

Varsano, Ricardo, Napoleão Luiz Costa da Silva, Elisa de Paula Pessoa, José Roberto Rodrigues Afonso, Erika Amorim Araujo and Julio Cesar Maciel Ramundo. 1998. "Uma análise da carga tributária do Brasil". Texto Para Discussão no. 583. Rio de Janeiro: IPEA.

Vejar, Dasten Julián. 2014. "Tendencias de un sindicalismo fracturado: Sindicalismo autoritario vs. sindicalismo movimientista." In Juan Carlos Celis Ospina, ed., *Reconfiguración de las Relaciones entre Estado, Sindicatos y Partidos en América Latina.* Medellín: CLACSO.

Vergara, Pilar. 1985. *Auge y Caída del Neoliberalismo en Chile.* Santiago: FLACSO.

Vergara, Rodrigo. 2010. "Taxation and Private Investment: Evidence for Chile." *Applied Economics* 42 (6): 717–725.

Vernon, Raymond. 1963. *The Dilemma of Mexico's Development: The Roles of the Private and Public Sectors.* Cambridge: Harvard University Press.

Vigna de Oliveira, Edélcio. 2007. "Bancada Ruralista: O maior grupo de interesse no Congresso Nacional." Brasília: INESC.

Villela, Annibal Villanova and Wilson Suzigan. 1973. *Política do Governo e Crescimento da Economia Brasileira 1889–1945.* Rio de Janeiro: IPEA/INPES.

Wagner, Adolph. (1883). *Finanzwissenschaft.* Third edition. Leipzig: Winter.

Wainberg, Miranda and Michelle Michot Foss. 2007. "Commercial Frameworks for National Oil Companies." Working Paper. Center for Energy Economics, University of Texas. www.beg.utexas.edu/files/energyecon/upstream-attainment /CEE%20National_Oil_Company_Mar%2007.pdf

Waisman, Carlos H. 1987. *Reversal of Development in Argentina: Postwar Counterrevolutionary Policies and their Structural Consequences.* Princeton: Princeton University Press.

Wallich, Christine I. 1981. "Social Security and Savings Mobilization: A Case Study of Chile." Domestic Finance Studies 67. Washington, DC: World Bank.

Waterbury, John. 1983. *The Egypt of Nasser and Sadat: The Political Economy of Two Regimes.* Princeton: Princeton University Press.

Weffort, Francisco C. 1978. *O Populismo na Política Brasileira.* Rio de Janeiro: Paz e Terra.

Weinstein, Barbara. 1996. *For Social Peace in Brazil: Industrialists and the Remaking of the Working Class in São Paulo, 1920–1964.* Chapel Hill: University of North Carolina Press.

Welch, Clifford Andrew. 2016. "Vargas and the Reorganization of Rural Life in Brazil (1930–1945)." *Revista Brasileira de História* 36 (71): 1–25.

Werneck Vianna, Luis. 1976. *Liberalismo e Sindicato no Brasil.* Rio de Janeiro: Paz e Terra.

Weyland, Kurt. 2002. *The Politics of Market Reform in Fragile Democracies: Argentina, Brazil, Peru, and Venezuela.* Princeton: Princeton University Press

1996. *Democracy Without Equity: Failures of Reform in Brazil.* Pittsburgh: University of Pittsburgh Press.

1997. "Growth with Equity in Chile's New Democracy?" *Latin American Research Review* 32 (1): 37–67.

Wickham-Crowley, Timothy P. 1992. *Guerrillas and Revolution in Latin America: A Comparative Study of Insurgents and Regimes since 1956.* Princeton: Princeton University Press.

Wilkie, James. 1967. *The Mexican Revolution: Federal Expenditure and Social Change Since 1910.* Berkeley: University of California Press.

Williams, Philip J. and J. Mark Ruhl. 2013. "Demilitarization After Central American Civil Wars." In Peter Stearns, ed., *Demilitarization in the Contemporary World.* New York: Oxford University Press.

Winn, Peter and Cristobal Kay. 1974. "Agrarian Reform and Rural Revolution in Allende's Chile." *Journal of Latin American Studies* 6 (1): 135–159.

Wolff, Jonas. 2016. "Business Power and the Politics of Postneoliberalism: Relations Between Governments and Economic Elites in Bolivia and Ecuador." *Latin American Politics and Society* 58 (2): 124–147.

Womack, John. 1968. *Zapata and the Mexican Revolution.* New York: Vintage.

World Bank. 2016. "Efectos Distributivos de la Reforma Tributaria de 2014." Washington, DC: World Bank.

2015. "The State of Social Safety Nets 2015."

2005. "Creating Fiscal Space for Poverty Reduction in Ecuador: A Fiscal Management and Public Expenditure Review."

1990. "Argentina: Tax Policy for Stabilization and Economic Recovery."

1986. "Arab Republic of Egypt: Current Economic Situation and Economic Reform Program."

1984. "Ecuador: An Agenda for Recovery and Sustained Growth."

1970. "Current Economic Position and Prospects of Chile."

1966. "Current Economic Position and Progress of Brazil: Volume 1."

1964. "An Appraisal of the Development Program of Mexico: Volume 1."

1962. "Current Economic Position and Prospects of Mexico."

1961. "Current Economic Position and Prospects of Chile."

1956. "Mexico: Current Economic Position and Prospects."

Wuhs, Steven T. 2014. "Mexico: The Partido Acción Nacional as a Right Party." In Juan Pablo Luna and Cristóbal Rovira Kaltwasser, eds., *The Resilience of the Latin American Right*. Baltimore: Johns Hopkins University Press.

2010. "From the Boardroom to the Chamber: Business Interests and Party Politics in Mexico." *Journal of Politics in Latin America* 21 (1): 107–130.

Yashar, Deborah. 1997. *Demanding Democracy: Reform and Reaction in Costa Rica and Guatemala, 1870s–1950s*. Stanford: Stanford University Press.

Zapata, Francisco. 1992. "Transición democrática y sindicalismo en Chile." *Foro Internacional* 32 (5): 703–721.

Zelaznik, Javier. 2014. "El comportamiento legislativo del peronismo durante el menemismo y el kirchnerismo: Cambio de agenda y adaptación partidaria." *Desarrollo Económico* 54 (213): 203–230.

2011. "Las coaliciones kirchneristas." In Andrés Malamud and Miguel De Luca, eds., *La Política en Tiempos de los Kirchner*. Buenos Aires: Eudeba.

Zepeda Martínez, Roberto. 2009. "Disminución de la tasa de trabajadores sindicalizados en México durante el periodo neoliberal." *Revista Mexicana de Ciencias Políticas y Sociales* 51 (207): 57–81.

Zhai, Qiang. 2000. *China and the Vietnam Wars, 1950–1975*. Chapel Hill: University of North Carolina Press.

Index

Abad, Alberto, 220
Ação Empresarial, 188
ACIEL. *See* Asociación Coordinadora de
    Instituciones Empresarias Libres
actor-centric theories, 11–13, 37–39
Administración Federal de Ingresos Públicos
    (AFIP), 222
agricultural dependence, 28–29
agricultural sector, 54, 71, 158–159, 180–181,
    203–204, 226–227
Alemán, Miguel, 110, 116–118, 121, 122
Alencar, José, 182–184
Alessandri, Jorge, 71–72, 74–75
Alfonsín, Raul, 205, 210, 213, 230–231
Algeria, 249–250, 253–254
Aliança Renovadora Nacional (ARENA), 171
Alianza Patria Altiva y Soberana (Alianza
    PAIS), 243–245
Allende, Salvador, 16, 53, 63–64, 86, 150
    backlash against, 97, 99
    business leaders and, 101
    Cárdenas, L., and, 55–56
    electoral victory of, 74–75, 105
    Goulart and, 169
    land reform and, 76
    Marxism and, 61
    mobilization against, 61, 77–78
    overthrow of, 66–67, 81, 99
    reforms pursued by, 55, 56, 57, 75–76
    sabotage against, 77
    transformations implemented by, 68
alliance for profits, 107–108, 117
Alliance for Progress, 246–247
Almazán, Juan Andreu, 115, 116
amparo fiscal, 143, 237

anti-statism, 15–16, 58, 60, 79, 132–133
    activism of, 131–132
    Alemán and, 122
    backlash against, 108
    Chile and, 48, 86–93
    coalitions of, 16
    economic elites and, 18, 38
    emergence of, 26–27, 56, 64–65
    influence of, 57, 59–60, 93–94
    institutions capable of sustaining, 66
    Mexico and, 48, 106–107
    neoliberalism and, 135–138
    path dependence and, 96–104, 105
    power of, 46
    power structure in favor of, 240
    private sector and, 206
    public sector expansion and, 147
    relative influence of, 27
    statism balance of power with, 44
    strength of, 48, 57–59, 62, 67
    tax policy and, 93–96
    taxation and, 39
    threats to property rights and, 52–59,
        72–79
    upsurges in, 41, 62
    weakness of, 72, 176–182, 190, 226
Árbenz, Jacobo, 240–241, 242, 247–248
ARENA. *See* Aliança Renovadora Nacional
Arenas, Alberto, 95
Arévalo, Juan José, 240–241
Argentina, 2, 4, 16–18, 60
    agricultural sector of, 226–227
    anti-statism and, 48
    business associations in, 39–40, 202–203,
        211–212, 226–227

Argentina (cont.)
  centralization and, 6
  democracy and, 31–33
  direct taxes in, 7
  distribution of seats in Congress of, 221
  economic liberalization and, 28, 62–63,
    210–211
  exports from, 193–194
  indigenous population of, 54
  inflation and, 29, 200–201
  ISI and, 202
  labor movement in, 41, 42–43, 195–196,
    201–202
  liberal interest groups in, 62
  middle class in, 202–203
  redistribution and, 26–27
  state oil company of, 60
  statism and, 47
  tax burden in, 4–5, 18–19, 22–23, 47, 65,
    191, 192, 194, 198–199, 201, 215–217,
    232–233
  VAT and, 200
  weak threats to property rights and,
    60–64
Argentine Industrial Union. *See* Unión
  Industrial Argentina
Argentine Agricultural Federation. *See*
  Federación Agraria Argentina
Argentine Chamber of Commerce and Services.
  See Cámara Argentina de Comercio y
  Servicios
Argentine Chamber of Construction. *See*
  Cámara Argentina de la Construcción
Argentine Industrial Movement. *See*
  Movimiento Industrial Argentino
Argentine Rural Society. *See* Sociedad Rural
  Argentina
Argentine Workers' Central. *See* Central de
  Trabajadores de la Argentina
Asociación Coordinadora de Instituciones
  Empresarias Libres (ACIEL), 202, 203
austerity, 83, 93, 123, 210–211
authoritarian enclaves, 11, 36, 37, 45, 87,
  97, 98
authoritarianism, 33, 36, 37, 98–99, 206–207,
  253–254, 258–259
Autonomous Technical Institute of Mexico. *See*
  Instituto Tecnológico Autónomo
  de México
Ávila Camacho, Manuel, 110, 116, 118–119,
  120, 121
Aylwin, Patricio, 84–85, 103

Bachelet, Michelle, 85, 90–91, 92–93
backlash, 256
  against Allende, 83–84, 97, 99
  of anti-statism, 108
  against Cárdenas, L., 147
  against neoliberalism, 217–221
  against property reform, 3, 234
  balance of power perspective, 15, 37–44, 48,
    62, 63–64
  cross-case variance and, 39–44
  policy outcomes and, 39–44
bancada ruralista, 180–181
Banco de México, 127–128
Banco Nacional de Desenvolvimento
  Econômico (BNDE), 155, 156
Banco Nacional de Desenvolvimento
  Econômico e Social (BNDES), 175,
  177–178
Beteta, Ramón, 117, 121
Beveridge Report, 163–164
BNDE. *See* Banco Nacional de
  Desenvolvimento Econômico
BNDES. *See* Banco Nacional de
  Desenvolvimento Econômico e Social
Bolivia, 1, 243, 245
Bolsa Família, 177–178
Bolsonaro, Jair, 176, 179
Brazil, 2, 4, 16–18, 63–64, 262–263
  business associations in, 39–40, 159,
    161–163, 169–171, 177–178
  current constitution of, 10–11, 36, 47,
    131–132, 149–150, 173, 184–187,
    189–190
  custo Brasil and, 149
  democracy and, 34
  direct taxes in, 7
  economic elites in, 150, 163–164,
    170–171
  economic informality and, 27–28
  economic liberalization and, 28, 181–182
  inflation and, 29, 154–155, 173
  labor movement in, 41, 42–43, 182
  land reform in, 60–61, 167, 180–181
  pension systems in, 4–5, 36, 173–174,
    184–185, 186–188
  redistribution and, 26–27
  relative political stability in, 151–152
  social reformism in, 61
  state economic activity in, 130
  state-led development in, 150, 153–154, 165,
    171–172
  subnational governments of, 35, 153

tax burden in, 3–4, 18–19, 22–23, 36, 65, 149–150, 151–152, 154–155, 163–164, 189–190
tax system decentralization and, 6
US and, 159–160
weak threats to property rights and, 60–64
weakness of anti-statism in, 40–41, 48, 169–172, 176–181
Brazilian Communist Party. *See* Partido Comunista Brasileiro
Brazilian Institute for Democratic Action. *See* Instituto Brasileiro de Ação Democrática
Brazilian Labor Party. *See* Partido Trabalhista Brasileiro
Brazilian military, 169
Brazilian Petroleum. *See* Petróleo Brasileiro
Brazilian Rural Society. *See* Sociedade Rural Brasileira
Brennan, Geoffrey, 34–35
brick, the (economic plan), 78, 81
Buchanan, James M., 34–35
Business Action. *See* Ação Empresarial
business associations, 39–40, 41
in Argentina, 202, 203, 226, 227–230
in Brazil, 161–163, 169–171, 188
in Chile, 57, 72, 76–77, 90–91
in Ecuador, 245–246
in Egypt, 254–255
in Guatemala, 238–239
in Mexico, 119, 128, 130–132, 136, 138–141
peak, 68.210, 71.150, 72.190, 101.50, 124.80, 235.210, 270.31, 296.90, 238
political parties and, 37–38, 41, 91, 136–137, 162
business leaders, 80–81, 101, 114–115
business mobilization, 74, 126–129
business organization, 17, 38, 44, 90, 159, 161–163, 170, 238. *See also* business associations

CAC. *See* Cámara Argentina de Comercio
CACIF. *See* Comité Coordinador de Asociaciones Agrícolas, Comerciales, Industriales y Financieras
Calderón, Felipe, 135, 138, 145–146
Calles, Plutarco Elías, 55, 112
Cámara Argentina de Comercio y Servicios (CAC), 227
Cámara Argentina de la Construcción (CAMARCO), 229

Cámara Nacional de la Industria de Transformación (CANACINTRA), 118–119, 128, 140
CAMARCO. *See* Cámara Argentina de la Construcción
Cambiemos, 216–217, 232
Cambodia, 252
CANACINTRA. *See* Cámara Nacional de la Industria de Transformación
capital, 254
controls, 29
flight, 9–10, 19, 29, 129
human, 261
national, 201–202
taxation of, 128–129
capitalism, 19, 57, 68, 105, 165, 252–253
attacks on, 96, 240–241
Capoccia, Giovanni, 50–51
Cárdenas, Cuauhtémoc, 138
Cárdenas, Lázaro, 16–17, 53, 55–56, 63–64
educational policies of, 56–57
labor militancy and, 113
land reform by, 113
major reforms implemented by, 112–113
Marxism and, 61, 114
Mexican Communist Party and, 156–157
mobilization against, 56–57, 61, 114–115, 147–148
Monterrey Group and, 56–57, 114–115, 119–120
PRI and, 123
private sector mistrust of state and, 163
property right threats and, 151
relationship to popular sectors, 156
tax exemptions and, 121
union leaders support of, 58–59
cardenismo, 116, 119, 126, 132, 155, 161
Cardoso, Fernando Henrique, 173, 180–181, 186–187
Carrillo Flores, Antonio, 117
case selection, 22–23
Castro, Fidel, 258–259
Castro, Sergio de, 82, 97
Catholic Church, 16, 61, 92–93, 198, 207, 241–242, 252–253
PAN and, 136
Perón and, 207
Vargas and, 159
Catholic University of Chile, 74, 78
Cavallo, Domingo, 210–211
CCE. *See* Consejo Coordinador Empresarial
CCTs. *See* conditional cash transfers

Center for Public Studies. *See* Centro de
Estudios Públicos
Central de Trabajadores de la Argentina (CTA),
211, 219
Central Intelligence Agency (CIA), 55, 75
Central Única dos Trabalhadores (CUT), 42,
182, 185
heavy taxation and, 189
strife within, 187
Central Unitaria de Trabajadores de Chile
(CUT), 42–43, 68
Centrão, 186
Centro de Estudios Públicos (CEP), 91–92
CGE. *See* Confederación General Económica
CGT. *See* Confederación General del Trabajo
Chamber of Deputies elections, Chile, 100
charros, 58–59, 116–117
Chicago Boys, 78–79, 81–82, 83, 99, 102
Chile, 2, 4–5, 16–18, 252, 257
anti-statism and, 48, 86–93
authoritarianism and, 37
business associations, 39–40, 90, 101–102
Chamber of Deputies elections, 100
Congress, distribution of seats in, 88
copper nationalization, 51–52, 73, 76
copper revenues, 30–31, 66, 69, 79–80, 86
designated senators, 37, 45, 87–89, 97, 98, 99
direct taxes in, 7
economic growth of, 93–94
economic liberalization, 28, 67–68, 79
Guatemala and, 238–239
labor movement in, 41, 42–43, 57
land reform in, 73, 76
light taxation in, 105
military coups in Brazil and, 164–165
military regime of, 79, 82
neoliberalism and, 66–68, 81
private sector of, 90
public sector growth in, 234
re-democratization of, 31–33, 84–85
redistribution and, 26–27
relative political stability in, 151–152
state-led development model of, 71
student-led protests in, 45
tax burden in, 4–5, 18–19, 22–23, 69
think tanks in, 91–92
threats to property rights and, 52–60, 64
wealth of, 66
China, 30–31, 249, 252
Christian Democratic Party. *See* Partido
Demócrata Cristiano
Christian Democrats, 73

CIA. *See* Central Intelligence Agency
civil society, 47, 92, 167
clientelism, 100–101, 119–120, 179,
219–220, 240
CMHN. *See* Consejo Mexicano de Hombres de
Negocio
CMN. *See* Consejo Mexicano de Negocios
CNC. *See* Confederación Nacional Campesina
CNI. *See* Confederação Nacional da Industria
COFINS. *See* Contribuição para o
Financiamento da Seguridade Social
collective bargaining, 105, 218
Collier, David, 52, 197
Collier, Ruth Berins, 52, 197
Collor, Fernando, 173, 179
Colombia, 6
Comité Coordinador de Asociaciones
Agrícolas, Comerciales, Industriales
y Financieras (CACIF), 238, 242
commodity boom, 215, 216, 217, 218–219,
261–262
communism, 101, 156, 159–160
Communist Party of Chile. *See* Partido
Comunista de Chile
CONAIE. *See* Confederación de las
Nacionalidades Indígenas del Ecuador
CONCAMIN. *See* Confederación de Cámaras
Industriales de los Estados Unidos
Mexicanos
CONCANACO. *See* Confederación de
Cámaras Nacionales de Comercio,
Servicios y Turismo
Concertación, 36, 44–45, 84, 86, 87–89, 90–91
1989 electoral victory of, 103
composition of, 43
labor reform under, 103–104
lack of legislative control, 87
leaders of, 92
seats of Congress controlled by, 98
tax reform and, 121
taxation and, 45
conditional cash transfers (CCTs), 144,
177–178, 261
Confederãçao Nacional da Industria (CNI),
158, 170
Confederación de Cámaras Industriales de los
Estados Unidos Mexicanos
(CONCAMIN), 117–118, 127–128, 130
Confederación de Cámaras Nacionales de
Comercio, Servicios y Turismo
(CONCANACO), 40, 56–58,
117–118, 121

Confederación de la Producción y del Comercio
(CPC), 39, 56, 57, 62, 72, 73–74, 90
rise of, 101–102
secondary role of, 130
support for Pinochet, 102
Confederación de las Nacionalidades Indígenas
del Ecuador (CONAIE), 244–245
Confederación de Trabajadores de México
(CTM), 42–43, 113–114, 137, 141
Confederación General del Trabajo (CGT), 42,
196, 211, 225
Confederación General Económica (CGE), 202,
203, 211–212
Confederación Nacional Campesina (CNC),
113–114
Confederación Patronal de la República
Mexicana (COPARMEX), 39, 114–115,
130–132, 138–140, 146, 147–148
creation of, 56–57, 114–115
ideology, 58, 130–131
membership, 130
Monterrey Group and, 56–57, 114–115,
130–131
PAN and, 41
Confederación Regional Obrera Mexicana
(CROM), 112
Confederation of Indigenous Nationalities of
Ecuador. *See* Confederación de las
Nacionalidades Indígenas del Ecuador
Confederation of Industrial Chambers of the
United States of Mexico. *See*
Confederación de Cámaras Industriales
de los Estados Unidos Mexicanos
Confederation of Mexican Workers. *See*
Confederación de Trabajadores de
Mexico
Confederation of National Chambers of
Commerce, Services and Tourism. *See*
Confederación de Cámaras Nacionales
de Comercio, Servicios y Turismo
Confederation of Production and Commerce.
See Confederación de la Producción y del
Comercio
Consejo Coordinador Empresarial (CCE), 39,
62, 128, 130, 131, 138–140, 145–146
Consejo Mexicano de Hombres de Negocio
(CMHN), 126–127, 128, 130, 138–140
Consejo Mexicano de Negocios (CMN), 39,
57–58, 126–127, 138–140
constitutional design features, 14
constitutional reform, 98–99, 186–187
consumption taxation, 120, 145

contingency, 50, 51–52, 55, 105, 106–107,
147, 255
Contribuição para o Financiamento da
Seguridade Social (COFINS), 174
Contribuição Provisória sobre Movimentação
Financeira (CPMF), 174, 222–223
Contribuição Social sobre o Lucro Líquido
(CSLL), 174
Contribution for the Financing of Social
Security *See* Contribuição para o
Financiamento da Seguridade Social
Convertibility Plan, 208–209, 210–211,
214, 215
Coordinating Business Council. *See* Consejo
Coordinador Empresarial
Coordinating Committee of Agricultural,
Commercial, Industrial and Financial
Associations. *See* Comité Coordinador
de Asociaciones Agrícolas, Comerciales,
Industriales y Financieras
Coordinating Council of Business. *See* Consejo
Coordinador Empresarial
COPARMEX. *See* Confederación Patronal de
la República Mexicana
copper industry, 53, 54–55, 69
Corporación de Fomento de la Producción
(CORFO), 70, 71
corporate income tax, 80, 85, 109, 145, 200
Corporation for Production Promotion. *See*
Corporación de Fomento de la
Producción
Correa, Rafael, 243–246
corruption, 142–143, 176–177, 190
Corruption Perceptions Index, 142–143
Council of Public Relations of the Pro-Mexico
Private Sector, 126–127
countermobilization, 56, 73, 105, 106–107,
114–115, 169–172
CPC. *See* Confederación de la Producción y del
Comercio
CPMF. *See* Contribuição Provisória sobre
Movimentação Financeira
Cristero rebellion, 115
critical junctures, 49–53
CROM. *See* Confederación Regional Obrera
Mexicana
CSLL. *See* Contribuição Social sobre o Lucro
Líquido
CTA. *See* Central de Trabajadores de la
Argentina
CTM. *See* Confederación de Trabajadores de
México

Cuba, 101, 123, 126, 252, 258–259
custo Brasil, 149, 178, 188
CUT. *See* Central Única dos Trabalhadores;
    Central Unitaria de Trabajadores de
    Chile

data sources, 23–24
de la Madrid, Miguel, 133–134
de la Rúa, Fernando, 211–213, 214, 217,
    218, 223
debt crisis, 133, 134
deindustrialization, 181–182, 203–204, 211
democracy, 9–10, 63, 75, 172–173, 178, 257
    Argentina and, 31–33
    Brazil and, 34
    income inequality and, 33–34
    indices of, 33
    light taxation and, 84, 132–133
    Mexico and, 33, 138
    role of, 230–232
    taxation and, 10, 27, 31, 84
    transitions to, 31–33, 34–35, 96, 97–98, 173,
        181–182, 236–237
Democratic Rural Union. *See* União
    Democrática Ruralista
Democratic Social Party. *See* Partido
    Democrático Social
democratization, 16–17, 46–47, 57–58, 67, 83,
    84, 105, 239
    of Mexico, 147–148
    re-democratization, 42–43, 84–85
    tax burden growth and, 173–176
    taxation and, 34–35, 66–67, 84, 133, 150
Departamento Inter-Sindical de Estatística
    e Estudos Socioeconômicos (DIEESE),
    182, 189
dependent variable, 21–22
developmentalism, 117, 163
developmentalist economic policies, 171–172,
    178–179, 246–247
Díaz, Porfírio, 108–109, 112, 114–115
Díaz Ordaz, Gustavo, 124, 128
DIEESE. *See* Departamento Inter-Sindical de
    Estatística e Estudos Socioeconômicos
direct taxes, 7, 12, 18, 38, 110, 135, 145,
    163–164, 215–216, 259–260
domestic consumption, 58, 201–202, 218
Dominican Republic, 1
Duhalde, Eduardo, 215, 217–218, 222,
    224–225
Duran Ballén, Sixto, 246
Dutra, Eurico, 154, 159–160

Echeverría, Luis, 45–46, 122, 129, 140
    business representatives and, 128–129
    business–state conflict under, 128
    López Mateos and, 124
    mobilizations against, 130
    political crises and, 123
    tax reform and, 124–125
ECLAC. *See* United Nations Economic
    Commission for Latin America and the
    Caribbean
Economic Charter of Teresópolis, 159,
    163–164
economic crisis, 154–155, 177, 209
economic development, 2, 13–14, 117, 120
economic elites, 12, 15, 37–38, 68, 161,
    247–248
    anti-statism and, 14, 18, 19, 38, 65
    in Argentina, 207, 230, 233
    in Brazil, 150, 163–164, 170–171
    in Chile, 67, 68–69
    Correa and, 245–246
    divided, 205
    fiscal contract and, 19
    fragmentation of, 39–40, 47, 72, 162, 178,
        188–189, 192, 243–248
    liquidation of, 248–250
    in Mexico, 106–107, 108
    in Middle East, 252–253
    redistribution and, 232–233
    social conservatism and, 158–161
economic informality, 27–28, 211
economic liberalization, 28, 62–63, 81,
    181–182
    cost of, 81
    of oil sector, 145
    private sector and, 177
    support for, 177
    tax burden and, 132
    of trade, 104, 133, 137–138, 212–213
    turn to, 82
economic planning, 155, 159
Ecuador, 235–236, 243–248
Egypt, 249–250, 253–255
Egyptian Businessmen's Association, 254–255
Egyptian-American Chamber of Commerce,
    254–255
ejidos, 113
El Salvador, 235
electoral system design, 13–14
Employers' Confederation of the Mexican
    Republic. *See* Confederación Patronal de
    la República Mexicana

equity-enhancing change, 256–263
Estado Novo, 153–154, 156–157, 159–160
   end of, 159
   income tax revenues and, 163–164
excise taxes, 124–125, 126, 133–134
export taxation, 153, 215–216, 222
expropriation of private property, 48, 53,
   64–65, 248–250

FAA. *See* Federación Agrária Argentina
Fairfield, Tasha, 12, 26, 38–39
Farouk (King), 254
Febres Cordero, León, 245, 246
Federação das Indústrias do Estado de São
   Paulo (FIESP), 39–40, 158,
   163, 170
Federación Agraria Argentina (FAA),
   226–227, 230
Federal Administration for Public Revenue. *See*
   Administración Federal de Ingresos
   Públicos
federalism, 10, 34–35
Fernández de Kirchner, Cristina, 47, 212–213,
   215, 217, 218–224, 230–232
FIEL. *See* Fundación de Investigaciones
   Económicas Latinoamericanas
FIESP. *See* Federação das Indústrias do Estado
   de São Paulo
First National Convention of Taxpayers,
   121
first-past-the-post (FPTP), 10, 22–23
fiscal centralization, 3–4, 23
fiscal deficit, 133–134, 199, 231–232
Fiscal Pact, 237
fiscal revenue, 30, 106, 135
fiscal systems, 1–2, 259–260
Flores-Macías, Gustavo A., 12
foreign aid, 1–2, 236
Forum for Business Convergence
   (Argentina), 228
Foundation for Latin American Economic
   Research. *See* Fundación de
   Investigaciones Económicas
   Latinoamericanas
Fox, Vicente, 134, 135, 140–141, 144–145
FPTP. *See* first-past-the-post
FPV. *See* Frente para la Victoria
France, 254
Franco, Itamar, 173
Free Officers (Egypt), 254
Freedom and Development, 91–92
Freedom House, 22–23, 33

Frei Montalva, Eduardo, 54–55, 66–67, 68, 70,
   73, 74
   land reform and, 76
   social security tax revenues and, 82–83
Frente Nacional del Área Privada (FRENAP),
   76–77
Frente Nacionalista Patria y Libertad, 77
Frente para la Victoria (FPV), 215,
   219–220, 229
Frente Republicano Guatemalteco (FRG), 237
FRG. *See* Frente Republicano Guatemalteco
Friends of Fox, 140–141
Frondizi, Arturo, 199, 203
Front for Victory. *See* Frente para la Victoria
Fundación de Investigaciones Económicas
   Latinoamericanas (FIEL), 226–227
Fundación Libertad (Liberty Foundation),
   226–227

GDP. *See* gross domestic product
General Confederation of Labor. *See*
   Confederación General del Trabajo
General Economic Confederation. *See*
   Confederación General Económica
Gerdau, Jorge, 188
Germany, 249
Goodin, Robert E., 255
Gordillo, Elba Esther, 141
Goulart, João, 74, 150, 154–155, 164–165,
   166–167, 172
   Allende and, 169
   attempts to veto assumption of power, 169
   ideology and program, 168
   impact of, 74–75, 169
   mobilization against, 170
   political weakness, 168
   popular mobilization and, 167
   reform failures, 167–168
Graham, Douglas H., 130, 171
Gramsci, Antonio, 38–39
Great Britain, 22–23, 254
Great Depression, 63–64
Green Environmentalist Party of Mexico. *See*
   Partido Verde Ecologista de México
gremialismo (Movimiento Gremial), 74, 77–78
gremialistas, 78, 81–82, 99, 100–101
gross domestic product (GDP), 1, 4, 23–24,
   151–152, 193–194, 244
Guatemala, 1–2, 235–242, 243, 252, 257
Guatemalan National Revolutionary Union.
   See Unidad Revolucionaria Nacional
   Guatemalteca

Guatemalan Republican Front. *See* Frente
    Republicano Guatemalteco
Guevara, Che, 258–259
Guisa y Azevedo, Jesús, 131
Guzmán, Jaime, 74, 77–78, 81–82, 97–98

Haiti, 1–2
human capital, 261
hyperinflation, 47, 186–187, 207–208,
    209–213, 230

IBAD. *See* Instituto Brasileiro de Ação
    Democrática
ICMS. *See* Imposto sobre Circulação de
    Mercadorias e Prestação de Serviços
IDB. *See* Inter-American Development Bank
IEDI. *See* Instituto de Estudos para
    o Desenvolvimento Industrial
IMF. *See* International Monetary Fund
import-substitution industrialization (ISI),
    70–71, 104, 108, 111, 118
    abandonment of, 122
    Argentina and, 202
    politically influential firms under, 212
Imposto sobre Circulação de Mercadorias
    e Prestação de Serviços (ICMS), 174
Imposto sobre Vendas e Consignações (IVC),
    153, 154
Impuesto sobre Ingresos Mercantiles (ISIM),
    110–111, 121, 124–125
Impuesto sobre los Ingresos Brutos, 216, 224
income inequality, 23, 33–34, 96–97, 251, 261
income taxes, 6, 7, 124–125, 237. *See also*
    corporate income tax; personal
    income tax
    declining role of, 200–201
    Estado Novo and, 163–164
    increase in, 135, 166
    kirchnerismo and, 223
    minimum, 145–146
    reform of, 83, 124, 128–129
    revenues from, 153, 154
    schedular, 121
    universal, 127–128
increasing returns, 49
Independent Democratic Union. *See* Unión
    Demócrata Independiente
India, 249
indigenous population, 54
indirect taxes, 6–7, 124–125, 153
Industrial Federation of the State of São Paulo.
    See Federação das Indústrias do Estado
    de São Paulo

Industriales, 226, 230
industrialization, 46–47, 71, 153–154
    deindustrialization, 181–182, 203–204,
        211
    inducing, 197
    limited process of, 251
    promotion of, 155, 205
inequality, 217, 236–237, 251, 256, 260–261
    centrality of, 256–257
    effects of, 251
    income, 23, 33–34, 96–97, 261
    reinforcing, 259
infinite regress, 51
inflation, 23, 28, 29, 194, 213, 223. *See also*
    hyperinflation; Olivera–Tanzi effect
    attenuated, 199–200
    economic crisis characterized by, 154–155
    fighting, 208
    minimum wage and, 187–188
    rate of, 200–201
    surges in, 191, 217
    tax burden and, 9–10, 29, 200–201
Institute for Economic and Social Research.
    See Instituto de Pesquisa Econômica
    e Social
Institute of Industrial Development Studies. *See*
    Instituto de Estudos para
    o Desenvolvimento Industrial
Institutional Revolutionary Party. *See* Partido
    Revolucionario Institucional
institutional theories, 10–11
Instituto Brasileiro de Ação Democrática
    (IBAD), 169–170
Instituto de Estudos para o Desenvolvimento
    Industrial (IEDI), 177
Instituto de Pesquisa Econômica e Social (IPES),
    169–170
Instituto Millenium (Millennium Institute),
    179–180
Instituto Tecnológico Autónomo de México
    (ITAM), 141, 180
Instituto Tecnológico y de Estudios Superiores
    de Monterrey, 141, 180
integralismo, 159
Inter-American Development Bank (IDB),
    23–24
interest rates, 194
International Monetary Fund (IMF), 21, 23–24,
    95–96, 208, 216–217
Inter-Union Department of Statistics and
    Socioeconomic Studies. *See*
    Departamento Inter-Sindical de
    Estatística e Estudos Socioeconômicos

IPES. *See* Instituto de Pesquisa Econômica e Social
Iraq, 249–250, 253–254
ISI. *See* import-substitution industrialization
Israel, 254
ITAM. *See* Instituto Tecnológico Autónomo de México ISIM. *See* Impuesto sobre Ingresos Mercantiles
IVC. *See* Imposto sobre Vendas e Consignações

Jaime Guzmán Foundation, 91–92
July Revolution, 246–247

Kaldor, Nicolas, 123–124, 127
Kelemen, R. Daniel, 51
Keohane, Robert O., 20
King, Gary, 20
Kirchner, Néstor, 47, 212–213, 215, 217, 218–224, 230–232
kirchnerismo, 215, 219–220, 222, 223, 224–226, 231, 232
Kubitschek, Juscelino, 154–155, 166–167, 169, 171–172
Kurtz, Marcus J., 35–36

labor codes, 63, 102–103, 104, 137–138
labor movement, 41, 42–43, 44, 182, 242. *See also* labor unions
  in Argentina, 42, 62–63, 191–192, 197–198, 211
  in Brazil, 42, 46–47, 191–192, 184
  in Chile, 42, 57, 70, 92, 102–104
  in Guatemala, 242
  ideology, 42–43
  in Mexico, 42–43, 57–58, 116–120, 137
  statism and, 18
  ties to parties, 46–47, 70–71, 94, 119–120, 137–138, 182, 197–198
  weakness of, 97, 102, 103, 137–138, 141
labor unions, 11, 39, 190. *See also* labor movement
  in Ecuador, 235–236
  force of, 104
  hindered revival of, 67
  ideology of, 62–63
  membership density, 42, 92, 102, 137–138, 182, 211, 225, 239, 244
  military rule and, 102
  repression of, 62
Lacerda, Carlos, 159–160
Lagos, Ricardo, 85

land inequality, 251
land reform, 16–17, 53, 54–55, 60–61, 71, 76, 254
  in Brazil, 60–61, 157, 167, 180–181
  in Chile, 54–55, 73–74, 76
  failure to fulfill expectations, 262
  in Guatemala, 240–241
  lack of in Argentina, 60–61
  market-assisted, 262
  in Mexico, 54–55, 112, 113
  in Middle East and North Africa, 249–250
  in urban areas, 262–263
landholding structures, 54
Laos, 252
liberalism, 78, 90, 99, 171–172, 178, 214, 230, 233
Libertad y Desarrollo, 91–92
Liberty Foundation. *See* Fundación Libertad
Libya, 249–250, 253–254
Lieberman, Evan S., 12
Lodi, Euvaldo, 158, 159
López Mateos, Adolfo, 45–46, 122, 126–127, 129
  COPARMEX and, 131
  Echeverría and, 124
  political crises and, 123
  reaction to dissent, 123
  tax reform and, 123–124
López Obrador, Andrés Manuel, 46, 135, 138, 140–141, 142, 179
López Portillo, José, 120, 122, 123, 125–126, 133, 140
  banks nationalized by, 136
  private sector and, 129
  VAT and, 126, 134
Lula (Luiz Inácio Lula da Silva), 175, 182–184, 186–187

Machinea, José Luis, 214
Macri, Mauricio, 47, 215, 216, 226, 231–232
macroeconomic instability, 199–205
Mahoney, James, 51, 58
Malvinas/Falkland Islands War with Great Britain, 22–23
Marxism, 15, 53, 56, 64–65, 247–248, 256
  Cárdenas, L., and, 61, 114
  UP and, 168
Massachusetts Institute of Technology, 95–96
Meltzer, Allan H., 33–34
MENA. *See* Middle East and North Africa
Menem, Carlos, 47, 63, 208, 209–210, 211, 212–213

Menem, Carlos (cont.)
Convertibility Plan and, 208, 210–211
hyperinflation and, 213
Kirchner, N., and, 218
legacy of, 217
structural reforms, 207–208
Mercantile Revenue Tax. *See* Impuesto sobre
Ingresos Mercantiles
El Mercurio (newspaper), 77, 78
Mexican Business Council. *See* Consejo
Mexicano de Negocios
Mexican Communist Party, 114, 156–157
Mexican Council of Businessmen. *See* Consejo
Mexicano de Hombres de Negocio
Mexican Petroleum. *See* Petróleos Mexicanos
Mexican Regional Labor Confederation. *See*
Confederación Regional Obrera
Mexicana
Mexican Revolution, 111–112
Mexico, 2, 16–18, 252–253
amparo fiscal in, 143, 237
anti-statism and, 48, 106–107
business associations in, 39, 40, 126, 128,
130–132, 138–141
corruption and, 142–143
Cuba and, 126
debt crisis in, 133
democracy and, 33, 138
democratization of, 147–148
direct taxes in, 7, 110
distribution of seats in Congress of, 139
especially light taxation in, 2–3
fiscal conservatism in, 130
Guatemala and, 238–239
labor movement in, 41, 42–43
labor weakness in, 141
land reform in, 54–55, 113
oil nationalization and, 113, 115
oil revenues and, 14, 29–31, 46, 106,
132–133, 146–147
pink tide and, 142
post-1940 conservatism, 107–108
post-revolution reforms in, 111–115
private sector of, 40
property reform in, 60
public sector growth in, 234
redistribution and, 26–27
right turn in, 116–120
socialism and, 111–112
tax burden in, 4–5, 14, 18–19, 22–23, 106,
109, 146–147, 151
tax system centralization, 6, 109–110, 126

threats to property right and, 52–60, 64
VAT and, 29
MIA. *See* Movimiento Industrial Argentino
Middle East and North Africa (MENA),
249–250, 252–254, 255
middle class, 176–177, 185, 202–203, 259
Miguens, Luciano, 229
military coups, 150, 153–154, 164–165, 197
military intervention, 198–199, 204, 231
military regimes, 47, 57, 167–168,
170–171
in Brazil, 165–166, 170–172
in Chile, 79, 82
management of economy by, 166
policies of, 68
taxation and, 165–166
UDI and, 99
military rule, 31–33, 46–47, 164–165, 178
income inequality under, 96–97
labor unions and, 102
repression under, 62
tax reductions and, 68, 79–84
taxation under, 67–68, 236–237
transformation of economic model under, 96
Millennium Institute (Instituto Millenium),
179–180
MIN. *See* Movimiento de Industria Nacional
minimum wage, 75–76, 156, 187–188, 218
Montero, Alfred P., 178–179
Monterrey Group, 40, 57–58, 115, 117–118,
119, 132, 147–148
COPARMEX and, 130–131
ideology of, 132
intellectuals associated with, 131
opposition to Cárdenas, 114–115
Montúfar, César, 245–246
MORENA. *See* Movimiento Regeneración
Nacional
Movement for National Unity. *See* Movimiento
de Unidad Nacional
Movement of Landless Rural Workers. *See*
Movimento dos Trabalhadores Rurais
Sem Terra
Movimento dos Trabalhadores Rurais Sem
Terra (MST), 180–181
Movimiento Industrial Nacional (MIN),
211–212, 226
Movimiento Regeneración Nacional
(MORENA), 44, 46, 135, 142
Movimiento de Unidad Nacional (MUN), 99
Movimiento Gremial (*gremialismo*), 74,
77–78

Movimiento Industrial Argentino (MIA), 211–212
Moyano, Hugo, 219
MST. *See* Movimento dos Trabalhadores Rurais Sem Terra
Mubarak, Hosni, 254–255
MUN. *See* Movimiento de Unidad Nacional
municipal revenues, 6, 153, 195

Nasser, Gamel Abdel, 254
National Action Party. *See* Partido Acción Nacional
National Bank for Economic Development. *See* Banco Nacional de Desenvolvimento Econômico; Banco Nacional de Desenvolvimento Econômico e Social
National Chamber of Manufacturing. *See* Cámara Nacional de la Industria de Transformación
National Confederation of Industry. *See* Confederação Nacional da Indústria
National Democratic Union. *See* União Democrática Nacional
National Industrial Movement. *See* Movimiento Industrial Nacional
National Party. *See* Partido Nacional
National Peasant Confederation. *See* Confederación Nacional Campesina
National Private Sector Front. *See* Frente Nacional del Área Privada
National Regeneration Movement. *See* Movimiento de Regeneración Nacional
National Renewal Alliance. *See* Aliança Renovadora Nacional
National Renewal. *See* Renovación Nacional
National Sinarquista Union. *See* Unión Nacional Sinarquista
National Society of Agriculture. *See* Sociedad Nacional de Agricultura; Sociedade Nacional de Agricultura
National Union of Education Workers. *See* Sindicato Nacional de Trabajadores de la Educación
National Union of Hope. *See* Unión Nacional de la Esperanza
nationalism, 60, 196
Nationalist Front for Fatherland and Liberty. *See* Frente Nacionalista Patria y Libertad
nationalization, 30–31, 54–56, 73, 76, 115, 175, 218–219
Mexico and, 115

Nasser and, 254
of banks, 136
of electric power generation, 123
of nonfarm assets, 243–248, 249–250
of oil sector, 113, 218–219
of railways, 206
natural resource extraction, 2–3, 26
natural resource nationalism, 54–55
natural resource revenues, 14, 23, 30, 134
neoclassical economics, 45, 56
neoliberalism, 56, 86, 92, 174–175, 177
backlash against, 217–221
Chile and, 81
consensus and, 94
counterrevolution and, 66–67
global ascendancy of, 192
hegemony of, 186–187, 210–212
light taxation and, 84–86
PRI and, 133, 137–138
public rejection of, 215
reforms of, 67–68, 178, 185, 204
tax burden stability and, 208–209
neopanismo, 136–137
New Majority. *See* Nueva Mayoría
Nicaragua, 258
Nigeria, 249
nontax natural resource revenues, 2–3, 14, 29–31, 106, 132, 134, 149, 250
North Korea, 249, 252
Nueva Mayoría, 43, 45, 84, 85, 86, 87
labor reform and, 103–104
platform of, 92
reform effort of, 95, 96
unpopular and internally divided, 92–93
Nuevo León, 114–115, 132

Obregón, Alvaro, 112
OECD. *See* Organisation for Economic Cooperation and Development
oil nationalization, 115, 218–219
oil prices, 132–133, 135, 146–147
Olivera–Tanzi effect, 9–10, 29, 154–155, 174–175, 200–201, 213, 214, 223
Organisation for Economic Cooperation and Development (OECD), 4, 18–19, 21
organized labor, 57, 147–148, 201–202. *See also* labor movement; labor unions
growth of, 234
kirchnerismo and, 219
Perón and, 205
Ortiz Mena, Antonio, 123–124, 127

PAN. *See* Partido Acción Nacional
Panama, 1
Paraguay, 243
parliamentarism, 13–14
Partido Acción Nacional (PAN), 16–17, 40,
    45–46, 56–58, 62, 145–146
  Catholic Church and, 136
  consecutive presidents of, 138
  creation of, 115
  fined after 2000 elections, 140–141
  liberalization of oil sector and, 145
  mistrustful attitude toward state embedded
    in, 147–148
  PRI and, 137, 138
  private sector and, 136–137, 146
  pro-business ideology of, 144–145
  social programs and, 144
  victory of, 134
Partido Comunista Brasileiro (PCB),
    156–157
Partido Comunista de Chile (PC), 43, 70, 73
Partido da Frente Liberal (PFL), 178, 179
Partido da Social Democracia Brasileira
    (PSDB), 41, 174–175, 187, 188
Partido de la Revolución Democrática (PRD),
    44, 138, 144–145
Partido Demócrata Cristiano (PDC), 66–67, 72,
    74, 84–85, 94
Partido Democrático Social (PDS), 171
Partido do Movimento Democrático Brasileiro
    (PMDB), 175, 176, 184, 185–186
Partido dos Trabalhadores (PT), 43, 46–47, 61,
    172–173, 175–176, 185–186
  dominance of presidential office,
    182–184
  electoral performance of, 183
  heavy taxation and, 189
  moderation of, 182–184
  rise of, 182
  strife within, 187
Partido Justicialista (PJ), 209, 211, 218
Partido Nacional (PN), 74
Partido Revolucionario Institucional (PRI),
    31–33, 44, 46, 116, 118
  ability to monopolize state power, 123
  acts of official repression of, 124
  business mistrust of, 119–120, 136
  CANACINTRA and, 119
  Cárdenas, L., and, 123
  hegemony of, 57–58
  moving left, 126
  neoliberalism and, 133, 138

return to presidency, 135
tax reform and, 145
Partido Social Cristiano (PSC), 245
Partido Social Democrático (PSD), 156–157,
    160, 162, 167, 168
Partido Socialista (PS), 70, 73, 85
Partido Trabalhista Brasileiro (PTB), 156–157,
    160, 166–167, 168
Partido Verde Ecologista de México
    (PVEM), 138
Party of Brazilian Social Democracy. *See*
    Partido da Social Democracia Brasileira
Party of the Democratic Revolution. *See* Partido
    de la Revolución Democrática
Party of the Liberal Front. *See* Partido da Frente
    Liberal
path dependence, 15–16, 48–52, 60, 62, 65,
    239, 255
  agreements about, 48–50
  anti-statism and, 96–104, 105
  disagreements about, 50–51
  mechanisms of reproduction and, 49–50, 58,
    96, 106–107
  property threats and, 52–53
pay-as-you-go pension system, 80, 82–83
PC. *See* Partido Comunista de Chile
PCB. *See* Partido Comunista Brasileiro
PDC. *See* Partido Demócrata Cristiano
PDS. *See* Partido Democrático Social
peasant political activism, 73, 76, 113, 124
PEMEX. *See* Petróleos Mexicanos
Peña Nieto, Enrique, 135, 138, 145, 146
pension systems, 4–5, 80, 82, 144, 260–261
  for private sector workers, 133–134
  privatization of, 214, 246
  reform of, 36, 82–83, 173–174, 176,
    186–187, 208, 223–224
  rural workers and, 165, 184–185
Perón, Juan, 60, 63–64, 191–193, 205–208
  labor movements and, 197–198
  leadership of, 201–202
  legacy of, 229–230
  military coup against, 61, 192, 207
  organized labor and, 205
  policy measures of, 196–197
  private property and, 61–62, 205, 206
  social security and, 194, 223–224
  SOEs and, 196
  working class and, 195–196, 197, 205–206
peronismo, 15, 42, 43, 47, 61–62, 192,
    195–196, 204–205
  anti-, 201–203, 231

austerity and, 210–211
authoritarian exclusion of, 63
clientelism and, 219–220
conflicts unleashed by, 64
culture of, 228
destabilizing force of, 207
influence of, 203
kirchnerismo and, 219–220, 224–226
military intervention and, 63, 204
roots of, 197
social conservatism and, 206–207
personal income tax, 5, 6, 80, 85, 223, 259–260
Peru, 235
PETROBRAS. *See* Petróleo Brasileiro
Petroecuador, 243
Petróleo Brasileiro (PETROBRAS), 155, 156, 176
Petróleos Mexicanos (PEMEX), 29–31, 106, 125–126
PFL. *See* Partido da Frente Liberal
Pierson, Paul, 50, 58
Piñera, Sebastián, 85–86, 96
Pinochet, Augusto, 44–45, 74, 79, 81, 97
Chicago Boys and, 81–82
detention in London, 98–99
institutional structures left over by, 67
legacy of, 101
pressure to stimulate recovery, 83
supporters of, 98, 102
tax policies of, 105, 165
voters for, 96–97
PJ. *See* Partido Justicialista
Plan Jefes y Jefas de Hogar Desocupados (Unemployed Heads of Household Plan), 217–218
PMDB. *See* Partido do Movimento Democrático Brasileiro
PN. *See* Partido Nacional
Polity V database, 22–23
Pontifical Catholic University of Rio de Janeiro, 179–180
popular mobilization, 47–48, 53, 113, 117, 167, 240, 248–250
Popular Unity. *See* Unidad Popular
populism, 18, 44, 94, 151
anti-populism and, 191
public revenues and, 195–197
social conservatism and, 155
taxation and, 192–193
porfiriato, 252–253
Portillo, Alfonso, 237
poverty, 236–237, 260–261

power resources theory, 2–3, 12, 37–38
PR. *See* proportional representation
PRD. *See* Partido de la Revolución Democrática
PRI. *See* Partido Revolucionario Institucional
private sector, 40, 71, 116–120, 224
accepting attitude toward state economic intervention and, 163–164
anti-statism and, 206
of Chile, 90
collective identity of, 90
Díaz Ordaz and, 128
elites in, 73–74
fear of alienating, 120
fragmentation of, 192
liberalization and, 177
López Portillo and, 129
mistrust of state, 121, 127, 163
mobilization by, 126
PAN and, 136–137, 146
political influence of, 137
relations between state and, 136
Vargas and, 158, 159, 161
privatization, 81, 83, 137–138
of pensions, 214, 246
revenues from, 173–174
of SOEs, 67–68, 173, 208
PRO. *See* Propuesta Republicana
Proceso, 204, 230–231
property redistribution, 249, 256–257, 262–263
property rights. *See also* threats to property rights
constitutional reform and, 73, 246–247
land reform and, 167
peaceful approach to restructuring, 257
redistribution of, 129
socialism and, 72–73
property taxes, 6, 153, 215–216
proportional representation (PR), 10, 22–23
Propuesta Republicana (PRO), 15, 41, 215
Proud and Sovereign Fatherland Alliance. *See* Alianza Patria Altiva y Soberana
Provisional Contribution on Financial Movements. *See* Contribuição Provisória sobre Movimentação Financeira
Przeworski, Adam, 21
PS. *See* Partido Socialista
PSC. *See* Partido Social Cristiano
PSD. *See* Partido Social Democrático
PSDB. *See* Partido da Social Democracia Brasileira
PT. *See* Partido dos Trabalhadores

PTB. *See* Partido Trabalhista Brasileiro
public enterprises, 124, 196–197. *See also* state-owned enterprises
public health, 111, 261
public revenues, 1–2, 195–197, 238, 261–262
public sector, 9–10, 15, 19, 80
  expansion of, 16–18, 38, 63, 70, 190, 217–221
  anti-statism and, 147
  limited, 119–120
  growth of, 67, 70, 224–230, 234, 236
  jobs in, 156
  redistribution and, 181–182
  size of, 18–19
  unions, 104
PVEM. *See* Partido Verde Ecologista de Mexico

Quadros, Jânio, 154–155, 166–167, 169
qualitative comparison, 20
qualitative research design, 22

Radical Civic Union. *See* Unión Cívica Radical
Radical Party, 73
Ranis, Peter, 207
reactive sequences, 51, 52–53, 56
redistribution, 7–8, 19, 26–27. *See also* land reform
  attitudes toward, 34
  conflict and, 150–151
  economic elites and, 232–233
  fiscal systems and, 260
  gains in, 259
  of income, 256
  of land, 54–55, 60–61, 73–74, 112, 157, 249–250
  pressures for, 29
  of property, 249, 256–257
  of property rights, 129
  public sector and, 181–182
  reform and, 52–53, 60, 66, 68, 164–165, 207
  backlash against, 105
  Vargas unwilling to pursue, 157
Renovación Nacional (RN), 15, 40, 62, 89, 94–95
Republican Proposal. *See* Propuesta Republicana
research design, 3, 8–9, 13, 19–20, 22, 23
revolutionary radicalism, 192–193
Richard, Scott F., 33–34
Riggs Bank, 98–99
right parties, 44–45, 57, 87, 89, 97, 99, 150, 235–236

rightwing actors, 37–38, 46
Rio de Janeiro, 162
RN. *See* Renovación Nacional
Rodríguez Lara, Guillermo, 245–248
Rodríguez Saá, Adolfo, 217, 220
Rossell y Arellano, Mariano, 241–242
Rousseff, Dilma, 175–176, 180, 189
Rubio, Pascual Ortiz, 112
Ruiz Cortines, Adolfo, 116–117, 120, 121–122
rural population, 54
rural workers, 168, 184–185

El Sadat, Anwar, 254–255
Salinas, Carlos, 133–134
Sanchez, Omar, 213
Sandinistas, 258
São Paulo, 157, 158–159
Sarney, José, 173, 186
Schmitter, Philippe C., 163
Schneider, Ben Ross, 12, 90, 170–171
Schneider, René, 75
Scioli, Daniel, 216
Secretaría de Hacienda y Crédito Público, 117, 127–128, 129, 146
Secretariat of Finance and Public Credit. *See* Secretaría de Hacienda y Crédito Público
self-reinforcing processes, 35.30, 26–27, 50, 51, 52–53, 63–64, 97, 106–107, 147–148
Servicio de Administración Tributaria (SAT), 146–147
sexenio, 116, 137, 146
SHCP. *See* Secretaría de Hacienda y Crédito Público
Sikkink, Kathryn, 163
Silva Lima, Mayrá, 76–77
Simmons, Erica, 51
Simonsen, Roberto, 158, 159, 163
Sindicato Nacional de Trabajadores de la Educación (SNTE), 141
Slater, Dan, 51
small-N approach, 20
SNA. *See* Sociedad Nacional de Agricultura
SNTE. *See* Sindicato Nacional de Trabajadores de la Educación
Social Christian Party. *See* Partido Social Cristiano
social conservatism, 40, 105, 206–207
  Catholic Church and, 99, 127
  economic elites and, 158–161
  economic liberals and, 230, 233
  political mobilizations of, 129, 190
  populism and, 155

Social Contribution on Net Profits. *See* Contribuição Social sobre o Lucro Líquido

Social Democratic Party. *See* Partido Social Democrático

social security, 2, 22, 61, 70, 82–83, 110. *See also* pension systems
  benefits, 156
  Brazil and, 153
  elite attitudes toward, 163–164
  expansion and legal consolidation of, 155–156
  incremental expansion of, 169
  Perón and, 194, 223–224
  Rousseff and, 175–176
  spending, 155
  tax revenues, 214
  universalization of, 159

socialism, 53, 72–73, 75, 117–118, 249
  Arab, 254
  fear of, 105
  goal of, 182–184
  Mexico and, 111–112
  property rights and, 72–73
  Soviet Union and, 252
  transition to, 168

Socialist Party. *See* Partido Socialista

Sociedad de Fomento Fabril (SOFOFA), 39, 72, 73–74, 90

Sociedad Nacional de Agricultura (SNA), 72

Sociedad Rural Argentina (SRA), 39–40, 203

Sociedade Nacional de Agricultura (SNA), 158–159

Sociedade Rural Brasileira (SRB), 158–159

Society for Industrial Promotion. *See* Sociedad de Fomento Fabril

SOEs. *See* state-owned enterprises

SOFOFA. *See* Sociedad de Fomento Fabril

Soviet Union, 252

Spain, 108–109

SRA. *See* Sociedad Rural Argentina

SRB. *See* Sociedade Rural Brasileira

stabilizing development, 116–117, 123, 125–126

state economic intervention, 15, 40, 57, 132, 163–164

state oil companies, 30–31, 60, 115, 218–219, 243. *See also specific companies*

state-owned enterprises (SOEs), 156, 171. *See also* public enterprises
  deindustrialization and, 181–182
  expanding, 165
  Perón and, 196
  privatization of, 67–68, 173, 208

renationalization of privatized, 175

state-led development, 71, 72, 150, 151–155

statism, 17–18, 72, 230
  anti-statism balance of power with, 44
  Argentina and, 47
  backlash against, 83–84
  in Brazil, 184–185
  business-friendly brand of, 63–64
  civil society and, 92
  deepening, 164–165
  fears of resurgence of, 67
  labor movements and, 18
  power balance of, 224–230
  predominance of, 184–189
  reaffirmation of, 169–172
  relative influence of, 27
  strength of, 63, 181–184
  supporters of, 38
  weak threats to property rights and, 60–64
  weakness of, 240

Suárez, Eduardo, 117

subnational revenues, 6, 10, 21–22, 35, 108–109, 153, 174, 216, 224

Suez Canal, 254

Syria, 249–250, 253–254

Tax Administration Service. *See* Servicio de Administración Tributaria

tax burden, 2, 4–5, 21–22
  in Argentina, 18–19, 22–23, 47, 65, 191, 192, 194, 198–199, 201, 215–217, 232–233
  average, 5
  in Brazil, 18–19, 22–23, 36, 65, 149–150, 151–152, 154–155, 163–164, 189–190
  in Chile, 18–19, 22–23, 69
  criticism of, 228
  determination of, 11, 15
  in Ecuador, 243–248
  in Egypt, 250
  fiscal centralization and, 3–4
  growth of, 70, 108–111, 150–151, 215–217
    democratization and, 173–176
    slow, 144
    sustained, 151–155
  increase of, 68–69, 86, 172
  instability, 198–199
  liberalization and, 132
  in Mexico, 14, 18–19, 22–23, 106, 109, 146–147, 151
  reducing, 71–72, 82
  richer societies and, 9–10

tax burden (cont.)
    stability, 132–135, 208–213, 215–217
    in Syria, 250
    theories of, 13, 26, 27
    threats to property rights and, 14–16
    trajectories, 59
    variance in, 4–5, 8–9, 14, 27–28, 36, 47–48,
        64–65, 234, 235
tax compliance, 189
tax evasion, 8–9, 165–166, 205, 213, 222
tax exemptions, 121
tax incentives, 166
Tax on Gross Receipts. *See* Impuesto sobre los
    Ingresos Brutos
Tax on Sales and Consignments. *See* Imposto
    sobre Vendas e Consignações
Tax on the Circulation of Goods and Services.
    See Imposto sobre Circulação de
    Mercadorias e Prestação de Serviços
tax progressivity, 6–8, 18–19, 153
tax reductions, 68, 79–84, 154–155
tax reform, 37–38, 84–85, 93, 165–166, 172,
    238, 259
    business mobilization and, 126–129
    Concertación and, 121
    Echeverría and, 124–125
    global, 188–189
    limiting, 142–147
    López Mateos and, 123–124
    PRI and, 145
tax revenues, 7–8, 14, 69, 195, 244
    Chile and, 67
    federal, 153, 194–195, 200
    frustrated efforts to substantially
        increase, 132
    increase in, 134
    in Mexico, 1, 109
    slow growth of, 121
    social security, 214
    stabilizing, 191
    stagnation of, 116
    volatility, 199
tax system centralization, 6, 69, 109–110,
    126, 216
taxation, 1–2, 120–122, 184–189. *See also*
    specific taxes
    anti-statism and, 39
    of capital, 128–129
    Concertación and, 45
    Convertibility Plan and, 214
    decentralization of, 200
    democracy and, 27, 31, 84

democratization and, 150
determinants of, 2
divergent levels of, 2
domestic, 69, 153, 196–197
double taxation, 95
economic conditions and, 9–10
export, 153, 222
federalism and, 34–35
fiscal deficit and, 133–134
growth of, 151
heavy, 68–72, 172–173, 243–248
increasing, 70, 189–190
judicial challenges to, 143
Kirchners and, 220–224
large-scale redistribution and, 3
light, 64, 66, 84–86, 93, 105, 106,
    236–242
democracy and, 132–133
under military rule, 67–68, 165–166,
    236–237
neoliberalism and, 84–86
populism and, 192–193
rates of, 5
rising, 163–164, 217, 228
theories of, 2–3, 8–9, 13–14, 65 (*See also*
    specific theories)
types of, 6–8
Technological and Higher Education Institute
    of Monterrey. *See* Instituto Tecnológico
    y de Estudios Superiores de Monterrey
Temer, Michel, 176
tenentes, 157, 159
Teune, Henry, 22
think tanks, 91–92, 141, 179–180,
    226–227
threats to property rights, 3, 14–16, 18–19,
    26–27, 52–53, 234, 248–249
    in Chile, 53, 56, 68, 72–73
    contingency and, 55–56, 105, 147
    countermobilization against, 56–57, 72–73,
        105, 108, 111–112, 240
    critical antecedents of, 53–55, 60, 147
    different effects in Middle East, 250–251,
        252–255
    in Guatemala, 240–241
    historical trajectory of tax burden and, 59,
        240–241
    lack of in Argentina, 17–18, 61–62, 198–199,
        205, 206, 234
    lack of in Brazil, 17, 60–61, 150, 151, 156,
        163, 205, 234
    lack of in Ecuador, 246–247

lack of in pre-Allende Chile, 71
in Mexico, 53, 108, 147
Tilly, Charles, 255
Toledano, Vicente Lombardo, 114
Tomic, Radomiro, 74–75
trade openness, 9–10, 23, 28
trade protection, 111, 118, 159
trade taxes, 68–69, 108–109, 151–152, 153,
193, 215–216, 222
Transparency International, 142–143
Turkey, 249
26th of July Movement, 258–259

Ubico, Jorge, 240–241
UCR. *See* Unión Cívica Radical
UDI. *See* Unión Demócrata Independiente
UDN. *See* União Democrática Nacional
UDR. *See* União Democrática Ruralista
UIA. *See* Unión Industrial Argentina
UNE. *See* Unión Nacional de la
Esperanza
Unemployed Heads of Household Plan (Plan
Jefes y Jefas de Hogar Desocupados),
217–218
União Democrática Nacional (UDN), 159–160,
171, 179
União Democrática Ruralista (UDR), 180
Unidad Popular (UP), 72–73, 75–76, 77
ideological change from, 96
Marxism and, 168
negative views of, 97
restructuring of property rights, 166
worker mobilization and, 101
Unidad Revolucionaria Nacional Guatemalteca
(URNG), 239
Unified Workers' Central. *See* Central Única
dos Trabalhadores
Unión Cívica Radical (UCR), 202–203,
205, 229
Unión Demócrata Independiente (UDI), 40, 58,
62, 89, 93
creation of, 99
military regime and, 99
as most right-leaning of major parties,
100–101
Unión Industrial Argentina (UIA), 39–40, 202,
203, 211–212, 229, 230
Unión Nacional de la Esperanza (UNE), 239
Unión Nacional Sinarquista (UNS), 115
unionization, 167–168, 197
Unitary Workers' Central. *See* Central Unitaria
de Trabajadores de Chile

United Nations Economic Commission for
Latin America and the Caribbean
(ECLAC), 21, 23–24, 117
United States (US), 9–10, 167–168, 249
Brazil and, 159–160
policy of isolating Cuba, 123
political dominance of, 248
proximity to, 29
University of Chicago, 56, 78
UNS. *See* Unión Nacional Sinarquista
UP. *See* Unidad Popular
URNG. *See* Unidad Revolucionaria Nacional
Guatemalteca
Uruguay, 1, 70, 235
US. *See* United States

Valdés, Rodrigo, 95–96
value-added taxes (VATs), 6–7, 27–28, 79–80,
165–166, 208–209
Argentina and, 200
broadening of, 135
centralization and, 126
creation of, 122, 125, 129
evasion of, 222
extension of, 144–145
increase in, 84–85, 94–95, 135, 145
López Portillo and, 126, 134
Mexico and, 29
rates of, 133–134
Vargas, Getúlio, 61, 150–151
agricultural sector and, 158–159
anti-Vargas military uprising by São
Paulo, 157
BNDE and, 155
business organization after, 161–163
communist influence stemmed by, 156
death of, 154, 160, 161–162
deposed, 153
Estado Novo and, 153–154
immediate post-Vargas governments, 154
military coup and, 153–154
opposition to, 158
PCB and, 156–157
pressured to resign, 169
private property and, 156, 205
private sector and, 158, 159, 161
pro-worker reforms and, 155–156
tax system inherited by, 152–153
two periods in power, 151
unwilling to pursue redistribution, 157
varguismo, 155–157, 159–161,
166–167

VATs. *See* value-added taxes
Velasco, Andrés, 90–91, 94
Venezuela, 6
Verba, Sidney, 20
vertical fiscal imbalance, 10, 35
Vietnam, 252
violent revolution, 256–257, 259

Waisman, Carlos H., 198
Washington Consensus, 178–179
wealth tax, 123–124
welfare states, 18–19

Workers' Party. *See* Partido dos Trabalhadores
working class, 12, 61, 151
  Perón and, 195–196, 197, 205–206
  Vargas, pro-worker reforms and,
    155–156
World Bank, 23–24, 110, 120
World War I, 64, 151–152, 193
World War II, 68, 70, 111, 117, 154, 192–193,
    200–201, 252

Zedillo, Ernesto, 133–134
Zürn, Michael, 256